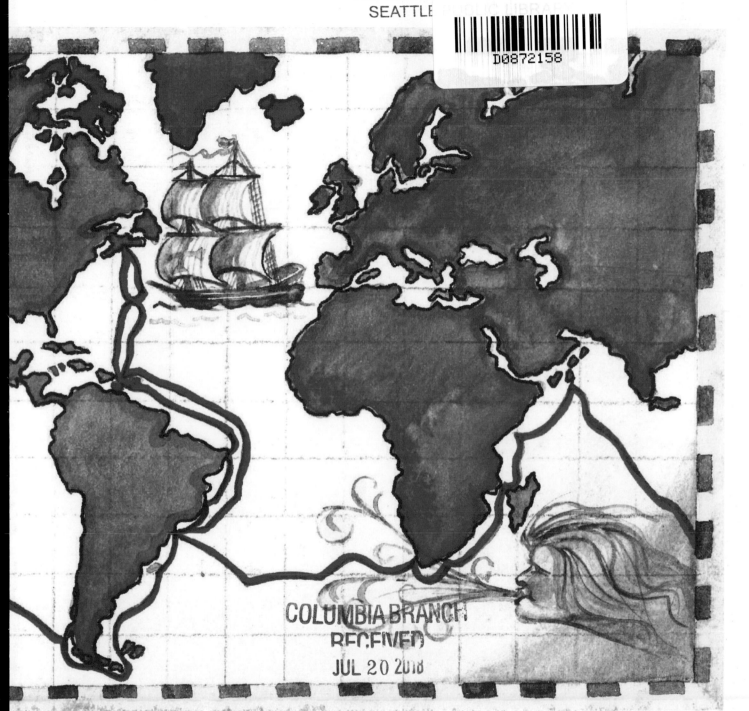

# THE SCHOONER
## *MAGGIE B.*

**A Southern Ocean Circumnavigation**

# THE SCHOONER
## *MAGGIE B.*

**A Southern Ocean Circumnavigation**

# FRANK BLAIR

Design and composition by Claire MacMaster, barefoot art graphic design
Cover illustration by Yuta Onoda.
Illustrations on pages ii, viii-ix, and 20-21 by Yuta Onoda

Printed by Printworks Global Ltd., London & Hong Kong

First Edition

ISBN: 978-0-9973920-8-1

## Dedication

This book is dedicated to my father,
Edward McCormick Blair, 1918–2010,
who taught me the love of Blue Water.

He never saw *Maggie B*, but he was with us
every mile of the voyage.

## *Author's Note*

Many geographic locations have many different names due to conquest, discovery, language, politics, nationalism and conflicting traditions. For example, the most southerly part of Africa is variously called: Cape of Good Hope, Cape Point, Cape Agulhas, Cape of Storms, and my favorite, Stormkaap. Charts, sailing guides, locals, and other sailors used various languages for port, cape, bay and such. Similarly, distances are in feet, meters, kilometers, miles and even fathoms. Gear that we had aboard and what we purchased might be metric, DIN, SAE, or some other standard. Weather reports could be in kilopascals, safety gear might be rated in newtons. I have abandoned consistency not to confuse but to share our direct experience and call all such elements by the terminology we encountered.

*Maggie B* running down the Chilean Canals.
Painting by Freddie Kellogg

# INTRODUCTION

**Mid-winter in the South Atlantic Ocean**

The sea today is a steely blue gray. Occasionally a wave will rear up near us, above the horizon, so that there is a thin "window" which is the bright azure of a South Seas lagoon. A lovely contrast, and a reminder of the marvels ahead in the Seychelles and the South Pacific.

We are beginning our approach to the African coast. Cape Town is 34 degrees South and we need to hold perhaps yet another degree (60 miles) south for room against a possible southeasterly blow. But each degree south of 30 edges us towards bigger weather. There looks to be an interesting break in the weather coming toward the end of the week, but we will not be far enough along to take advantage of it.

One Blue Water emotion that is hard to explain is how nice it is to be a thousand or so miles from land. Yes, we are all on our own in the South Atlantic in winter, with a series of gales not too far off to the south. But so much of a sailor's fear of gales is due to the danger of getting driven ashore because of an anchor not holding, or a mooring parting, or getting dismasted with the engine conking out. In Blue Water you have the ability to work on your problems without crashing breakers to reduce your options. Out here you have the ability to run a hundred miles in one direction or another to stay out of trouble and time your exposure to the storms.

## The Start

While sailing around the world had been my dream since I was little, it came into focus during the summer of 2003. My son Alden worked in the sea program of the Hurricane Island Outward Bound School in Maine, as I had for twenty years. Two days before he went back to college for his junior year, he came to see me and said words that would chill any father's blood, "Dad, you have to promise me something."

I said that I would do my best, though I feared what a 20-year-old might want to get his father to promise. He said, "By the time I graduate from college, I want you to buy or build a boat that you and I can sail around the world, together with friends."

Before I could answer, he added, "by Cape Horn." Relief, delight with the challenge and pride in being asked rushed through me and I said, "OK, but going west to east." And we shook on it.

My son, Alden, in the galley with fresh bread.

In fact, the *Maggie B*, in many ways, started years earlier. I had been sailing when I was two years old, reportedly, while staying at my grandmother's house in Maine. Subsequent summers were spent in rowing class and sailing school on Mount Desert Island, Maine, about halfway Down East toward the Canadian border.

My brother Ed and I got a Herreshoff Bullseye called *Waterbug* in our early teens, sailing and racing as often as we could. Later I worked as boat boy for a variety of captains in gradually larger boats in the sailing fleet. My father bought a Hinckley Bermuda 40, called *Belisarius*, and then a Tripp-designed Hinckley 48 called *Norumbega*. I sailed, raced, and cruised them along the coast, up to New Brunswick and across to Nova Scotia. My Blue Water experience was limited to a Bermuda Race on a friend's boat.

Sailing in Maine taught me about fog, cold water, sharp and unpredictable granite ledges, the value of good foul weather gear, the smells of land and sea, the comfort of a tight cove, and the joy of going Down East with a fresh southwesterly breeze in a sound boat with good friends.

Five years in the Navy followed college. I served as a carrier-based fighter pilot, flying F-8 Crusaders off the USS *Shangri-La* in the Mediterranean and the USS

*Hancock* in the Western Pacific. The second tour was flying low-level photoreconnaissance over North Vietnam in an RF-8G.

Flying taught me the glories of distance; that impossible, unbelievable things might be tried and accomplished; that time/speed/distance really matters; and that the worse things get, the calmer you need to be.

I returned to Outward Bound, as a student and then as an instructor. There I learned that all my hard skills, like knowing all about time/speed/distance, didn't really matter if I didn't have the soft skills of communication, team building, trust, and respect for everyone's talents. It also taught me that I didn't need a feather bed, a hot meal, and clean clothes to be happy.

I filled out my resume by getting my Coast Guard Master's License and becoming a Registered Maine Guide.

Every sailor who is exposed to a variety of boats sees things that they like and dislike in every boat they get near. You admire a stem or despise a complicated and dangerous mainsheet arrangement. Balzac said, "Everyone has a novel in their belly." I believe that every sailor has a boat that is building in his belly, head and heart. Certainly, it was so with me.

## The Design and Build

In November of 2001, my shipmate and close friend Bill Brewer invited me to go with him to see the boat he was building in Nova Scotia.

On the way to Covey Island Boatworks in Petite Rivere, Nova Scotia, the owner, John Steele, asked if we would like to see the schooner he was just starting for himself. She was being built in a clearing on the shore near his house.

There were only a few frames completed. They were made up of thin, very long strips of Douglas fir, epoxied together to make the strongest, lightest, most beautiful structure you could have for a boat. They looked like Danish Modern furniture for giants. I almost couldn't imagine that anyone would be so profane as to take that beautiful sculpture and plank it and hide it in the hull of a boat.

I was hooked.

Bill's boat was handsome and being handsomely built. Some boats are museum-quality works of art, others are slap-dash plastic snap-togethers. Real sailors' boats are somewhere in-between. I most admire boats that are well designed, well thought out, solidly constructed, and well finished. Covey Island seemed to be the place to do it.

While looking around the shop in Petite Rivere, I noticed some photos of earlier boats built by Covey to their Westerman designs. They were a collaboration between the boatyard and an English naval architect named Nigel Irens. The boats were very good looking but a bit too traditional for me, being recreations of 1890s Bristol pilot cutters.

I kept Nigel's name handy and was stunned when I went on his webpage. Rather than being a stiff traditionalist, the kind who would snort, "If it was good enough for [fill in the name of someone dead for at least 100 years], it is good enough for me!" Nigel's principal clients were unlimited trimaran racers, whose boats were perfectly comfortable averaging 20 knots in any weather.

Nigel has a remarkable range, scale, flexibility and creativity, coupled with a modest ego and great experience with ships, sailors, and owners. This is not always true, even among the greats: a Herreshoff is a Herreshoff is a Herreshoff. Frank Lloyd Wright built houses for himself, not his clients. Nigel has the rare ability to listen to his client, understand his or her needs, and then design the boat for the client, not for the designer.

Nigel and I happened to be in Paris at the same time in February 2004, six or seven months after Alden gave me my instructions. I had looked at lots of available boats, but none quite spoke to me.

Over a bottle of wine, I asked Nigel for a boat that would be fast, safe, and comfortable going around the world in the Southern Ocean. He said, "You usually only get one or two of the three!" I told him that was why I was talking to him.

We shook hands at the end of it and he got started sketching. He had the preliminary plans ready on March 30, 2004.

Nigel and I considered other boatyards, but the fix was really in to build *Maggie B* at Covey Island. Every boatyard has its own way of doing things, and often they have in-house designers. Showing up with an "outside" designer runs a serious risk of "Not Invented Here" (NIH) behavior on the part of both the designer and the boatyard. Adding an owner who might have his or her own ideas could make the ingredients for a toxic cocktail.

To me, the essential way that we should be able to relate to each other was that all of us could ask, suggest and chime in without fear of put-downs, pulling rank or NIH behavior. I wouldn't say, "I'm the Owner and I say so." Nigel wouldn't say "This Is A Nigel Irens Design And That's The Way I Want It." And John wouldn't say, "We don't do it that way here in Nova Scotia."

A huge advantage at Covey Island was that John Steele, his son Dorian, and several of the workers were experienced sailors. Thus, their suggestions weren't just

Nigel Irens considering a new schooner's hull.

from woodworkers; they were calibrated with wind, waves, and salt spray.

In my case, I was a customer with a focused purpose: to build a boat that would take us around the world: fast, safe, and comfortable. I didn't approach building my boat by saying that I wanted one "just like Joe's, but in blue and two feet bigger." Nor did I admire a race boat of the 1930s and want an exact copy in spite of what might have been learned in the last 70 years.

We lofted the first frame—the first rib—in June 2004. The frames of a boat are built on a lofting table that for us was about 25 by 25 feet, perfectly flat, made of plywood, and ruled off in one-foot squares. Each rib has its shape drawn out following the latitude and longitude of the curve, sized up from the computer-drawn plans. Right-angle irons were screwed in temporarily at each step. The wood for the frame had been sawn into long, thin pliable strips that were three-inches wide. Enough strips were assembled and glued together with epoxy and wrapped in plastic so the strips would stick only to each other. Then the whole bundle was clamped to the right-angle irons. Actually, two identical bundles were prepared, one for the port and one for the starboard rib. The builders left the bundles clamped for 20 hours, and then they did it again for the next rib, after changing the location of the angle irons.

The wood we used was recycled old growth Douglas fir. It had been the roof beams from a U.S. Army armory that had been built in 1932 outside Philadelphia and had just been torn down. Old growth is highly desirable because the grain is much denser than that of new plantation wood. The advantage of recycling is that the wood has had a good time to dry out and to do whatever twisting or splitting that fresh timber might eventually do. Our wood had had 72 years to get ready to be a hull. Recycled wood is also less expensive than virgin wood of the same quality.

I happened to be at Covey Island shortly after the wood arrived. It looked just awful. It had been painted every year for the last 70. It was full of bolts, fasteners and holes from fittings. The pile made a bunch of used railroad ties look like a display at Home Depot. It seemed like money down the drain.

But Covey Island carefully went over each huge piece, pulling out every piece of metal with the help of magnetometers to find each nail and hidden screw the way the TSA finds the keys in your pocket at the airport. Then they sized it and sliced it, and out of the ugly pile came hundreds and hundreds of lovely strips.

The frames are attached in order and held together by temporary staging. This is all done upside down. Why upside down? To make it easier to plank. Think of the shape of a boat and imagine your job is to lay, fasten, and glue hundreds of long strips, 1¾-inches square, butted up against each other. Would you like to do it over your head, getting glue in your eyes and having sticky strips dropping on you? Or laying them down along a nice slope?

Inside an inverted, planked hull, it is like a small, perfect chapel. It is no surprise that there are a whole series of small churches on Prince Edward Island whose roofs are made like boat hulls upside down.

Once planked, the hull is rolled over, slowly and carefully.

After the hull is turned over, it gets filled up, some say filled up with money. First come fuel and water tanks, engines, systems, and then she is decked and partitioned into cabins and public spaces.

We built *Maggie B* with two watertight bulkheads forward. The first was the

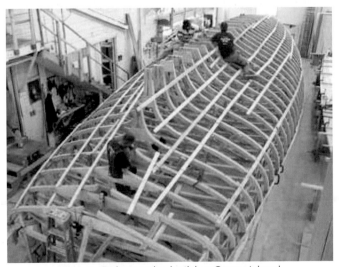

*Maggie B* during the build at Covey Island.

very front compartment—the forepeak—that held only the chain locker. The next forward area, the fo'c'sle, also could be sealed off. I was, frankly, afraid of running into some semi-submersed piece of flotsam or jetsam like a cargo container. It was a very real risk with all the junk in the oceans and I was determined to do my best to survive a collision.

One area where I may have pulled an "I'm the Owner and that's the Way I Want It!" on John and Nigel was refusing a navigation station. Such nav stations are an essential part of almost every boat made in the world. Everyone has the picture in their head of the navigator with the huge chart spread out on a big specialized table—measuring angles with a protractor or parallel rules and checking distances with dividers, while occasionally fiddling with the nearby radar, listening to the weather on the VHF and calling up to the helmsman "Come starboard 10 degrees!"

That was not an image that I had for the *Maggie B*. I wanted information to be where you needed it. That place is on deck, at the elbow of the watch officer. If you have to scamper below to check the radar you aren't going to do it as often as you should, especially in bad weather, when you need it the most. I wanted each watch officer to not just be able to follow an assigned course, but to have what airplane pilots call "situational awareness."

Down below, popular charter boats are set up with as many individual private cabins as they can stuff in the hull, each with its own head and doors that lock: the bigger the double beds, the better. Far too many boats are really set up to be funny-shaped apartments that happen to be floating in marinas or, very occasionally, on anchor in a sheltered harbor.

The *Maggie B* was made for passagemaking. This meant that the bunks were adequate in length, but snug in width. If you are at sea, you want a place to snuggle down and sleep, not a king-sized trampoline that will toss you onto the cabin sole at the first wave. All the bunks had strong canvas lee-cloths to keep you in your bunk when the boat was heeling. The two tight doubles also had lee-cloths down the middle like a bundling board, to keep you separated.

We had room for eight, if both doubles were fully occupied.

While the accommodations were relatively tight for a 62-foot boat, much of the room on the boat was consciously given to "public space." The first space as you went below was the crew mess and galley.

If an army travels on its stomach, sailors sail on theirs. A good galley makes for good food, which makes for happy sailors, which makes for a happy captain. The galley was the primo spot on the *Maggie B*, with the best air, light, and access. It

A ship is merely decorative without the crew.

was big enough so that two could work in it and not get in each other's way, but tight enough that you could brace yourself in any conditions. The "galley alley" was oriented fore and aft, so that you could brace for lurches and not get catapulted across the boat.

The crew mess table had space for five or six, if squeezed in. This table, and the saloon table, were made from a big piece of black walnut that had come from a tree on my parents' property in Illinois.

A few steps down, and forward of the crew mess, was the saloon. It was the library, music room, occasional movie palace, and general snuggery to curl up off-watch. The seating was soft, the backs were deep, and every shipmate had a nap there one time or another. In port, it was entertainment central.

Across from the saloon was my cabin. Next forward was the ship's office, with computers, long- and short-range radios, Sat phone, and many of the gauges and switches to control the ship's systems like the watermaker and generator. It also held half a dozen three-ring binders with the instructions and parts manuals for everything on board. To be a successful modern skipper, you have to be a good librarian. Right from the start we had saved and categorized every piece of paper that had come with every piece of equipment. We had perhaps a thousand different pieces of instructions, parts catalogs, and trouble-shooting directions.

Next forward was head and sink on the right and shower and sink on the left. Then the second double on the left, the good single on the right with pipe berth above and finally, the fo'c'sle, with the rarely used pipe berth. On the starboard side of the fo'c'sle was a whole wall of spare lines and gear, and assorted big plastic bins, some full of tools, screws and bolts, and others with wine, whiskey, and rum. There was a vise tucked in the corner, which got regular use.

On deck, the *Maggie B*'s cockpit was quite large. It was comfortable with a dozen people in it when in port. You definitely felt that if you were in the cockpit, you were going to stay in the cockpit, something critical offshore. At sea, there were helmsman's seats on either side that you could tuck into and see and control everything. In the middle of the cockpit there was a lovely foldable table.

I have always hated canvas dodgers on boats. If they were big enough to protect you, they limited your ability to see forward. If they were small enough not to be in the way, they didn't do much to protect you and were often a pain to get past going below or forward, especially if you were in full foul weather gear.

While I was determined not to have a dodger on the *Maggie B*, I still wanted to have adequate shelter for the crew. Nigel came up with a typically elegant solution. The roof of the house for the galley and crew mess continued aft about two feet, and there was a comfortable seat on either side beneath it, facing in. There were big windows, usually open both forward into the galley and crew mess and aft into the cockpit. You were out of the weather but still on deck, and could access all the instruments and screens. In very heavy weather, the thick Plexiglas outer windows could be dropped in and the companionway boards inserted and locked off. Charmingly, Nigel called the crew shelter "the winter porch."

The cockpit was graced by the helm, which had been rescued from a Southern California nautical antiques store. The wheel came from a 1942 Liberty ship, and had many miles on it. We stripped and redid the old varnish and added a stainless outer rim, which was finished off with French braid fancy work, applied during quiet evenings in the kitchen of the crew house before launch.

Light for the interior spaces was provided by portholes, traditional skylights, and old-fashioned (but incredibly successful) round deck prisms. All the interior electrical lights were LEDs, which after an initial bad lot, lasted forever and used almost no electricity.

The deck was carefully designed to be long lasting. Nigel specified a sandwich where the middle layer was Corecell, a structural hard foamcore material that was invulnerable to seepage. The top decking was Douglas fir, which was quarter-sawn so that it did not produce splinters.

The masts, sails, and rigging were an optimized blend of very modern and traditional. The masts were perfectly round and of constant diameter most of their heights. They could have been made of cellulose, grown in a Nova Scotia forest a hundred years ago, but instead they were formed of a modern carbon fiber in a loft in Rhode Island.

The standing rigging was made up of modern fibers also, soft instead of the hard metal of most boats. Our rig was mostly adjusted with the pulley advantage of bronze deadeyes rather than steel turnbuckles. Steel turnbuckles are notorious for being "fine" one day and cracked and broken the next (often with a lost rig). Unlike the old days, the Vectran lanyards were strong enough to lift the whole boat, while they had the honesty of fiber and would show fatigue and wear.

The sails were made by North Sails and turned out excellently. The material was Spectra Dyneema, laminated together. With sails, you worry about them ripping, stretching out of shape, deteriorating with the UV from the sun, and chafing and wearing. We used the same three basic sails for 38,400 nautical miles over two years, two months. We raced at the Antigua Classic Yacht Regatta in 2006 with the suit of sails and then took them around the world in the Southern Ocean, then raced again with them at the 2008 Antigua Classic—and they still looked great!

We checked the sails every watch, and had a few rips and blown cringles, but they were our most dependable engine. North Sails did a wonderful job of supporting us all around the world.

Most sloops will have perhaps a half-dozen to a dozen different jibs. We had only one, which could be roller-reefed in the heaviest weather. Besides the three basic sails, we had an asymmetrical lightweight downwind sail that we called "the Bird," and two storm sails called Cathy and Sally for the women who made them in the North Sails Lunenburg loft.

We would practice regularly with the storm sails, but never needed them. We had about 40 knots of wind for a day or so, but the *Maggie B* was very comfortable with the main with three reefs, the foresail down, and the jib rolled up to just the size of two winter overcoats.

The only part of the rig we had trouble with was the jib furler. Everything except the furler liked the soft rigging. It was constructed out of long aluminum sections, joined by short inner pieces, all attached by short grub screws. The forestay would flex and the little bolts would be spat out like teeth in a bare-knuckle fight.

Other systems included the Yanmar engine, Onan generator, Spectra watermaker, Dickinson cabin heater, Force Ten galley stove, and Sea Frost refrigeration system.

But all of the above is just wood and steel, fiber and systems. A boat is just a

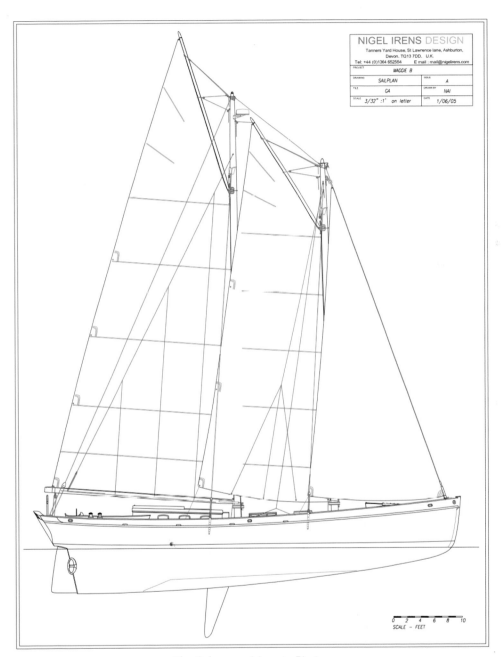

The Schooner *Maggie B*'s rig.

13

fixture until you have your crew. Whenever I give my talk about the circumnavigation, the two photos I emphasize the most are of the crew mess. The first one is a stock "magazine" photo of the space, done to show off the fit and finish. The second one is of the space populated with the happy crew of Gail, Paul, John, Bori, and Ann-Louise sitting down to Gail's fish stew, en route to Bermuda on our maiden voyage.

During the two years, two months that it took us to get around, we had 26 crew-members (nearly evenly comprised of men and women). All were volunteers. Some stayed for just a leg, some more than a year. Ages were from early twenties to older than I am. One I had known since I was 12 years old, others came from fortuitous meetings in ports. Only three didn't work out, which is probably average for any endeavor.

The crew varied from highly skilled and experienced in the marine trades to new sailors. Nationalities included American, Canadian, English, French, Dutch, Hungarian, German, Australian, and New Zealander.

I am delighted that most all of the crew have kept in touch since the voyage, that at least five shipmates are going for their captain's licenses, and that many are already in contact to sail on the next boat.

Joseph Conrad, in *The Mirror of the Sea*, probably made the most eloquent description ever of a gathering of schooners:

"A fleet of fore-and-afters at anchor has its own slender graciousness. The setting of their sails resembles more than anything else the unfolding of a bird's wings; the facility of their evolutions is a pleasure to the eye. They are birds of the sea, whose swimming is like flying, and resembles more a natural function than the handling of man-invented appliances. The fore-and-aft rig in its simplicity and the beauty of its aspect under every angle of vision is, I believe, unapproachable. A schooner, yawl, or cutter in charge of a capable man seems to handle herself as if endowed with the power of reasoning and the gift of swift execution. One laughs with sheer pleasure at a smart piece of maneuvering, as at a manifestation of a living creature's quick wit and graceful precision."

\* \* \*

This isn't a how-to-sail book, nor is it a textbook on navigation or meteorology or marine systems. While we had excellent adventures in Cape Town, Buenos Aires, Hobart and many other places, there are plenty of great travel books written by others. We didn't have any near-death experiences, nor did we spend 93 days in a liferaft drinking seagull blood. This isn't a compilation of Cape Horn stories dosed with a little dab of personal salt water.

I set out to fulfill every sailor's dream of a circumnavigation. Simply, I want to give a sense of the joys of Blue Water, and the hard and soft skills necessary to sail around the globe fast, safe, and comfortable. We all sharpened our sense of wonder, our joy in accomplishment, and the rediscovery of patient sailors' skills.

At sea, we kept the log every four hours. It recorded position, weather, sail configuration, ships sighted, and the like. Each day the noon position was the most important. Each afternoon I would write up the working details of weather and position as well as expectations, worries, triumphs, breakdowns, meals, books, and delights.

*Maggie B* was the first boat I ever helped to build. I learned something new every day. Her plans were finished in March 2004. Her first rib was completed in June 2004. She was launched in January 2006.

So, what follows is our adventure as it unfolded day-by-day—what we learned, what we were taught, the good and the bad as we experienced it. There are occasional sidebars that attempt to distill learnings in a variety of areas, but the core intent is to share the adventure as it happened, not smoothed and polished later. Come along!

## Starting Out—Nova Scotia

I had vaguely thought that when you launch a boat, she is ready to go. I learned that launching is just the start of the work to finish her. The engines have never run; the radios have never radioed; the batteries have never provided power; the centerboard has never moved; the watermaker has never made water; the refrigerators have never cooled; the lights have never lit; the sails have never been hoisted; the hatches have never kept out water; the stove has never cooked; the heater has never heated; the rudder has never steered; the anchor has never been lowered; the radar has never scanned; and the toilet has never flushed.

Nova Scotia can be harsh in winter. Several people asked why I bothered to launch in January—why not wait until the weather is nice to fit her out? My reply was that I wanted to be somewhere in June, not sitting at the dock in Lunenburg.

Fitting-out that winter was an experience. Most days started in the morning with shoveling the previous night's snowfall, sometimes a few feet worth. Then we tested, aligned, greased, and ran everything. We would motor around the harbor, go for a sail, and run all the equipment. We took her out for the 65 NM (nautical mile) run up to Halifax in February to try her in some sea, and got a big dose of ice on the way back.

We loaded on all the gear. Anchors and chain, tools, water, fuel, lights, batteries, life jackets, blankets, towels, books, fire extinguishers, emergency gear, portable radios, our tender, *Reepicheep,* charts, liferaft, extra oil, filters of every sort, spares for everything—even an extra propeller. Food for the first week's trip to Bermuda, with canned food in case we were delayed en route, and liferaft food in the event of a disaster.

The big plan was to sail around the world, from west to east, in the Southern Hemisphere. That meant heading south to perhaps 30 or 40 degrees south to pick up the westerlies. Wind is power for a sailboat. If you are headed east around, having the wind from the west is good. No wind is bad, east wind is worse. Our plan was to go by the great capes: Good Hope in Africa, Southeast Cape in Tasmania, and Cape Horn.

### BLUENOSE, GERTRUDE L. THEBAUD AND WANDERER

In 1920 in Halifax there was major derision at a note in the newspaper that the New York Yacht Club had canceled a race because of a 23 mph "gale." Besides knowing that a gale starts at 28 knots - 33 mph, the Nova Scotians sneered at sailors who ran for port in what they considered to be just the start of a decent breeze.

The *Halifax Herald* subsequently sponsored the International Fishing Vessel Championship for "real" boats. One of the rules was that the entrant had to have spent a season on the Grand Banks fishing, a requirement designed to eliminate the kind of yachts the NYYC sailed and raced. All the boats that raced were schooners.

Unfortunately for Nova Scotian pride, in the first race, *Esperanto* from Gloucester beat the Canadian entrant, *Delawana*.

The yard of Smith and Rhuland in Lunenburg was commissioned to build a fishing schooner that could beat the Americans. *Bluenose* was launched in March 1921. The name represented the self-applied nickname for a Nova Scotian.

After a required season fishing the Banks, *Bluenose* went to Gloucester in the fall of 1921 to recapture the Fisherman's Cup from *Elsie*. *Bluenose*, sailed by Captain Angus Walters, was able to keep the Fisherman's Cup in Nova Scotia for the next seventeen years.

In the last race in 1938, the American challenger was *Gertrude L. Thebaud*. The *Thebaud* tied the *Bluenose* 2-2, out of five in the series. The event was somewhat controversial with races canceled at the last moment, Captain Walters scandalizing his

There is a marvelous Atlas of Pilot Charts that contains 300 years of wind data. One book for every ocean—one page for every month. Plotted out for each 300 by 300 NM of ocean is a plot of the average wind direction and speed plus waves, visibility, ice, and chance of very strong winds. We had great tactical guidance from a weather router in New Hampshire, Commanders' Weather, but for strategy it was critical to stand on the shoulders of all the great sailors over the years.

There were some places I wanted to go: the Caribbean islands, Brazil, South Africa, the Seychelles, Sri Lanka, Australia, New Zealand, French Polynesia, Chile, and Argentina. There were others I wanted to stay away from—places where piracy was a long-standing occupation—such as the Red Sea, the Straits of Malacca, much of Indonesia, and Papua, New Guinea.

home province by agreeing to race on Sundays, and outraging the Americans when he was caught sneaking ballast off the *Bluenose* to give her an advantage in light weather.

In the final race, the *Bluenose* won by two minutes and 50 seconds. The foretopman and navigator of the *Thebaud*, Sterling Hayden, gave the day's light wind the ultimate fisherman's insult as being a "New York Yacht Club" breeze.

Sterling Hayden had gone to sea when he was 15, in 1931. He worked as a doryman on the Grand Banks out of Gloucester, had gotten his Master's license and had sailed around the world by the time of the last Fisherman's Cup.

Photographs of Hayden in the articles about the *Bluenose/Thebaud* races got him discovered by Hollywood. He became well known to movie audiences from his roles in 58 movies, especially *The Asphalt Jungle*, *Johnnie Guitar*, General Jack D. Ripper in *Dr. Strangelove*, and Captain McCluskey in *The Godfather*. But sailors cherish him for his autobiography, *Wanderer*.

*Wanderer* was the name of his 98-foot schooner. He became the hero to every sailor and many landsmen, when, in 1959, he threw away his hated Hollywood career, defied his ex-wife, judges, magistrates and sheriffs, and took his four small children, a volunteer crew of 13 and three other children, on a voyage to the South Seas.

His beautifully written book is about his experience of actually doing what so many dream of – chucking everything and sailing a big wooden schooner with friends away to a distant tropical paradise.

The route south from Nova Scotia to Bermuda and then on to the Caribbean was obvious. After that it was down the coast to Brazil, then across to Cape Town. It was a route traveled often over the years. There weren't many alternatives, given the winds and currents. Perhaps we could have gone the Great Circle Route from Nova Scotia to England and then south to the Azores and then across to Brazil, but that was way longer.

John Steele also tempted us to enter the Antigua Classic Yacht Regatta. Many of the most beautiful and historic sailboats in the world end their season in the Caribbean at that gathering each April. John had many friends there and he wanted to show off his newest, fastest schooner. How could we resist?

In the circumnavigation, I wanted to move, to make miles, to cover the long legs. I also wanted to enjoy the places we stopped. Race boats go when the gun goes off. Conversely, some cruisers stop for months or years when they get to a nice spot. We were somewhere in between. We ended up spending two days in port for each day we spent at sea over the two years, two months that it took us to get back to Lunenburg. I loved Cape Town, and Hobart, and Bahia, but after a few weeks, I would get itchy and was ready for the next passage. Mostly we went 24/7 when we got going. Only in Chile did we work our way day by day south to the Horn.

## RULES

The English Royal Navy established the famous 35 Articles of War in 1757. The first was that captains should "shall cause the public worship of Almighty God, according to the liturgy of the Church of England established by law." The 35th was, "All other crimes not capital committed by any person or persons in the fleet, which are not mentioned in this act, or for which no punishment is hereby directed to be inflicted, shall be punished by the laws and customs in such cases used at sea."

Captain Bligh nailed his rules to the main mast of the Bounty, though unfortunately he had no Royal Marines to enforce Number 18 – "mutinous assembly… shall suffer death."

The rules of a ship, though, from time immemorial, are the captain's. He or she has complete responsibility and thus complete authority. The captain's word is law.

That said, we didn't have many rules on the Maggie B. They were:

1. Always carry a knife when on deck at sea.

2. Wear a harness/lifejacket when on deck at night. Snap it into the jackline when going forward at night.

3. No drinking at sea, except for a glass of wine or a beer on rare lunches when all the conditions were perfect.

4. No drugs aboard – ever.

5. Do your share.

6. Say please and thank you.

"Starboard!!" Photo credit: Tim Wright, Photoaction.com

*"I had to call "STARBOARD" on Altair
and we missed getting crushed by 15 feet."*

# 1

# NOVA SCOTIA TO
# DESHAIES, GUADELOUPE

## 28 MARCH 2006

The schooner *Maggie B* departed Lunenburg, Nova Scotia, for Bermuda on March 27th at 1:20 p.m. on her first leg of the circumnavigation. We are headed out of Nova Scotia winter to a lovely spring in a semi-tropical paradise. Aboard is a real Blue Water crew: John Steele, Anne-Louise Dauphinee, Gail Atkinson, Bori Kiss, Paul Basket, and myself. All are highly experienced, cheery, "the glass is half full" shipmates. It is about 700 NM to Bermuda.

It is 40 degrees and generally fair weather. The wind north-north-west at 15–20 knots. There is a long swell of 8 to 10 feet, with a chop of 2 to 3 feet. We are headed south-southwest at 8 knots, on a nice broad reach. All is well.

No sooner had I typed the last sentence on the boat than the main peak halyard let go due to chafe at the saddle. Crash, down came the mainsail! But within an hour we had the foresail up with one reef and the main halyard repaired and re-hoisted with one reef and were back doing 7–8 knots.

Last night we had another "starting out" problem when the engine's oil filter came off during charging and blew out six quarts of hot oil all over the engine room before it was shut down. John and Anne-Louise were total heroes to dive into the engine room to clean up the hideous mess. Now it is all cleaned up and repaired. Also, there is something caught in the prop and it will not feather. We hope that these are just teething problems.

We had a big troop of dolphin playing around us as we were fixing the main and a tired bird, a junco, aboard for a few hours rest.

## 29 MARCH 2006

We have 408 miles to go to Bermuda and have gone 312 miles from Lunenburg. We are making 6 knots under a light easterly. The main is up with one reef together with our beautiful G2 gennaker, AKA "the Bird." The sea is smoothing out with just a long northeasterly swell.

The seawater has warmed up from 36 F to 60 F since yesterday noon. We expect to enter the Gulf Stream around midnight tonight.

Saw many VLSs (Very Large Ships!) last night. They seem to appear only after full dark.

A large pod of pilot whales passed by us but didn't stop to play.

First sail trials with the gennaker, called "the Bird" up.

## 30 MARCH 2006

We have averaged 6.9 knots VMG (velocity made good) since leaving Nova Scotia. VMG is not speed through the water (STW) or speed over the ground (SOG). VMG is how fast you are going towards your destination. SOG is how fast you are going—in whichever direction you are going—which may or may not be towards Bermuda. STW is how fast you are going through the water, which can be affected by current or tide. We ran somewhat west of our rhumb line (shortest route) for the first half of the voyage, trading speed in the northwesterly for angle. Now we are heading east of the rhumb line in a fresh northeast by east breeze.

Our passage through the Gulf Stream took place during the midnight to 6 a.m. watches. We regularly hit 10 knots SOG with about half a knot assist southerly and some easterly set from the Stream. I used to think that the Gulf Stream was simply a tight current rushing north up the coast. In fact, it has lots of swirls, so even if you are headed south from Nova Scotia to Bermuda, you can get a boost on your way if you hit it right. We hit it right, with guidance from Commanders' Weather.

Our estimated time of arrival at St. Georges, Bermuda, is about midnight on Friday, March 31st. We hope for a relatively fast turnaround (one week?) then depart for Antigua to participate in Race Week. It is strange to be out in Blue Water, headed to Bermuda, such a prized destination for so many sailors, but for us it is just the first stop in a 30,000 NM-plus trip. It is hard both to glory in the speed and success of this first leg, and to look ahead.

It is March in the North Atlantic, but we are stunned by how fast it has gotten warmer. John Steele was the first crewmember on deck in shorts, and many were barefoot today. John was disqualified, however, because he put his "took" (toque—French Canadian for knit hat) back on within half an hour.

Lovely sailing.


## 31 MARCH 2006

At noon, we were about 120 miles from St. Georges, Bermuda. We motored this morning because the wind is light from the northeast, with no sign of it backing to the northwest as expected. At about 10 a.m. we realized that there was no reason to go fast and arrive at St. Georges at 3 a.m. tomorrow. We played with "the Bird" (G2 gennaker) until about 5 p.m. in fine conditions. But Bermuda is right downwind of us so we started slow motoring, planning to arrive at 8 a.m. It makes no sense to rush to arrive during the night, and risk the reefs and tight passages.

I talked to Bermuda Harbor Radio on SSB (single sideband) and they will coordinate with Customs and Immigration for our arrival.

The Furuno autopilot has been working hard for us. It is adaptive, meaning it learns from experience (unlike some of us humans), and does a great job. Autopilots are often given nicknames on boats. The naming of ours has caused serious discussions among the crew. John Steele voted for George, in honor of a longtime friend. Frank favored Oscar, the name of famous sailor Peobo Gardner's professional captain, who was skilled at bringing his boat back from far-flung places. A stand-off ensued until Gail suggested naming it after the mythical *contrabandista* who steered *Spray* when Joshua Slocum was ill on his renowned solo circumnavigation in 1895. We whipped out the ship's copy of *Alone Around the World* and found a picture of the fevered illusion, but, alas, no name was mentioned. So, we agreed on Jorge, a reasonable contrabandista helmsman's name.

Cathy sewing our storm sail
in the loft in Lunenburg.

We tried out the storm staysail today. It was made in the North Sails loft in Lunenburg. It is always good to try these things before you really need them. I got tired of saying "storm staysail," so we agreed on calling it Cathy after the person who made it. Right now, "Cathy" is flying as a handsome stabilizer. No storms are in sight. The smaller storm trysail is nicknamed "Susan," who works with Cathy at North Sails.

We expect to experience Bermuda customs at about 9 a.m. tomorrow, April 1st.

## 2 APRIL 2006

We arrived at Town Cut—the way into St. Georges Harbor—at 8 a.m. on April 1st (no joke!). We had dogged it a bit to allow for a safe daylight approach, and also for the fun of seeing the island appear over the horizon.

*Maggie B* at Captain Smokes Marina, St. Georges, Bermuda.

Customs clearance was easy and quick, with only the flare gun being impounded until our departure. We are currently moored Mediterranean style (bow tied to moorings, stern lashed to bollards on the wharf with a gang plank from the stern to the wharf). Our landing site, Captain Smokes Marina, is an easy five-minute walk from the center of St. Georges, and well protected by a huge fort right up the hill.

Celebration of our arrival after our first Blue Water trip started early and ended late at the White Horse Tavern in St. Georges, Bermuda. The Gosling Brothers, makers of Bermuda's Black Rum, have been significantly enriched.

We are completely thrilled with the *Maggie B*'s first Blue Water leg, her maiden voyage! We averaged 6.2 knots for the 720 NM trip and were only the third sailboat to reach Bermuda this year from North America. The first two each lost a mast, and one person was killed.

We are learning that we have a fast, crew-friendly ship. Even doing 10 knots crossing the Gulf Stream in March, the off watch was able to sleep comfortably below.

We have a busy week ahead with lots of little things to fix before we depart for Antigua. Bermuda is so marvelously positioned: just where a sailor would want a pit stop, there she is!

Cleanup in Bermuda.

# BERMUDA

I smelled Bermuda half a day before I first saw it. It was on a race in the late 60's from Newport and we had been somewhat roughly handled along the way. We were very eager to finish. We were beating to windward and the smell of the island – jasmine – was clear and strong more than 30 miles out.

Bermuda is so strange, perched all by itself, circled in the far distance by the North American coast. It is 750 NM from Halifax, 670 from Boston, 630 from Norfolk, and 910 from Miami. Sailors making the passage must cross the sometimes fearsome, always interesting, Gulf Stream. It is a perfect destination in itself, but also an excellent pit stop when traveling from Nova Scotia to Antigua or Charleston to Europe.

A Blue Water captain's first experience with Bermuda is often with the very powerful Bermuda Radio. They want to know everything about you, your crew, your ship and your rescue gear. It is a good reminder that Bermuda has been saving endangered sailors for hundreds of years, and knows its business.

It was discovered in 1505 by Juan de Bermudez, a Spanish explorer. First settled, unintentionally, in 1607 by Admiral, Sir George Somers, who wrecked his flagship, *Sea Venture*, on the very scary Bermuda reefs, saving his whole crew as well as the ship's hound. Shakespeare wrote *The Tempest* after he read the story.

Many, many vessels have been shipwrecked on Bermuda. Some are now popular tourist diving sites; others are just visible in St. Georges Harbor, poking a bit above the waves. But if you work your way safely through the

A formal crest.

passages into Town Cut and into Saint Georges harbor, you know that you are safe from whatever is going on outside.

Bermuda is used to taking care of the passing sailor. Sail lofts, engine overhauls, and hydraulic refit – just ask. Also there are great bars like the White Horse Inn, that has been making Dark and Stormies for many, many years.

Bermuda is also used to taking care of itself, and has the secure feeling of a windward shore. The houses, churches, fortifications, trees and walls are all very well attached. For the tourists, there are golf courses, umbrellas, sun porches, and pink sand beaches; but you can also see everywhere that it is quick and easy to clear the decks, batten down the hatches and ride out the next storm.

## 9 APRIL 2006

At noon on April 9th, we were about 10 miles southeast of Bermuda, on our way to Antigua. We probably surprised onlookers by doing two 360-degree turns on our way out to calibrate our electronic compass.

The wind is fresh at 15–25 knots from the south. We got our main up in the harbor, with one reef and the full jib, and sailed out of Town Cut for the fun of it.

The time in Bermuda was well spent. St. Georges is a very friendly town, and we got lots of work accomplished, both repair and improve.

Now offshore, we are close hauled on the starboard tack, heading about 110 degrees at 7 knots. Seas are 7–8 feet and somewhat confused. Antigua is about 920 NM away on a heading of about 185 degrees.

Most sailors' instinct would be to tack and head more for Antigua, rather than heading so far east, but the weather pattern shows our strategy. We are trying to stay ahead (east) of the next cold front coming off the American coast and get into easterly winds. Our plan is to stay on starboard tack until we are really headed, and then tack for Antigua. In a day we hope to be on a comfortable beam reach on port tack, charging along right for Antigua, catching fish for dinner!

## 10 APRIL 2006

Our noon position was about 170 miles southeast of Bermuda. We are chasing the easterlies and hope to be in them by nightfall. Currently the winds are south-southwest at 10–12 knots. We are still making 6.5 knots to the southeast.

Last night we put a second reef in the main and kept the foresail furled as the winds rose to about 25 knots. During the night, we had the stars to guide us: Arcturus and Deneb in the Swan to starboard, and Vega in Lyra to port.

On leaving Bermuda waters, we took down the Bermuda courtesy flag. In a burst of enthusiasm, we hoisted up "Bravo Charlie" which in the International Code of Signals means "Full Speed Ahead."

Two fishing poles are in action with a Nova Scotia "Ballyhoo" lure on one side of the boat and a Bermuda "Insane Squid" lure on the other.

The centerboard had been making big clunking noises from time to time. We tried to raise it to see if we could stop the noise, but it is jammed down. We nominated Paul, as a representative of Covey Island, to check it out (at 7 knots), but he declined. I guess that we'll get hauled in Antigua, though we'll try again on the other tack to see if it can be moved.

## 11 APRIL 2006

We are motorsailing, mostly motoring, as the wind is only 5 knots. It is from the southeast, a direction that we have been hoping for, but we need a bit more pressure.

At about 8:30 this morning, our fishing lines were hit by very big Wahoo *(Acanthocybium solandri)*, who gave us a couple of lovely jumps before taking the Nova Scotian lure, leader, and line.

The centerboard is not exactly fixed, but it will go up and down now with some complaining. It has some sort of hang-up at the full-down position, so we don't use more than 75% down.

What We're Eating:

Lunch today was "29th Parallel" sandwiches: canned salmon dosed with fresh onion and mayo, laid on a bed of snow peas, with mustard and mayo on 12-grain bread. Needless to say, Paul added a good dose of Tabasco. Delicious!

What We're Reading:

Paul: *1421: The Year China Discovered America* by Gavin Menzies

Bori: *Edge Seasons: A Mid-Life Year* by Beth Powning

Anne Louise: *Ocean Sea* by Alessandro Baricco

Frank: *Caribbean* by James Michener

We are all also spending a lot of time with hot topics such as the *2006 Nautical Almanac*, the Furuno operator's manual, and *The Cruiser's Handbook of Fishing* by Scott and Wendy Bannerot.

I sent this email from the boat to the Reverend Calum MacLeod at my church in Chicago:

Dear Calum:

Now about three in the morning. We have finally picked up the easterly trades and are about 300 miles out of Bermuda and 600 to Antigua, rolling along at eight knots, hardly touching a sail.

I like standing the first watch—midnight to 4 a.m. It is quiet and focused and important and sometimes hard. I have my iPod with me and burned in Elam Davies CD of his sermons. It really is something to listen to "God is Love" as you sail with Arcturus as a guide (GPS also...) and the sails lit by the moon.

Hope all is well in Chicago.

Best to John and all.

Frank

# CREW

Traditionally crew were part of your family or tribe or village. Some were along for the fun or food or travel or money or to get away from the law. Some were slaves. The English Navy used a Press Gang. Many stories tell of First Mates going through brothels and jails to fill out their crew. Melville famously described going to sea as a way of "driving off the spleen and regulating the circulation" when he had "a damp, drizzly November in [his] soul."

Six on deck.

Being crew on a sailing boat is hugely romantic and can be a wonderful life. It also can be misery and dangerous. The skill and attitude of the captain and the other crew matters hugely, as does the condition of the vessel and where she is going.

On board *Maggie B,* our crew was male and female; early 20's to late 60's; one I had known for fifty years and others were new acquaintances.

People go to sea for a break, for an adventure and to fill out their maritime resume. Many would come up to the boat when we were docked to enquire if there was space. I paid no salary, only a token amount of "walking around" money. I would fly people home if they stayed for a passage. Some boats hire crew and captain and pay a fair wage, some charge crew for the honor and training of being aboard a great ship. So we were somewhere in-between.

For me, the main criteria for crew are that they be interested and interesting. Also non-pukers. Mostly it was a question of whether you wanted to live with them in close quarters for a passage.

Many think that you have to be an experienced buoy racer to be a good sailor. But really not so. The skills you want are mostly what you would want in a good roommate. Plus a reasonable sense of technology.

One of the most essential skills in a shipmate is to know when to call the captain. I would always say that if you were uncomfortable, call the captain. If you were wondering if you should call the captain or not, call the captain. I missed sleep sometimes, but I was the most concerned was when they didn't call me and should have.

In vetting potential crew, we would, when we could, all have a few meals together and a sail. Otherwise he or she would need to have a strong endorsement from somebody on board.

*Maggie B* was a fast, complicated sailboat. But the skills to run her were more common sense than knowing how to splice a main brace. I could teach a new person how to be a good sailor in a week or two, but I couldn't teach a great sailor who was a jerk, how not to be a jerk.

## 12 APRIL 2006

Winds have been variable from the east from 5–20 knots. We have been getting occasional tradewind rain showers with wind before and calm afterward. Nice freshwater wash-downs.

Yesterday we had a pod of about 30 striped dolphins playing around our bow. Their Latin name is *Stenella coeruleoalba* (cerulean and white). They have beautiful racing stripes on their flanks. A third of the pod jumps perfectly together at a time.

Today we saw our first Yellow-billed Tropicbird *(Phaethon lepturus)*, which seemed interested in our fishing lure. Not the sort of catch we had in mind.

The big excitement was seeing a whale (a migrating humpback perhaps?) doing a series of acrobatics to celebrate the arrival of a big rain shower. Lots of tail slaps and a few breaches.

We have 522 miles to Antigua. We are about 1,000 miles east of Miami.

What we are eating: Breakfast this morning was 4-minute soft-boiled eggs with strips of prosciutto over and salsa on the side, washed down with cranberry juice and lots of French roast coffee.

## 13 APRIL 2006

So much for easy tradewind sailing. The wind has veered to 150–160 degrees and increased to 25 knots with gusts to 30. Rain squalls come and go. We are reefed down to two reefs on the main and one on the foresail. Our course is southwest and speed 8 knots. There are moderate swells from the southeast and 4-foot waves on top. The sea is building.

Our expectation is that this low will pass north of us and the wind will veer further. The east side of Antigua bears about 195 degrees, at 365 miles. Our plan is to tack if the wind veers much past 195. Plan B is to make for Anguilla Passage between Anguilla and the British Virgin Islands, but that choice is about a day away.

The barometer has fallen to 1014 from 1019 mb yesterday.

Lunch today was *lecso*, a traditional Hungarian dish of eggs, tomatoes, and mushrooms. Bori is a bit cranky because no paprika was available in Bermuda, so the dish lacked full authenticity. It is a tribute to the *Maggie B*'s seakindliness that we could all sit down and have a comfortable hot lunch in these conditions.

Last night at 5 a.m., the second watch (Paul and Bori) woke me because we had a meeting situation with a VLS. We had right of way both for being a sailing ship as well as being off their starboard bow, with them being at our nine o'clock, with a steady bearing angle.

We were finally able to contact them (wake them?) when they were about one mile away. When the groggy voice announced, "Yes, I am seeing you, I will go to your left behind but maybe I am OK crossing you." We began to reach for the flare gun. Paul dogged it, heading up and luffing, and the VLS passed about one-quarter mile ahead.

Two tropicbirds made repeated passes to alight on the main gaff peak, but it was just too smooth for them to land. Two flying fish came aboard in the night and were hooked up as bait, but without success. Next time we should better appreciate our place in the food chain and just fry them up for breakfast.

## 14 APRIL 2006

Well, we got spanked last night.

We made good only 75 miles towards Antigua in the last 24 hours. But we sure did a lot of sailing. There is a developing low in our area and it seemed to develope right over us.

The Captain at the helm on a dirty day.

We knew we were in trouble when we saw the 70-foot maxi race boat ABN AMRO go past us, northbound, at about 20 knots with a huge spinnaker up. They reported on the radio that they were currently in first place in the Rio to Baltimore leg of the Volvo Ocean Race. Two things can be surmised by this: first, that they are going in the opposite direction than we are, and second, that they have sought out the worst possible, strongest area of weather to push them to Baltimore.

Shortly after seeing ABM AMRO, we commenced to reenact the role of Joe Btfsplk, the Li'l Abner character who always had a raincloud over his head. As darkness fell, we had about 6 hours of a southerly gale, with winds steady over 30 knots with higher gusts. Good news for ABN AMRO, bad news for us.

We had the jib rolled up halfway (nice roller reefing design!) and two reefs in the main. The foresail was doused. We stayed on a close reach for better control, sometimes headed east to get clear, then back west as it seemed possible to head for the Anguilla Passage. The waves were quite sharp, 9 to 12 feet with occasional breaking crests. It was a long night. *Maggie B* stayed controllable and steady. Below decks was mostly dry and warm. All gear worked fine and only one glass was broken. Dinner was scones and chocolate.

We regretted not making suitable toasts to the gods on departure from Bermuda.

We're still learning. On this leg from Bermuda to Antigua we got reminded that a little paranoia is a good thing.

We had set out from Bermuda for the 940-mile trip to Antigua with three good pieces of weather advice: 1) the excellent four-day forecast from Bermuda Weather Service, 2) a trip plan from Commanders' Weather, and 3) advice from the marvelous Canadian weather sage, Herb, of *Southbound II*.

We also left with the expectation (gee, it's in all the brochures, isn't it?) that we would quickly get into the easterly trades and bowl on down, reading our novels at leisure and never touching a sheet.

All three professional forecasts said that we would pick up the easterlies at about 29 or 30 North, and we did on Tuesday, two days out.

The weather and the sailing were just like the brochures…for a while.

Our forecasts generally covered four days and were right on…for four days. The plan had been to give Herb a call each day at 2000 to update, but propagation was terrible and we didn't get through.

Four days out the barometer started to fall modestly (to 1011 mb from 1019 mb the day before) and the wind picked up from the south-southeast.

That evening we had a fresh southerly gale, Beaufort 8, with winds at 34–40 knots. The boat and crew handled it fine, but we should have anticipated it better. We would not have done much different, though it would have made sense to have run east a bit more to get further away from the developing low when we had an easterly wind to moderate the impact. When unable to contact Herb, I should have spent more time with the difficult-to-understand USCG SSB weather reports, called Commanders' Weather on the Sat phone, and gotten the weather fax working in Bermuda, or all three. We're still learning.

Now we are about a day's run to Antigua, bowling along in a nice 15-knot westerly, reading our novels, and improving our tans. God and Herb know where the easterly trades are.

## 16 APRIL 2006

The Schooner *Maggie B* arrived safely at Nelson's Dockyard, English Harbor, Antigua, at approximately noon on April 16th. Almost one week from Bermuda to here. We are at the dock that the Hero of the Nile, Lord Nelson himself, blessed.

Last night the excitement was catching a nice, small (4 foot, about 25 pound) wahoo. Almost no fight until close to the boat. Frank cranked in, Paul handled the boat with Bori, and Anne Louise handled the gaff. Not too much mess on the stern and Anne Louise only gaffed herself a bit ("just a flesh wound" as they say in Monty Python). The fish was cut up and sautéed in oil, butter, garlic, and a bit of lemon and was on the table in an hour. Absolutely delicious.

English Harbor is full of Big Dogs: 100-foot sloops with tons of brightwork and professional crews. There are also lots of white plastic sloops with more bimini than sail area. We should have lots of fun. The next step is to put our tender, *Reepicheep*, in the water and row around to see the other boats.

Crowded after the races in Antigua.

Single-handed sailing in Antigua. Credit: Tim Wright, Photoaction.com

### 18 APRIL 2006

Antigua Classic Race Week is quite something. Some of the most beautiful sailing yachts on the planet are here. It is marvelous that *Maggie B* is a little part of it.

I raced *Maggie B* yesterday in the single-handed race and we were first through the course, but only third on corrected time. One might ask how you can handle a 62-foot gaff schooner by yourself, and the answer is "not too well."

The rules are that you can have extra crew to get your sails up; John Steele, Dorian Steele, Sandy MacMillian of North Sails, and Paul Basket got us going. They have to be off the boat before the ten-minute gun and Paul and Dorian exited in great style with cannon balls into the warm sea. John and Sandy stepped off into a passing outboard. There were about 30 boats of all sizes and we got a good start and just stayed out in front. Nigel Irens, the boat's designer, was my safety crew aboard. I had great difficulty keeping him from touching anything.

Today was the "Old Road" race and we finally had a nice blow. Huge boats around us, such as *Ranger*, one of the famous J-Class boats. There were lots of photo boats and helicopters about.

Racing with a full crew in Antigua. Credit: Tim Wright, Photoaction.com

It was just marvelous to have the builder, the boat designer, and the sail designer aboard. We all learned so much about *Maggie B,* as well as seeing some of the coolest sailboats in the world rocketing around us. I have never participated in such a spectacle. And we get to do it again tomorrow!

### 20 APRIL 2006

Antigua Classic Race Week was such an experience. Wouldn't have missed it for the world and thought I would never be able to do it again.

Many of the race photos are taken by a guy named Tim Wright. He goes out in a tiny high-speed boat strapped to his feet and gets right into the action with his cameras. He also is a really nice guy. He has stunning photos of *Endeavor, Ranger, Altair* (the most beautiful schooner in the world), and *Mariella.* I had to call "*STARBOARD!*" to *Altair* as we were doing about 9 knots and she was doing 15 as we came to a mark simultaneously. We missed getting crushed by 15 feet.

We came in third in the single-handed competition, third in the Classics, and

Passing *Lion's Whelp* while racing in Antigua. Credit: Tim Wright, Photoaction.com

*"Marinas may be bad, but being hauled out
is worse. I may be sick of marinas,
but this is a big step forward from being hauled out
for the weekend in English Harbor."*

first in the gig races—men's doubles—in *Reepicheep*. But best of all were the interesting and wonderfully favorable comments from the best professionals. There was a boat parade in English Harbor after the second race, during which a famous local commentator announced the boats as they passed by. *Maggie B* was described as "a wolf in sheep's clothing." A real high point for us was, as we passed *Altair* (which came in first), the crew lined her rail and gave us three cheers. We were thrilled.

But all is not glory. Backing into our slot at Antigua Yacht Club Marina, we caught an anchor line in our prop, wrapped it, and slashed up our rudder and king post doing it. The line fused onto the shaft and had to be chiseled off. Right now, we are hauled out to fix the damage to the rudder and king post (can't let water in under the epoxy). When we hauled we found that the huge (6 inches across) pin for the centerboard had bent its restraints and was in the process of popping out. Sigh. But at least we are on it and it won't come out in the middle of the Indian Ocean. We hope to be back in the water soon and off to other islands. I want to move the boat along the circumnavigation route, but have fun and see beautiful places along the way. The current thought is maybe St. Barts, then down to Isle des Saints, Martinique, Barbados, the reefs around Trinidad, and then on to Recife, Brazil.

## 3 MAY 2006

All was more or less finished this morning and back into the water we slid. *Maggie B* is back at the dock in Falmouth Harbor. Marinas may be bad, but being hauled out is worse. I may be sick of marinas, but this is a big step forward from being hauled out for the weekend in English Harbor.

Work continues on chafe issues. Ah, the smell of epoxy in the morning! We perhaps have another day or so in port to finish the various fixes. Then onwards to the further islands!

## 5 MAY 2006

We are now right where we planned to be, two years ago. Anchored off our own little deserted Caribbean island. We finally kicked the last of the workers off the boat at noon today. Lots of great work by an Antiguan company called Woodstock. Chafe guards, fix-ups for dings, and the first step in solving our centerboard mysteries. But enough of yards and having wood and stainless steel chaff on the decks.

Three of us (Bori, Henry, and me) motored (5–10 knot wind right on the nose) an hour and a half to Green Island, just on the south side of Nonsuch Bay on the eastern side of Antigua. We are in 20 feet of water in a perfect cove with three little sand beaches, perfectly protected off a wild island where the only noise is from hundreds of doves. It is so great to get out of Falmouth Harbor, the insanity of Race Week and the noise of dueling bands along the waterfront.

When we arrived, Bori swam, Henry rowed around, and Frank tested the Bermuda rum. Tomorrow we'll try out the changes to the foresail and the main, to see what new complications the "fixes" may have brought us. Maybe onto to Nonsuch Bay and Harmony House for dinner, maybe not.

The grand harbor at Les Saintes.

*"Our favorite restaurant was
'The Creole Garden of the Saintes
at the Inn of the Farting Rat.'"*

## 2

# DESHAIES, GUADELOUPE
# TO NATAL, BRAZIL

**13 MAY 2006**

The schooner *Maggie B* is in the port of Deshaies (pronounced *duh-high*), Guadeloupe. We arrived last night after an eight-hour run from Antigua. As before, we anticipated the normal northeasterly trades, but got quite the opposite—namely, a light southwesterly—and ended up motoring about half the way.

From Antigua to Brazil we had a variety of crew. Of these, three—Max Hoffman, Bori Kiss, and Valentine Michon—I would have and could have sailed anywhere. Of the others, two took off after a day or so on board for unknown reasons and two I wish I had never met. The mess was my fault. I was naïve and casual about this critical aspect of a captain's job, I thought that everyone would "get it," but perhaps the Caribbean lowers everyone's guard.

Bori, Frank, and crew in Deshaies.

Our passage south from Antigua was marked by the smoking, hulking presence of the island of Montserrat, where the volcano was still putting out steam and ash. We also had a school of 30 dolphin greet us as we approached Guadeloupe. One specialized in belly flops near the boat.

Deshaies is a port of entry and we attempted to register with customs (closed until further notice) or the police (closed at 5 p.m.). A marvelous waterfront restaurant accepted our business for dinner, even though we were incompletely documented. There are about 40 sailing vessels of all descriptions anchored in the harbor.

## 15 MAY 2006

*Maggie B* is in the lovely Bay of Bourg des Saintes, in Les Saintes. We are just south of Guadeloupe, just north of Dominica. We have still not cleared in with French Customs.

Iles des Saintes, in addition to having wonderful beaches and being a fine bastion of France (good croissants, great cooking, and inexpensive wine), has quite a number of iguanas—very astonishing, even when you are expecting them. The people here are largely Breton, and the architecture reflects it. The food is marvelous, especially at our favorite spot, *Le Jardin Creole des Saintes, a l'Auberge du Rat qui Pete* (The Creole Garden of the Saintes at the Inn of the Farting Rat).

Iguana on Les Saintes.

The sun is now north of us at noon. We are at about 16 degrees north and the sun is at about 19, so we are sailing into winter, though it doesn't seem like it.

## 16 MAY 2006

*Maggie B* is at anchor in Martinique, off a beach called Anse Mitan, and across the bay from Fort de France. We had a nice reach down from Iles des Saintes, needing just 12 hours to cover the 90 miles. The wind was a proper stable easterly trade, blowing 10–20 and pushing us along at speeds up to 9.5 knots.

We slid past Dominica on the way. That island country has impressive mountains, soaring up to 4,000 feet. Even though we were well offshore, we experienced some interesting wind shifts. We were sorry to go past without stopping…next time.

Coming into a new port at night was a bit of a challenge, especially a complicated one like Fort de France. The wind piped up when it was time to take in the sail, but the crew got everything stowed efficiently, and we anchored in a nice protected spot without any particular fuss. The overlay function on the Furuno radar/GPS was most useful. It made it easy to sort out the buoys and boat traffic; it overlays the radar picture on top of the electronic chart, so you can compare the chart to reality.

Last night at Iles des Saintes, we were introduced to "boat visiting" by a nice couple from California. They cruise on *Orion,* an 80-year-old steel schooner that was formerly a Belgian tug (really!), and invited us over, together with another boat's crew. Hors d'oeuvres, a nice bottle of wine, and great conversation. There had been many boats around in Antigua, but it was so crazy that there really wasn't a chance to visit and make friends. We are going to see a nice boat, row over, say 'hi' and ask them over, whenever we can from now on.

So, another lovely day's run…but off the top of our heads, Bori and I came up with a list of 15 things that we should do to/for *Maggie B* while we are here in Martinique before our next leg to Barbados.

## 17 MAY 2006

Today we moved from the bay of Fort de France about 20 miles down the coast of Martinique to the charmingly named Cul de Sac des Marins (sailors' dead-end). This is the sailing center of Martinique, if not the Caribbean. There was a forest of masts as we came in. It is a big charter center, with at least 500 sailboats for rent each week. Falmouth in Antigua is empty in comparison.

We somehow ripped out a cringle on our foresail during the sail from Antigua to Guadeloupe. North Sails has representatives everywhere and they had a guy on the dock here to evaluate the problem, pick up the sail (actually it took four of us to lift it), and put it on a plane to Guadeloupe tomorrow to be returned fixed in two days. Just in time for a promised northerly (yes, sometimes it blows from the north here) to take us to Barbados.

We're still learning. Backing down your boat is a necessary skill in European countries. Most marinas in these parts don't allow you lie alongside a dock: you toss your anchor out and back into a narrow slot between other boats, or there is a mess of buoys and you somehow put a line on one as you back past it, then snubbed up just before you crash into the dock.

*Maggie B* doesn't have a bow thruster and I simply don't yet know her characteristics when backing down. Is speed your friend? Does she "sidestep" and, if so, which way? What effect does the rudder have, fast or slow? It looks as if I'll have to find some peaceful spot with a few buoys to practice my reversing skills.

## 25 MAY 2006

*Maggie B* is now in Barbados, in Carlisle Bay. We arrived May 25th after a reasonably fast overnight run, 130 NM in 18 hours. Carlisle Bay is right off downtown Bridgetown. There is a long lovely beach that is well used. We are on a mooring associated with the Barbados Yacht Club, which has been very welcoming.

The bay and the beach have fine, soft sand, but anchor-holding conditions are terrible. Our mooring gives some appearance of safety, but we can't really tell what is under the sand holding us. Some of the moorings around us (visibility in the water is about 200 feet!) are huge ancient anchors, one with 10-foot flukes. In a protected area near us, new scuba divers dive on a variety of wrecks. What can the prudent mariner deduce? Abandoned anchors, wrecks, terrible holding conditions? We are going to check out a new artificial harbor on the northwest side of the island in St. Charles, which might be more secure.

We have seen lots of turtles swimming around the boat, and they are entirely calm around humans. We have also seen some fascinating fish, Flying Gurnards (*Dactylopterus volitans*), which are about a foot long and rather boxy. They root around along the bottom with two fins that work as hands to scrape for food. If alarmed, they spread other fins that are about the length of their body that look like an iridescent blue cape, like the Phantom of the Opera taking his departure.

During our swims, we have been rubbing off the little marine growth that accumulated in the bio-rich water of the Cul-de-Sac des Marins marina. We're keeping Maggie B a clean machine!

Our strategic planning for Brazil is somewhat complex. A direct route puts us right against an adverse current (up to 4 knots) that runs along the Guianas, and once we cross the Intertropical Convergence Zone (ITCZ—see Lexicon), a strong head wind is usual. Our current thinking is to head east as best we can, with whatever we can get of northerlies, perhaps as far as 5N/28W, cross the Zone, probably motoring, and then loop back towards South America in the southeasterly trades. There is relatively little current out in the middle. Recife is about 8S/34W, so we have 21 degrees of southing and 26 degrees of easting to do. From Lunenburg, we have done 31 degrees of southing and only 5 degrees of easting.

## 26 MAY 2006

We are in a new, artificial harbor called St. Charles at a so-called mega-yacht dock. The chart calls it Six Men's Bay, but probably the developer was named Charles. The beach is perfect, the turtles are all around, and the coral is healthy.

We are staying here until June 5th, when Max Hoffman, 30, from England arrives. We are dragging him away from rebuilding a 1950 Bentley engine, which shows that

Max, shipmate and engineer, contemplating the Yanmar.

he is either mechanically inclined, or nuts. We had met Max in Antigua, and he will be a fine shipmate.

In getting ready for the passage to Brazil, one of the first things we thought about was water (coffee and chocolate came first). While I'm enormously encouraged that we can make water on our own (the system is now fixed), and I expect to catch rainwater, we have to set up the discipline, and understand our limits. We carry tankage for approximately 350 gallons of fresh water. If you assume 20 days to Brazil: no rain; no watermaker; six people; add 50% extra; convert it to liters, you get about 7 liters per person per day—or cooking, drinking, showering, laundry—everything. Today I went around with all crew to show how quickly you can use a liter. In the shower, 11 seconds. All were impressed. We have a saltwater tap in the kitchen for rinsing dishes and to add to soups. I am also going to rig a tarp with a hose tap so that we can efficiently get water in the tanks during the inevitable rain showers in the ITCZ.

## 8 JUNE 2006

At 10 a.m. today, we were about 140 miles east-southeast of Barbados. Leaving Barbados was hard due to the endless details, but we were all eager to get going. Even with our "slippy bottom" anti-fouling paint, algae were growing on *Maggie B*'s bottom at an alarming rate. We would scrub in the morning and the growth would be an inch or two long by evening.

We had a marvelous time provisioning in Barbados. We made friends with Pierre, owner of our favorite Mango Restaurant, and he put us in contact with his best suppliers. Unfortunately, most of the crew is now eating only dry crackers; perhaps we lost our sea legs from being ashore. The waves are rather big and confused. There is a 10-foot swell mixed with a sharp southeasterly chop, which makes even a big boat like *Maggie B* move around a bit.

We are close hauled on the port tack and have been for the last day. The wind has been steady at 20 knots. Right now, we are going more south than east, and we would like to be doing just the opposite. We are headed towards French Guiana (Devil's Island penal colony). If we get too close to that coast, we will find a strong adverse current. We probably don't have to worry until we get south of about 10 degrees north, but that is not too far. The course to our planned turn point is about 120 degrees, and the wind would have to back a lot for us to make that.

## 9 JUNE 2006

We are about equidistant from Barbados, Trinidad, and French Guiana, 270 miles. Hazy bright sun and still sloppy seas. Crew is stronger, but not all at 100%.

We were concerned about adverse current as we approached the Guyana/Suriname coast, but last night we had a favorable set, adding about a ½ knot to our speed and 10 degrees favorable lee-bow push. The wind has backed to favor us about 20 degrees since we left Barbados, and we hope it will continue as we make our easting. That would allow us to get to our turn point for Natal before we hit the doldrums—

on the far side of which are the most unfavorable southeasterlies.

The sea is empty here with only occasional shearwaters and long-tailed tropic-birds. No sign of any boats of any size. The only radar echoes last night were small rain showers, some of which came to visit.

## 10 JUNE 2006

The wind has favored us by backing to about 080 degrees and lightening to 15–18 knots. Seas are still confused and *Maggie B* will, from time to time, launch herself off of a big one to flop like a breeching humpback. Possibly she is trying to break off the last of the algae from Barbados.

Our course should allow us to make our doldrums turn point of 5N/28W, but that is still some ways off. We have gone about 420 NM and Natal is about 1420 NM, as the shearwater flies. With this course, we will be able to head off the coast gradually. We have about a half-knot of adverse current. The farther off the coast, the less current.

We can tell that we are downstream from the Amazon because we are already seeing pieces of huge trees float by. The mouth of the great river is about 650 NM away.

We saw one small fishing boat rather close to us last night, 200 miles off the coast! We sail with our LED deck lights on, which give a moon glow to the sails. The night watch had spotted a white light ahead, and as we closed on it, they put on a red light above, signifying "fishing at night."

A container ship passed on a reciprocal course only two miles away and we just had a low-flying four-engine plane check us out.

The crew has all recovered and there is talk of a chicken stew this afternoon!

Max with dinner.

## 11 JUNE 2006

We are sailing with jib, full main and one reef in the foresail, which probably will come out soon. We appear to have a half-knot favorable current, a real blessing where we were anticipating at least that much adverse current. We continue to see pieces of trees, presumably flotsam from the Amazon River.

The weather remains mostly clear with a high haze and occasional passing rain showers. The barometer is off just a bit to 1010 mb, which seems right as we move away from the Bermuda High.

Yesterday afternoon we saw a marvelous sight as a whole gaggle of 200 ocean birds circled what must have been a "bait ball" close by. The water was just frothing with little fish as large wahoo and tuna flew through the air in every direction. I suppose that we should have circled back with some lines out, but I was not in a circling mood and the crew was not hungry for anything more than crackers and soup. Putting the lines out will come after trying to overhaul our red and green navigation lights which have shorted out, probably due to having spent quite a bit of time fully submerged (note: they are usually about 6 feet out of water, high up on the rail).

I have just finished *Telegraph Days* by Larry McMurtry—perhaps partially for the pleasure of contemplating dry, dusty Tombstone, Arizona. Now I'm on my third re-read of Patrick O'Brian's *Blue at the Mizzen*—trying to alternate sailing books with their land cousins. Valentine is reading Pierre Desproges's *Chroniques de la haine ordinaire*. I hope that there is no *haine* [hate] left over for the Captain....

## 12 JUNE 2006

We are some ways northeast of our last position. We tacked over onto starboard last night to take advantage of a short southeasterly that must have been associated with the last modest tropical wave that slid by on the ITCZ. It gave us the advantage to head off the coast for half a day. We are squeezing out every little bit of easting we can from the modest changes thrown to us.

After four and a half days sailing close hauled on port tack, it was a surprise and pleasure to switch over to sailing close hauled on starboard. Last night was as pretty sailing as I have ever known: full moon with distant rain showers to give the horizon character, *Maggie B* slipping along at 6 knots in only 10 knots of true wind, not touching a sheet for hours at a time. The swells have mostly laid down and give a nice regular motion.

Doldrums.

By noon our southeasterly wind ran out and the regular easterly has set back in, but not yet in any force, so we are motorsailing to get into the wind. We have gone about 700 NM so far and it is 1250 yet to Natal.

Lunch today is shrimp in garlic and oil with special spices from our friend Pierre, owner of Mango Restaurant in Barbados, and a salad of mixed greens with tomatoes and goat cheese.

Yesterday we had a family of about 6 to 8 false killer whales *(Pseudorca crassidens)* come hang out with us. They clearly were interested in us, but didn't quite have the energy, speed, or enthusiasm to ride our bow wave. They hung out in formation, about 200 yards away for perhaps 15 minutes before heading off for their next appointment. Their heads are rather rounded, but not as dome-like as a pilot whale, and the rounded, curved dorsal helps with the identification. The whole impression is of a group of active but slightly overweight Southern matrons bustling to a church tea, while groups of dolphin are more like teenagers on skateboards.


## 13 JUNE 2006

First the good news. Yesterday evening, Max our resident dinghy racer, experimented sailing *Maggie B* with a fixed helm. We were sailing close hauled at 6.5 knots in 18–23 knots true wind in a 5–8 foot swell with mixed waves. The *Maggie B*, without autopilot and with the helm locked, kept herself sailing at about 38–40 degrees off the relative wind, with a variation of only 5–6 degrees, for two hours.

But then, at about 10:30 on the moonlit night, I came on deck where Max had the watch. We were bounding along under full sail and she seemed a bit over pressed. Literally just as Max said, "Do you think I'm driving her too hard?" the block at the top of the main throat halyard let go with a bang and down came the sail. All hands on deck had it sorted out in a jiffy and we proceeded at 5 knots and a bit off the wind with foresail and reefed jib.

On inspection of the failure, the upper block was a hefty-looking Lewmar 80 "three-wheeler" but it had a pathetic spindle connecting it to the shackle. While small to begin with, the spindle had been bored out and further compromised by the hole to allow for the shackle pin. It is surprising that the trivial remaining amount of metal could hold up the block, let alone a mainsail. Our other blocks appear all to be Lewmar 80 HD, which have a much heavier spindle.

Going up the mast this morning with the new halyard and spare (heavier!) block was a challenge. Still blowing about 20 knots with a moderate confused sea. We

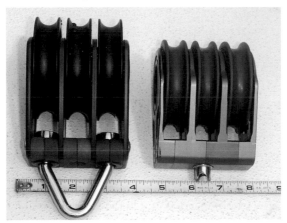

Antal block on the left, broken Lewmar on the right.

set her on course paralleling the rollers, but it still felt like a beating by a big guy (Neptune?). My inner arms and thighs are black and blue; I am snacking on industrial strength Ibuprofen.

When I was up there I thought of my hero, Ellen MacArthur, who set a new solo speed record sailing around the world. She got similarly (but much, much more) thrashed in the Southern Ocean and I knew that I could, that I must, hang on and finish the job. But I also thought of Jack London's hero in *To Build a Fire*, whose hands finally failed him in the cold as he tried to light a match.

But now the sails are back up and we are bowling along to Natal.

All is well.

## 14 JUNE 2006

The mouth of the Amazon is southwest about 460 NM and Natal is 1060 NM. We are still close hauled with the wind 075 at 9–10 knots. We are on a course of 120, making 4.5–5 knots through the water with 1 knot of current against us.

We have updated waypoints from Commanders' Weather, our routing and weather advisor. Our next point is 5N/40W, where we should encounter the start of the ITCZ, somewhat broken up by a weak tropical wave. From there we make a grand curve south towards Natal. This is cutting the corner from our earlier plan to go as far east as 5N/28W. The reason is an expected softening of the breeze, requiring some motoring for a day or so.

It is another lovely day. The sea is down to mostly 5–7 foot swells, which gives us an easy motion. Today was "boat day" with lots of vacuuming, washing down, fixing, tightening, stitching, etc.

Last night we started learning our stars with two hours of full darkness before the mostly full moon came up. Arcturus was right over us, seemingly wrapped in the top of the mast. Venus greeted the morning watch.

Preparations are already underway to greet Neptune when he boards us as we cross the Equator southbound. It is going to be a rough go with five pollywogs (sailors who have never crossed the Equator) aboard, but I'll do my best to arrange for the proper ceremonies.

## 15 JUNE 2006

By 2 p.m., we were motoring at 8 knots towards our next turn point on the north side of the ITCZ. The wind has fallen off to 3–4 knots. So, as captain I have to start worrying about how far can we motor and when we might have to turn for some earlier Brazilian port if we don't get any wind. We left Barbados with about 350 gallons of diesel. In the last 7 days, we have run the generator for 39 hours (20 gallons) and the engine for 7 hours (14 gallons), so we should have about 315 gallons left or somewhat over 1,000 miles motoring. We also have an emergency 10 gallons tucked away aft in the propane locker.

It was discouraging to start the engine because it has been such lovely sailing, even though slow. We had the second half of the wahoo for lunch on deck under the awning: fillets marinated in ginger and lime juice, done quickly in a hot frying pan. The sea is sparkling all around with distant rain clouds showing rainbows. There is a gentle swell from the northeast giving the *Maggie B* a light calm motion.

Our trip log is now at 1028 NM—not all in a straight line as we are no motor-boat. Belem on the Amazon is 500 NM away, and Natal is 976. Africa, Sierra Leone, is just under 2000 NM to the east.

I mention Africa because one of today's surprises was having a big butterfly around us. Since we are downwind from Africa, it must have ridden a Tropical Wave across 2,000 miles! This morning at first light, the watch saw a 2-meter blue marlin (*Makaira nigricans*) close aboard.

We have "air cover" from a group of sooty shearwaters (*Ardenna grisea*). Today they displayed unusual behavior by landing quite close to the boat, three or four

## THE CAPTAIN

I started off the cruise fully inculcated with the Outward Bound view of a captain – from Lao Tzu: "The good leader talks little, when his work is done, his aim fulfilled, the people will say, 'We did this ourselves.'"

This maybe works well in China. I started out spending a lot of time in consultation with everyone: what about this, what about that, what if we go this way or that way? But I ended up perhaps not all the way to being an 18th century Navy captain, but a good ways in that direction.

The captain's first job is to recruit and train the crew. Training was not necessarily sail training – you do surprisingly little actual sail work on a big passage. Training was safety, maintenance, communication, systems, lookout, navigation, meteorology, and comradeship. Please and thank you. How can I help?

Most days at lunch I would do a presentation of where we were, where we were going and what weather I was expecting. I would assign jobs and take my share. We all would cook. We all would clean.

I felt that my biggest responsibility was safety. My second was to put the boat where we could get the most favorable wind to move us fastest towards our destination. No wind meant no progress or the use of precious fuel; too much wind was unsafe.

The captain's hardest decisions were when to leave port. Your crew was never fully ready, your food was never complete, the weather was never quite right; there was always some system or another that needed something. But if you didn't leave port, you wouldn't ever get anywhere.

---

meters, and then immediately ducking their heads underwater to look for goodies. We must have an interesting following of fish under the boat.

Last night "Jorge" the autopilot was acting out a bit and we were hand steering. The mostly full moon was in perfect position to lock in the shrouds and sail right on until morning.

## 16 JUNE 2006

First a quiz, with answers at the end. In a perfectly flat sea with perfect visibility, how far can you see something right on the surface (such as a person's head or the strobe light on a life jacket) if you were standing 10 feet (3 meters) above the water, before it is over the horizon, literally? Write your answer down. Second, if you are 10 feet (3 m) above the water, flat sea, perfect visibility, how far away could you see a bright light (like on the bow of a container ship) 40 feet (12 m) in the air? And finally, if the *Maggie B* is doing her usual 7 knots and the aforementioned container ship is doing 28 knots (like the one we saw last night) and they are closing, how long from the first glimpse of the ship's light to impact?

We are 870 NM from Fernando de Noronha, our next planned stop. The archipelago is on our way to Natal and is described in the *Lonely Planet* guide, which is not prone to exaggeration, as the prettiest place in Brazil, if not the whole world. It has three of Brazil's top ten beaches. Access to Fernando de Noronha is tightly controlled, with a limited number of tourists, and escalating daily fees. It is mostly a national park and has tight restrictions. It is not exactly a port of entry, but we have heard that yachts are allowed to stay briefly in certain areas, especially if it is a "port of necessity." We expect that Bori with her Portuguese, suitable crew uniforms, a nice bottle of French wine, and cheerful payment of the official fees will make our arrival a success.

In Barbados, many sailors tried to discourage us from our proposed routing to Brazil due to the current along the coast, which would push us back into the Caribbean. The reality is much different. We have had as much favorable (2 knots behind us last night) as unfavorable current. I suspect that if this current were as much analyzed as the Gulf Stream, it would not be so scary to sailors and, with good updates, a navigator could work the eddies to speed their way southeast.

Answers to the quiz: 1) 3.6 miles (5.8 km); 2) 11 miles (17.6 km); 19 minutes. Yikes! Thank goodness for radar.

## 17 JUNE 2006

We appear to be on the south side of the ITCZ, with the wind at 180 degrees at 10–12 knots true. We haven't had much in the way of rain showers or calms. Since setting out 10 days ago we have run the engine only 25 hours, with my general rule being to motor only when the boat speed is under 4 knots.

Last night it looked as if we were going to get a real frog-choking, gully-washer of a rain so we rigged our rain-catcher, which is an 8 by 10 foot tarp with a drain set in the middle leading to a short pipe to plug into the water tank filler. Some of us got into bathing suits for a free shower, but alas, it passed us by at the last minute with only a little spritz.

Bori and Valentina.

We are on course for, and 100 miles from, our first turn target from Commanders' Weather, where we'll start arcing south to plug into the southeasterlies. We have a southerly already, we may not be able to do much arcing, but so far so good.

Today was washday and the boat looks like hippie-patched blue jeans from the 1960s, with every color and kind of cloth hung up everywhere. We will not be seen by any other boats.

Bori is starting our Portuguese lessons today, so that we can learn essential phrases such as hello, thank you, and where is the internet cafe? Noontime music is all Brazilian. Samba lessons next?

**18 JUNE 2006**

Last night we had one rain shower after another. The rain showers would bring wind and water! then leave us with no wind after the squall passed. Our routine was to stop the engine, roll out the jib (foresail stowed), adjust sails, close all hatches, get a big cold shower, run out of wind, start engine, roll up jib, open hatches. Repeat on half-hour intervals. Fun at 4 p.m., less so at 4 a.m.

At noon, we were sailing along at 6.5 knots, heading 175 degrees, with a wind from 120 at 12 knots. Great if it lasts, but more southerly winds (on our nose) are predicted ahead so we are doing our best to keep east for the wind shift.

We have gone 1420 NM since Barbados. Natal and Fernando de Noronha are both about 680 NM away.

Last night we were treated to a very rare (first time I've ever seen it) moon-bow. After one short but intense rain shower, the half moon popped out, and behind us was a perfect arc against the clouds—whiter than the clouds, with just a little touch of pink.

One pleasure of having the skies relatively clear to the south is that we have been learning our southern stars. There is the Southern Cross, which despite all the hype looks more like a kid's kite. More interesting are Alpha and Beta Centauri. But the most interesting, if one is up from midnight to 4 a.m., is to watch the well-defined Scorpio do a slow somersault around bright blue Spica in Virgo. We have also had the Twins setting in the west behind us, looking sometimes like a pair of ship's masthead lights bearing down on us.

Today was another first. I made scones and they came out pretty well—after you have been at sea for a while, anything is delicious. The recipe caught my eye by being called "Fool Proof Scones." I was happy that my son Alden had insisted on installing a nice slate bread-making surface next to the stove.


## 19 JUNE 2006

The southeasterly trades seem to have set in. The wind has been 120–140 degrees at 10 to 25 knots. Rain showers are more frequent. Our course is about south at 4–6 knots. We have full jib up and full main, which is too little for the lighter breezes and too much for the little blows that come with each shower. We are probably going to switch to one reef in the foresail and main, to keep two "slots" where the overlapping sails help power us along. That will give us more balance and flexibility. The sea is bigger and confused with a fair southeasterly swell with a cross chop.

We need power to push through the waves, but we also want to go to Fernando de Noronha, which is about 550 miles at 160 degrees. When in doubt, go for power.

We put our fishing lines over today and landed a nice wahoo about an hour later. Somewhat bigger than the last two, this one will probably make three meals for the six of us. Thanks to great advice from my friend Richard Postma (of the fishing catamaran *Taravana* in French Polynesia) and killer lures from Melton, it seems as if we just have to decide when we want fish for dinner and "reach in the tank" for a nice one. I suppose it helps that no one else has probably fished this area.

It looks as if we are going to have a hard slog to windward. I have forgotten what it feels like to sail *Maggie B* off the wind.

We are having some filter problems. For oil, we have lots of spares for both main engine and generator, but not for fuel filters. I have a vortex fuel filter on the main engine, which only needs flushing. But the Yanmar has another fuel filter that we have just discovered. It seems blocked up and we don't know where a replacement cartridge might be found

*"Then they turned on an additional white masthead light. Yikes! Two masthead lights in a vertical line means a towboat! Towing trumps sailing."*

## 20 JUNE 2006

We are headed south at 6 knots, sailing under one reef in both main and foresail with the jib partially furled/reefed. She balances perfectly, with zero rudder angle. The wind is from 120–130 at 15–22 knots, with a fairly sloppy 8- to 10-foot sea, increased in confusion by a ½ to 1-knot southerly (favorable) current. We are thrashing along in a less than elegant fashion, but now after 13 days, essentially all close hauled on port tack, we are all accustomed to it, and know just when to reach out and catch the espresso pot as it hurtles across the galley.

Fernando de Noronha is 435 NM away. We will probably keep these conditions the rest of the way unless we get some sort of unexpected break. We should be there in perhaps four days. The trip log is 1670 NM.

Fish stew is simmering away on the stove, with the last of our tomatoes, lots of onions, frozen peas, canned corn, and herbs.

I'm reading *My Name Is Red* by Orhan Pamuk. Valentine just finished *Le Grand Secret* by René Barjavel, which is about a great secret—an immortality drug.

Neptune should arrive on board this evening, if he can grab on as we slip and slide across the Equator. The pollywogs are increasingly nervous.

Neptune aboard, Crossing the Equator.

**21 JUNE 2006**

The Schooner *Maggie B*'s noon position on June 21 was 0 deg 44.0S/37deg 54.0W. "S" means SOUTH! We crossed to the Southern Hemisphere on the very same day that the Northern Hemisphere goes into summer and the Southern goes into winter.

We got our wind shift this morning, after twelve days waiting for it. The wind is now 160 degrees at 10–12 and we are headed about 105–110 degrees at 6 1/2 knots. Fernando de Norunha is 375 miles away and we are about 240 miles off the Brazilian coast. We have about a knot of adverse current and the seas have laid down a lot. The weather is marvelous—scattered clouds and enough breeze to sail perfectly balanced, but no spray on deck or rain showers. Last night we did have a heavy rain with winds up to 30 knots.

We crossed the Equator last night at about 2000 hours. I was temporarily absent, but I understand that King Neptune came aboard to interview, test, mark, and accept all five pollywogs, who are now true schoonermen shellbacks. Bori took some scary pictures.

We are now in a fine topsail breeze with all plain sail up. It is strange to be on the starboard tack after the better part of two weeks on port tack.

Lunch today was wahoo fish cakes. We have eaten wahoo raw, grilled, in a stew, and now in fish cakes. One more meal of wahoo left and the competition is on for another recipe.

## 22 JUNE 2006

The wind is from the south at 15–30 knots. The 30 knots come in the regular rain showers that really should be called squalls. You suit up for one and it is over by the time you are all strapped in, you get out of the foulies, settle in, and the next one is on you.

We are having teething problems. People say that it takes a year or two to settle in a custom boat and we have only been at it for five months since launching and have done a lot of miles in that time. Teething sounds trivial, but I remember that with my kids, there was a lot of crying. Our recurring problem is the attachment for the main throat halyard. It was originally too low and chafed through before Bermuda and then we had some new pieces put on in Antigua and one of them popped off at 4:30 this morning, dropping the main a bit and causing us to lower it the rest of the way.

We got things fixed up with a jury rig so that the main is up with one reef, and it will be fine until we can get a little more work done on the mast when next in port. These carbon fiber masts are modern marvels—strong and light—but you can't just screw something into them like a wooden mast.

We are also having some concerns about the engine. Somewhere along the line we seem to have gotten some algae in the fuel. We dosed it with algicide in Barbados, but the dead stuff seems to have partially clogged one of the engine filters (the one filter that we <u>don't</u> have a spare for!). The engine still runs, but at reduced revolutions per minute. The latest anomaly with the engine is that it runs satisfactorily, the gearbox is fine and turning the prop shaft in both directions, but we are getting no thrust at all from the prop. We have a feathering prop, which may be doing something clever, but the more likely probability is that the propeller has come off. When the weather calms down a bit, I'll be going over the side to check. We do carry a spare prop, but no spare prop nut.

We have changed our destination back to Natal. Fixing the boat trumps beautiful beaches. I'm already studying Natal harbor to find a nice, open, safe spot to anchor if we have to do so under sail.

Never a dull moment.

## 23 JUNE 2006

We have 204 miles to go to Natal. The wind is 170 degrees at 15–20 and Natal is bearing 170 degrees. We are headed in towards the coast of Brazil, hoping to get a break on the current that is pushing us northwest. The coast is about 100 miles away and we should pick up soundings at about ten o'clock tonight.

I have been emailing for advice about the propellor. Everyone says that the prop cannot come off. They say that the prop must have somehow eaten its internal gears and the three blades now are essentially free floating. Why? Who knows? One possibility is that we picked up some sort of trash, which fouled the prop and as it worked it had some sort of extra stress that caused it to fail. Or it may have come off. The weather is still too rough to stop and check it.

We may try to replace it at sea if we find some quiet spot along the coast before we get to Natal. The town is spread along a river that looks from the chart to be friendly for anchoring under sail.

We have plenty of water, plenty of food, but must make port soon as we are running low on chocolate.

It is amazing to me that, while on deck it might be a real thrash, with rain and spray in equal (industrial strength) parts, wind blowing 20–30 knots, yet down below it is mostly quiet, warm and dry, and the off-duty crew sleeping soundly.

## 24 JUNE 2006

Yesterday I went over the side to check the prop and found…no prop. The makers and the installers said that it couldn't come off, but…it did. It is now sleeping with the fishes. *Maggie B* is no longer an auxiliary schooner—she is just a schooner. It was strange to dive in the deep ocean. The water was very clear and I felt quite vertiginous to be in 10,000 feet with this little boat floating nearby. It was a great relief to get back on board and set sails for port.

We are where Brazil sticks furthest out towards Africa. They call it *Esquina do Conti-*

*nente*, the corner of the continent. This Cape, Calcanhar, is where the coast of Brazil changes from East/West to North/South. The wind and the current are both against us. Once past this cape all will be easier, but we are not there yet and progress is slow.

Last night was a surprise. We worked our way into the coast to try to get out of the adverse current and maybe get a favorable wind shift. It was very dark. We made soundings for the first time in two weeks and sailed in to a depth of 100 feet though we were still 20 miles off the coast. In the last ten days, we have seen perhaps three boats but now we were in the midst of dozens of fishing boats. Most of them carried only a single white light, which made it challenging to determine their speed and distance. Since they were small wooden boats, they hid in the swells and didn't show up well on radar.

One medium-sized motorboat did show up on radar. As it came within five miles we were able to "acquire" it. Acquiring a target on radar means that we can highlight it with a pointer, push a button or two, and the computer will work out the target's course, speed, and closest point of approach. This boat was coming right for us. It was on our right, so in general it would have right of way. But we are a sailboat, under sail and would thus have right of way over a motorboat. But would they realize we were a sailboat? I turned the deck lights on to light up the sails, hoping they would adjust their course to pass behind us. There was an announcement on the radio in Portuguese but Bori, who can speak the language, was asleep. Then they turned on an additional white masthead light. Yikes! Two masthead lights in a vertical line means a towboat! Towing trumps sailing. I spun *Maggie B* downwind to avoid the hypothetical barge, though there turned out to be nothing else there, other than a

After six months at sea, the windlass didn't work.

game of "Brazilian one-up."

We expect to be in Natal tomorrow or the next day. Life on board has an end-of-school-term-at-school feeling. I am anxious about finding a good place to anchor under sail up the River Potengi, and then all the bureaucratic problems of checking in with the fabled world's worse bureaucracy, getting the supplies we need, getting *Maggie B* hauled to put on a new propeller, etc.


## 25 JUNE 2006

We are about five miles off the beach at Cape Calcanhar, the turning point. The black and white striped lighthouse is visible through the rain showers. Cape Sao Roque, better known but less important, is another 20 miles south. We currently have tacked to a course of 110 degrees at 6 knots. We are just 40 miles from Natal, but we are beating into a strong southeasterly, so we probably won't be there until after dark.

The mouth of the Potengi River at Natal seems wide and well marked. There is a nice breakwater at the mouth, inside of which we should be able to anchor for the night. The chart does have a caution about varying currents and shifting shoals, so if it looks chancy when we get there, we'll just hold off for the night and enter at dawn.

Last night was a long one of beating our way down the coast through rainsqualls amid strings of tiny fishing boats, impossible-to-detect on radar, all lit up by oil platforms and petrochemical works.


## 26 JUNE 2006

The Schooner *Maggie B* anchored off the Yacht Club do Natal at 0930 on June 26th, 17 days out of Barbados. The trip log is at 2408 NM, for an average of 141 miles a day, not in a direct line. It seems as if we were close hauled on port tack for 99.7% of the time.

The last bit into the Potengi River without a motor was difficult. The wind was light, 5–8 knots, getting lighter and more variable, and the current out was about a knot and a half. This was all complicated by the construction in midstream of a new bridge, reducing the room to tack. We had to anchor in the middle of things for a bit to wait for more breeze, which was complicated by failure of the windlass. But quick thinking by Max had us "nipping" the chain and pulling it back, length-by-length, to the electric cockpit winch, when a bit of a favorable breeze came up. It took us almost an hour to go the mile from the mouth of the breakwater to the yacht club.

Once anchored, we were told that we were too far out in the stream and had to tuck in further. As we were launching *Reepicheep*, a small Brazilian fishing boat capsized nearby. We rowed over and dragged them to safety into the beach. Then we rowed our #2 anchor up into the requested position and kedged our way out of the channel. Then lunch and now we are off to deal with the fabled Brazilian bureaucracy.

## THE SCHOONER *ATLANTIC*, WHOSE RECORD LASTED 100 YEARS

"Wee" Charlie Barr was the racing superstar in 1905. He had won just about every ocean race there was to win, including the last three America's Cup races, sweeping every race. In 1904, he won 19 of 22 races in British and German waters.

The New York Yacht Club had been challenged by Kaiser Wilhelm II to a wide-open Trans-Atlantic Race. No handicaps. Few rules, though all propellers had to be removed and engines sealed. The Kaiser had begun to rebuild the German Navy and was eager to challenge British domination of the seas in every way. Ocean racing was hugely popular in the press, and the closest thing to open war to show off your high seas prowess.

The German entry was the *Hamburg*, a new black two-masted schooner, 158 feet overall with a 116 foot waterline. She was designed and built in Great Britain and crewed by German Navy officers and sailors.

While the British were the focus of the Kaiser's challenge, American millionaires were the most eager to show off their boats. Eleven boats were entered. The British entries included the largest boat, Lord Lindsay's 245 foot ship-rigged super luxury yacht *Valhalla*. The other British entry was the topsail schooner *Sunbeam*, at 170 feet length overall. *Sunbeam* was perhaps the most famous boat in the race, having been the first private yacht to circumnavigate the globe. Her owner, Lord Thomas Brassey, was a naval expert and skilled sailor who had sailed her 300,000 miles by the time he arrived for the race.

The American entries were *Apache*, *Utowana*, *Thistle*, *Endymion*, *Hildegarde*, *Ailsa*, *Fleur de Lys* and *Atlantic*.

Wilson Marshall, owner of *Atlantic*, had inherited his father Jesse's fortune, made running the Broadway Surface Railroad Company, originally a fleet of horse cabs. His wife Jessica was the favorite granddaughter of P. T. Barnum. *Atlantic* was 184 feet overall and 139 on her waterline. She was relative light at 206 net tons and narrow with a beam of only 30 feet. Contemporary writers declared "*Atlantic* is not an Atlantic boat."

In the spring of 1905, Charlie Barr came back from a season in the Mediterranean as master of the 127-foot *Ingomar*, navigating her, racing her and managing the floating palace for her owner and his guests. On returning, he found his wife sick with tuberculosis and not expected to live. The last thing he wanted to do was to turn around for a no-holds-barred race across the North Atlantic early in the season, starting May 16th.

But the New York Yacht Club wanted to win the Kaiser's Cup. Barr was the best racing skipper and the *Atlantic* was the boat with the best chance. He was offered a double salary, huge bonus if he won, and full-time doctors for his wife. He was also dependent for his career on the goodwill of the members of the New York Yacht Club.

The North Atlantic in May is tough sailing. There are basically two routes to get across: either short or safe. The Great Circle Route is the shortest at about 2875 NM. But it takes you close along the Eastern Seaboard, close past Cape Cod, Nova Scotia, Newfoundland and the ship's graveyard known as Sable Island. It also takes you into ice. You get relatively unstable weather rolling right off the continent, both foggy calms and fierce gales.

Steamers favored the Southern Route: further from the ice, more stable weather and the chance of some help by the Gulf Stream current. But that way was about 300 NM or 10% longer.

The start of the race was almost a disaster with light winds, a very short starting line, and eleven blue water yachts ranging in size from 86 to 648 net tons. The huge spectator fleet and numerous press boats made for tense confusion. But by night-fall, *Hamburg* had blown away all the competition, which was especially unnerving because the conditions favored the lighter, finer American boats.

The Germans had the advantage of long experience working with each other and closely knowing their boat, like a jockey who grows up with a racehorse. Charlie Barr had just been hired a few weeks before and only had a few days practice to get to know *Atlantic* and her crew.

*Hamburg's* lead evaporated when she broke the attachments to her main sheet, crippling her for a few hours, and allowing Charlie Barr to drive *Atlantic* about 20 miles ahead.

And drive he did. He put up the biggest and lightest sails he could carry, until they blew out. It was Marshall's money he was spending, and Marshall had hired him to win the race, not spare the sails. Another danger was that he was sailing in the west-bound steamer track and at night one huge boat after another would pass as close as half a mile, with all lights on and orchestra playing. It must have been like riding a motorcycle the wrong way on a freeway full of trucks, in the fog.

Charlie Barr had no way of knowing, but he was holding about two degrees or 120 NM north of the *Hamburg*. It was a shorter course, but brought him into the ice sooner. In the morning of May 22, the air temperature was 63 F and the water 57 F. By that evening, it was 37 F and 35 F respectively. Every sailor knew what that

The original *Atlantic*. Credit. Charles Edwin Bolles, Library of Congress.

meant: ice. Barr doubled the watch and kept driving *Atlantic* – 11, 12 and then 13 knots through the hazy, dark night. They spotted ice that night and then a huge berg the next morning – half a mile long and 300 feet high. The log entry put it at almost the exact spot where *Titanic* sank seven years later. In the heart of the ice field, *Atlantic* made an incredible 341 NM day's run. That day *Hamburg* did 303 NM along a longer, more southerly route.

On the 25th a gale blew in from the southwest. Among the fleet, spread along the track, it split sails, broke yards and bones. *Hamburg* ran north with the gale, covering more miles than the *Atlantic*, but Charlie Barr held straight for the finish line, despite all the punishment *Atlantic* was taking and the pleas from the owner and his guests, locked below in their seasickness.

Charlie Barr crossed the finish line at 9:16 PM on May 29, 1905, having averaged 10.32 knots, for an elapsed time of 12 days, 4 hours, 1 minute. *Hamburg* was second, almost a day slower. Barr returned to New York where he found his wife recovered thanks to the careful tending by the NYYC doctors.

*Atlantic* was sold and resold over the years, but never again had a real success. She served as an anti-submarine patrol boat in WWII and sank at her moorings in New Jersey in 1968 after being derelict for many years.

Wilson Marshall smashed the Kaiser's Gold Cup during WWI. It turned out to be gilded porcelain rather than the promised solid gold.

*Atlantic's* race record for monohull sailboats was finally beaten in June, 2005, by the schooner *Mari-Cha IV*. No other such record has lasted for 100 years.

Frank, Bori, and Max with natural face paint in Natal.

*"The Southern Ocean gales move around the world
unrestricted. Prudent sailors ride the pressure gradients.
If the glass is falling, go north, if it is rising, ease south.
Low pressure systems rotate in the opposite direction
from those in the Northern Hemisphere,
but that is probably the only sure truth of the weather."*

# 3

# NATAL TO SALVADOR, BRAZIL

**29 JUNE 2006**

We are in Natal, Brazil, learning the town, fixing things, and generally recovering.

But first, a short quiz for the celestially inclined (don't skip ahead!). The sun on June 28th is about 23 degrees north of the equator. The *Maggie B* is about six degrees south of the equator. When we look at the sun at noon, it is about 29 degrees north or down from overhead. So, the question is: where, up north at noon, will someone look at the sun and see it about 29 degrees south or down from overhead? As a clue, 23 degrees north means that the sun is directly overhead in Cuba, Oman, and Taiwan.

Natal is a fast-growing city of perhaps a million people. Hard working, rich in parts, poor in parts, and seemingly generally successful. The interior is reportedly very poor due to long-term drought, and has been depopulated. One Brazilian described Brazil as "rich south, poor north, with the dividing line at about Salvador, and Natal the capital of the poor north." Natal has been helped by tourism and the beaches have impressive hotels, which are apparently filled in season. June is not the season. Some of the "scene" and the tourist trade have reportedly been spoiled by sexual tourism, and active and aggressive prostitution. We have not seen any of that, but then we have been steered to specific areas (and away from others) by our friends at the Iate Clube do Natal.

Today is going to be a big workday. Our to-do list has 27 items. Some are easy, like "re-glue paper towel holder," some hard, like "clean boat." Our hope is to finish by 4 p.m. and get a cab to the nicest beach area, the Ponte Negra, which is NOT one of the bad areas mentioned above. It is about 10 km away, and we hope to go for a swim and generally hang out and have dinner and reward ourselves for a hard day. Tomorrow we are going to hire a driver and a dune buggy to explore the area north of the river, which apparently has fascinating dunes and wild beaches. Then the weekend to finish things up and set off for Salvador on Monday. We plan to head south in short stages, checking out the little out-of-the-way beach towns. At least, the beach towns that are accessible by a boat drawing 2 meters. The coast is sketchy, with both electronic and paper charts being full of the symbol for wrecks. We should have fun.

As the crow flies, Salvador is about 475 miles—by sea, perhaps 550.

The crew is now down to the hard core, Max Hofman and Bori Kiss; essentially, the watch officers from the last leg. The French girls are gone (two of whom will not be missed). Valentine will be much missed.

Answer to the quiz: London, North of Newfoundland, Canada, Kiev, Ukraine, Warsaw. So, we are getting less sun in Brazil than ALL of the US!


## 3 JULY 2006

We are beating our way, close hauled along the coast of Brazil, headed south to Salvador. At noon, our course was southwest at 6 knots. Recife is 90 miles away and Salvador is 435. The wind is from the south at 15–20 knots.

We left Natal at 3 p.m. on July 2nd. We had finally gotten our spare propeller fitted and attached. The key for the prop and the two bolts holding it were hand machined, and looked like fresh gold when they arrived with the skilled diver who helped us. Our delight at getting the prop on was totally dashed by the diver telling us that it didn't fit the opening, which had been made for the vanished feathering J-Prop. Max, in a tour-de-force, realized that our jackshaft (an extra piece of shaft between the engine and the shaft to the prop) could be extended by the few inches we needed. He took it off and carried it to nearby primitive local machine shops, where he was able to get it adjusted so that all fits and works now.

Our departure was delayed by the two hours it took to take on 180 gallons of water at the yacht club.

We find it good to be back at sea after Natal, though the first night was a bit of a thrash to get back in the routine. There are many, many boats along the coast. "Meeting situations" with very large container ships, when surrounded by local fishing boats, can get a bit too exciting.

We are thinking about stopping at what is described as a lovely island and beach about 20 km south of Recife—Ilha de Tatuoca—but all depends on weather and progress towards Salvador. Maceio sounds interesting. The bay around Salvador will be great fun to explore.

## 4 JULY 2006

We are about five miles off the coast of Brazil, ready to slide by Recife, which is about 15 miles ahead.

Recife looks a little like Chicago from the water, with rows of varied high-rise buildings. The difference is that south of Chicago is the end of Lake Michigan and Gary, Indiana—south of Recife is the Great Southern Ocean, as well as the rest of Brazil and Argentina.

We have wind at 170 degrees at 10–12 knots and a half-knot foul current. We are paralleling the coast and making about 5 knots. Since Natal, we have been sailing well, though slower than when we had our slippery J-Prop. However, the combination of being close hauled, tacking out regularly, a foul current, and fair residual seas has made our VMG a pathetic 3 knots.

Salvador is less than 400 miles away, but we are going to have to speed things up a bit if we are going to have time for fun before Bori goes back to Hungary. But we have almost turned the corner.

Another Lewmar block broke this morning. I'm getting concerned about whether we have the right size or whether they are manufactured adequately. This one just gave up in 20 knots of wind.

Another failed Lewmar block.

I want to take a moment to mention some of our stars on board. The Furuno radar/GPS/plotter system has been great. "Jorge," our Furuno autopilot, has learned how to steer by relative wind and is a true star. The icebox system, a pair of Sea Frosts, has been flawless. The Spectra watermaker works tirelessly. The Force 10 stove has made endless tasty meals. The Iridium Satellite Phone with UUPlus has made staying in contact with the rest of the world effortless. And once we discovered that our "leak" problem was water coming back *in* the bilge pump outlets, the hull has been perfectly dry.

## 5 JULY 2006

We are booming along with 12–15 knots of wind on our beam, with "the Bird" flying, doing 8 knots! This is after thousands of miles close hauled. We are all a bit stunned. The wind is 100 degrees at 12–15 and our course along the coast to Salvador is about 220 degrees—perfect!

We are about 10 miles off the coast, 45 miles from Maceio and 300 from Salvador. Towns passed by last night included Dos Milagres, Ponta do Patacho, Ipojuca, Ponta des Pedras Pretas. This last town seems to translate "The Bridge at Black Rock"—great name for a Western!

Yesterday was for ship cleaning and today things look nice. We may even do laundry, as we have plenty of water and power.

What we are reading: I just finished *My Name is Red* by the Turkish author Orhan Pamuk; Max is reading the operating manual for our ZF marine drive.

Max has made a culinary success out of Wahoo Fish Cakes, adding egg and corn meal to make a delicious and durable meal. Delicious in that they get eaten up promptly, either at the time of making or as a marvelous midnight snack. Durable in that if we had an emergency leak, they could be stuffed in and would hold for a week or so. More! Soon!!

## 6 JULY 2006

Yesterday was lovely and clear; today reminds us of English weather, with poor visibility, continual rain and less wind than we want. We are also battling up to 2 knots of foul current, which makes everything even drearier. We are moving in closer to the coast to try to get out of the current, but this area has a lot of offshore oil and gas exploration and we don't want to get up close to a rig. "Isabel" is the name of the next drilling platform, though, which sounds nice.

We have 188 NM to go to Salvador, and are about 20 miles off the coast, just passing the Rio Sao Francisco, and coming up on Aracaju. Rio Sao Francisco was the site of the last great battle for Brazil between the Dutch and the Portuguese. The Dutch controlled much of northeast Brazil in the seventeenth century. Aracaju

*"Our delight at getting the prop on was totally dashed by the diver telling us that it didn't fit the opening, which had been made for the vanished feathering J-Prop."*

should be familiar even to Nord Americanos from the song of the same name by Bebel Gilberto.

Sigh, another system has given up the ghost. We had a nice, compact, inexpensive Italian clothes washer/drier in the fo'c'sle. It seemed like a great idea and we had used it successfully several times. Never again. It was obviously made for an upscale apartment near the Spanish Steps, not in the bow of a Blue Water cruising boat, diving into waves. It got a full douche of salt water through its exit pipe, which it really didn't like. But, basically, it beat itself to death inside, as the drum banged into everything, breaking piles and controls. It will become a treasure of Salvador's dump, and will not be replaced.

Lunch today in the rain was comfort food: little steak filets well marinated and then done in garlic and butter, with baked potatoes and frozen peas.

We have been doing solo watches, two hours long and four hours off, but are going to try three and six, to try to ensure that we all get REM sleep, so that nobody is cranky.


**7 JULY 2006**

We are about five miles off the coast and 37 miles from turning the corner into Baia de Todos os Santos (All Saints Bay). We should be tucked into the Bahia Marina by sundown.

Today has been a perfect sail. We are doing 7–8 knots with one reef in the main and the foresail, on a broad reach with only moderate swell and waves. We were head to head with a fast-moving empty coastal tanker at dawn, but since then we haven't seen a single boat, large or small. The sun is out and the temperature is perfect for just a t-shirt and shorts.

We have been reading up on Salvador and are quite excited to arrive. The Raivavae Marina seems to be a safe base for us to do the boat work while being close to things. The town sounds interestingly historic and somewhat wild. The *Lonely Planet* guide clearly likes the city, but is full of cautions ("don't go to this or that area, take a taxi,

The Captain on the street in Bahia.

don't fight back when you are pickpocketed, don't carry a bag," etc.).

Max showed his dinghy sailing background and put together a bunch of "tweakers" to improve the trim of the sails and he got at least another half a knot out of her. I didn't do my homework well enough on what was where when I went on for the midnight to 3 a.m. watch. When the usual rainsquall came through at about 1 a.m. with 25–30 knots of wind, I got tangled in various ropes and we went for a bit of a sleigh ride before all was settled.

## 18 JULY 2006

The Schooner *Maggie B* docked safely at Bahia Marina, Salvador, Bahia, Brazil, at approximately 7 p.m. on July 7th. We are safe and in a fine spot.

The days after arrival passed in the usual blur of finding help for systems and gear, discovering restaurants and bars and entertainments in a new city, and deciding whom to trust.

We were hauled out at Bahia Marina on July 18th to clean the hull and fit a new propeller. *Reepicheep* has gone off to get fixed and cleaned up a bit.

The Travelift that took us out is rated to 40 tons. The *Maggie B* is 35 tons before water, tuna fish cans, diesel, foul weather gear, etc. The hoist did fine, though the tires looked like those of a gypsy truck whose owner had just scored a huge pile of scrap lead.

We are still learning. If you send something important to Brazil via FedEx or DHL, customs essentially charges 100% import tax. Yes, 100%. Officially it is ONLY 70%, but there are extra handling fees, etc. If, however, you use a freight forwarder, and add the magic words "Temporary Importation, Boat in Transit," the taxes are…zero. Why not refuse the FedEx and send it back and have it immediately resent? Because Brazil customs has already collected from FedEx as soon as it was sent to Brazil. Live and learn.

We have had two Lewmar blocks fail under routine conditions. I believe that any engineer or innocent bystander would look at them and say that the Lewmars are poorly designed. I am concerned that I still have dozens of them up in my rigging. I am currently replacing the Lewmars with Antals, which appear to be much sturdier. Perhaps other people have had bad experiences with Antals, but I hope that the photos will help any sailor to look at a block and consider the possible weak points.

Tonight, we are hauled out on dry land, up in the yard. We are VERY well protected. In the Bahia Marina area (which includes four restaurants and a number of shops) there are at least eight security guards with guns. But in our particular area of the yard, between 10 p.m. and 6 a.m. there are huge Rottweilers that prowl the grounds. I feel as if we are in a safe anchorage, patrolled by huge sharks, which will keep the pirates away, but will also eat me if I go for a swim. I hope that they can't climb the ladder up into the boat!

We are still enjoying and learning about Salvador. It is fascinating and complex. Bori has headed back to Hungary for a break. Max and I are waiting for crew to answer and commit for the next leg. We know that we can handle the boat just us two, and do a good job (together with "Jorge"), but it will be so much more fun, easy, interesting, and safe with two more. Once we relaunch [*mañana, mañana*], we will shift to another marina nearby (Centro Nautico da Bahia) that is a bit more sailor-oriented and closer to the fun in the Old Town. Also, we may go exploring around the bay and down the coast.


**23 JULY 2006**

The Schooner *Maggie B* hasn't moved much in the last two weeks, but lots has been going on, including lots of exploring of Salvador. We have been hauled out and back in again, have a new J-Prop to replace the one that went to swim with the fishes

Centro Nautico in Bahia.

somewhere between Barbados and Natal, and have cleaned off all marine growth so we are again in a go-fast mode.

Work on the boat has included plugging the usual minor leaks, checking and replacing some rigging pieces, getting fresh secondary fuel filters for both the engine and the generator, off-loading our failed clothes washer (we are trying to find a traditional wash board), getting more minutes for the Iridium satellite phone, etc. Brazil is marvelous, but everything takes more time and inevitably has complications.

One big step now is getting our tender *Reepicheep* fixed up. *Reep* is a Moosabec Reach Wherry of the Whitehall class, built by two apprentices at The Apprenticeshop of Rockland, Maine. She has been admired from Nova Scotia to Brazil. The varnish needed redoing and the hull paint has suffered too many insults. I also mixed up the jib lead one night when *Reep* was on deck, and the jib sheet wore into the hull in two places. So, she is out for a Salvador makeover, and was due back yesterday so that we could go exploring the huge Baie de Todos Santos. But now it is "maybe tomorrow." Sigh.

But the exciting news is that we are now crewed up with excellent hands for the trip to South Africa! A week ago, when we were in the Bahia Marina waiting to be hauled, we saw a nice little sloop arrive with an obviously fatigued crew of two. She was the *Plume d'Ange*, a Belgian boat, just in from the Azores with a couple, Bart and Lieve, sailing her. We got talking and have stayed connected as we both moved over to the Centro Nautico. Bart and Lieve are in their late twenties and are both maritime professionals, now on a sailing holiday/leave. Lieve has her ticket as "Chief Mate, All Ships, All Oceans." She runs the huge dredges that replaced the beach at Acapulco after the hurricane, or the levees in New Orleans. Bart is "Chief Engineer to 3000 kW engine power"

Boat watcher for *Reep* on the beach in Itaparica.

(about forty times our horsepower). He works as the mechanic for the supertugs that can hold a drilling station on position within a few centimeters in a hurricane.

They became interested in, and then excited, about *Maggie B* and the trip to Cape Town. After a few dinners together on *Maggie B* and *Plume d'Ange*, we four felt that we had confidence in each other's plans, priorities, and skills. The *Plume d'Ange* is going to stay in Salvador in a safe yacht club up the coast to be hauled for new anti-fouling. A local sail loft will remake their genoa, which blew out on the way down.

The route to South Africa from Salvador is interesting. If you go straight, the southeasterly trades are in your face the whole way, so the trick is to head south to pick up westerlies. But not too far south, because it is winter here and the Roaring Forties is not just an expression. Also, as we go south, we will need to stay clear of the area around Montevideo and Buenos Aries due to the winds they call the Pamperos, which have wrecked many a ship.

The logical route, south but not too much so, should take us past the island of

*"... we know to ready the emergency bilge pump,*
*we know to practice rigging the storm sails,*
*we know to load food for 30 days*
*plus everybody's comfort food—chocolate!"*

Tristan da Cunha, where we should be able to resupply...with potatoes. So, from Salvador, we will head south to south-southeast, depending on the winds, until we reach the westerlies, which should be found at about 25 or 30 degrees south. It is about 2,000 miles to Tristan da Cunha on a heading of about 160 degrees, and then 1,500 miles from Tristan da Cunha to Cape Town on a heading of 105 degrees.

The Southern Ocean gales move around the world unrestricted. Prudent sailors ride the pressure gradients. If the glass is falling, go north, if it is rising, ease south. Low pressure systems rotate in the opposite direction from those in the Northern Hemisphere, but that is probably the only sure truth of the weather.

## 26 JULY 2006

We finally have *Reepicheep* back from her Brazilian makeover. She looks good and has only lost a little of her panache and gold paint, but her broken frames are now sistered, and her hull looks a lot better.

We are off this afternoon to explore the island of Itaparica, which is only about 20 miles across the bay. It is one of 56 islands in the 1,000 sq. km. bay, and is the weekend escape for many Salvadorians. Itaparica served as headquarters for the Dutch in 1711, and then was the base for Bahian independence in 1823. For us it is a break from the bright lights of Salvador and the Pelo—the old town with all the restaurants, bars, music, and dancing in the street.

Itaparica also has a famous mineral water fountain, Fonte da Bica, constructed in 1842. We hope to fill our tanks there for the crossing. We will rendezvous with Bart and Lieve and *Plume d'Ange*, and further our plans and timing for Cape Town.

We're still learning. Few people realize how difficult it is to learn Portuguese: it takes TWO translations, first from Portuguese to English, and then to the real meaning. Thus:

Portuguese=English=Meaning
*Agora*=today=tomorrow
*Amanha*=tomorrow=next week
*nao problema*=no problem=it is complicated
*Esta sabado*=this Saturday=next Wednesday

But it is mostly fun along the way.


## 30 JULY 2006

We are now in full prep mode. Everyone has had the experience of preparing for a big, complicated, family road trip, when packing and supplies are checked and double-checked. A big ocean crossing is like that but much more complicated. It is about 4,000 NM across to Cape Town. No stops, no 911, no hardware stores, no supermarkets.

In talking about the Iraq war, Don Rumsfeld said something about the "known knowns, the known unknowns, and the unknown unknowns." We are right there, wondering about how to get ready for the unknown unknowns. We know to check the rig for wear and loose pieces, we know to change the oil and filters, we know to ready the emergency bilge pump, we know to practice rigging the storm sails, we know to load food for 30 days plus everybody's comfort food—chocolate! We know to watch the scary lows rolling off the Pampas into the Southern Ocean, we know to calibrate backup GPS units, but…how do you prepare for the surprises? Sharpen your knives, get extra sleep, and listen to lots of advice.

One fun sign that we should start saying goodbye to Brazil (we arrived in Natal almost five weeks ago!) and think about Africa was meeting a neat couple, Allan and Anya, who had come in from South Africa on their boat. They traded us a South African courtesy flag for a case of beer. Now we are ready!

We are going to have an interesting series of challenges to pick the right course. There is a perfect spot with great winds to move us to Cape Town, but edge too far south and you get hammered and too far north there is no wind. Easy to say, but the systems are moving shockingly fast, so you have to position yourself way before the systems arrive. We go 150–200 miles a day. The systems move at least twice as fast.

The moon is getting fuller every night, which should make night watches more pleasant. We have a strong crew: all four of us are experienced Blue Water sailors, all are shellbacks. With four, each of us stands only one 3-hour watch during the night. Positive luxury, though I expect that there will be some nights when we all will be up.

Looking at the Pilot Charts, we will be running along the line that is the northern limit of glacier ice in August (record from 1772!), plus the line that has a historic record of having waves exceeding 12 feet 30% of the time. The *Maggie B* can do 10.5 knots at hull speed. We'll see what she can do surfing!

Filling up for this leg has been fun. We took on water at Isla de Itaparica's mineral spring. The dock is only 200-feet away and the water is delicious and cheap (10 reals—about US$5—for all you can take). We fueled up with 700 liters of diesel at the Centro Nautico floating service station. Diesel costs about US$3.20 per gallon. With about 300 gallons of diesel aboard, we can motor about 1,200 NM. With 350 gallons of water on board, we can splurge on two gallons per person per day for 44 days, before we catch rainwater or use the watermaker.

It turned out to be a huge ordeal to get our cooking gas tanks refilled. Lots of reasons, with explanations changing daily but, in the end, we bought a Brazilian tank and jury-rigged the connection. They use butane rather than propane, but it seems to work fine, protected behind all our regulators and safety systems.

This was a very hard five weeks in Brazil. The arrival in the Potengi River without engine was one of the most difficult sailing challenges of the whole trip. Brazil was fascinating and almost always fun, but it could make the simplest tasks monumental. ATMs, phone calls, FedEx, refilling cooking gas. The boat had a bunch of things to fix, like installing a new propeller, but there were a host of underlying worries about the fitness of the whole system. So many unanswered questions! Why did the prop come off in the first place and will this new one stay on? Why are we busting so many Lewmar blocks and what will fail next? The roller furling foil for the jib spits out the grub screws that connect the sections—will it stay together in the Southern Ocean? And there is the Southern Ocean and our first big crossing to Cape Town staring at us outside the calm and beautiful bay of All Saints. How would *Maggie B* do in the Roaring Forties in winter?

But the biggest uncertainty had been crew. The two people that I had originally counted on for the crossing had changed their minds. I only had Max, who was being seduced and distracted by the many charms of Salvador. My emails of the time have perhaps a hundred "asks" of friends, friends of friends, acquaintances of friends, acquaintances of acquaintances. It seemed for a time that perhaps Salvador was the end of the trip, at least for a while. Running into Bart and Lieve was perfect. We left Salvador for Cape Town with probably the most competent crew I had during the whole voyage.

## ON WATCH AT SEA

The human race ended up with a 24-hour day from the ancient setting of the night watch. Hours were originally counted only from sunset to sunrise and divided so as to make it easy to split up the night for watch. Ten isn't a very useful number for watch because it is only divisible by two and five. Twelve, of course, can be divided by six, four, three and two. Different situations of the number of watchers or the degree of alert would cause the captain to split up the night differently.

When we had four aboard, we generally did three hours on and nine off. When we were three aboard, we would do "two-twos" – four hours on and eight off during the day and two hours on and four off during the night. So you had a long watch during the easier day and two two-hour watches at night.

But what do you watch for? The instructor who taught me to fly said about preflighting an airplane, "Look for what's there that shouldn't be and for what's not there that should be." Boats are the same.

First and foremost, the watch was there to ensure that we didn't run into anything. Other boats, shipping containers, nets, trees. We could spot big boats on radar first, perhaps as far as 25 miles out. Little boats and flotsam and jetsam were harder. At night it was much trickier. One marvelous, traditional, mistake that I and many others have made, is to think that the planet Venus, rising, is the bow light of a huge ship about to hit you.

Gail on watch.

The watch should also check below. Is everybody OK, is some pump running that shouldn't be, is there some new sound? Are there any more cookies?

But what do you see when you look out at sea? Certainly rosy-fingered dawn and the shimmer of moonlight on the waves. While offshore is called Blue Water, the color of the sea is always changing, as is the sky. You look out to consider the clouds to see if they promise rain or wind or a quiet day. You look for sea animals – whales or dolphin or tuna. You watch the birds – the great albatross or darting petrels. At night there is often phosphorescence, sometimes little creatures, sometimes fantastic big shapes.

I would generally take the midnight to 3 am watch. It was the hardest, perhaps, to stay alert for, but also often lovely and peaceful with the boat going along and your shipmates snugly asleep below. I was never bored. Every 15 minutes you would run the radar and take a hard look in every direction. Each half hour I would check below and go forward on deck to adjust and check the sails. It was a good time for exercise and stretching. We had an almost bottomless supply of good books which I read by headlamp. If clear, you could always learn a new star. I won't say that 2:45 am, the time to wake my relief, ever came too soon, but the three hours almost always passed quickly.

Photo Credit: Bart Gabriel

*"I think that most things that go wrong
can be treated in the same way—either fix it
or work around it. A perfect boat never sails."*

4

# BRAZIL TO CAPE TOWN

## 1 AUGUST 2006

We welcomed August by getting underway from Salvador for Cape Town. We realize that we know so little of Brazil, and had quite an adventure there, but we are happy to be headed for Cape Town.

At noon, we were about 10 miles off of Salvador. It is a lovely clear day. The wind is 135 degrees at 12 knots and we are making 195 degrees at 6.3 knots. The direct course to Cape Town is about 135 degrees (wind on the nose again!) for 3363 NM, but we are going to run south along Brazil's coast to pick up the back side of a high-pressure system that is just getting ready to exit the coast, and then ride its northwesterlies across—circulation here is opposite from the Northern Hemisphere's system.

Crew for the crossing—Brazil to Cape Town.

The floating gas station in the Bahia harbor.

## 2 AUGUST 2006

We are about 150 miles from Salvador, heading south along the Brazilian coast, about 50 miles off shore. We are motorsailing in light easterly winds, heading 155 degrees at 6.5 knots.

We have started fishing and caught dinner after only an hour and a half, a 20-inch skipjack tuna or bonito that will fry up nicely in garlic, lime juice, and oil. We knew that these waters are rich because the flying fish are back in squadrons, and a gannet followed us all morning.

Brazil is a lovely country, but so bureaucratic. To clear into Natal, we had to visit 1) the Federal Police (Immigration), 2) Customs, 3) the Health Ministry (are you bringing yellow fever?), and the *Capitainerie* (Harbor Control). It took us four hours, supplying similar information in each spot. We were told that when we left Natal, all we had to do was check out with the Capitainerie, which we did.

On arriving in Salvador, we went at once to the Capitainerie, and checked in. No problem. Soon the Federal Police showed up and wanted to know why we hadn't checked out of Natal. We said we were told we didn't need to, they showed a line on one of our forms which said we had to. We asked why we had to check out with the Federal Police when we weren't leaving the country and they said because we went to another Federal State, and they wouldn't check us into Salvador because we were still officially in Rio Grande del Norde. They *would* check us out when we were ready to leave for Cape Town. It made perfect sense to them. At least they didn't send us back to Natal to check out. And, no, nobody asked for or hinted about "special fines" or "processing costs."

We had a somewhat interesting ship track us from ahead last night. Around sunset we saw a small Brazilian Naval vessel about six miles ahead. During the night, regardless of our course changes and variation in speed, it kept position at our one o'clock at exactly six miles distance. Only when we got to 30 miles off the coast, at about 3 a.m., did it peel off and head back. It must have been some anti-smuggling or Coast Guard patrol, but I did nervously think that we might have missed something in our checkout from the various Brazilian bureaus—Police, Federal Police, Harbormaster, Customs, Health, etc.

At noon today in light breezes, we practiced putting up our storm sails, so that we won't fumble too much when we need them.

One t-shirt we saw when we left Salvador said "Belgium: Small Country, Great Beers." We have shipped enough beer for one can each, every other day for 24 days. Because today is an even day, we will toast our first fish of the voyage with Brazilian Skol beer. But just one can each.

## 3 AUGUST 2006

We are motorsailing at 7 knots on a course of 156, which is a direct course for Tristan da Cunha. The wind is still a light easterly. It is a lovely day with rain showers off to the south. We are working our way east to stay clear of Brazil's coast and south to pick up the promised westerlies. The barometric pressure is at 1019 mb, down very little from the 1021 when we left Salvador.

Absolutely fresh tuna steaks.

Max has proven himself to be an efficient fisherman. We had our lines out for only two hours yesterday and he got a lovely jack that was fishcakes for lunch today and a 30-pound yellowfin tuna that was sashimi and dinner (garlic and oil, lightly warmed in the frying pan, served with fresh lime) last night. We'll eat our way across in luxury!

It is great having a crew of efficient, experienced Blue Water sailors. Everything is kept clean and put away. Nobody is sick. Confusing systems are subdued, watches are easy and the boat is well kept.

J-Props are one of several kinds of propellers that offer less resistance when the engine is turned off. A fixed propeller, if stopped in the water while you are under sail, can reduce your speed by half to 1 knot, perhaps 10% of your boat speed. A rotating prop causes even more drag, and, if the engine is not working, can cause damage to your transmission and the through-hull fitting.

The blades of the J-Prop, however, are supposed to feather when the engine is off, to minimize drag. If the shaft isn't turning, either in forward or reverse, the blades should go to neutral just from the pressure of the water flow.

Our new J-Prop propeller doesn't seem to feather the way it should. We have tried the usual tricks (such as putting the engine into reverse before shutting down) to no avail. Last night we "roped" the shaft to stop it from turning (our transmission is hydraulic, so putting it into gear does nothing). Today at noon I went diving to check if there was anything caught in the prop, and if it was still flexible and free. We stopped the boat and I hopped in (water temperature a lovely 78 degrees). The sun was bright and I was immediately struck with vertigo as I looked down the light shafts through the incredibly clear water towards the bottom 10,000 feet away. Fortunately, there were no predators higher on the food chain around. The prop turned out to be perfectly clear and smoothly flexible, so we will have to try something else. It eventually unstuck from whatever problem it was having.


## 4 AUGUST 2006

We were motoring last night in light breezes, but the wind has now filled in from 110 degrees at 10–15 and we are sailing close hauled on port tack at 6.5 knots on a heading of 180 degrees magnetic.

The latest forecast from Commanders' Weather is quite favorable. We are headed south down the coast of Brazil (about 200 miles off) but making some easting because 180 degrees magnetic is about 160 degrees true here. We hope to rendezvous with the back side of a high-pressure system at about 27S/32W, which should give us nice northwesterlies to blow us across. We should be able to make the turn east in two or three days.

We are just coming to a series of seamounts, the *Cadeia Vitória-Trindade*, where, in places, the bottom rises from 4,000 meters to 30 meters in a matter of a few miles. We expect interesting sea conditions. The seamounts reach out 700 NM off the coast to Isla da Trindade, which pokes up 600 feet above the water.

We are now fully at sea with *Maggie B* heeling over comfortably. Everyone is used to bracing themselves and knowing what will slip and what will stay in place. Finding a place to sleep or nap becomes more specialized. We have railings or battens stretched part way up the sides of the bunks. Thus, if you sleep on the low side, it makes a comfortable corner to wedge into. It is easy to sleep with the water gurgling inches away and the rig creaking above. For those berths on the high side, we have heavy canvas lee cloths, which tie into place to keep sleeping bodies from flying through the air into the companionway. The pipe berths have the cleverest arrangements as one can adjust the supporting ropes to set the bunk at the perfect angle. You do need warning of a tack, though. Max bought a hammock from a street vendor in Brazil, but has not tried it out yet.

Lunch today was shrimp in a garlic white sauce followed by fresh yellowfin tuna steaks with potatoes and broccoli. Yum!

Plate-leveling scheme.

## 5 AUGUST 2006

This is idyllic sailing. We have 9–12 knots of wind, the sheets are started from close hauled as we are 45 degrees off the relative wind and *Maggie B* is slipping along at 6–7 knots. The sun is out but not too hot, t-shirt weather, and there is a gentle, long, 8–10 foot swell from the south. Occasional, rare, whitecaps show off the deep, deep blue of the ocean. There are no reefs or islands to run into for hundreds of miles. We haven't seen a ship in a day and our "Sea-Me" Active Radar Target Enhancer, which can sniff a ship's radar perhaps 100 miles away, is quiet. Puffy fair-weather clouds are scattered around, and the moon is now two-thirds full, promising a bright night watch.

Lunch was fish stew, with the last of our fresh yellowfin tuna, onions, carrots, potatoes, a tomato, lots of garlic, and one-third of a bottle of a 2004 Graves (for the stew, not the cook).

The only frustration of the day was trying to get the Dell computer to talk to the Furuno Ethernet, so that we can get the MaxSea software to talk to the GPS and boat performance system. If we could get it to work, MaxSea will help us work out routing, given the ship's performance and the wind data that we download each day. But MaxSea is French and Furuno is Japanese and we all get a little hazy when assigning the components different IP addresses. Perhaps there is a guru in Cape Town.

We seem to be on schedule to pick up the southwest quadrant of the next high coming from the west. The barometric pressure is rising here, which should presage the high coming. In the southwest quadrant we should have nice 20-knot northwest winds, which we can ride across. Our turn point, from south to east, is about 26S/32W or 340 NM away, just over two days.

## 6 AUGUST 2006

We have gone 786 miles so far. Tristan da Cunha is 1345 NM and Cape Town is 2800.

Today is splendid. I know that I may run out of adjectives, having used "idyllic" yesterday. But today is different from yesterday. The swells of yesterday have organized into long 8–12 foot South Atlantic rollers, that slip easily under us every 12 seconds or so. The white caps are more general, the Beaufort scale having eased up from Force Three to Force Four, and the wind waves are more sharp and angular. It is cooler, with the water at 70 degrees from a tepid 83 in Barbados. More hatches are dogged down, *Reep*'s lashings are rechecked, t-shirts have given way to polypro, favorite blankets are searched out from the linen locker, and knives are re-sharpened.

We have started our turn to the east. At noon the wind was 080 magnetic at 10–14 knots, now at 3 p.m. it is 060 at 15. Sheets have eased more. At noon we were doing 7.8 knots, now we are up to 9.0. We are in the high, with the pressure up to 1021 mb, but we need to make a bit more Southing to keep the coming northwesterly as long as possible.

Great shearwaters *(Ardenna gravis)* with their 4-foot wingspan have joined us, preparing us for albatrosses, if we are so lucky to see one. Last night I ran a surface krill troll, picking up some tiny fish, many fish eggs, as well as red, orange, and white tiny shrimp. I will use longer line and some weights tonight to see what wonders are a bit lower down.

Last night's disaster was spilling Coke onto the computer. This morning I switched to the backup computer, which, as always, was not well backed-up. Max has made a keyboard transplant and is working to de-Cokify the bad one.

Max scrubbing the computer keyboard.

## FAVORABLE GALES

At their centers, the Southern Ocean lows might be blowing 60-70 knots. What we wanted for good sailing was 25-30. Too far north, no wind – too far south, too much. We checked the barometer every hour and logged it every four hours. 1017 millibars – OK; lower, go north; higher, go south.

In the Southern Ocean, the powerful lows, driving hard around the planet, circulate clockwise. If you are north of the low, you first get a northwest wind, then west, then southwest. The strength depends on how close you are to the center.

You want a favorable gale. Really. People ashore perhaps forget the obvious point

Sea between sails.

– to sail you need wind. You don't want the wind on your nose; you want it helping you along. In my great-grandmother's hymnal are two "traveling" hymns from more than a hundred years ago that have verses with "Oh, Lord, do send us a favorable gale."

In the South Atlantic, before a gale you get what our weather router calls "large waves," which means 15-20 feet. But they are long rollers, Southern Ocean waves that keep moving around the planet, without any land to obstruct them. They look huge, they are huge, but they are so long that you slide up, surf down and then do it again. This is much different from waves against a current or, perhaps, across a river mouth, which can be very vertical. Inshore a 15 foot vertical wave can destroy a big boat, it the open ocean a 15 foot swell is usually just a comforting roller.

Today you can get pretty good weather forecasts up to five days out. In five days we could go 1000 miles. At sea, every hour of every day of every passage I would think about the wind and waves – what was forecast versus what we are experiencing, and what was forecast coming next. I often woke from a sound sleep when there was a significant change in speed, boat direction, wind or waves. Keeping us safe was my first job, putting the sailboat in the right breeze was the second, and a close second.

## 7 AUGUST 2006

We did 195 miles in the last 24 hours, in winds of 15–18 knots! During my 9 to midnight watch, I saw hull speed, 10.2 knots, from time to time. As planned, we are just south of our first high. The wind is now 15–18 knots at 340–350 degrees and we are "making hay while the sun shines" and heading right for Cape Town on a course of 120 M (magnetic) at 8.5 knots. At this speed, we would make Cape Town in 13 days, but that is optimistic.

There is a steady series of highs and lows forming and moving rapidly across the South Atlantic. I have decided to name them as they come along, to better keep track and not get caught either in the lack of wind in the center of a high or too much wind in the center of a low.

As this first high (Hank) passes ahead east of us, the wind should back more and get light. Later in the week the next low (LaVerne) will track off the continent. LaVerne should have winds of 60 knots in her center, and we will aim, as best we can, to be about 200 miles north of the center in 20–30 knots from the northwest backing to the southwest.

Right now, we will head east as long as this nice northwesterly lasts, then make some more Southing in what should be light westerlies backing to southerlies, as we wait for the low. Our aim is to be at about 31S for LaVerne.

We record the wind, waves, barometer, and clouds each hour. It seems that 1018 mb of pressure is about right—less and we ease north towards the high, more and we go south for the breeze. If we do this right, we will have a good passage.

With the wind behind us and the sun out, we are back in t-shirts and the hatches are open.

Max's attempt to salvage the keyboard failed, though he applied heroic measures. We hope that Dell will part with a new one.


## 8 AUGUST 2006

At noon our speed was 6.2 knots with a course of 150 degrees. The wind was 240 degrees at 8–10, but fading. We are headed to Commanders' next turn point (30S/26W), which is 185 miles away.

Tristan da Cunha is 991 miles, Cape Town is 2,462, and we have come 1,170 miles since Salvador. Yesterday's run was 189 miles.

We are still headed south and east, to get to 30 degrees South to stay below the next high (Herb), which is forming just about over us here at 28 degrees South. We

Max's mahi-mahi.

have our eyes peeled to the southwest for a small low (Lacie), which is preceding a relatively intense low (LaVerne). The barometer is holding up at 1021, which provides this great weather, but we are headed south for lower pressure and more wind.

Yesterday's afternoon excitement was catching a beautiful mahi-mahi. Max reeled it in and Bart landed it: 49 inches! It will provide marvelous meals for some days. Today's lunch was mahi-mahi steaks marinated in oil and garlic, lightly poached, with roasted potatoes and a cabbage/carrot salad. Landing the mahi-mahi almost upset tea time, where chocolate chip muffins were in the oven when the fish struck. There was some multi-tasking to handle the boat, to help land the fish, while checking the muffins. All went well.

We officially switched to Greenwich Mean Time (GMT) minus 2 today to move us towards being ready for our eventual arrival in Cape Town, which is on GMT plus 2 (unless there is some "daylight saving" foolishness).

Email to my son, Alden:

Subject: Crew Wanted

Baker and Able Seaman wanted for long sea voyage. Long hours and low pay. Safe return probable, but timing unknown. Must stand watches as well as make fresh bread daily. Exotic locales and variable weather. South Africa to Australia via Indian Ocean Islands. Sound boat and happy, skilled crew. Mid-September departure.

Please reply to:
Captain, Schooner *Maggie B*.


## 9 AUGUST 2006

Our course is 155 degrees magnetic at 7.8 knots and Max is making mahi-mahi fish cakes for lunch!

Last night surprised us all. It was forecast, but shocking nonetheless. It was flat calm. Not a light breeze, but Beaufort Zero—a glassy calm. At 29 degrees south in mid-winter! The next high was forming over us (Herb) and we motored south to get on the right side. The wind is now 290 degrees at 10–12 knots and we are continuing southeast to make some easting while setting up for the next big blow.

But right now, the weather is warm enough that shoes are off and shorts on, hatches are open, and laundry is hanging out to dry. The barometer is nice and high at 1023 mb. The seawater is down to 66 degrees and we have lots of shearwaters around us.

When I went on watch last night at 2100, I brought up my concertina for practice. I told Max, who I was relieving and sleeps in the pilot berth, that he should tell me if I bothered him. He replied that he had good earplugs and was going to use them. Fortunately, my attempts to work through "Spanish Ladies" did not keep him awake.


## 10 AUGUST 2006

The wind is northwest at 10–12 knots and we are heading 115 degrees at 7.3.

The noon position using GPS was confirmed by sun sight, which came up with latitude of 31 degrees 35 minutes South. Right on!

During the morning watch, it was noticed that we were getting an increased amperage draw from the Furuno GPS/radar/plotter, so it was shut down. After

Lieve getting our noon sight.

breakfast and a few extra cups of espresso, Max and Bart went on the chase of the electrical fault like junior versions of Inspector Morse and Hercule Poirot. Instead of *"Ah-ha, it was a left-handed woman between the age of 45 and 50!"* it was *"I have a ground fault in the secondary DC negative bus!"*

All was cleared up by lunch (mahi-mahi baked with potatoes and cauliflower), with the culprits being a damaged circuit breaker (poor construction) and some loose fittings. For the few hours while the ship's power was off, Lieve and I brushed off our musty memory of sun sights and cleaned up the sextant. We will try for star sights tonight at dusk. We also broke out the battery powered GPS #2.

The weather today is what in Maine we would call a smoky southwester, except here it probably would be called a *norte/oeste fumaria*, being Brazilian and from the northwest. We are watching to the southwest for LaVerne, but the wind is staying light and the barometer steady at 1024 mb.

Staying in shape on a small boat isn't hard. At sea, walking to the bow is more like playing on a jungle gym than walking down a street. Even sitting to read or eat, you are always tensioned or braced in some fashion. Now while wedged into the ship's office to type, my left leg is braced against the step and both elbows have to actively keep me relatively level with the keyboard. Certainly, raising, lowering and adjusting sails give you a regular upper-body workout, as does coiling lines, polishing the binnacle, etc. During night watch, I do some yoga to stay flexible, dimly remembered ballet exercises using the binnacle grab rail as the barre, and occasionally pull in and let out the mainsheet by hand to get the muscles moving. We also probably eat less than when on land. Generally, our big meal is all-together at lunch. Dinner, due to different watch schedules, is usually pretty light—cold potato and a cup of soup, or a few slices of salami and cheese with some crackers. We don't have many sodas on board, so a Coke is a small celebration and we drink almost no alcohol—just a glass of wine or a beer every other day.

> ## *"This is just what the* Maggie B *was designed and built for: 30 knots of wind (Beaufort 7 or Near Gale) at 120 degrees relative."*

We stay in contact with the rest of the world pretty well. The inexpensive Dell laptop is connected to an Iridium Sat phone. Email is handled by an organization called UUPlus. When you finish a letter and click send, UUPlus takes the file, compresses it, and stores it in a "send queue." The program does not allow fancy formatting, different fonts, "smilies," attachments, photos, or anything but basic letters and numbers. On the other end, ashore, UUPlus will regularly sweep any email accounts and collect your mail, compress it, and strip off fancy coding and most attachments. Big files are sent back to the sender with a note. Then when you are ready, you press "connect" on the computer and it takes over the Iridium phone, dials up the UUPlus connection, dumps your mail "ashore," and grabs the packet ready to go. It will also pick up specific web files, like weather charts. Connection is usually pretty slow for land-based, perhaps 4800 bytes, but with the compression and simplification, I can uplink five to ten messages, get the same back, plus a big weather file, all in perhaps a minute, which costs about $1.50 (plus the cost of the Sat phone). I could do all this on the SSB radio, where there is generally one fixed charge, but connection is chancy, notably slower, and the weather charts less usable.

I smell chocolate chip muffins ready for tea.

## 11 AUGUST 2006

Our course is 090 at 9.1 knots. The wind is 320–330 at 20 knots. Cape Town is 2,014 miles away, Tristan da Cunha is 545, and we have come 1,650 miles so far.

Even here in the South Atlantic, we got the news about the airline bomb plot using liquid explosives. It makes dealing with a Southern Ocean gale seem relatively simple and nice.

We are just rushing along in a brisk northwesterly. It is still fairly warm on deck in the sun, and shorts and bare feet are the order of the day…but not for much longer. As the GRIB files and Commanders' Weather report show, we can expect this NW'er to build–perhaps 30 knots with gusts to 40. Commanders' predicts swells of 12–18 feet and confused seas. We are moving north a bit and will reef down by sunset, even if the wind isn't up by then. The barometer is only just beginning to fall, down to 1022 mb from 1024 last night at midnight. Cold frontal passage is due about dawn tomorrow, when the wind will shift to the southwest and we will jibe over to starboard tack and head back south to keep on track for Cape Town and milk what we can out of this system.

Chicken ravioli for lunch with broccoli—can't have fresh mahi-mahi every day….

## 12 AUGUST 2006

We did 236 NM in the last 24 hours, for an average of 9.83 knots, not bad for a 35-ton gaff schooner with a design hull speed of 10.2 knots!

This is just what the *Maggie B* was designed and built for: 30 knots of wind (Beaufort 7 or Near Gale) at 120 degrees relative. We are also getting a nice assist from some major southwesterly swells, averaging 12 feet with many much higher. The *Maggie B* surfs along the wave, like a pro, not just diving down them. We have seen 14.3 knots on the GPS whilst surfing.

We were on port tack last night, with the northwesterly, but anticipating the cold front passage. It came at 5 a.m. during Lieve's watch (just like the last one), and we all turned out to jibe over in the pre-dawn grayness and 28 knots of wind. All went smoothly.

The boat is nicely steady. The lee rail is mostly about two feet out of the water and only occasional packets of spray come off passing waves. The sails are balanced with two reefs in the main and one in the foresail with a full jib. The wind has been 25–35 knots with a gust or two to 40. Jorge, the autopilot is doing an excellent job in very tough conditions, probably better than the humans on board. Both yesterday

A confused sea in the Roaring Forties.
Photo credit: Bart Gabriel

and today we were able to sit down at the crew mess and have a nice hot meal while she was at hull speed and surfing occasionally. Today's lunch was mahi-mahi steaks breaded and done in a hot pan, with fried onions, and coleslaw with tomatoes, pine nuts, apple, and raisins.

We are joined by a dozen or so seabirds—petrels and shearwaters—with today's newcomer being the dazzling pintado petrel *(Daption capense)*, the fighter pilot of the Blue Water birds.

We are heading right for Cape Town or actually 100 NM south of Cape Town. Many have advised us to hold south until a bit past lest we be blown back west by the regular southeasterly

A shearwater looking for lunch.

gales and the additional push of the very strong westerly current. It looks as if we will have another day of riding LaVerne—this low—before she leaves and is replaced by Hector, our third high of the passage, which will again give us no winds or a light head wind, while we wait for Libby, the next low that is racing east.

## 13 AUGUST 2006

We did 202 NM in the last 24 hours. We have gone 2,078 miles since Salvador and Cape Town is now 1,627 miles away. Tristan da Cunha is just 350 miles south of us.

The wind is backing around as forecast. Currently it is 120 degrees at 12–15 knots. We have shaken out our reefs and are under all plain sail. The barometer is way up to 1030 mb as the next high (Hector) forms just south of us. We should have easy sailing for the next three or four days with the wind backing to northwest and steady at 15–20 knots. The next big wave of pressure should catch up to us on the 17th or 18th.

As Commanders' Weather says, we are seeing a bit of a large sea, up to 20 feet, generated by the storms to the south of us. While the waves sound big, they really are not a concern as they have a long set, and rarely combine with the other series to peak up. Occasionally *Maggie B* will be perched like a skier just at the top of a Black Diamond run, looking rather far down, but then the wave passes smoothly on its way to Africa, perhaps just leaving a little splash of water in the face of the duty watch.

We have flocks and flocks of sea birds around us—petrels and shearwaters— probably all nesting on Tristan da Cunha.

Lunch was mahi-mahi fish soup, done Chinese style with rice and ginger. Lieve used just a bit of the famous Susie's Hot Sauce from Antigua, which was enough to light our fires.

Birdwatching in the Southern Ocean. Photo credit: Bart Gabriel

## 14 AUGUST 2006

We have a lovely northwesterly (340–350 degrees at 18–25) and are headed 120 degrees, right for Cape Town, at 10 knots. We only did 177 NM since yesterday noon due to a very slow period (my watch...) while the high was forming south of us.

We seem to have a southwesterly current helping us a bit, adding half a knot to our speed and a bit of a lee-bow push (moving us north a bit).

Tristan da Cunha has slipped off our plans. We are having a great South Atlantic winter passage and dropping that extra 300 NM or five degrees further south just seems to be asking for trouble.

The waves are mixed up as there is a big southerly swell, the remains of the southwest swell, all enlivened by the wind-waves kicked up by the strong northwesterly breeze. But we are riding them well and little spray comes on board.

Lieve on watch.

We are beginning to plot our approach to the African coast. Cape Town is 34 degrees South and we need to hold perhaps another degree south for room against a possible southeasterly. But each degree south of 30 edges us towards bigger weather. It looks like an interesting break coming towards the end of the week, but we will not be far enough along to take advantage of it.

In the last two weeks, we have run the main engine for 47 hours and the generator for 48. Very conservatively, this means that we have used about 115 gallons of diesel, leaving us about 200 gallons: 100 hours with the main engine or 700 miles steaming. Plenty for our approach!

## 15 AUGUST 2006

We did 218 NM in the last 24 hours. Cape Town is 1266 NM away, heading 120 degrees magnetic. We have come 2473 NM so far. Our clocks are now set to Greenwich Mean Time.

The wind is fairly steady at 330 degrees magnetic at 15–20 knots. It is a nice dry day and ports are open, bedding is airing out, people are showering, and some

Close hauled for Cape Town.

laundry is getting done. The cabin has warmed up to a relatively comfortable 65 degrees F. The barometer is up to 1028 mb and it is partly cloudy.

Our electronic compass differs from our electronic heading sensor by about eight degrees, and the handheld compass is in between. We have been trying for the last three days to get a bearing from sunrise, sunset, or moonrise to check the compasses from the predicted azimuth (Zn for you star-sighting types), but, alas, it has been cloudy.

Last night's culinary success was "Alexandra's Best Ever Lemon Cake," from *Maggie B*'s cookbook. It had mostly disappeared by dawn. I had to make it with limes because we had limes but no lemons, and also in honor of all the caipirinhas we enjoyed in Brazil. Lunch today will be chicken in garlic and oil with a bottle of Entre deux Mers (between two seas—get it?) white Bordeaux.

Today's excitement, which perhaps shows that we have been at sea too long, was Max exclaiming, "Oooh, the spread legs rig!" To Lieve's and my surprise, Bart was showing Max an esoteric sailing rig with two masts set up like an A-frame. Ah, well.

We are about a week away from landfall and are watching our weather systems carefully. It is too early to nail anything down, but it looks as if we will have this nice northwester only for another day or so and then a big and confused high will form around us, which we will just have to work our way through, with lots of wind shifts. The next low seems to be setting up more to the south, perhaps blocked by the high. We shall see. We are keeping the reef in the main for now.


## 16 AUGUST 2006

After an unsettled night, we are back to the usual 15–20 knot northwesterly, booming along at 8–9 knots, heading 110–120. Cape Town is now 1096 NM on a bearing of 128 degrees. *If* we can keep this speed, we will be there in five days; a passage of 21 days from Salvador. It looks as if the door might be open for us to slip into Table Bay without a southeasterly gale beating us up. Maybe. It is too early to tell for sure. A very big storm well south seems to be taking most of the energy.

Today is mostly cloudy with occasional light drizzle. We have a big westerly swell, enhanced by the remains of the southwesterly from the last storm. Jorge is steering well, with occasional wild stupidities as it puts the requested heading 50 degrees right or left of what we humans entered. At least it peeps pathetically when it goes stupid (the deviation alarm), but it would be nicer if it just kept us on course.

Last night's excitement was running out of the gas for the stove and having the Brazilian tank not work. The prospect of no coffee for breakfast put the whole team to work. Regulators were dismantled, cleaned, and reassembled. Systems were checked up and down. Finally, a wire running to the switch-off solenoid was found to be imperfectly installed, and the heat shrink fitting had filled with salt water and only a strand or two was left. Once that was fixed, it was espresso all around!

We have had a lot of delicious fresh fish—almost too much. Max has not been allowed to put a lure into the water since the last mahi-mahi. I recalled that we had loaded some lovely filet mignon in Barbados and there were four left in the freezer. Getting to them was like an archeological project, as Bart worked his way down through layers and layers of ice and frost. Finally, he pried them out, and we got a defrosted freezer in the bargain. They are now marinating in olive oil, garlic and herbs, and Bart has requested Lieve's peppercorn white sauce. Maybe we will let Max fish tomorrow.

## 17 AUGUST 2006

We did 214 NM in the last 24 hours, and have gone 2872 NM since Salvador.

We jibed at dawn and are now on starboard tack, heading 170 at 9 knots in a fresh northwesterly. Heading south may allow us to catch the tail end of the southwest breeze from the last big low to come through south of us. It appears as if we are in for three or four days of unsettled weather, including the possibility of some fairly strong winds on our nose. We will probably have lots of tacks and jibes, reefing and shaking out of reefs, before we are tied up at the Royal Cape Yacht Club.

Now that we are getting close (yes, 1000 NM is close), we are looking hard at charts of approaches to Cape Town. One interesting spot is a sea mount about 500 miles off the coast of South Africa. The bottom goes from about 5,000 meters to 11 meters in just a few miles. Bart says that it must be a great place to watch whales, but I think that we'll stay clear. The Agulhas Current runs strong southwesterly past Cape of Good Hope; here 1000 NM west of the Cape, we are on the edge of the strong easterly current and the equally strong Benguela Current runs northwest. Enough currents to brew the whole ocean into froth!

The swells and waves are now coming at us broadside. The boat is riding them well, but occasionally they rear up alongside, as if they trying to peek into the cabin. Sometimes it is like driving in the Rocky Mountains or the highlands of Scotland, where you go in a moment from being in a nasty tight gorge to popping out to see a lovely open meadow.

We are seeing lots of big boats now, as we are crossing the tracks of every steamer that comes around the Cape of Good Hope heading for North or South America. Radar watches have been increased.

We are down to our last six eggs, all of which have been assigned to baking. Blueberry muffins baked yesterday for tea did not survive to see the sunset.

Besides getting GRIB weather files daily, we get updates from Commanders' Weather every couple of days. We are trying to contact some South African weathermen on our SSB radio. Nothing like local knowledge.

*"It (Lucille) should be our last low before Cape Town and we hope to ride the north side of it like a remora attached to a basking shark. We just hope that it doesn't turn out to be a hammerhead!"*

## 18 AUGUST 2006

We are motorsailing, heading 136 at 7.6 knots for our point off of Cape Town. The wind is variable, but generally south at 5 knots. Cape Town is 754 NM away. We have come 3063 NM so far and covered 191 NM in the last 24 hours.

It is not a great sailing day today. Long, confused swell, no wind, cold and drizzling. This morning we did what any hard-core South Atlantic shellback sailors would do—we put Jimmy Buffett and his Coral Reefer Band on loud, picked cleaning stations (floors; walls; head and shower; vacuum) out of a hat, cleaned up the boat, made blueberry muffins, and decided on lunch (a kilo of steamed shrimp with four dipping sauces—garlic, mustard, curry, and spicy tomato). It made for a great morning. On top of that, the engine has heated up the water and we have made lots more with the watermaker, so we all are clean and even clean-shaven!

Yesterday I got an amazing email. As previously mentioned, I ruined the keyboard of one of the Dell laptops by spilling Coke on it. A computer is critical for us to receive weather information, useful to plan routing, and nice to have for email. Max fixed the computer by switching keyboards (the backup was not sufficiently backed up) and we went on our way. Yesterday, out of the blue, I got an email from

Dell Customer Service saying that they had seen my posting about needing a new keyboard. Could they help and was everything OK? Amazing support. And a new keyboard has been shipped to Cape Town and should be waiting for us at the Royal Cape Yacht Club!

## 19 AUGUST 2006

We are close hauled on the port tack, getting beaten up a bit in 25 knots of wind and a confused, rough sea. Cape Town is 630 NM on a bearing of 124 degrees magnetic. We are headed 124 degrees at 6.5–7 knots. The wind has been backing all morning and is about 080 magnetic at 20–30. We have a reef in the foresail and the main, and the jib is partially furled. We will probably put a second reef in the main after lunch (steak filets wrapped in bacon with garlic butter, mixed vegetables, and rice).

A new low is quickly forming just south of us, and is the cause of this rough weather. It (Lucille) should be our last low before Cape Town and we hope to ride the north side of it like a remora attached to a basking shark. We just hope that it doesn't turn out to be a hammerhead!

This morning's surprise was a 10-inch squid on deck. It must have jumped six feet to get aboard. Despite having an eye as big and sad as Bambi's eye, it was fried up in butter and tasted delicious.

According to the GRIB files and Commanders', this should be the worst of it, with the wind clocking around to the north, west and then south, all at 20–35 knots. We should have a pretty good ride in. Did I mention moderate rain also? You can't tell if the water on your face is salt or fresh until you taste it. A real test of foul weather gear! Fortunately, we are all pretty well suited for the conditions.

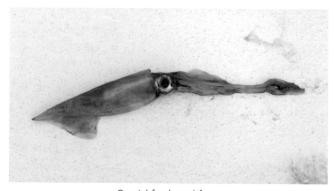

Squid for breakfast.

Double-reefed foresail and main.

## 20 AUGUST 2006

We had our first strong gale, Beaufort Force 9, last night—winds to 44 knots. We ran Lucille a bit close.

Probably our first inkling was at 5:30 p.m., about sunset, when the 1-inch high-tech foresheet parted in only 25 knots, in a sail with one reef. We quickly secured things, and Lieve remarked, "Cape Town comes with a price."

We had been happy at 9 p.m. with the barometer at 1015 mb and the wind about on our beam at 30 knots. We were running along with two reefs in the main, one in the foresail, and about half the jib. The centerboard was halfway down to help with stability in the confused sea.

The second clue came about 9:30 p.m. when the *Maggie B* jumped off a large wave and the impact on the centerboard burst one of the hydraulic lines. We wedged the centerboard down with a handy two by four.

By 10:30 p.m. the sea was becoming large and confused and all hands were called to take in the foresail, which was done quickly and efficiently. The jib was further reduced to the size of two overcoats. By midnight the barometer was down to 1010 mb, with the wind steady from the north at 30. By 1 a.m. the barometer dropped to 1005 and the wind peaked up to 44 knots. The *Maggie B* swam fine over the very confused sea with her double-reefed main and scrap of a jib. Sail area was down to about a quarter of the full sail hoist.

> *"We hope to arrive by sunset on the 23rd, so that we can find the Belgian Brew Pub in Cape Town, to celebrate Lieve's 27th birthday with lots of Belgian beers!"*

This night was part of the price for Cape Town that Lieve mentioned. We were caught between the need to hold south for the Cape aim point, and the low that had caught up with us. We talked about the possibility of heaving to—dropping the sails, except for the small storm sails, and crossing sail and rudder to stop any progress while bobbing on the waves. But I felt that the crew had good energy and *Maggie B* was handling the waves and wind well. Everything was wet on deck and below wasn't much better. No one had any dry gear left and well-wrung-out socks were the best one could hope for.

By noon we were back on course, close hauled on port tack again, with the wind from 045 at 15, doing 8.3 knots directly for Cape Town.

We hope to arrive by sunset on the 23rd, so that we can find the Belgian Brew Pub in Cape Town, to celebrate Lieve's 27th birthday with lots of Belgian beers!

## 21 AUGUST 2006

We are only 304 NM from Cape Town! This last bit still seems like a lot, even though we have gone 3565 NM since Salvador. The wind is piping up from the south, currently 210 degrees magnetic at 18–25. Just another southerly blow.

We are on course for our aim point 100 NM south of Cape Town, at 7.5 knots. This wind is due to freshen and come more easterly, so we will probably need every yard of southing we have saved up. Together with the wind backing to the southeast, we can count on the Agulhas Current to push us back to the west and north. We are saving up our southing like a skier holds a little high on a hill before a long traverse, or as a cautious pilot would save some altitude on approach to a tight runway.

We are beginning to see some smaller seabirds, which must be land-based on South Africa. I believe that we saw an immature albatross yesterday. Identification will have to wait until we get a South African seabird book.

Last night was not as bad as the night before, but it was wearying. All foul weather gear is damp. Favorite clothing has become painted on—worn night and day. Knit hats may never be dry again. The cabin was a little nicer by noon today because we used the main engine for battery charge and ran the heat as well, so at least the pilothouse is dried out and the bunks are warm. My favorite piece of clothing, which I have been wearing for days, is a top of fine Merino wool, made in New Zealand. It is warm when things are cold, feels fine when wet, and not hot when under layers of foul weather gear while working hard on halyards.

We are sailing under full jib and two reefs in the main. Foresail stowed away. Pounding hard close hauled on starboard tack. The seas have organized somewhat, but a 1.5 knot current from the southwest has made them peak up a bit. If the wind lightens any more, we will put the foresail up with two reefs, to help us go to weather. Right now, that would be too much sail.

What we are reading: I just finished a lovely book, *American Sea Writing: A Literary Anthology*, edited by Peter Neill. It was given to the boat by my friend and future shipmate, Robert Farrar. It has pieces by obvious authors such as Melville, Dana and Twain, but also lovely pieces by James Fenimore Cooper, James Agee, Eugene O'Neill, Langston Hughes, and many other less likely. Well worth it!

Two days!

## 22 AUGUST 2006

Our wind is steady from the south at 15–20 knots. We have eased sheets a bit, but are heading for a conservative turn point about 100 NM southeast of Cape Town.

Our weather advice says that we should be fine coming in, with the strong southeaster holding off for a day or so, and that the current between Cape Town and us is weak and disorganized. We will hold a bit of our southing in reserve. In any case, we are about 175 NM from Cape Town, an average day's run. At this speed, or a bit faster (when we are reaching), we should arrive tomorrow morning. No need to rush the turn.

Spaghetti Bolognese for lunch with a fresh Beaujolais. We have to drink up the French wine shipped from Martinique to make room for all the great South African wines!

It is a bright sunny day. Smaller terns are around us now, together with the shearwaters and petrels from the further reaches. As Commanders' has predicted, seas are "quite rough with wind-waves and a southerly swell" but the *Maggie B* is handling them well, only throwing occasional buckets into the cockpit to keep the watch alert.

Three weeks from Salvador—Cape Town tomorrow!


## 23 AUGUST 2006

We sighted the Cape of Good Hope through the rain clouds right at noon. Bart was on watch, called me up on deck, and in a marvelous formal manner said, "Captain, I give you Africa!"

We arrived Cape Town going hull speed with two reefs in main and foresail.

*Maggie B* tied up to the Royal Cape Yacht Club dock at 4 p.m. on August 23rd. We had gone 3903 NM in 22 days, averaging 177 NM per day, or 7.4 knots. The crew is happy to be ashore, but also rested and fit, and ready to go out and celebrate Lieve's birthday.

Table Bay lived up to its reputation and we had gusts to 38 knots as we furled sails on approach. The wind was only 30 knots in the RCYC marina.

The *Maggie B* was launched on January 16, 2006, and set out on her first voyage on March 27th. Since then she has sailed about 9,000 miles, and been at sea 84 days. She has spent about half her time in port and half at sea.

Last night I asked Bart and Lieve for their observations on the crossing. Their answer surprised me—it was essentially "Just Do It!" Their point was that so many people wait for just the right weather forecast, or to perfect their rig, or to find just

Our first view of the Cape of Good Hope.

the right crew, and they never get going. "Pretty good" and going sailing beats not sailing because things are not perfect.

One man in Nova Scotia had a lovely new boat, but never went out sailing. I asked him why and he said that he hadn't been able to get the proper-sized anchor rode for his #2 anchor.

I was very lucky to have crew with the sailing and mechanical skills of Max, Bart, and Lieve. Things would have been much more difficult if they hadn't been able to jump on our different breakdowns—and we have a lot of redundant systems. I think that most things that go wrong can be treated in the same way—either fix it or work around it. A perfect boat never sails.

In terms of gear, one of my mistakes was not assuring that we had spare filters for everything. I should have prioritized between items nice to have (such as extra lightbulbs) as opposed to items "gotta have" (such as fuel filters).

One real surprise for me has been the toll taken by chafe and corrosion. I knew that things chafe when they rub together and that metal corrodes in salt water, but I have been astonished at the speed with which this happens. The windlass control become totally corroded and useless after five months tucked high up in the anchor compartment. The incredibly strong main throat halyard parted after three days of rubbing—just *touching*—the gaff saddle. Corrosion eats up the little pins in electrical connectors like a reaper cutting hay.

But here we are in beautiful Cape Town!

*"Table Bay lived up to its reputation and we had gusts to 38 knots as we furled sails on approach. The wind was only 30 knots in the RCYC marina."*

Table Bay and Cape Town.

## FOOD AT SEA

We ate well on the *Maggie B*. Best of all was the fresh fish – tuna, wahoo, and mahi mahi, plus occasional flying fish and squid. It is hard to mess up perfectly fresh fish. We had it as sushi, lightly browned, steaks, fish cakes, and in stew.

We had a good cooler and a big freezer. There were bags for oranges and grapefruit, piles of garlic, every spice we could find and at least six different kinds of hot sauce. In French Polynesia we bought a whole stick of a hundred bananas, and hung it from the boom gallows.

Flying Fish for breakfast in garlic and butter

Before the trip, I had feared that we might have to set up cooking "the big meal" in a formal rotation. But, as it turned out, essentially all the crew wanted to contribute a great meal, and the only arguments were to let everyone try. The biggest food crisis we had was when one cook used up all the paprika and another was anticipating that spice for her big meal. And occasionally as we got low on eggs at the end of a passage, they would be officially saved for baking.

Our longest passages were perhaps three weeks. We would eat the freshest stuff first and then get into frozen and finally canned. You can get canned everything: butter, milk, nearly every kind of meat and, of course, sauces.

Shopping was usually interesting. Some places were gross, like the meat market in Madagascar where one had to shoo the flies off to see the cuts, and we didn't buy anything. Some places had unusual rules, like eggs only offered on Thursdays, and warm, straight from the hen.

One of the strangest experiences was in the capitol of the Seychelles, where currency controls had completely distorted the market. You never knew what might be in, and where. We would be quietly working on some boat repair and another sailor would row by and say, "The Prix Fixe has yogurt!" and we would jump into our tender and head for the Prix Fixe to load up on yogurt, which had been missing for two weeks.

Thomas, our French Canadian shipmate had many recipes. The only problem was that he loved to flambé things, which made the galley a scary place, as the flames would rise to the overhead. But he was very skilled and safe.

Willis and Bori. Birthday lunch.

"Where the South Atlantic crossing was mostly about strategy,
this section is mostly about tactics."

5

# CAPE TOWN, SOUTH AFRICA TO MADAGASCAR

THIS LEG NORTH from Cape Town to the Seychelles was a huge contrast to the crossing from Brazil. The South Atlantic was a big leap—but we were Lords of the Ocean! Booming along in big weather, surfing the waves, and playing the storms. I had a great crew and *Maggie B* was performing all out. It was a huge success. Now we had an utterly different challenge—working our way north up the East Coast of Africa. No longer in depths over 10,000 feet, no longer thousands of miles from land. Now it was reefs everywhere, stay close to land, watch out for 100-foot waves, watch out for gunboats and pirates. Lots of unfamiliar countries, languages, practices, and customs. Many sailors head on to Australia to keep clear. We are going to dig in and get a good dose of the shores of the Indian Ocean. Where the South Atlantic crossing was mostly about strategy, this section is mostly about tactics.

## 27 SEPTEMBER 2006

*Maggie B* has moved a bit, but not too far. The Royal Cape Yacht Club is wonderful, welcoming and efficient, but they had no good place for us to tie up and it is about three kilometers to the nearest bar. We are now in the inner harbor, in Cape Grace Marina.

In the marina we are about a hundred feet from Bascule, one of the best bars in Cape Town, (with 407 different Scotch whiskies!) let alone the rest of the waterfront area with perhaps a hundred restaurants, two hundred bars, and much better protection for *Maggie B.*

Cape Town is a wonderful place. I knew that South Africa was nice and scenic and "First World," but I had no idea how great it is. When we arrived from Brazil, we had a bunch of things we needed to fix. At the Royal Cape Yacht Club there is a company called Action Yachting, whose business is to help sailors. My list for them was to take down and repair the roller furler, sew up a rip in the jib, redo the lashings of the standing rigging, rebuild the damaged hydraulic system, install MaxSEA release 12.5 and get it working with the Furuno Ethernet, repair two stove-in planks in *Reepicheep*, etc. I gave them the list on Monday, and by Friday almost everything was done. I don't believe that I've been in any town, anywhere, with more depth and breadth of maritime skills and experience. And while you are getting fixed up, you have the great view of Table Mountain and other gorgeous scenery, as well as fun spots to go at night.

One continuing theme in different seaports is the persistent presence of the Dutch influence. In the United States, we are so inculcated with the primacy of the British Navy, we forget that in so many places the Dutch were there first. It is certainly easy to see this in Cape Town with the footprint of the Afrikaans, as it was in Natal, Brazil.

Cape Town is a hard-working port. There are many container ships coming in and out, but also strange diamond dredgers, deep-sea cable layers, Japanese and Chinese fishing trawlers, Norwegian research ships, South African Navy stealth frigates, and on and on.

They are also exceptionally serious sailors here. Kids are out in 35 knots of wind doing their weekly races. The Cape Doctor is the name for the strong southeasterly wind that blows much of the year. The RCYC has an entrant, *Shosholoza*, in the America's Cup. A single-handed race to St. Helena, 1,000 miles away across an empty ocean, is considered to be "fun."

We went down to the Cape of Good Hope National Reserve and found the scenery to be stunning. Bigger and wilder than the Mendocino coast or parts of Oregon. We saw a rare troop of baboons who had adapted to collecting shellfish at low tide.

As of early this morning, we have the crew for our next leg: Frank, Bori, Willis, and Hannah. Since it is a new crew and we have had a lot of things worked on, we are going just 50 miles, around the corner to Simon's Town in False Bay. After that, we plan to head for Durban, then clear out of South Africa, on to Nosy Be in Madagascar and then Mahe in the Seychelles.

A South African stealth frigate in Simon's Town.

I am beginning to get anxious about getting out of the Indian Ocean before the typhoon season gets cranked up; pretty soon we will be putting our miles in and watching the sky.

The weather of the southeast coast of Africa is notorious—this is where they invented 100-foot waves. The Agulhas Current runs southwest down the coast at speeds up to 6 knots. Big gales slide by south of Africa, one after another. A gale to the southeast will sometimes team up with a second, later one from the southwest. While each gale will produce waves of perhaps only 15–20 feet, waves can sometimes get very big when one set meets another, even before they meet the opposing Agulhas Current. All this makes for dangerous conditions. We will be doing a lot of listening to experienced sailors....

Hannah on watch as we pass the Cape of Good Hope.

### 4 OCTOBER 2006

*Maggie B* is currently moored in Simon's Town, South Africa, at the False Bay Yacht Club. We doubled the Cape yesterday, covering about 55 NM along some of the most interesting water on the planet.

Simon's Town has been a naval center since 1741, when the Royal Navy set up here after the strong winds blow them out of Cape Town. This was their base for operations against the Dutch. Today it is the headquarters of the South African Navy. Many of the buildings remind us of English Harbor in Antigua.

The False Bay Yacht Club is organized and active. As I write this, 17 boats are slamming around for the Wednesday night Beer Races, a great showing.

One of the fun things to do here is go a few kilometers up the coast to Boulders Beach to see a colony of two thousand African (AKA jackass) penguins *(Spheniscus demersus)*.

As we came around the Cape of Good Hope (AKA the Cape of Storms), we heard a routine *securite* call on Channel 16, announcing that a South African Navy ship was conducting a live-fire exercise at lat/long whatever. It dawned on us that the numbers were amazingly close to our current position. We had to alter course and admired

Surf's Up!

a spanking new stealth frigate shooting up targets. After we passed that interesting sight, and were most of the way into the harbor, another ship hailed us on Channel 16 to announce that they were conducting flight operations and were restricted in their ability to maneuver, and that we must keep clear. With that introduction, we spotted a fast ship coming at us out of the twilight with a buzzing horde of helicopters around it. We did a smart jibe to avoid causing an international incident.

Under current South African regulations, foreign ships can only enter the country via designated Ports of Entry, except in emergencies. After we cleared out of Cape Town (Customs, Immigration, Health, Port Authority, etc.), we are only supposed to stop at Durban, where we have to go through the same rigmarole to check in. I do feel a bit nervous having most of the maritime power of South Africa only a few hundred meters away. Most sailors told us not to worry about stopping in other places, that no one ever gets caught. We would hate to be the first, and we are not flying the US flag here lest it attract some grumpy functionary.

We have the usual minor breakdowns—a jammed block, overheating genset, and some craziness with the GPS. We hope to be all sorted out tomorrow.

On Friday, a front is supposed to come through and bring a northwesterly to carry us up the coast. We have been repeatedly advised to stay within the 100-foot depth line to minimize adverse current and monster waves. We didn't have to be told twice.

## 6 OCTOBER 2006

We have just passed the beautiful Kaap Hangklip, Cape Hanging Rock, en route to Durban. The cape defines the northeastern end of False Bay. We are making 8 knots on a course for Danger Point (really!) and then on to Cape Agulhas, which is about 60 miles. We have gone 25 miles since leaving Simon's Town this morning and 81 since Cape Town. Durban is about 700 miles away. The wind is a perfect due west at 12–15 knots.

We were almost unable to leave Simon's Town this morning because the southern right whales had come in to play. There are strict rules to keep at least 300 meters away from them. The whales were so thick that there was almost no way to get past. We had a significant part of the South African Navy watching us leave, as well as houses full of whale lovers with telescopes.

False Bay and Simon's Town are famed for great white sharks. Seal Island is in the middle of the bay and is where the usual seal whelping carnage occurs each spring. Many of the National Geographic Magazine photos of great whites breaching are taken here. We thought that there might be some exaggeration until we met a local sailor who came over to talk to us about the *Maggie B*. He had a funny handshake, which he explained was due to having BOTH HIS ARMS IN A GREAT WHITE'S MOUTH! His arms were scarred but somehow still attached. He had been catching lobsters and was attacked and put his arms up in defense.

Yesterday we did a lot of preventative rigging work. We also found that the genset wasn't pumping raw water for cooling anymore and changed the impeller with some help. Not sure how long they are supposed to last, but this one made it to 335 hours.

All the loveliness of Simon's Town was somewhat marred by a bad case of red tide. But, perhaps associated with the algal bloom, there was incredible phosphorescence at night.

The False Bay Yacht Club was incredibly welcoming, with lots of interest and appreciation for both *Maggie B* and *Reep*. Besides hot showers and an active sailing program, the club had the marvelous institution of offering huge glasses of excellent cold beer for only 7 Rand (US$0.90) during happy hour. Vice Commodore Colonel Lionel Dyck and his wife, Clair, invited our whole crew up to their lovely home for

Cape Point Lighthouse.

apple pie and lively conversation. Colonel Dyck was the last colonel of the Rhodesian Paratroopers and had many interesting stories.

We are pushing to get around the corner of Cape Agulhas before dark. It is supposed to get quite lumpy in all conditions. We should be there right at dusk, at current speed.

## 7 OCTOBER 2006

Last night Hannah and I saw one of the most magnificent sights imaginable. We were on the 1800 2200 watch (we have doubled-up watches—four hours on, four off— for this difficult section of the coast). The full moon had risen and the path of the moonlight was bright silver against the deep black of the ocean. One of us had just

*Maggie B* at Cape Grace Marina, Cape Town.

commented about the beauty of the light when a huge humpback whale breached three times in succession right in the path of the moonlight about 300 yards away. My heart almost stopped. Then it came right alongside to breathe once or twice before taking off. It was astounding.

At noon the wind was southeast at 10–12 knots and we are motorsailing towards Knysna. The barometer is dropping rapidly and a full northwesterly gale is forecast for the Table Bay to Cape Agulhas area behind us, with seas above 15 feet. If it sounds as if we are running for cover, we are. It is a fair blow coming. Knysna is a very interesting port. The British Navy has long described it as the most difficult harbor entrance in the world. If the swells are up much, waves break across the entrance.

We are going be very safe and only enter if Knysna Control, which has an active Sea Rescue Station on the headlands, recommends it. We think we will be fine otherwise, running down the coast ahead of the northwesterly storm.

Yesterday we were smoking along at hull speed and had porpoise playing in our wake as well as at the bow, jumping fully out of the water in twos and threes. As we came around Cape Agulhas, it was fascinating to watch the 10-foot southwesterly swells from the South Atlantic meet the 10-foot easterly swells from the South Indian Ocean. Sometimes they proved that 10+10–30.

Last night and early this morning it was foggy and cold—more like Maine than my conception of South Africa. It burned off by ten o'clock, but we were quite chilled.


## 8 OCTOBER 2006

*Maggie B* is tucked safely in Knysna. Last night the weather closed in with gusts to 42 knots and a major electrical storm. The barometer dropped seven millibars in three hours. We arrived at the headlands at dusk and, fortunately, the Sea Rescue boat came out to guide us in. The current out was 7.5 knots against us, so we barely had the power to make any headway. After the entrance, there was a long torturous route to a safe spot on the waterfront pier, with lots of very tight turns made difficult with the high wind.

The yacht club was absolutely hopping with the Commodore's birthday party, and we went over and did our best to support the celebration.

We may be stuck here for a bit as the southwesterly swell is coming in and the harbor will be closed by surf across the headlands. We could be stuck in worse places.

Today we were joined at the pier by an English Royal Signal Corps world sailing boat called *Adventure*. She is on her way to Australia and stopped in here on the way. We make a handsome pair in the tight harbor.

In Knysna we made a bunch of friends at the yacht club, as we had at False Bay. Many were former residents of Zimbabwe or Rhodesia, who had been driven out and lost property and possessions to the new government. They are still nervous here in South Africa, not trusting how things will play out. Who could blame them? That makes yacht clubs and big Blue Water boats more attractive. One couple that we met has an exceptionally salty sailboat that has a motoring range of 4000 NM. They keep it stocked and with full tanks. When I asked the owner why such a range, he simply replied: Australia.

The *Maggie B* and *Adventure* in Knysna.

## 14 OCTOBER 2006

*Maggie B* is underway again! We are making 6 knots with full main and "the Bird," in 12–15 knots of wind from the northwest. We are about 8 NM off Cape Seal, at the entrance of Plettenburg Bay. So far, we have only one-fifth knot of adverse current, with little swell.

Knysna was so kind to us. Such a lovely place! Quite hard to leave. We made good friends at the Knysna Yacht Club and three boats accompanied us out the heads (the mouth of the harbor) to make sure we were safe. The headlands looked fearsome but we hit the bar right at high tide and had plenty of depth and no breaking waves. Whew!

To celebrate the Captain's birthday today, we are underway with Mick Jagger and the Rolling Stones singing their hearts out over the ship's sound system. The boat is rocking!

Durban is about 500 NM away. The weather forecast is so variable that we will just have to take what comes and do the best with it. We will need to progressively stick closer and closer to the coast, with old hands at the yacht club recommending straying not more than one-half mile off the coast as we get around to the Transkaii Coast, after East London.

Lunch is just on: chicken breasts poached in white wine with garlic, onions and peppers, with rice on the side. Plus, a lovely bottle of South African Buitenverwachting Cap Classique sparkling wine. *Buitenverwachting* means "better than expected" in Afrikaans.

I was just about to type "all is well" when the gennaker block (another @#$%^& Lewmar!) failed and "the Bird" had to be recovered from the water. We had just checked all the rigging in False Bay. It appears to have separated and spat out the center core in 15 knots of wind!

Now…all is well.

## 15 OCTOBER 2006

Knysna is 131 miles behind, Durban is 356 ahead. We are motorsailing, mostly motoring, with 5–10 knots of wind from the south. Right now, it is lovely, but last night it was cool, foggy, and drizzly. The fog didn't burn off until late morning. We have averaged about a half knot of adverse current—not enough to make the effort to duck into bays in the hope of a back eddy. As we get further down the coast, we will be really hugging the inshore.

The KwaZulu National Reserve.

## CAPE OF GOOD HOPE

The south end of Africa was called the Cape of Storms. Later it was rebranded as the Cape of Good Hope. It is, in fact, both.

We were warned to stay well south of Cape Town when making our passage from Brazil. At least 100 NM. When there is a blow, it comes from the South and can team up with a strong current with a southerly set. If you aim right for Cape Town, you can find yourself set well North, with a tough job to work your way back.

Bartolomeu Dias, the Portuguese explorer, made the first mention of European discovery of the Cape, in 1488, though Herodotus makes a good case for the Phoenicians being there in ancient times. Cape Town was developed by the Dutch East India Company

Cape Point.

For us, it was a big passage to get there — some 4000 NM from Brazil. We had a fair blow when we were about a week out and used up all of our 100 NM "insurance." Seeing Cape Point through the fog and rain was a complete thrill after three weeks at sea. It was blowing 40 knots from the south when we took down our sails before docking.

We pushed hard the last week as it became clear that we might arrive on our shipmate's, Livet's, 27th birthday. All the talk was about which beer would be the first when we celebrated at the famous Den Anker (The Anchor) restaurant. All of the 20 to 30 beers on the menu came in their own special glass, which must have made the bartenders crazy. One, Pauwel Kwak, came in such a special glass that you had to turn in one of your shoes as guarantee to return it.

The Royal Cape Yacht Club was very hospitable to us, but had a hard time accommodating a schooner our size. We moved to the lovely Victoria and Albert yacht basin where we were totally snug, and also closer to Den Anker.

Coming into Table Bay, you leave Robben Island to port. Happily it is now a museum, but we all knew its history as a prison island for political prisoners like Nelson Mandela.

Cape Town has been taking care of ships for five hundred years and they know their business.

*"There have been whales around us, sometimes exceedingly close, since rounding The Cape. Today Willis upped the ante by spotting a number of giant rays on the surface."*

We are just past Port Elizabeth, cutting inside via the Bird Island Passage. The shore is dramatic with huge sand dunes mixed with deep green vegetation. We have seen tens of thousands of black and white gannets (…Bird Island), some humpback whales, and a number of penguins chasing fish. The sea is made up with long 2–3 meter swells from some distant storm. The barometer has been steady, but we are watching the start of a cloud system drawing in from the south.

Lunch today was a hearty tomato and beef soup with yesterday's rice in it, and a cold chicken salad with avocado, tomato, and shaved carrots, topped with a garlic vinaigrette. We finished yesterday's sparkling wine, eating on deck in the sun.

Durban in two days?

## 16 OCTOBER 2006

We are about a half-mile off the beach (Big Surf!) along the Transkai Coast in KwaZulu-Natal, about 201 NM from Durban and 633 from Cape Town. We are motoring at 7.3 knots on a course of east-northeast, with the wind behind us from the west at 10–12 knots.

Normally we could sail fine in 10–12 knots, but here we have to carefully pick our way along, hugging the coast to keep out of the strong adverse current. Even the container ships are within three miles of the shore, roaring past us like express trains.

After lunch today, we put up our two storm sails. Not because we expected any storms, but to put up some simple sails to slow the rolling in the swells and chop. It was also a good exercise so that we would know how to rig them in a big blow.

I was interrupted from writing this by a call from Hannah: a humpback whale breached alongside, perhaps 50 feet away. I came on deck and saw it breach another twenty times as it got behind us and disappeared in a small rain shower. In the last two days I have seen 200–300 humpback breaches, ten times what I have seen in the rest of my life.

The Transkei Coast is part of the KwaZulu-Natal province, another part of the failed apartheid effort. It was given to the Zulu nation with the thought that it could operate successfully, independently, essentially without any government support or infrastructure. Without any employment in the province, the men left for work wherever they could find it, leaving the women and the old behind in very hard times. But from here it looks green and lovely, with many classic Zulu round houses and numerous cattle.

*Maggie B* runs on computers, and not just those in the GPS, plotter, and auto-pilot systems. Last night this was amusingly clear: I was on one computer watching the TV series *House*, Bori was on another burning tracks from CDs onto her new iPod, and Hannah was on a third doing her email. And Willis? He was on watch using the ship's three other computers to steer and navigate. Must have been rough in the old days.

What we are eating: besides the great meals (garlic shrimp on multicolor pasta for lunch), we eat lots of nuts, South African beef jerky called biltong, instant soup with leftover rice, granola bars and, of course, chocolate.

We expect to arrive Durban tomorrow afternoon.

## 17 OCTOBER 2006

At noon, we are about 46 NM to Durban and should arrive in time for a late dinner, tying up at the International Wharf on the Victoria Embankment. We will check into the Point Yacht Club tomorrow, which is right nearby. We have gone 792 NM since Cape Town. We have all sails up but are getting very little help from the wind, as it is northeast at 5 knots.

I don't mean to complain about having to motor most of the way here. We could have had a much worse time. Right now there is a strong gale back between Table Bay and Cape Agulhas. Our currents—we have a display set up on the monitors comparing speed through the water to speed over ground—have varied from plus 2 knots to minus 2 knots.

Hannah has continued to see the humpbacks flying through the air. There have been whales around us, sometimes exceedingly close, since rounding The Cape. Today Willis upped the ante by spotting a number of giant rays on the surface.

The current coastline, as we approach Durban, is called the Hibiscus Coast. It really looks like South Florida, with endless summer homes, condos, and high-end destination resorts, in contrast to the empty Transkei Coast with its occasional Zulu hut.

*Maggie B* at the International Dock in Durban.

As we came along the coast this morning, we ran one of our two diesel tanks dry. It should have been totally routine, but we didn't really have any sails up (just the two stabilizing storm staysails) and we were a bit less than a half mile from huge breakers on a starkly unforgiving coast, with a light breeze blowing us ashore. The engine would not restart on the new tank. We ran around like the Marx Brothers for a bit, but eventually got things sorted out, sailed away from shore, drained gunk out of the filters, and got the engine started again.

We are busy reading guides to Durban and making plans. It looks as if some rain is coming, but we have happily watched the temperature of the seawater rise from 61 degrees at the Cape to 75 here. We are planning to take at least one surfing class. If you don't surf in Durban, you aren't really there!

Arriving at Durban was quite intimidating. It is the biggest port in South Africa, and the ninth biggest in the world. The entrance is fairly narrow and you must have clearance to enter. After motoring most all the way up from Knysna, we arrived here in a proper squall, with lightning and 40 knot winds. Once we got the sails wrestled down, Durban Harbor Control put us fourth in line for entry, behind three huge ships. I felt like tiny Air Blair Flight #211 in the daisy chain of 747s for approach to Chicago O'Hare.

The harbor itself wasn't too complicated, with excellent mapping from the Furuno and a clear description in the South Africa Coastal Pilot. But the International Pier, while very grand sounding, turned out to be a slip about 70-feet long in an incredibly cramped spot right up against the wall. It was not visible until we were a boat length away (at night in 25 knots of wind), and we would not have found it in the dark if there had not been helpful voices from the shore encouraging us to come further in. It did cross my mind at the time that they might have a local tradition of wrecking foreign yachts for profit.

## 18 OCTOBER 2006

*Maggie B* is safely docked at the International Pier in Durban, at the Victoria Esplanade. This is the first time we have been north of 30 degrees South since August 9th.

Last night at the local fish restaurant we celebrated our arrival with four different kinds of calamari—Cajun, wok-fried, deep-fried, and grilled—plus a bottle of Southern Right Sauvignon Blanc that was not nearly as good as the sight of the whales.

Durban is slightly smaller than Cape Town (2.5 million vs. 2.9 million) but right now it seems bigger and somewhat tougher. We look forward to exploring it.

## 22 OCTOBER 2006

Sunday in Durban. We have the usual pattern of repairs and resupply going on. We are conscious that while we probably will not be a long time at sea on the next leg, that there isn't the prospect of First World resupply until Australia.

Yesterday was lovely. We took an all-crew surfing class with a marvelous instructor. John was probably somewhere between forty- and sixty-years-old, but hadn't aged a day since he was nineteen. The surf was terrible (trashy 2–3 meter shore breaks due to the easterly wind) but he got almost all of us up on long boards with no more damage than nasal saltwater douches. That evening we hit the Gateway Mall (biggest in Africa) and saw *Roar*, the IMAX film about a pride of lions in Botswana. The girls cried when the old king was driven out. Then we had dinner at our new favorite restaurant, Bean Bag Bingo, which is right next to a boutique hotel called (quaintly?) La Bordello. Then to bed/bunk early so as to be fresh for today, when the wind was due to shift to the west.

It has been fascinating to compare Cape Town with Durban. They are both about the same size and have lovely, active harbors. But they are at different stages of development. Durban's city center has essentially been abandoned by most whites and most of the money. Downtown is deserted, and dangerous at night. The yacht clubs and a tiny strip of land are OK, but guarded by dozens of police with machine guns. Redevelopment is taking place slowly out towards the beaches. But as a fun place to stroll at night like the Cape Town waterfront? Forget it.

Our current plans are to leave with the next westerly, which should come through

Durban harbor.

on Wednesday. The winds are shifting and the northeasterly is beginning to come in, which would make it very hard to get up to the Seychelles. This new wind will bring typhoons to this area of the world, so we really need to get moving. The Seychelles are north of the typhoon tracks for the last 40 years, so we should be safe there. This is the end of the typhoon season for the Northern Indian Ocean and the start for the Southern Indian Ocean.

We plan to stay close to the African continent as we go north until we get even with southwestern Madagascar, then cross over when we get a favorable breeze. The cycles seem to be every four or five days. If we get a big northeasterly against us, we'll just anchor along the coast. The west coast of Madagascar has the positives of being out of the current and being very beautiful. It has the disadvantage of being poorly charted, full of reefs and without navigational buoys. We plan to stop at Nosy Be (Big Island) on the northwest tip of the island for a bit, and then head for the Seychelles.

On the way to Nosy Be, we also hope to stop at Bassas da India, which is out in the middle of the Mozambique Channel—a deserted atoll with perfect diving and fishing. It is associated with Europa Island, "owned" by France, which has a two-man weather station.

We are rigging the *Maggie B* with a forward-looking sonar to help us find our way around places like Bassas da India and the west coast of Madagascar. It is built by a company called Interphase and is a civilian knock-off of military technology. It will supposedly show us the contour of the ocean bottom up to 1,000 feet ahead. It will be cool if it works.


## 25 OCTOBER 2006

At exactly at noon on October 25th, *Maggie B* cast off her lines from the Durban Marina Fuel Dock, underway for Nosy Be, Madagascar. We have a light southeasterly and the prospect of rain. We are headed northeast, going up the coast, trying to take advantage of any favorable back eddies in the current.

South Africa has managed to edge out Brazil in a tough race to have the most difficult and stupid port clearance system. To be fair, it took only three hours, but it was stuff that could have been done in 15 minutes without sacrificing anything except for a few excess bureaucrats. Here are the steps:

1. Pay your marina bill.
2. Get letter from marina, saying your bill was paid.
3. Get receipt for money paid.
4. Go to Port Control (2 miles away) and fill out flight plan—three pages which include questions like, "What frequencies can you receive on your Single Side Band Radio?"
5. Get Clearance Certificate from Port Control.
6. Go to Immigration (15 miles—all crew must come). Submit Crew List.
7. Passports reviewed and stamped.
8. Fill out Request to Leave.
9. Fill out Departure Report.
10. Get Immigration Clearance Certificate.
11. Go to Customs (12 miles). Fill out another Departure Report. Questions include, "State name of Approved Container handler."
12. Fill out "Report Outbound."
13. Get asked for Safety Certificate and Skipper's Competency Certificate,

> *"South Africa has managed to edge out Brazil in a tough race to have the most difficult and stupid port clearance system. To be fair, it took only three hours, but it was stuff that could have been done in 15 minutes without sacrificing anything except for a few excess bureaucrats."*

but point out that it does not apply to foreign vessels.

14. Get Customs Certificate of Clearance.
15. Return to Port Control (2 miles). Everything is stamped and permission granted to leave.
16. Return to Marina. You have 36 hours to leave or you do it all again.

We have an addition to our equipment, a lovely little single surf kayak. It is made by a Durban company, Stealth (www.stealthpp.co.za). It is about 22 feet long and 1.5 feet wide. It should be fun. *Reepicheep* sniffed a bit when it came on board, but we hope they will be friends. It is named *Strika*.

We filled up with diesel for the first time since Brazil. We took on about 250 gallons after covering 4,800 miles, for both main engine and genset. We carry a total of 325 gallons. Seama-rine Services, the fuel dock at the Durban Marina, proved that there are still pirates active in South Africa. They managed to put 216 gallons in a tank that only holds 200, they added 5% to the already high price when I used a credit card, and they refused to sell the diesel without 14% VAT (Value Added Tax), even though I had all my clearance papers.

Bori in *Strika*.

## 26 OCTOBER 2006

At noon we were motorsailing in a light southerly along the wild coast of Swaziland, in the St. Lucia Marine Reserve. We have gone 1009 NM since Cape Town and have 1317 to go to Nosy Be, Madagascar.

The plan had been to work our way close in to the coast, up until we were able to make a dash across. Things have changed a bit. By the afternoon, we had a smart southwesterly at 23–30 knots: perfect weather to cross. We are now on a beam reach for Bassas da India, which is about two days or 500 NM away. With luck, we will be able to ride this low, first a southwesterly and then from the southeast, as it passes us to the east, before the north-easterly returns. We are doing 9–10 knots. Adverse current is only one half to three-quarters of a knot, just the same as inshore. While this sets up the possibility of big waves with wind against current, the current is relatively modest at this point and the south-wester has not had enough time to blow up much in the way of waves. We are closely watching the wind speed and direction as well as the baro-metric pressure.

Bori's moth attack.

Bassas da India is a large reef enclosing a shallow lagoon full of coral heads making a six-miles-across translu-cent green pool in the bright blue ocean. The diving is reported to be fantastic, if you like sharks, which are prolific. The lagoon is also famous for the number of ancient and modern shipwrecks!

The names along the coast have changed from Anglo or Portuguese to fully African. No more Simon's Town or Port Elizabeth or Richards Bay. Now it is Maputo and Inhambane and Sihangwana.

While Hannah is the champion for spotting whales breaching, Bori has claimed a new category: moths. Last night during Bori's watch (9 p.m. to midnight), we were swarmed by moths. They looked like monarch butterflies, but behaved like moths.

*"We are getting ready to start on our malaria meds in preparation for Nosy Be. Supposedly they produce strange psychotropic effects in some people. I hope that the crew will not have to tie me to the mast like Odysseus's crew."*

There were not hundreds, not thousands, but tens of thousands, everywhere. To turn a headlamp on was to get mobbed, to turn this computer on was to lose the screen.

## 27 OCTOBER 2006

At noon the wind is from the south at 10 knots and we are making boat speed of 6.1 knots and 6.7 knots over the ground with a favorable reverse current.

We are about 25 miles off the coast at Xai Xai, Mozambique.

The wind has been up and down, with small rainsqualls marching through. As I write this in the afternoon, we are doing hull speed (10 knots) with a half knot of favorable current. Excellent!

Last night we started out towards Bassas da India, but got about 35 miles off shore and the wind and waves were making up a bit and a big electrical storm was lighting up the sky to the south, so we did the prudent thing and jibed in towards Inhaca and Maputo. Now we are back, tracking along at full speed towards Bassas da India. We round the corner near Inhambane in 70 miles, when we will fully enter the Mozambique Channel.

This unsettled weather apparently is typical of the time between the end of the southeast trades and the start of the northeast trades. We will do our best to exploit every change and anchor if it is too tough.

We are getting ready to start on our malaria meds in preparation for Nosy Be. Supposedly they produce strange psychotropic effects in some people. I hope that the crew will not have to tie me to the mast like Odysseus's crew.

Hannah is making apple crisp for us this afternoon! It will more than make up for her spilling body powder all over the floor of the bathroom, which tracked up the boat worse than a scene from CSI with ultraviolet light.

Rainy season clouds in the Madagascar Channel.

## 28 OCTOBER 2006

We are booming along at a boat speed of 9 knots, with a speed over the ground of 9.4. This is the perfect point of sail for the *Maggie B*—20 knots of wind on the beam. We will be at Bassas da India at dawn tomorrow.

We did 195 NM from noon yesterday, not bad for "going the wrong way" up the Mozambique Channel.

It is warm again, with the seawater up to 78 degrees F (25C) and the air is warm enough for bathing suits during the day.

The patterns on a boat sailing 24/7 are interesting. We all have two 3-hour watches a day: Frank midnight–3; Hannah 3–6; Willis 6–9; and Bori 9–noon. It seems as if each thinks that their watch is the easiest, but in any case three on and nine off is pretty light duty. Of course everybody's sleep patterns are different. At any given time one to three of us (hopefully never four!) are asleep. We all make a big effort to be up together for the mid-day meal. With this schedule, it is easy to get eight hours of sleep a day—just not all at the same time. It seems to take one's body two to three days to accept the change, but after that there is plenty of energy all around.

Off-duty time is for ship's work: cleaning, polishing, vacuuming, food prep, stitching, making fancy work, repairs, systems maintenance, and planning. Plus personal work: emails, reading, letter writing, watching videos. Half the books we are reading are closely ship-related such as *The East African Pilot*, or Brandt's *Madagascar*, or *Pilote Cotier des Seychelles*.

Where we are headed is navigationally complicated. You would think that with GPS and radar all would be easy, but every storm reconfigures sand banks that stretch up to 30 miles off the Madagascar coast. Buoys are non-existent. Even the position of Bassas da India varies by two miles on different charts and reference books. Somewhat tough as it is only six miles across and the highest point two meters, except for the, gulp, shipwrecks.

We hope to play in the lagoon tomorrow. We will also be doing ship repairs that can only be done in calm water, such as those up the masts.

## 29 OCTOBER 2006

The Schooner *Maggie B* is safely anchored at Bassas da India. The charts are about two miles off. No wonder that there are so many wrecks along the reef!

This is an atoll totally out in the middle of nowhere. At high tide it is mostly all underwater, except for the wrecks. The water is incredibly clear. We anchored in 50 feet of water and can clearly see the bottom.

As we came around we were hailed by another boat. It turns out they are shark researchers and film crew. We felt our way around to consider trying the entrance if it looked open. Hannah, high up in the rigging with Polaroid sunglasses, saw two big sea turtles and then a little hammerhead shark that came over to check us out. We found the entrance, or at least an entrance, but the water was so clear that it looked about 10-inches deep. We passed it by. Perhaps we will explore tomorrow in *Reep*, carrying portable GPS so that we can set better positions.

Last night was marvelous for all watches. There were lots of shooting stars. The moon as a guide for the early watches, then Orion for me, and then Sirius, the Dog Star, to guide Hannah.

We saw some strange humpback whale behavior. Two whales were motionless vertically with their tails sticking out of the water, but the tails were bent back 90 degrees so that the white underside was facing straight up. They stayed in that position for five minutes or so, and only stopped because we disturbed them. A singing position? Sunbathing?

## 30 OCTOBER 2006

We moved today, but not far. We are on the other side of the atoll, the southwest side. When we woke up this morning we found that the wind had picked up to about 15 knots from the northeast and was kicking up a bit of a sea and pushing us uncomfortably close to the reef, where the 2–3 meter waves were breaking with much ado.

As happens sometimes, we made a bit of a thrash of it. I always anchor with a float attached to the front of the anchor to mark the anchor's position, and to aid in its retrieval if it gets stuck under coral or whatever. The tide had come in and the anchor buoy was hidden underwater. As the anchor came up, we searched for the buoy. The prop found it first, immobilizing the engine just as we needed it most to avoid going ashore. The retrieval line tightly attached to the prop, of course, also immobilized the anchor. Willis immediately jumped in, knife in teeth and cut the line free of the anchor. I rushed forward to set the anchor before we went ashore. As I was about to drop it, I notice that Willis was attempting to re-board the *Maggie B* by climbing the anchor chain. I believe that I said something emphatically impolite, to suggest that he use the midship ladder as I had other use for the chain.

We re-anchored promptly and then Willis and I took turns pulling and cutting the turns of the rope off the prop, which was accomplished with some difficulty due to *Maggie's* stern working hard to bash our heads in whenever we came up for air.

After all that excitement, we had a peaceful motor around the island to rejoin the shark researchers in their catamaran, *Aerandir*, on the leeward side of the island. It was a lovely spot with the breeze off the atoll. The anchor is in 35 feet of water and we are 200 feet of chain away, in 70 feet. We do have the sound and fury of 3–4 meter southerly swells lifting us up and breaking on the reef that is only about 500–600 feet away. We are going to stand anchor watches tonight because a wind shift could have us in the surf zone.

Once we set the anchor, I jumped in to check it. I have never jumped out of the water so fast! A 10–12 foot white tip shark cruised by just beneath me. We then had a peaceful salad Nicoise lunch. Hannah decided to go for a swim afterwards. She had a religious experience—walking on water—as three sharks showed up. So, no more swimming. I decided to try out the new surf kayak *Strika*. I felt perfectly confidant,

*"As I was about half way over*
*I noticed that they were actively chumming*
*a big group of sharks into a feeding frenzy!"*

Sharks near the boat at Bassas da India.

but dumped. Hannah's sharks came to see what the fuss was about. I got back in, but was pretty shaky, which I'm sure was the malaria medicine. I decided to paddle over to our neighboring catamaran, with the three sharks as escort. As I was about half way over I noticed that they were actively chumming a big group of sharks into a feeding frenzy! It just seemed to be a better idea to go back to the *Maggie B* and curl up in the cabin with a good book.

Off to Nosy Be tomorrow.

## 31 OCTOBER 2006

It is about 690 NM to Nosy Be. We are about 100 NM off the coast of Madagascar, angling in towards the western hump of the island. The wind is about 12 knots on the nose and dying out so we will be motoring soon. We have gone 1623 NM since Cape Town.

Last night we had a party on board the *Maggie B* together with the crew of the *Aerandir* (from the Lord of the Rings?). Chris and Monique, who own the boat, work out of Simon's Town in False Bay, the White Shark Capital of the World. The lovely couple takes tourists out to see the Great Whites eat baby seals, while they do serious research on the side. Chris and Monique stayed on *Aerandir*, but sent over their crew of five, together with a present of five kilos of just caught sushi-grade tuna.

Their crew included: Reiner, who is an ecologist researching Hawksbill Turtles; Kim, his girlfriend and also a researcher; Guy, a big South African Dutchman, who is captain of the ship; Greg, a rocket scientist from San Diego, who is building a plasma engine for the manned trip to Mars. He is the ship's engineer. And Shamus, an Irish cameraman documenting the trip.

We had such a fine evening, perfect weather for sitting outside in the cockpit. It was the best party for miles around. In fact, we were the only people for a hundred miles, except for Chris and Monique, who apparently turned in early. The crew of the *Aerandir* was thrilled to be aboard the *Maggie B* because their boat is dry and they had been out for three weeks. We were well supplied, which was good because the crowd was thirsty.

Some glimpses of the fine evening: Hannah starting the singing off by leading us in "Barrett's Privateers" ("I'm a broken man on a Halifax pier"). Shamus, a shy non-singing Irishman, was not so shy that he didn't, unsuccessfully, proposition both Bori and Hannah. They argued over the question of whom he asked first. Guy, singing a sad Dutch song, repeatedly, with a different translation each time. Reiner telling me how we can sneak into Aldabra, the UNESCO World Heritage site with 100,000 Giant Indian Ocean Tortoises, where he used to work. Guy telling the tale of the *Santiago*, one of the many ships to run aground on Bassas da India, and how more than 2,000 people have died on the reefs—the very reefs that were producing huge breakers only 600 feet away. Me forgetting the last verse of Janis Joplin's "Mercedes Benz" ("Oh, Lord, won't you buy me a night on the town, I'm counting on you, Lord, please don't let me down. Prove that you love me and buy the first round").

We should be in Hellville, the capital of Nosy Be, November 4th or 5th. Hellville is named after a French Admiral, not the after effects of the local rum. The main street used to be named Cours de Hell (Highway to Hell), and a street sign is still up, painted on the side of the church.

## 1 NOVEMBER 2006

We are slipping along at 6.3 knots in an easy 10–12 knot northwester, heading for a turn past the westerly hump of Madagascar, near the French Island of Juan de Nova. We have gone 1761 NM since Cape Town and have 569 to go to Hellville.

It has become hot and muggy and we are looking forward to the beaches of Madagascar almost as much as seeing the lemurs.

Today was one of those very routine days at sea that makes the life of a sailor comfortable and steady. Being a quiet day, I called for "The Hat" which means four jobs written on slips of paper in a hat, to be chosen by everyone at random. Vacuum, wash floors, wash verticals, and, everybody's favorite: The Head and Shower. Hannah chose the short straw, so she was rewarded at lunch with the tiniest flying fish as a main course. The rest of the meal was fresh tuna marinated overnight in soy sauce, lemon juice and ginger, followed by stir-fry shrimp, onions and peppers over rice.

Willis and I had been separating trash by the rail and had made a bit of a mess. I got a bucket on a rope to wash it down and caught a wave just wrong and it was snatched out of my hands. I called for All Hands and we did Man Overboard drill. The chart plotter was able to immediately retrace our path within yards. Even so it was astonishing how quickly a bright red floating bucket can disappear. Hannah was on the foredeck with the boat hook looking like Queequeg the harpooner in the bow of Starbucks' boat, all of us being guided by Bori for the final approach. Hannah got it on the first pass and the bucket will live on to do another lifetime of wash downs.

Bori has been given the responsibility of reading a poem a day to us. We have lots of books of poetry on board. Yesterday she read Fernando Pessoa's *The Tobacco Shop*. It was met with only limited enthusiasm from Frank and Willis, and led to the discussion of what poetry should be. I believe that Pessoa must have been crippled by a bad translator. Today I read Sasha Moorsom's *Jewels in My Hand* ("I hold dead friends like jewels in my hand") to some success, at least with Willis, the self-described cynical lawyer.

## 2 NOVEMBER 2006

At noon on November 2nd, we were about 30 NM south of Juan de Nova, a French island off the coast of Madagascar. We are sailing along on a close reach in a 10–12 knot north-northwesterly breeze, making 6.25 knots through the water and 7.4 knots over the ground with a favoring current.

The barometer has fallen a bit to 1009 mb, enough to remind us that the weather can change quickly here, though not enough to be of concern yet.

One navigational difficulty in this part of the world is the names of places. It seems usual to have a town with three different names, the official Malagasy, the French name from the period of occupation, and the Portuguese "discovery" name. So Diego Suarez is also Antsiranana; Fort Dauphin is Taolagnano. Most towns start with An- or Am- which means "the place where" and Island is Nosy, which comes first. Imagine looking up in an alphabetical list of towns where two-thirds are An-something, or finding an island where the format is "Island Long" rather than "Long Island" so it is Nosy This and Nosy That. Sigh.

Bori's Spanish omelet.

Bori made a lovely Tortilla de Patatas for lunch. It is a traditional Spanish dish, made with potatoes cooked slowly in olive oil with garlic, eggs and onions.

## 3 NOVEMBER 2006

Today is a big day astronomically as the sun is right over us at 15 degrees 06 S. We are in some ways now heading into winter, the same season as our family and friends in the northern hemisphere. The sun will be in the southern sky again.

We haven't quite decided on our first Madagascar landfall. At current VMG (velocity made good) towards Nosy Be, we would arrive at approximately 0500 on November 5th. There are some wonderful islands south of Nosy Be, and currently we are making for them, specifically Nosy Saba, which the East Africa Pilot describes as:

"stunningly beautiful... beautifully clear water... large game fish... pleasant walking... plenty of wildlife." But, then there is the lure of Nosy Be and "the boisterous disco-theque at La Vieux Port—Rendezvous des Marins. There you will be educated in the wild art of Malagasy dancing until 0800 or so the next morning." Decisions, decisions.

The one island that we won't be stopping at is Nosy Lava (Long Island), which is the site of Madagascar's maximum-security prison. It became famous in yachting circles in 1993 when two murderers broke out, killed the crew of the yacht *Magic Carpet* anchored nearby, and escaped to the mainland.

I have asked our weather routers, Commanders' Weather, for strategic advice. With the marvelous complexity of Madagascar in front of us and then the beauty of the Seychelles after that, the chances of making Australia in time to go home for Christmas leave, seem remote. I asked Commanders' three questions: 1) is it safe from typhoons to leave the *Maggie B* over Christmas in the Seychelles, 2) what is the best way to get to Australia from the Seychelles, and 3) any chance of going by Bali on the way to Australia. Their answer was: 1) Yes, 2) the same as from Brazil to Cape Town, go south and pick up the westerlies, and 3) No.

Yesterday at lunch we continued our poetry readings. Hannah read John Mase-field's excellent *Sea Fever*. A future shipmate, Robert Farrar, added to the discussion with an emailed copy of Octavio Paz's marvelous *Towards the Poem*, which I read. Today Bori read Thackeray's delicious *The Ballad of Bouillabaisse*, which made us salivate even though we were having a perfect meal of chicken breasts poached in white wine with onions and carrots.


## 4 NOVEMBER 2006

Nosy Saba is 46 NM away. We are motorsailing with a light Westerly.

Tonight we should be safely anchored off the beach at Nosy Saba, the "almost perfect island" according to the *Bradt Travel Guide*; "stunningly beautiful," *East Africa Pilot*. We should arrive in time for sunset, ready for rum and Cokes and a piece of the chocolate cake that Hannah is making while I try to concentrate on typing. We plan to stay there all day tomorrow, then leave Sunday evening for the 90 NM trip to Nosy Be, with the plan to arrive at about 9–10 a.m. to check into Madagascar, with the help of Anderson Jaomanina.

Six months ago, when we were in Cul de Sac des Marins, Martinique, Yvon, Captain of the beautiful yawl *Darwin Sound*, gave us the name of a former shipmate, Anderson Jaomanina, from Madagascar, and encouraged us to track him down when we got to this part of the world. Happily we were able to make contact and Anderson will be meeting us at the pier in Nosy Be, to introduce us to the delights of Madagascar. Anderson should be of significant use because the East Africa Pilot says, "Nosy Be is famous for the determination and cunning shown by port officials in pursuit of bribes and fictitious port charges."

The sun is right overhead and is a killer. We rigged our collapsible Bimini sunshade today for the first time in a while.

> *"Speaking of clearing customs, it was a breeze. ... Everyone was friendly and quick. There wasn't even a hint of extra fees or bribes, we got receipts for everything and it was fairly inexpensive."*

One fascinating story about this area concerns the area called Russian Bay, which is between Nosy Saba and Nosy Be. In 1905, a Russian warship named the *Vlotny* was sent out to harass Japanese ships as part of the Russo-Japanese War. The officers and crew got to Madagascar and decided that both war and Russia weren't nearly as interesting as Madagascar girls. Sort of like the *Bounty* mutiny, but as if Bligh went along with it. The ship hid in the bay, emerging from time to time to pirate trading vessels in the Mozambique Channel. Eventually they ran out of coal for the boilers. Then they built a dormitory in Andassy Be, and settled in as fishermen, trading off parts of their vessel. The last one lived to 1936 and they are buried in a section of the local cemetery.

One integral piece of equipment for night watches is the iPod. We all have one, with lots of trading where we have the music either on disc or burned into a computer. What we are listening to: Frank: Bob Dylan, *Modern Times and Kate Melua*; Bori: Indigo Girls and Chopin; Willis: books on tape, Julien Stockwin, Kydd and J.R.R. Tolkein, *The Hobbit*; Hannah: Irish Descendants and David Usher.

## 5 NOVEMBER 2006

We spent a lovely peaceful Sunday anchored off Nosy Saba. Now we are underway for a 90 NM night passage, planning to arrive Nosy Be tomorrow morning about 9 a.m. Why travel at night? We're good at it, and why not? It will give all day to play paper chase with the Nosy Be bureaucrats.

When we got anchored last night, we settled in to have a little party, celebrating the arrival with Hannah's chocolate cake. The cake was nautical, as the pitching of the boat had set it in the oven in a wave. The evening was perfect with Hannah discovering that dark rum went well with our tropic fruit drink, Frank testing the South African wine, making sure it was still good in another country, Willis drinking all the cold beer, and Bori acting as designated driver.

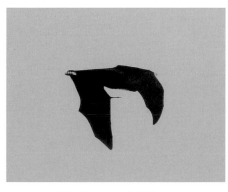

Madagascar fruit bat.

I slept on deck, as the temperature was just right. Waking at 3 a.m. to check the anchor and to pee, I was surprised to see large birds flying close to the boat. When I shined a light on them, I was surprised to see that they were crow-sized bats somehow attracted to the boat. It was like Hitchcock's *The Birds* but creepier. I woke the crew so that they could get a good sense that we weren't in Kansas anymore.

During the day we snorkeled all around and saw wonderful fish. Then I took *Reep* to row around the island, which is about three-quarters of a mile by 2 NM. Hannah, Bori and Willis went to walk over it. The three met a construction watchman and saw the site of a future rustic hotel. The watchman gave then some coconut milk and announced that there were exactly 15 lemurs on the island, but very hard to see.

As we raised the sails just after sunset we were greeted by the marvelous full moon, which will light our way to Nosy Be.

## 6 NOVEMBER 2006

We are safely at anchor in Hellville, the main harbor of Nosy Be. It is a small but active commercial port. There are about a dozen other cruisers at anchor here. We saw some harbors nearby with greater concentrations of sailboats, so Hellville is clearly where you shop, clear customs and get diesel, then go somewhere else for fun.

Anderson was a great help checking in. I'm sure he earned a week's salary just this morning. It is so strange to connect with him from a chance conversation, months and thousands of miles ago, in Martinique with another captain.

Speaking of clearing customs, it was a breeze. The East Indian Pilot and Nigel Calder have it wrong. Everyone was friendly and quick. There wasn't even a hint of extra fees or bribes, we got receipts for everything and it was fairly inexpensive. The local currency is the Ariary, which is 2,000 to US$1. Health clearance was $12, each visa was $15, Police clearance of the boat $7, and a month-long cruising permit was $24. I will write the authors and update them, though there is a presidential election coming up and perhaps all will change.

Nosy Be is quite exotic. The faces are variable: one Arab, the next Somali, the next Congolese, the next Polynesian. The taxis are tiny old Renaults with Mercedes trucks and zebu (humped cattle) carts thrown in.

As with most ex-French colonies, the food is very good. Hannah had her first octopus for lunch today and enjoyed it. We are going to try our best to balance high-speed city life (at Rendezvous des Marins Disco) with the outdoors (picture Hannah with a baby lemur).

Rue George V, in Nosy Be.

*"Here in the Seychelles, they make new islands all the time.*
*Coming in here, my paper and electronic charts,*
*both only six months old, indicate we sailed over solid ground,*
*and there is lots of solid ground where clear water used to be.*
*It has been dredged and reclaimed and filled."*

# 6

# HELLVILLE TO
# MAHE, SEYCHELLES

## 9 NOVEMBER 2006

*Maggie B* is happily moored at Nosy Komba (Lemur Island), just a few miles from Nosy Be. It is peaceful, with only three cruising boats in the harbor and not much in the way of comings and goings. We have come 2377 NM from Cape Town. Aldabra Island (a World Heritage site in the Seychelles) is just 268 NM away and Mahe, the capitol of the Seychelles is 676 NM.

People talk of the smells of the East; they are so much with us now. The whole boat smells of vanilla since we bought a big handful of pods for $5. We have lots of fresh ginger and garlic for perfume, as well as ylang ylang (*Cananga odorata*, an essential oil widely used in the perfume industry) and citronella perfume/anti-mosquito oil. From ashore, there is the smoke of charcoal from the cooking fires, as well as the complex dense humid smells from the forest. Enchanting.

We have become a bit concerned about water. There is town water in Nosy Be, but everyone says not to take it. The cruising guides said that Nosy Komba is the place to get water, but now that we are here, the locals say that it has been dry and that they have none to spare. Indeed we saw a group of perhaps a dozen women gathered around the one tap that was working. We had been a bit profligate with water (not to name names, but some people

Hiking out.

were taking two looong showers a day). Our watermaker makes six gallons per hour, though the engine or the generator needs to be running. But there will be none from "outside" until Mahe, if then. So the pressure pump is turned off and we are washing with Dr. Bronners soap in the ocean before a freshwater rinse. Of course, as I write this, it is raining hard. I suppose we should be collecting from the awning.

For boat work we are scraping weed off the hull and patching and sealing a few spots. One lifeline chafed through at a gate and Hannah had a new splice and eye back in it in a jiffy.

We are planning to spend much of tomorrow at Tane Kely Island (also known as Nine Pin) that has terrific snorkeling, then back to Nosy Be Friday night for the Rendezvous des Marins and Malagasy dancing.

## 10 NOVEMBER 2006

This afternoon, it was raining hard and I went on deck and put a bucket under the edge of the awning, which filled up fast. Then I stripped, jumped in, got out, soaped up, jumped back in, got out and poured the bucket over me. I think that I spoiled the cocktail hour for the English boat near us. Serves them right for parking right on top of us with only 3 other boats for miles around.

I put snorkel gear on and dove down to the centerboard yesterday. When down fully, one can move it fore and aft perhaps 6 inches. At half up, you can move it fore and aft 3 inches. I replaced a broken bolt and tightened the others so the butt of the hydraulics isn't bouncing and creaking any more. Something somewhere that once was tight has been worn or beaten out of shape. Right now we probably have the worst of all: it can move some and then fetches up and beats the bejesus out of whatever stops it.

## 11 NOVEMBER 2006

We are back in Nosy Be getting supplies, including food and diesel, with the hope of leaving for the Seychelles on Monday. Sunday was the plan, but you can only clear in or out on weekdays.

The weather remains hot and humid, but the wind blows fair for the Seychelles.

We see 30 to 50 sailboats around us each day. These aren't for the tourist trade, nor do they belong to the poorest fishermen. They are the backbone of commerce here, moving people and goods from island to island, as well fishing.

Refueling in Nosy Be.

We had a hard day today to get 70 gallons of diesel on board. The taxis are the ridiculously small Renaults of the 1950s. Imagine the back compartment full of 35 gallons of diesel in various nondescript jerry cans. Then they have to be carried down to the pier, then down a slippery ramp to the *Reep*, then rowed out, then carefully poured in the tank, then go back and do it again.

But the big story of the day is about another boat in the anchorage. There are only ten cruisers here, so we noticed it early on, a well-kept blue sloop with a prominent fleur-de-lys on the bow. The German owner was found four months ago with his head cut off with one blow of a sword, and placed in his lap! The Police arrested the Swiss-German owner of a nearby boat, and put him in the local jail. But the German Police came out and tested the DNA of some of the blood on the dead man and it did not match the Swiss-German's, so he was released after what must have been a very long three months. Reportedly, the Swiss-German uses his boat as a rumrunner, filling his water tanks with Malagasy rum and sailing to one of the French islands for trade. Local gossip is that the headless sailor had gotten seriously behind in his bills for recreational drugs, a situation not well tolerated in most places.

## 12 NOVEMBER 2006

Email to Robert Farrar, future crewmember

Dear Robert:

You won't need a lot of gear. The best foulies you have, breathable better because sometimes it is very wet but hot also. Some poly pro because it will get cool when we head south to pick up the westerlies. Certainly, night watch means foul weather bottoms and some sort of jacket possibly with poly pro under it. Bathing suits and shorts. White t-shirts and some long sleeve for if/

### BLUE WATER NAVIGATION

Blue Water navigation is easy. Now with GPS you know exactly where you are and can plot exactly where you are going. Even the cheapest equipment will tell you which way to steer and whether you are on track.

It is so easy it can kill you. In the old days before GPS, a good navigator had to be somewhat paranoid. If one had a good star fix, you wanted it confirmed by a radio range and a deep-water depth sounding and agreement by another passing boat. You were ever alert to changes in the pattern of the swells, bird traffic, double checking your helmsman and the compasses, even for unusual smells from perhaps a fire ashore or guano on a rock.

Today, the danger is that modern humans tend to think that information on a computer screen is right. The navigation system on a well-equipped American Airlines jet on approach to landing in Columbia, wrongly turned the plane into a mountain and everyone aboard died – because a fix had been incorrectly entered in the flight system.

Similarly, on boats, plotters can be wrongly configured. Due to a software bug, our Furuno GPS and autopilot kept trying to sail us on a rhumb line rather than the shorter Great Circle Course, which would have been a difference of about 250 NM on the route from Tahiti to Puerto Montt in Chile.

Some charts and plotters work in degrees, minutes and seconds of latitude and longitude while others work in degrees, minutes and hundredths of minutes. Thus 30° 29' 56" is about 1000 yards from 30° 29.56" – certainly enough room to run aground in a fog. I bet that 90% of sailors don't know which way their GPS navigators are configured.

when you burn. One specialty item is a headlamp. Maybe get one that is LED so you don't have to replace batteries too often, but it should do red as well as white. All hands have to have a ready sharp knife when on deck. Having a fid with it is good, not because you will be splicing on the fly, but because it is good to break out a knot that has jammed. Hats are great—warm as well as anti-sun. Probably want sea boots. If there is some food you live on (Kit-Kats, chewing gum?) you should bring it. Water jug to keep handy. iPod with all your favorite songs plus books on tape. Polarized sun glasses plus a spare for when you lose the first pair. Lots of reading glasses if you need them. Some great novels. We don't have every great sailing book on board, but we have most. We have lightweight sleeping bags and sheets and blankets, but if there is a "sleep system" that makes you comfortable, bring it.

Best, Frank

New compass.

Also, chart plotters also don't necessarily show all the information. A long leg plotted on one scale may show troubling details, like shoals, only on another scale. New deepwater construction, such as oil rigs or wind farms may not be on recent charts.

Sometimes the charts are just wrong. Bassas d'India, a six-mile wide lagoon in the Mozambique Channel is two miles out of position on all the latest charts. In some of the *cannales* of Chile, major features are moved or misrepresented on charts to make invasion more difficult. And nature moves things. Recently a beautiful sail training ship was wrecked trying to enter a California port, running aground on a sand bar deposited across the channel by a recent storm.

Finally, the accuracy of the GPS makes you complacent. My favorite example was a few years ago, four young men were bringing a new yacht up to Maine from Massachusetts. They chose Mount Desert Rock as their landfall across the Gulf of Maine. The Rock is 20 miles out to sea and only perhaps 200 yards by 400 yards in size. The Coast Guard light on it is 75 feet above sea level and can be seen from many miles away, if you are looking for it. It has been a great landfall for thousands of cautious navigators over the years.

But these boys had GPS on board running a fine chart plotter. Accuracy to 30 feet! They set a waypoint on the Rock and commanded the autopilot to navigate the boat to the waypoint. All was safe and secure and in control. But the Watch fell asleep and the next thing that they knew was that the doomed boat had run itself aground right on the waypoint, within 30 feet of the midpoint of Mount Desert Rock.

*"The bigger news is that the main shaft bearing for the engine, where it goes through the hull from the engine to the prop, seems to be failing."*

## 14 NOVEMBER 2006

*Maggie B* got underway from Nosy Be, Madagascar, about noon on November 13th. The southeasterlies have filled in and we are making 6.3 knots close hauled, heading about for Mahe.

We are in the grips of the South Equatorial Current, which is pushing us west, but it should trouble us for only a hundred miles or so.

This morning about 10 a.m., a very black rainsquall jumped us. We quickly took in the foresail, partially furled the jib and put one reef in the main before it hit. In the end it only produced about 30 knots of wind, so soon we had the jib shaken out and the fore back up with one reef. The squall did provide torrential rain, though, and a big swimming pool formed in the bunt of the mainsail, and we got about 20 buckets of fresh rain water transferred into our tanks. Showers tonight!

The bigger news is that the main shaft bearing for the engine, where it goes through the hull from the engine to the prop, seems to be failing. Last night, while motorsailing under only 2,000 revolutions, it started to make a horrible metal-on-metal noise. We shut down to troubleshoot as best we could, but now are waiting on advice from Covey Island, the builders. So again, as in Natal, Brazil, we have a great engine, but can't put it to use.

Our suspicion is that we have had some lines around the prop from time to time, and I suspect one has fused in and somehow restricted cooling of the shaft bearing.

The joke is that we had been considering going by Aldabra Island, which is highly restricted for yachts, and saying that we had a failure and needed to stay a day or so for repairs. Now we actually have a serious failure, but the only responsible thing to do is to head for Mahe, the capitol, and the technical support there. We will be passing the Farquhar Islands on the way to Mahe, and I briefly imagined troubleshooting our problem while anchored in a lovely lagoon. But then I read the cruising guide, which says that the only way in is through the marvelously named 25 Franc Passage, which has tidal bores of up to 8 knots with coral heads all around. No thanks!

Willis with double rainbow.

## 15 NOVEMBER 2006

We are just 10 NM west of St. Pierre Isle in the Farquhar Group of the Seychelles. We have taken down the Madagascar courtesy flag and put up the colorful Seychellian flag, with the yellow "Q" flag, which means that we have not yet cleared customs. Formally, it means, "I am healthy and request a free pratique."

We have come 2694 NM since Cape Town and the entry point of the Seychelles is 406 NM away. We are sailing on a beam reach in 15–18 knots of wind, driving us along easily at 8.5 knots, with one reef in both the main and fore. Now that we are in the islands, currents are swilling about, sometimes with us, sometimes against.

St. Pierre Island is circular and about a kilometer across, mostly bare except for some thin pines. It is a big seabird-nesting place, and we are surrounded by excited terns. It was neat to watch a hovering gannet take several flying fish that the *Maggie B* drove into the air. We passed the island at lunchtime and I read an excerpt from Anne Morrow Lindberg's *Islands in Time*: "How wonderful are islands. Islands in space, like this one I have come to, ringed about by miles of water, linked by no bridges, no cables, no telephones. An island from the world and the world's life. Islands in time, like this short vacation of mine."

We passed within 500 yards of St. Pierre and were still off soundings even with a very good depth sounder that will read up to 500-foot depths.

Hannah made the afternoon marvelous by baking a peach/apple crumble.

We have three guidebooks on the Seychelles and we are reading up on the delights in front of us. We should be in Mahe in 2 or 3 days. With some troubleshooting, the main shaft seems better and should be able to provide some propulsion when we get there, pending some more work.

## 16 NOVEMBER 2006

We are slopping around in very light southeasterlies, with intermittent rain. The seas are 2–3 meters and irregular in adverse tidal/current flow. In front of rain showers, the wind picks up to 10–12 knots, which drives us along, then it rains in biblical fashion (all our water tanks are full now!), then the wind dies out. This is typical weather as the southeasterly trades meet the ITCZ (Inter Tropic Convergence Zone). Normally, we would motor when the boat speed is less than 4 knots, but we have fewer options now and we don't know if the shaft bearings will work for 5 minutes or 5 days; I want to save power for when we need it, like arrival in Port Victoria, Mahe.

Sunset in the Seychelles.

Nigel Irens, the *Maggie B*'s designer, has a school chum in Mahe. He is the president of a company that is agent for port activities. He has sent me information on how to get ready to be boarded by Sechellian Officials on arrival. Among other things, they say we will need:

1. 6 copies of Crew Lists
2. 3 copies of Crew Effects Declaration
3. 3 copies of ship's stores
4. 3 copies of IMO Health Declaration
5. 3 copies of Certificate of Registry
6. 2 Declarations that we have no firearms
7. 3 copies of last 10 Ports of Call

I am panicking that they might try to take away our lovely South African Wine. Perhaps I'll declare it medicinal. "Ship's Stores" is a bit scary. Will they take all our food? And what are "Crew Effects?" Ah, well, I'm sure it will be fine. The Seychelles has apparently done a lovely job of protecting their environment, and I'm sure it will be sensible.

We are just off of Saint Francois Island, part of the Alphonse group. There is supposedly the one of the best resorts in the world on Alphonse, which is the #1 spot on the planet for fly-fishing for bonefish. I wonder what the guests, who pay $600 per night for a standard room, are thinking in the downpours? Probably happy that they are not on that schooner making her way past them...

## 17 NOVEMBER 2006

The wind has been light and variable. Last night during my watch, midnight to 0300, I was able to move the boat exactly three nautical miles. With no engine, you take what you get. As I write this in the afternoon, though, we are making 8.5 knots in a fresh southeasterly, with rain clouds all around.

At noon we were 46 NM from DesRoches Island, home of the famous Desroches Island Lodge. We hope to anchor in their lagoon for tonight and Saturday night, and attempt to clear up the problems we have with our propeller shaft. They have a top dive operation, so I should be able to get a tank and poke around for a bit. Our ETA is about sunset. Hopefully we will be able to slip into the lagoon. Our first real trial of the forward-looking sonar. It will be a challenging experience to sail in to the right spot without relying on the engine.

Properly we are not supposed to land anywhere before we clear in Port Victoria, Mahe, but I'm of the opinion that this is a "safety of the vessel" issue, and anyway, hopefully, it won't come up. We hope to eat ashore tonight at the lodge!

## 18 NOVEMBER 2006

We sailed into DesRoches Island, named after Francois Julien DesRoches, governor of Mauritius from 1767 to 1772, on Friday night, slipping into the lagoon with the help of our forward-looking sonar. It was so strange to come in from big waves and weather, past a hidden reef, to anchor off an island barely visible in the inky black. We cleaned up a bit and rowed into the five star Desroches Island Lodge, to be turned away from dinner by the manager who was appalled that people could just show up and expect to join them. But he did agree to allow us to have lunch and dinner the next day.

I spent a lot of time at DesRoches with the serrated blade of a bread knife and ice picks, trying to get the burnt plastic remains of rope out of the shaft. The space-age ropes fuse themselves into a solid black plastic that is almost indestructible. I'm afraid

*Maggie B* anchored between local vessels and the "Sugar Loafs".

A US Coast Guard cutter on pirate duty in the Seychelles.

Japanese fleets, and then require them to process their catch here in the Seychelles. Fifty percent of their GNP!

### 24 NOVEMBER 2006

We are comfortable, well protected, well supported, and provisioned. But we are stuck in a marina. We have a Hertz car to get into town and around the island. It has remained hot, muggy with intermittent rain, sometimes heavy. The Wharf, despite its rather pedestrian name, has a snappy hotel, restaurant and bar.

The Seychelles has made the decision to focus only on the top-end of the tourist trade. Camping is illegal. There are no big hotels; one with 170 rooms is the biggest. They do not allow discount airlines to fly here and airline tickets are expensive. On a tour around the island we saw a very nice hotel where the cheapest room was 1,000 Euros a night. It was nice, but there are a number of resorts where on private islands scattered around, the prices are considerably higher. Helicopter is the usual connection from the airport for these folks.

Other costs are high too. It was a bit of a shock after Madagascar to be charged $10 for a rum and tonic (10 times Nosy Be prices). The official exchange rate is 5.7 SR (Seychellian Rupees). If one chose to change money "informally" one would get 10 SR to the dollar, but it would be illegal. Many of the hotels price everything in dollars or Euros and sneer if you try to pay in SR.

*"Other costs are high too. It was a bit of a shock after Madagascar to be charged $10 for a rum and tonic (10 times Nosy Be prices)."*

The supermarkets are a bit strange. One market will have apples, and there will be a huge pile and a bit of a feeding frenzy around it. But no oranges or tomatoes or pears; but "maybe peaches tomorrow." The next market will have a huge pile of Pepsi but no Coke or Sprite or root beer. The open-air markets have piles of every sort of fish you can imagine.

We toured the island of Mahe yesterday with a local guy. It seems prosperous, with the apparent success of a government plan to provide a house for everybody. The government employs about half the workers, both in the usual professions—education, streets, sanitation, etc.—as well in many government-controlled organizations like the national tea company and the Island Development Corporation.

One strange development in the harbor of Port Victoria is the reclaiming of land by filling in the shallow areas. It seems to be going full blast and the islands change their shape daily. The Seychelles puts itself out as being environmentally focused, but nobody talks of the impact of filling up the bay or dredging all the material for the new islands. The islands are used for sport complexes, the new airport, subsidized housing and very high-end condos. It must be frustrating for someone with waterfront property to wake up to a new island with condos for rich foreigners in what used to be open water.

We are tied up next to a superyacht, *Northern Lights*, which belongs to a Swedish family. It is off for Thailand on Monday. There is also a famous, highly successful, ocean racing yawl here, *Stormvogel*. They will soon be off for the Mediterranean, the America's Cup, and all the classic regattas next season.

Crew in a Coco de Mer preserve.

*"Joseph Conrad called Mauritius 'the sugary pearl of the Indian Ocean.' For us it is a handy re-provisioning stop on our way to Australia."*

7

# MAHE, SEYCHELLES
# TO MAURITIUS

## 27 NOVEMBER 2006

We are anchored in Baie de la Raie on Curieuse Island, named for the French frigate that discovered it. We have been exploring the islands around Mahe. On Saturday, we had lunch at St. Anne in Victoria Bay and then on Sunday we sailed the 30 miles to Praslin, and anchored off Anse Volber, just next to Chauve Souris (Bat) Island.

Today we had a lovely outing ashore to the World Heritage site of Vallee de Mai, where they have saved a big area of Coco de Mer palms, which grow up to 50-meters high and produce nuts of up to 17 kilos. The nuts, besides being huge, develop into the shape of women's buttocks, while the male plant appears to have an organ bigger than an elephant's, though, unlike the elephant, the Coco de Mer palm has small yellow flowers on it. We spent a marvelous two hours wandering in the park, feeling as if we were on a Hollywood set for a prehistoric movie.

These islands are granite, in pinks and greys, like the islands of coastal Maine that I know well. It is strange to see familiar weathered granite shapes, with palms clinging to the soil instead of pine trees.

We have had a problem of mast hoops sticking, as we raise the main and the foresail. We noticed one day when it was raining as we hoisted, that all the hoops went up smoothly. So now we get a half-bucket of water and throw it on the hoops before hoisting and all is smooth and easy.

## 4 DECEMBER 2006

*Maggie B* is safely moored in the inner harbor in Port Victoria, Mahe, the Seychelles. We are sitting on a mooring that apparently belongs to a big game-fish boat, which usually stays at the commercial dock. How long we can use it is up for question. Possibly a few hundred Seychelles Rupees will solve the question.

There are two fascinating Seychelloise specialities: uniforms and dangerous roads. Uniforms are everywhere. Every school, not just the Catholic ones, has its uniform and as the schools let out, different

Mermaid shirt done by Hannah.

patterns sweep by, probably like the Montagues and Capulets in Shakespeare. But it doesn't stop there. Every woman clerk, assistant or secretary dresses rigorously like her colleagues, like coveys of airline stewardesses. The same is true of the men in boat yards or automobile parts stores. It is all a great leveler, but seeing a cop or soldier is unremarkable because each hotel doorman also has a precise uniform like a colonel of the Marines.

The roads are worth a whole report by themselves. The essential scary part is not that they are in bad shape, quite the opposite—most are well paved and clear. The scary part is that because it rains hard from time to time, they have deep ditches at the edges: four feet deep in many places, a foot or two wide, and right at the edge of the road. Besides making a perfect way to break an axle, it causes dogs, cats and people to walk in the narrow paved part of the road due to lack of sidewalks. Furthermore, the government busses are supersized, and the bus drivers appear to have gotten exemption from Parliament from following the lanes. And many of the streets were designed with whiplash curves, in the middle of which one finds a car or bus stopped to chat with a pal.

Today, Sunday, was a wonderful day. Our morning was uplifted by a 500-person Christian Evangelical meeting in the park, 100 feet from the boat. The service started at 8 a.m. and was going full blast when we left the anchorage at 11 a.m.

*"The Maggie B may be the perfect blue water fast cruiser, but today she was an excellent picnic boat."*

Bori had made pals with some of the young people in the French Embassy and the Alliance Francaise. We put on a Sunday picnic and gathered a crew. We were 14, which is a new record for the *Maggie B*. We motored (no wind at all) about two hours around the north end of the island, to a wild cove called Anse Jasmin. We all swam ashore to a wonderful beach where a Schellois pal climbed a coconut tree and threw down a dozen coconuts, which we drank and ate. Then more swimming and a lovely salad lunch and some sunning and more swimming and then motoring back as the moon came up. It was a lovely day. The *Maggie B* may be the perfect blue water fast cruiser, but today she was an excellent picnic boat.

Sunday picnic in Anse Jasmin.

A picture for Bori from a Seychellois artist.
Credit: Allen Gervais Comettant

## 9 DECEMBER 2006

One of our least favorite new Seychellois shopping expressions is "It is Finished." It means out-of-stock. "Yogurt, it is finished." Then, when something comes in, there is a feeding frenzy.

Those who have been following us may think that much of our life is like last Sunday's delightful picnic, but they should have seen us working in the boat yard this last week. *Maggie B* was hauled last Wednesday, to check the shaft and prop, and to clean the bottom and repaint with anti-fouling. The prop and shaft check went fine and minor adjustments seem to have fixed everything. The bottom was something else.

We were covered with barnacles, white hard wormy formations, and green weed: a real mess. Paint scrapers peeled off most stuff, and that was followed with a high-pressure wash, followed by scrapers, followed by sanding end to end and every inch. She really is a HUGE boat. Working overhead meant barnacles in the hair and every nook and cranny of clothing, working low on the boat meant being in the mud and slime of the shipway, bumping into metal scraps or huge timbers. Staging was rickety (I fell six feet when a board broke, happily not breaking anything else), ladders were chancy and the yard was filthy. I suggested to the owner that he perhaps was waiting for the next tsunami to clear it out like the Augean Stables.

We were staying in a little old-fashioned 20-room hotel down the beach a ways, but we were too tired at the end of the day to do anything other than flop in the water and then shower, have dinner and sleep 12 hours, with Ibuprofin for tired muscles. Even noisy Christmas parties at the hotel didn't keep us up for long.

But now we are all clean and *Maggie B* is slippery again and ready for a fast trip to Australia.

The "after" photo with a clean bottom.

Grande Anse, Seychelles.

## 13 DECEMBER 2006

Back in Port Victoria we are going through supplies, planning for what we will need on the trip to Australia this January and doing some of the endless boat tasks such as chipping the hidden rust off the windlass and putting hard plastic protection up to give the fore gaff saddle something to chew on other than our expensive foremast.

Spices for sale in the market.

We are looking forward to having Owen Baker join us (Frank, Hannah and Bori) in January for the trip to Australia and beyond. One of his many accomplishments was designing and building a mechanical amphibious vehicle that looked like an elephant.

## 16 DECEMBER 2006

*Maggie B* is well settled at a mooring in the inner harbor. I dove on the mooring this morning to be sure of it. The mooring is about 100 pounds of granite plus some unknown piece of machinery about half the size of a Volkswagen Beetle. I added a few ropes and a shackle and we should be fine. I have paid up my Seychelles Yacht Club dues, hired a local boatman to look after *Maggie B* (for a new pair of Oakleys from the US) plus made friends with nearby Aussie yachties.

Our favorite menu experience here in the Seychelles was last Sunday on La Digue at a Restaurant called Chez Marcel. The specials were listed on a big board. 1) Squid Curry; 2) Squid in garlic and butter; 3) Deep fried Squid; 4) Squid pasta. After these specials was CALAMARI! in excited capitals. It reminded us of the great "Spam, spam, spam" Monty Python sketch.

We all took off for Christmas holiday. Hungary, Nova Scotia and Chicago. Getting out of The Seychelles was expensive and complicated. But fortunately not too crowded, as most everyone else was coming in.

## 7 JANUARY 2007

Today we are converging from all over the world into the Seychelles. Frank from Paris and Chicago, Bori from Paris and Budapest, Hannah from London and Halifax, and Owen from Baltimore and London. We should all arrive in Port Victoria within a few hours.

My bags on the plane include: the correct toilet repair kit; lots of different epoxies; touch-up paint for the hull; an air compressor so we can dive down to 60 feet to work on the hull; specialty hoses; etc. Owen is bringing some pine tar to seal some spots on the deck. I bet the TSA found that—can't hide the smell! He said his girlfriend was eager to get it out of the house.

We hope that we will find *Maggie B* in the same shape as we left her. There had been some high winds and she dragged a bit, so our friends had to put together a new mooring, as well as tossing out our anchors. I think that she was missing us and went looking for her crew.

## 8 JANUARY 2007

*Maggie B* is now re-crewed in Port Victoria! Frank, Bori, Hannah, and Owen all made it to Port Victoria safe and sound, and more or less on time.

The two anchors and the mooring lines will take us a week to sort out—a Gordian knot. The boat has only a few minor dings. We were lucky to have good folks watching her while we were gone.

We're unpacking today, and sleeping. Tomorrow we'll start loading and sorting and stowing. The weather is cloudy and rainy, on and off, and forecast to continue the same.

Owen started his Seychelles experience right with octopus curry for lunch. Even though warned by his shipmates, he took some of the hot sauce; steam came from his ears, which was fun to watch.

Moorings and two anchor rodes, a mess.

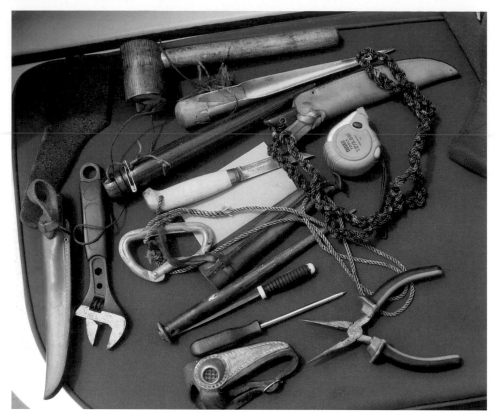

Hannah's rigging kit.

## 14 JANUARY 2007

We had a very successful Friday in Mahe, which included filling up on diesel and water. For those of you used to pulling into a marina and saying "fill her up!" you have no idea of the complications of getting fuel and water around the world. First was a serious negotiation with the Marine Charter Association as to whether they would sell us diesel at all. Then a 3 hour wait for the right bit of the float to open up. Then spinning *Maggie B* (in front of the lunch crowd of professionals) in a space with barely a foot to spare in any direction and 10 knots of crosswind to make it interesting. Then an hour to get the 1053 liters of diesel. Did I mention paying in cash? Also negotiating with a fishing boat to "borrow" their water. But, to be fair, the price was reasonable at about 6 SR a liter or US$2.26 a gallon, if you exchange your crisp US$100s on the "informal" market.

We noticed that while the bottom was still clean with its new anti-fouling, the propeller was totally covered with barnacles. But I had brought a hookah back with me: an electric air pump that plugs into the *Maggie B*'s 110 volt AC, and supplies air to a mouthpiece at the end of a 60-foot tube. It enabled me to slide down to the prop with a paint scraper and wire brush and get it all sorted out in about 20 minutes. The system worked marvelously and seemed to particularly fascinate the fish, especially a very serious 6-foot barracuda, which really wanted to slide in and get a close look, though a poke in the nose by the wire brush dissuaded it.

Owen has already proved that he will be a fine shipmate, standing tall on the shoulders of the *Maggie B*'s great Maritime Mechanics, Max and Bart. He was able to replace the salinity probe in our watermaker in less than an hour despite it being positioned in a place a little harder to get at than the transmission of a 1954 Austin Healey. Tomorrow we are going to try to replace the impeller of the Yanmar. It hasn't broken but it has been spinning its heart out for 640 hours. The generator's impeller destructed after 335 hours.

*"I'm glad that the Coast Guard didn't check us, but if they came by, they probably would have joined the party."*

## 17 JANUARY 2007

The *Maggie B*'s first anniversary last night was epic. She was launched in a snowstorm on January 16, 2006 in Lunenburg, Nova Scotia. No snow in the Seychelles! Bori baked a cake and decorated it with a schooner, Hannah baked delicious cookies, some shaped as Maple Leafs in honor of the Nova Scotian birth. We invited yachtie friends, Seychellian friends and all our French friends, and made new friends that night. At one point I counted 35 people visible from the cockpit and I missed some. We had 11 dinghies tied up, looking like a nursing sow with piglets. I'm glad that the Coast Guard didn't check us, but if they came by, they probably would have joined the party. We had a half case of nice South African champagne saved for just such an emergency. It disappeared even before we got to light the one candle on the cake.

171

The game plan is to head south to pick up the westerlies on the south side of the South Indian Ocean High. It should take us to about 35 South. In general we will have light 10–15 knot easterly winds for much of the way. Mauritius is about 850 NM away, south and a little east, and we are going to head in that direction. It is about 4200 NM to Perth and we have about 1200 NM of fuel for motoring. If, as I suspect, we will have to motor a fair amount between here and Mauritius, we will stop there.

Checking out of the Seychelles was relatively easy—two hours and about $300 in fees for the two months we were here, which seems fair for the marvelous time we had.

We are off tonight for a last meal at our favorite restaurant, La Perle Noir, also the name of a famous ship. Then 4,000 Rupees of food arrives from the wholesaler at 8:30 a.m., top up our diesel and water, and, after a check by the Coast Guard, we are off for Australia!

Captains from America, Australia, Sweden and Mauritius.

## 19 JANUARY 2007

We are headed due south for Port Louis, Mauritius at 8 knots, motorsailing. We are scampering across the historical tracks of South Indian typhoons. It is typhoon season, but our winds are light and there is nothing happening at least according to the three different 5-day forecasts I have reviewed. We will be in Port Louis in four days at this speed, where we will refuel, buy a few fresh veggies and be off for Perth. Once we are about 200 miles—a day's sail—south of Mauritius, we will be clear of the historic typhoon tracks.

## 20 JANUARY 2007

Today was a big "ship work" day. Hannah sewed and fitted a storm cover for our deck box; Owen fixed the "Sea-Me" active radar reflector and sewed a Mauritius flag out of some colored sailcloth we got in Lunenburg; Bori fixed and glued up two places where wood had split in our skylight and in the frame for the cover of the *Reepicheep*; I overhauled, brought out, put away and organized all our paper charts, and trouble-shot a Yanmar oil pressure concern.

Mauritius is an independent country, attaining independence from Britain in 1968. It was Portuguese first—they ate all the dodos, then Dutch, then French, then English. There are 1.2 million inhabitants, mostly descendants of imported Indian laborers. A small minority of French descent forms the wealthiest group. Joseph Conrad called Mauritius "the sugary pearl of the Indian Ocean." For us it is a handy re-provisioning stop on our way to Australia.

Hurricanes in the North Atlantic tend to curve north and then northeast as they approach the US coast; typhoons in the Southern Indian Ocean tend to curve southeast and then south as they approach Madagascar. The islands of Reunion and Mauritius historically have

Owen free climbing the main mast.

acted like giant slalom ski gates for the turn to south and then finally southwest. Are we concerned at being here right now? You bet! But the storms form far away to the north and east of us, and we are watching that area closely. We get three different forecasts that cover five days out. If something formed, we would have five days warning of the birth, and the storm would still be at least a week away, once developed. So we should have at least 12 days warning of any developments. In 12 days we can go 2,000 miles, which is plenty of distance, even though we would be in the SW—the danger quadrant. Nevertheless, we are going to fuel up as soon as we arrive and stay ready to leave—even without the blessing of Customs and Immigration—on the first notice of developing lows.

Most sailboat engines have an idiot light to indicate low oil pressure. *Maggie B* has the most sophisticated panel that Yanmar sells for this engine, which includes an electronic oil pressure gauge as well as an idiot light. Right now the oil pres-

## PIRATES

I had my usual midnight to 3 am watch. We were sailing easily down the coast of Brazil, perhaps only five miles offshore. It was a dark night with occasional rain showers, but with a favorable breeze driving us south at 7-8 knots.

We were headed for Salvador after a stop in Natal. We were close to shore because that is where Brazil sticks out most to the East, and staying inshore is the shortest route. Even big ships were close in. There was every sort of ship and boat around, from small wooden fishermen to big tankers, all trying to make good time south or north.

Our radar had the capability of highlighting and tracking targets. If you clicked on them, you could get relative speed, closest point of approach, time until you got close, etc. On this night, the sailing was easy and there were no navigational challenges—you just had to make sure not to hit anything or anybody.

There were perhaps a dozen targets within the 20-mile range. I had particularly been watching one smallish target heading south with us. It had been a mile or so away for the last hour or so, going about the same speed. My readout said that it was slowly closing on us. When the boat was about a half mile away, suddenly it turned off all its lights and started closing on us fast.

I immediately lit it up with our 2 million candlepower searchlight. For me it was bright as day, but for them it must have been dazzling. They immediately turned their lights back on and turned away. Shortly thereafter, another dense rain

sure gauge is reading very low, though the idiot light has not illuminated. Tough to troubleshoot. An urgent inquiry to the Halifax Yanmar dealer came back with the advice that the electronic gauges weren't very accurate and should only be considered advisory. What does that mean in the middle of the ocean? I went all over the engine with a laser thermometer and found only normal temperatures, so we are declaring it a gauge error. If we can, we will get an old-fashioned "steam" gauge installed in the oil system in Port Louis, so that with a bit of effort, we can check the accuracy of the electronic gauge.

Food continues to be top quality. Lunch today was Hannah's hard-boiled egg and potato salad, with a fresh Seychelles avocado, topped with Frank's mustard vinaigrette dressing. Sides included Prosciutto di Parma, Jarlsburg cheese and Hannah's fresh baked biscuits. Served with a cold bottle of South African Sauvignon blanc. Dessert was apple and orange slices with Kit-Kat chocolate chasers.

shower came through and I turned off all our lights, gybed and headed another five miles offshore. I didn't see the mystery ship again.

Was he a pirate? Not in the sense of a full-time profession. But probably opportunistic like your average big-city mugger. What would I have done if he had continued to come at us? I'd have gotten our Portuguese-speaking crew member on the emergency channel 16 and had her yell bloody murder; fired flares in the air and at the other boat, (I had 60 shots for the flare gun) turned lights out and gone to maximum speed away, dodging being boarded; while continuing to light up his ship with every searchlight.

In the reports of piracy on the high seas, two things stand out. First is that there are some areas that are very dangerous – off of Somalia and the Red Sea, the Straits of Malacca, the drug islands in the Caribbean. If you stay away from them, all other reports over the years are essentially of simple muggings that appear to be random and opportunistic. We were an alert, prepared boat and had no trouble other than the single event described above.

Some cruisers carry weapons. Those that do have to be both skilled and practiced in their use, and also ready to kill all the people in the other boat. One of our heroes, Sir Peter Blake, tried to break up a robbery on his boat in the Amazon by waving a rifle at six armed pirates. He was killed. The robbers took a 15 HP outboard and a few watches.

Pirate Fremantle.

Long-tailed Tropicbird.

## 21 JANUARY 2007

The day is fine, but a little frustrating. The wind direction will vary from 080 to 130 degrees, wind speed from 5 to 20 knots. One little rain shower will dump on us and bring wind, then a dry stretch, then another dump. We are aiming to get to Port Louis before 6 p.m. in two days. The port is reportedly closed from 6 p.m. each evening to 6 a.m. the next day. That means we must average 8 knots. Sometimes the wind is powering us at 10 knots, so the engine goes off, then the wind poops out and back on comes the Yanmar.

We are having the usual chafing challenges. One is at the main throat halyard, where it rubs on the bolster that holds the stays on the mast. Owen showed his gymnastic abilities by scampering up the rope hoops along the main luff, as if they were proper ratlines or even a ladder.

The other serious operation of the day is iPod care. Getting them full of just the right music, podcast, poetry or books-on-tape, as well as fully charged, is almost a full-time duty. Having something fun to keep you company on solo night watch is marvelous, as well as a good safety against sleeping.

## 22 JANUARY 2007

We are under all plain sail, making 6.2 knots in nine knots of wind from the east. We have come 717 NM from the Seychelles and have 229 to go to Port Louis, Mauritius. The weather remains good. We should be in Port Louis by tomorrow afternoon.

Last night's delights were celestial. Owen and I sat up the first part of the evening watching Venus, our evening star, set with the two-day-old moon not far behind. Then during the night Saturn was pretty much overhead, watching our progress. Finally, when Hannah came on deck to relieve me at 3 a.m., we admired Jupiter rising out of the eastern sky, looking like a locomotive headlight roaring right at us.

What we are reading: I'm working on Conrad's *Lord Jim*, the story of a merchant marine officer who panics and abandons his ship and its passengers, thinking it is sinking and then later seeks redemption in the Far East, and is killed. Owen is reading Jared Diamond's *Collapse* about how nations fail. Hannah is reading *The Butter Box Babies* about a Nova Scotia institution that engaged in infanticide, baby selling and child abuse. And Bori is reading *101 Alternatives to Suicide*. The Captain's "spider sense" went to 100% alarm on hearing this last title, but supposedly it is uplifting.... Actually, all these books are a bit dark.

However giggles and guffaws are the order of the day. We are sharing Garrison Keilor's *Prairie Home Companion Comedy Theater*, burning the CD's into our iPods, and watching *Monty Python and the Holy Grail*, and *A Fish Called Wanda* on the laptops.

Despite today being Monday here and in most of the rest of the world, we declared it Sunday so that we could start the day with French toast. Owen was at the controls in the galley and got an A+ for taste (Madagascar vanilla, cinnamon, and crushed cashews) but alas, a D- for execution as most of the batter went into the cooler, spreading itself over 30 days of supplies. But he got up, dusted himself off and the second round was a great success.

## 23 JANUARY 2007

After a quick run down from the Seychelles, 950 miles in five days, we are moored at the Caudan Marina in Port Louis, Mauritius.

Mauritius is a handsome island, looking like Cape Town or Mahe on approach. Lots of tall buildings and the harbor approach is very industrial, but it opens up to a somewhat schizophrenic waterfront, trim Navy ships next to messy Chinese fishing boats next to grain elevators next to five star hotels. We are mixed in with the latter.

*"It is so funny to get up in the morning,
have a crew meeting over the first cup of coffee,
work out a reasonable timeline for the day,
and then watch it totally unravel
when faced with the realities of the tropics."*

Clearance with Customs, Immigration, Health and Coast Guard was relatively quick and pleasant. The usual 40 different forms asking the same questions in tiny different ways, but all the officials were smiling, helpful and efficient. English is the official language, but everyone seems to speak French to each other. All the professionals I have met so far look South Asian, rather dark, and speak good English with a charming French accent.

We hope to refuel tomorrow and have minor engine problems looked at, and sightsee. We are now about 3200 NM from Perth, though our trip will probably cover more distance, as we will head down to about 35 South to get on the south side of the high pressure. Departure for Perth on Thursday or Saturday, hopefully.

## 26 JANUARY 2006

It is so funny to get up in the morning, have a crew meeting over the first cup of coffee, work out a reasonable timeline for the day, and then watch it totally unravel when faced with the realities of the tropics.

We are still in the harbor. Today was the day to get engine work finished, fill up on diesel, and load food resupply. Surely also plenty of time to go to the famous garden in Pamplemousse? No.

It is noontime and we are at the Taylor-Smith yard across the harbor from the marina. It is a famous old yard, with twin 160-year-old dry docks. We are here to get some minor engine work completed and to get diesel: 200 gallons. There is a big Shell fuel dock nearby, but they only talk in tons of fuel and in any case it is closed today for some reason. So our contacts at Taylor-Smith, who have been very helpful, offered us 200 gallons from their supply. No problem? Not really. We had thought that after refueling in Madagascar from a town filling station and carrying jerry cans all over, and then the Seychelles where there was endless negotiation and very difficult access, that we had seen it all.

Here it is amazingly complex. Rube Goldberg would be proud. The fuel is put into 55-gallon drums, carried by a forklift to the edge of the dock, pipes and tubes are fitted. A 5-ton crane lumbers over, the drum is chained up horizontally, and hoisted alongside the *Maggie B*, the fuel is slowly drained out into our tanks. Another drum is brought over, ready to be hoisted. STOP! It is eleven o'clock—lunchtime—we have been here since 8:30 a.m. We fear that there might be a siesta in the union contract. Did I mention payment is cash only?

Our engine is in good shape. We have changed the oil, plus oil and fuel filters on both the Yanmar and the Onan generator. We had been having oil pressure indicator problems and the mechanics at Taylor-Smith were able to replace the pressure indicator, and now it works fine. They have also made a T-junction, so that on the side of the engine we will continue to have the electronic sensor, which reads out in the cockpit, but also an old-fashioned "steam gauge" that will sit on the side of the engine to confirm the electronic reading—belt and suspenders.

Mauritius fill-up.

We had a water pump impeller failure on the Onan generator back in Durban after about 335 hours. No impeller, no water circulation, and the engine over-heats. The Yanmar had gone about 750 hours on its first impeller, and their manual suggests changing after 1,000 hours. But we had a spare, we were here with good mechanics, why not change it now? We pulled it out and, horrors! it had lost one vane, which we found, and another was torn and ready to come off. Whew!

We hope to finish up here directly, go get food supplies, have some tourist fun this afternoon, have a great dinner, and be off for Perth sometime tomorrow, Saturday. The winds are favorable. Mauritius is marvelous and worth weeks to explore, but we are Blue Water sailors, bound for South Australia!

## 27 JANUARY 2007

Today was not such a good day, on many levels. The plan was to leave today for Perth. We went in the morning to the Botanical Gardens, which were stunning. We had lunch at our favorite restaurant, the Captainerie. Then a long torrential, gully-washing, frog-choking downpour. But we were on *Maggie B* more or less on our time-line to depart for Perth. We motored proudly out of the Marina for the Customs dock. Big, open harbor with lots of Blue Water boats coming and going, but no channel markers. Dredged to 17 feet, per the chart.

We ran aground solidly just 200 feet off the five-star hotel that had sheltered us. Maybe only 20 yards from mid-channel. No buoys. But on one chart that I reviewed afterwards, there was a three-foot spot. Distracted, inattentive, concern about Customs, maybe a bit of pride and bravado, put us high and dry.

We stuck hard at dead low tide. No problem in Maine where you get a tide with 12 feet of rise and fall. Here the tide is less than a foot. We got marvelous support from another yacht, but the Mauritius Coast Guard came over to be sure nobody was dying.

We ran one line ashore to drag us back out, like a kedge, attached to a huge piece of granite. We ran one line from the main tops to heel us over. Finally, after local advice and lots of soundings with the leadline, we finally kedged, warped and heeled us off the rock. Whew! It took four hours. It was awful.

We returned to the Marina, invited the French couple that had helped us over for drinks and dinner, and had a group hug.

The Crew on a fig tree in the Sir Seewoosagur Ramgoolam Botanical Garden.

Bori near Balaclava Beach, Mauritius.

## 29 JANUARY 2007

The nice French couple that helped us out of our disgrace on Saturday were Didier and Celine with their marvelous ship's hound, Nane, off the boat *Neurone*. This morning, Didier came by, as we were getting ready to head off, to suggest a Sunday picnic a little way down the coast at a beach called Balaclava. He suggested that it would be smart to dive on the bottom of *Maggie B* to check for any damage. We didn't need much persuading.

It was a marvelous day. We motored about 45 minutes down the coast to a lovely little bay, caught a mooring, dove, swam, snorkeled, kayaked, walked ashore, visited ruins and giant tortoises, snuck into a marvelous hotel swimming pool, and generally had a great time. Didier and Celine (and the dog, Nane!) took us to a lovely small river with waterfalls. We inspected the romantic ruins of a former naval ammunition factory nearby.

The bottom of *Maggie B* was a little scraped, but as per plan, her keel is made to take the ground with minimal damage. The air compressor was very useful.

Monday morning, after clearing Customs and Immigration, we hoisted our sails in the Inner Harbor, and sailed out the channel with all flags flying. I believe that it probably has been many years since a schooner left under sail from the Inner Harbor. We were cheered by the crew of a Coast Guard boat and several Taiwanese fishing boats.

*"... we hoisted our sails in the Inner Harbor, and sailed out the channel with all flags flying. I believe that it probably has been many years since a schooner left under sail from the Inner Harbor."*

At noon on Monday, *Maggie B* was at about two miles off the Point aux Sables lighthouse on the west coast of Mauritius. We are finally underway for Perth in a nice southeasterly, making 6.5 knots just about due south. We expect the wind to back a bit to the east, which might help us make a bit of easting as we head south to pick up the westerly wind. The waves are a bit choppy and *Maggie B* is working a bit, as if she had lost her sea legs from the long time in port in the Seychelles and then the essentially flat conditions on the run south to Mauritius.

The forecast for us for the next five days is what we have, an easterly at 15 to 20 knots. In five days we should be on the south side of the high and picking up our westerlies. We are watching a low that is forecast to develop about a thousand miles east of Madagascar. In five days it is forecast to have 40 knots of wind. We will be well south before it gets here.

Perth is about 3200 NM away, though we will cover more distance on our way there. We should be there in three weeks.

Bori and Owen with a tuna.

*"February has been good to us so far.*
*We are wondering what Groundhog Day means*
*in the Southern Hemisphere."*

## 8

# OFF TO SOUTH AUSTRALIA

**30 JANUARY 2007**

We are headed about due south magnetic at 8.5 knots, with wind from 120 degrees at 22–28 knots. The seas are sloppy, made somewhat peaky by a one knot current from the north. We have come 1130 NM from the Seychelles and have about 3110 to go to Perth. We have one reef in both the main and the foresail.

While we could be close hauled and make some more easting, both the crew and the boat were taking a bit of a pounding when we tried it. Now with the sheets started a bit, we are making better speed to the south and life is more reasonable on board as *Maggie B* has a chance to handle the waves and not just jumping off one wave and slamming into the next. Green water carried away a ventilator next to the fore hatch and tried to snatch the boat hook. *Reep* and *Strika* are riding well on deck. The watch in the cockpit gets a steady refreshing saltwater misting.

It is good that we left Mauritius when we did. They will be getting a low with 30–40 knots of wind by February 3rd. We should be well south by then, starting our turn for Perth.

We had a new, interesting experience last night. A French warship intercepted us. We were within about 40 NM of Mauritius and about 100 from French territory (Reunion). They came within about two miles at about midnight and called us on the radio. We saw a long, big, grey warship. They had lots of questions, which I answered with increasing irritation, partially because they refused to identify their ship at all ("Eet is no possible"). They were satisfied with our MMSI and IHO numbers, Radio Call, Port of origin, date and time of departure, destination, cargo, number of crew, national origin, etc. I was prepared to refuse boarding and call the Mauritius Coast Guard for assistance, but, happily, it did not come to that. The French warship then went after another boat that accelerated from 15 knots to 28 knots when hailed. I'm sure they were more interesting than we were.

## 31 JANUARY 2007

The sea has laid down and gotten more regular, but we are still taking a fair amount of water over the deck, certainly enough to keep the helmsman salty.

Last night's excitement came when Owen was sitting up talking with Bori during her 9 p.m. to midnight watch. When he was in mid-sentence, a flying fish hit him in the face. Only an inch to the left and it would have been a hole in one!

Tropical Cyclone Dora is forming about 850 NM north-northeast of us. It has winds of 40 knots so far. It is headed southwest at 11 knots and we are headed southeast at 9, so we should be well clear. Our barometer is rising.

The variation here is 25 degrees west. In many places in the world there is a significant difference between magnetic north and true north. This is one such place. We steer *Maggie B* on magnetic courses, so when I say we are headed 180 degrees, that is 180 degrees magnetic or 155 degrees true, and making some precious easting. The support we get on weather forecasting gives headings in true, so we have to be sure to make the proper correction. Sailors have memorized "Can Dead Men Vote Twice? (Add East)" or "True Virgins Make Dull Companions." That is to help remember "Compass; Deviation; Magnetic; Variation; True."

## 1 FEBRUARY 2007

February has been good to us so far! We are wondering what Groundhog Day means in the Southern Hemisphere. We are headed 180 magnetic at 8.3 knots. We did 208 NM in the last 24 hours, 402 in the last two days! We have gone 1532 NM since the Seychelles and have 2769 to go to Perth.

We are still on a close reach, sailing easy with a 15–18 knot breeze at 60 degrees relative wind. The seas have laid down and there is only an occasional "Wake Up!" splash into the cockpit. Some hatches are open, making below decks much nicer.

Today is an "after the storm" sort of day, though we just had a good blow, not a real storm. We are doing what sailors always do when the sun comes out—laundry, clean the mess in the fo'c'stle, check and empty all bilges, check and run engines, fix damage. We had one sheet part and one ventilator taken away. We see a few minor problems with the sails, which will have to be tended in Perth, if not before. We are in very good shape.

Tropical Cyclone Dora is giving us a great advantage to go south as she will pull the normally southeasterly trades back to northeast and then north. We may have

> *"We are doing what sailors always do when the sun comes out—laundry, clean the mess in the fo'c'stle, check and empty all bilges, check and run engines, fix damage."*

to continue south to 38 or 40 degrees to stay in westerlies, but we won't know for a couple of days. Essentially we are taking advantage of great meteorological information to slingshot around a very dangerous storm.

## 2 FEBRUARY 2007

We are making 8.3 knots on a heading of 170 degrees magnetic. The wind has been fairly steady in direction at 080–090 magnetic, with the speed slowing from 15–18 yesterday to 12–15 today. The barometer is slowly rising as we work our way down south of the Southern Indian Ocean High (and away from T/C Dora!).

Last night was beautiful with the full moon rising as the sun set, and then keeping us company all night behind a veil of complex high cirrus clouds.

T/C Dora is now about 850 NM north-northeast of us, scheduled to pass a little south of Mauritius early next week. It is no factor for us, other than to pull the southeasterly trades more to the northeast, which is a great help.

A building ridge of high pressure is modeled to set up along 36–37 degrees South early next week, and we will have to be south of that if we want to get our westerlies for Perth. We may head as far south as 40. Already being at 31 South should make that an easy target.

We may come near to, or possibly land at a French island at 38 degrees South, which is about 750 NM ahead of us on our current course. The island was first known as Isle Amsterdam, then La Roche Godon, now Martin-de-Vivis. Correspondents tell us that it is volcanic, with the last eruption in 1792, the year the mobs ran free in Paris in the rising against Louis XVI. It has an area of 21 NM and the highest mountain is 2,844 feet. There is a French weather station and a UN atmospheric research station on the island, plus many, many fur seals. In 2002 there were 145 scientists and support personnel on the island. Anchoring and landing challenges are unknown. I wonder if they have a French warship protecting them from itinerant American schooners?

It is getting cooler. The watch last night needed a warm top as well as full foulies, and ... shoes! Hard on feet that are used to being barefoot. The crew started digging for the blankets. Seawater temperature is down ten degrees Fahrenheit from the Seychelles.

Yesterday we experienced our fifth Lewmar block failure. Another poor design. Hopefully there is a cut-rate Antal distributor in Perth/Fremantle and we can get this Lewmar junk off the boat before someone gets hurt.

The Captain got injured today in perhaps the most ridiculous fashion possible. We usually play some music loud when we are getting ready for lunch, our big communal meal. I put on the soundtrack from the musical *Spamalot*. When it came to "We Are The Knights of the Round Table and Dance Whenever We're Able," I was doing a sailor's jig with Owen, and misjudged the overhead in the pilot house and almost knocked myself out on a beam. Ah, the sailor's life.

## 3 FEBRUARY 2007

We are headed 155 degrees magnetic at 8 knots with one reef in the fore and main despite the wind lightening to 12–14 knots from the northeast. We did 188 NM in the last 24 hours.

The barometer is rising steadily, up to 1016 and the wind is backing and easing. But we are watching multiple layers of clouds, with the high ones coming in from the west and the low ones blowing across from the east. Clearly something going on. But the GRIB files predict a nice 10–15 knot beam reach as we slide down to our westerly highway to Fremantle at about 38 degrees South. So far so good.

I don't want to miss the chance to laud, once again, the marvel of Nigel Iren's design and the success of North Sails-built sails, and the work of everyone else involved. Here we are in February in the Southern Indian Ocean with an easy close

*The Captain got injured today in perhaps
the most ridiculous fashion possible. ...
I was doing a sailor's jig with Owen,
and misjudged the overhead in the pilot house
and almost knocked myself out on a beam.
Ah, the sailor's life.*

reach in 12–14 knots of wind, with a reef in the main and fore, doing eight knots! It is comfortable enough even in 5–8 foot chop and swells to have Bori's excellent Tortillas de Patatas for a sit-down lunch, chased with Hannah's chocolate and banana bread for dessert.

We are scrubbing and sanding the decks, and going through all the bilges to pump them dry and clean them out.

Logs of my dreams are maybe not a great idea, but my waking dream was so cool I want to share it. I was Captain of a square-rigged sloop in about 1780 and had been caught by the British for smuggling (rum? arms?) and taken into Boston, tried, convicted and sentenced to be shot. It was a very rich dream, in color with full details. Somehow I persuaded the British that it would be more impressive to take me and the crew back to our ship, anchor it close in the harbor and execute us there. Sort of like the heads on Traitor's Gate in London. But we seized the ship from the poorly trained execution squad, threw them overboard and made off for blue water. I was woken by Owen sanding the deck above me, rather like All Hands at 6 a.m. in the Old Days.

This morning we were also happy to hear from sailing friends: our shipmate Willis arriving safely in Georgetown, SC, after a very difficult winter run from Long Island, and South African friends we met in Knysna, made it to Trinidad from Cape Town on a catamaran delivery to French Polynesia. Their Shellback skipper put his pollywog crew over the side on ropes and dragged them across the Equator as part of their initiation.

Wash on the line, Southern Ocean.

## 4 FEBRUARY 2007

We are motorsailing, heading 160 degrees at 7 knots. The wind is 035 magnetic at 10 knots. There is 5–8 foot swell from both north and southeast. The sky is partly cloudy with a textbook variety of forms, at all levels. The barometer, while still high-ish at 1015, has started to fall.

We got a rather alarming weather update from Commanders' Weather at midnight last night. It starts out with "Summary—Very Impressive Tropical Cyclone Dora…." These are words you don't want to read at midnight, or at any other time, except maybe in a historical novel. Apparently Dora has intensified, now with winds at 120 knots, with gusts to 150. Fortunately 1) it is very compact, 2) it is 850 NM away 3) it is moving slowly to the southwest and 4) we are moving quickly to the southeast.

## OFFSHORE RISKS

Offshore is safer than inshore. The simple fact is that there is less to run into, and most of the time sailors get hurt is when they run into something – a reef or another boat.

And there is probably something else going on beyond having a lot of running room. Captains check themselves, their boat and their crew more carefully if they are going 1000 miles than if they are going ten miles, though one can drown just as easily in ten feet of water as in 10,000. Offshore you get into a more professional state of mind. You focus on the boat rather than texting about a party at the next port. You have a chance to really "get your mind in the boat."

People fear storms - rightly. But a huge storm might be only 100-150 NM across. Today you can get good weather forecasts five days out and *Maggie B* could cover 1000 NM in five days. If you are paying attention and have sea room, there is no excuse to sail into a storm.

I had two big offshore fears. One was running into a semi sunken shipping container. The other was a medical emergency that I couldn't handle, like a burst appendix.

For the former, I had two levels of watertight bulkheads forward, so we could, in theory, crash and survive. For the latter, I subscribed to a medical service that you could call by satellite phone or email and get right through to an ER nurse and doctor at George Washington University Hospital. I never needed the former – the three times we ran aground, we were never more than 1000 feet from shore. The latter I used only for the relatively boring issues of defecating too little or too much.

Claus Heinrich

Offshore dangers are mostly emotional. We live in a country that takes pretty good care of us. Highways are clear, doctors are close. Somebody will deliver heat and electricity. At sea, offshore, it is you and your crew and your ship; and that can become overwhelming.

I was surprised because I had been getting GRIB updates twice a day (usually only once/day) and they were only showing 40 knots maximum wind. When questioned, Commanders' said, "GRIB files do not handle tropical systems well, especially small, compact ones." We will be well clear to the south and east, but we worry for our friends and acquaintances in Mauritius, who may get a real walloping. It is forecast to pass south of Mauritius, but there is a fairly energetic cold front approaching from the West, and the interaction of the cold front and the tropical cyclone is tough to model.

We spent the morning shaking out the reefs in the main and the fore as the wind is getting light, and we made some minor repairs to the sails and running rigging. We are continuing south and east to get on the far side of the ridge that should form with the passage of the cold front, which should give us nice westerlies.

What we are reading: Hannah is reading *Explorers: Journeys to the Ends of the Earth* by Jon Balchin; Bori is reading *Tibetben a lélek (The Soul is in Tibet)* by Tovaly Ferenc; Owen is reading Jared Diamond's *Collapse: How Societies Choose to Fail or Succeed*; and Frank is reading *Heavy Weather Guide*: Kotsch & Henderson; *Weather for the Mariner,* William Kotsch, and the famous section 3909 from Bowditch that starts: *"The passage of a tropical cyclone at sea is an experience not soon to be forgotten..."*

On a more fun note, our watches have been immensely improved by the liberal sharing of a series of Garrison Keillor CD's of his *Prairie Home Companion* show. Giggles on watch can be heard at any time of day or night.

We have noted with some concern that we have come all this way but have not yet settled on a *Maggie B* work song. Certainly we need one to help us raise the sails. It must have a "haulaway" refrain like "Way, hey! Up she rises." It could have a question and response style like "What shall we do with the sea-sick sailor?" Or it could give various geographical tributes (first verse Canadian, second Caribbean, third Brazilian, fourth South African, fifth south Asian, sixth Australian). Of course, there is also Gilbert and Sullivan: "He polished up the binnacle so carefully that now he is the Captain of the *Maggie B*!"

## 5 FEBRUARY 2007

We are under sail at 7.5 knots with the G2 "Bird" up, headed for Ile Amsterdam. We have some high cirrus clouds coming in from the north and a long northerly swell, mixing with a southeasterly set. We have come 2258 NM from the Seychelles and have about 2120 to go to Perth. A short visit to the Beakers (scientists) at Ile

Amsterdam is still a possibility.

Today was The Hat Day. Four major cleaning jobs—vacuum, wash decks, wash walls, and....The Head and the Shower—were put on little slips of paper and put in a hat for all to choose. The Captain got The Head, but all's fair.

Just as we were congratulating ourselves on a great cleaning job, there was a funny "static" sound, which I thought was something on the VHF. Bori correctly identified it as the fishing reel buzzing out! We all went to our stations—grab the fishing pole and reel, control and slow the boat, get the wash down pump hose, ready the gaff, ready the killing instruments and sharpen the knives, clear the afterdeck, ready the cutting and cleaning board, etc. In a little bit, with minimum of commotion, we had a lovely fat 35-pound blue fin tuna aboard, killed and bled out. This is perhaps the 20th fish caught on a beat up "hurt squid in blue and pink hula dress" lure from Bermuda. Priceless! In another half hour it was cleaned and cut up and packed in the fridge, except for the part that is marinating in lemon juice and other good things for tuna ceviche this evening.

The scraps that went overboard made us very popular with the albatrosses that were following us.

T/C Dora is going its way and we are going ours, and it appears as if our paths will not cross. The barometer is staying up at 1017 mb and the significant clouds are behind us. The challenge is how far south we should go to pick up our westerlies. Right now it looks as if we will have to go into the forties, but we will not need to make that decision for a few days.


## 6 FEBRUARY 2007

We are under all plain sail, making 6.2 knots close hauled, heading 160 degrees magnetic. The southwesterly has come in for us, at 10–12 knots, the wind having backed all the way around from the northeast last night.

We are about 80 miles from the French weather station at Ile Amsterdam. With this wind we can't reach it unless we either tack up to it, or drop sails and motor. Right now we don't know 1) if there is any safe anchorage there, 2) if they are friendly and welcome visitors and 3) how long this "the wind blows fair for Australia" will last. We will try to reach them by radio at sunset to get answers to #1 and #2. If we stop, we'll get there about midnight.

We have had an occasional albatross follow us. Yesterday, when we were cleaning the tuna and tossing bits over, we saw two albatrosses land in the water to gobble up

A new albatross.

some tidbits. The word must have gotten around because today we have two squadrons of albatrosses, apparently waiting for the next feed.

Not sure which albatross: wing span about 4–5 feet, wings black across the top,
white on the underside. Body and head white except for the tail, which is black. Big
head. Beak large and faintly hourglassed, orangish with black below.

One of our safety devices is a "Sea-Me" active radar transponder. It gives out a
strong pulse as it senses ship radars, making us look very big. It also can "peep" when
it hears a radar. We haven't seen a ship since the French frigate near Mauritius, but we
have been hearing a steady radar sound on the "Sea-Me," which has remained consis-
tent in pulse and strength. Think of the sonar man in *Hunt for the Red October*. I have
become convinced that it is the French frigate, tracking us, but staying just out of
our visual and radar range. *"Sacre Bleu! Cette goelette etrange vont direct a notre station
meteo a Ile Amsterdam!! Elle doit etre mechante! Preparez les missiles!!!"* Or: "Sainted
blue heavens! This strange schooner is going directly towards our weather station on
Amsterdam Island!! She must be evil!! Prepare the missiles!!!"

At about sunset I contacted Ile Amsterdam on the VHF radio. A nice French
woman with a lovely accent answered. We no longer had the opportunity to land

as we were 55 NM north and the wind had shifted to the South, but I thought that it would be fun to check in. She reported that there were 30 French people on the island, that there was no protected anchorage, and that we were very welcome to come by. It made me think of the Sirens, or that we would land and the crew would be turned into pigs as Circe did with Odysseus, or that it would turn out to be a Super Secret French listening post, and that we would drop anchor and the French Frigate that had been tailing us, would appear from behind the island and we would never be heard from again.

Last night the watches had tuna cerviche (lemon juice, tomato, onions and spices). For lunch we had fresh tuna, flash-seared in a hot pan with butter and garlic.

## 7 FEBRUARY 2007

We are headed due east magnetic at 7.2 knots, close hauled under all plain sail, with the wind from 160 magnetic at 12 knots. The wind has been backing steadily, and lightening up. By midnight tonight, we expect to be motoring southeast against a 5–10 knot easterly.

Essentially we have to wait a day for the first in a series of cold fronts to catch up with us. The further to the south and west, the earlier we catch our ride to Perth. Ideally, we should be about 150 NM to the south, but we will do fine here. The fronts should bring in great wind for us. Maybe 25–30 knots, on the beam or quarter. We should have a fine ride into town.

In the Northern Hemisphere, one says "backing" if the wind is shifting counter-clockwise and "veering" if it is shifting clockwise. We are wondering if we should say it the other way around in the Southern Hemisphere, because everything rotates the other way.

Last night was wonderfully clear, at least after midnight. The celestial high point was seeing Scorpio laid out like a cat on a sofa arm, with Jupiter coming up from underneath, as if working on a rendezvous with red Antares in the scorpion's belly.

One correspondent has written to us to say that there is a special, endangered albatross living on Ile Amsterdam, the Amsterdam Albatross. It is identifiable by dusky brown upper wings, rather than dusky grey. We immediately decided that our following albatross squadron REALLY had dusky brown wings. We did see a tag or two, which perhaps were just missing wing feathers.

On researching our delicious tuna, one reference book said that tuna schools sometimes follow along with boats, taking advantage of what the boat does to frighten flying fish and squid, making them easier to catch. It is funny to think that we have accompanying tuna, just as we have accompanying albatross.

Hannah today made what used to be her "Nova Scotia tea biscuits." This time, she added some of our fresh vanilla beans from Madagascar, in a vanilla butter swabbed on top, to make "Madagascar Sea Biscuits." We had them at lunch in a lovely tomato-based fish stew. Chocolate chip cookies for teatime!

One can't ignore it is getting colder. We have chosen favorite blankets from the storage closet. Some are considering a second one. Night watch means "Tooks on."

Perth/Fremantle in perhaps ten days!

## 8 FEBRUARY 2007

We are motoring directly towards Perth/Fremantle at 7 knots, on a heading of 116 degrees magnetic. There is no wind, but a long, big swell is making up from the south-southwest. The sky is generally clear. We have come 2766 NM from the Seychelles and have 1691 to go to Perth/Fremantle.

Today is the calm before the storm. The first in a series of cold fronts should arrive about noon tomorrow. Winds, maybe to 30 knots, should be on our quarter, allowing for great speed and a relatively comfortable ride. We are seeing the swell already, but no significant clouds yet. The barometer topped out at 1022 mb, and now is down slightly to 1020.

One option is to head south to get in a better spot for the next storm. I puzzled over it, making complex "what if's" and Velocity Made Good analyses. Finally, I decided that with all the variables, we could do a lot worse than heading right for Perth/Fremantle, so that is our plan. We may have to wait a bit longer for the wind pressure, but we won't have wandered all over the Southern Ocean.

We have been motoring a bit since Mauritius, but we are still on our first tank, 120-gallons of diesel, with the second tank holding about 200 gallons. We use 1 1/2 to 1 3/4 gallon per hour at 7.5 knots, so have at least 850 NM of motoring available. From the look of the weather charts, we won't be using a lot of fuel the rest of the way in.

Some have asked how we keep clean at sea. Very nicely, thank you, we reply with a check of our underarms. In fact, we are in good shape for fresh water. We started out from Mauritius with about 350 gallons, and I have been making water with our desalination unit pretty much every day, when the engine or generator is running. We can make six gallons an hour and we still have full tanks. So, one daily freshwater

Shearwater in our wake.

shower per person is easily supplied though I occasionally growl at shipmates who I suspect of taking "country club" showers.

Washing clothes is a little more challenging. We have lots of salt water. "Cold Water Tide" suds up nicely in cold salt water. The system is two buckets, and a bucket full of dirty clothes: perhaps three t-shirts, three underwear, and a pair of shorts. Suds and wash in the first bucket of salt water, rinse in successive buckets of salt water until all the soap is out and then finish rinse in fresh water, hang on the rail and you are ready for a few more days! The only drawback is seeing how dirty your clothes are, judging by the color of the rinse water…hard to figure with no real dirt within 1,000 miles….

Lunch today was Hannah's tuna noodle casserole. Some may not find that very special, but when Hannah makes it with fresh sashimi-grade tuna and whole-wheat rotilli, it comes out marvelously. Dessert was fresh-baked cinnamon cake. Best of all, there's lots of leftovers for the night watch!

It always seemed to rain on Hannah's watch.

## 9 FEBRUARY 2007

We are headed right for Fremantle at 8 to 12 knots. The variability on speed depends where we are on the swells, which are now up to 10–12 feet—sometimes surfing, sometimes recovering. But nice long swells with no nasty habits. We are headed 120 degrees magnetic and the wind is pretty stable at 20–25 from 270 degrees. The day now is mostly clear with just occasional rain showers…concentrated, as usual, on Hannah's watch.

It looks as if we now have our ride to Fremantle (Freo). The weather forecast suggests that the wind will build to about 30 knots by midnight, and then back a bit more and settle in 15 to 20 knots from the south for at least several days—until the next front. At this speed, we are six or seven days to Freo. We have come 2938 NM from the Seychelles and have "just" 1522 NM to go.

The *Maggie B* is looking a little like a "hobo" boat. Some halyards are several lines spliced together, our sheets don't match any more, and many have sheetbends holding them together. Many working parts of masts, gaffs and boom have "protection" glued on at one place or another. There are even some places with, *gasp*, duct tape, holding something on or together. We are not ready for a Concours d'Elegance. But we are ready for a week's 1500 NM run to Freo! So many boats are like the Harley Davidson motorcycles that are polished and cherished and only drive two miles every other Sunday, and not if it is raining, to the nearest Starbucks Cafe. Then you see the bike, maybe a BMW 1975 Boxer or Norton 750 with banged-up saddlebags and a variety of paint under the dust and dirt, down the street outside a bar with cold beer and good pizza…that's the bike that's been somewhere.

## 9 FEBRUARY 2007
Email from the Weather Router

> To: Cap't Frank Blair on SY "*Maggie B*"
> From: Commanders' Weather Corporation
> Route: Port Louis, Mauritius to Perth, Australia

> Summary: Very rough conditions developing late today and Saturday.
> Improving conditions Sunday/Monday. Watch for conditions to deteriorate

again Tuesday night/Wednesday.

## 10 FEBRUARY 2007
The wind is 230 degrees magnetic at 30 gusting to 40 knots. The seas are 20 to 30 feet from the southwest, very large, but rarely breaking on us. The sun is out and the conditions are improving.

Last night we watched the barometer fall rapidly and realized that after all the quiet time, we were in for a summer Southern Indian Ocean Gale. We doused the foresail, double reefed the main and jibed over to head north as fast as we could go. During the night the wind blew 35 knots steadily with gusts to 52. Dawn was welcome; though it did show the large seas, which had been a physical feeling rather than visual experience during the night.

At noon we jibed back to starboard tack and are headed for Fremantle, which is 1380 NM away, doing ten knots.

This low is moving ahead of us quickly and our wind should be down to 15 knots by this evening. We'll see.

There is another, bigger low and cold front following this first one in a few days. We will take more timely avoidance maneuvers for the next one. We are six days out of Fremantle at this speed.

We are mostly dry and warm below decks. The off duty watches can sleep.


## 11 FEBRUARY 2007

The wind has calmed down a lot. We are headed 130 degrees magnetic at 6.7 knots with a wind of 15 knots at 275. There is still a big southwesterly swell, which is throwing us around a bit, but is of no danger. We expect to run off to the southward a bit and then jibe about midnight as the wind veers more northwest, with the beginning of development of a high just north of us. The barometer is well up to 1017.

Today was exciting: we got to dry everything out! We looked like a gypsy boat with foul weather gear, boots, socks, long johns, everything crowding for space in the sun. All hatches open and all is now aired and dried out. Bliss!

The latest system to test us is the stove gas solenoid. It should electrically shut off the gas at the propane tanks, which are safely set back in a vented stern locker. The solenoid that shuts off the gas seems to be a problem. We had to replace the first on in Cape Town after it failed while crossing the South Atlantic. The replacement failed today and now has been removed from the system. We will try to oil, clean and reinstall it tomorrow.

I spent most of the day working on the Australian Customs "Small Boat Report." It is four pages long, and has questions like "List the make, model and serial number of all electronics gear." The report has to be submitted 96 hours BEFORE arrival. One recent yacht that didn't submit the report before arrival apparently was fined A$10,000!! I'm sure that the Australian Customs are nice people, but it does seem a bit ridiculous.

Regular readers know that I have been having issues with Lewmar blocks. Five have failed so far. Well, now it appears that perhaps I just have issues with blocks. Yesterday a small Harkin failed, and we replaced it with a brand new Barton. The Barton was making some noise today and I went to oil and inspect it and found a little pile of brass shavings under it as it apparently is in the process of self-destruction. Completely new!

QUOTE OF THE DAY: Today's quote is from Don Bamford: "Only two sailors, in my experience, never ran aground. One never left port and the other was an atrocious liar."

### 12 February 2007

We are headed due east for Fremantle at 8.9 knots with a lovely northwesterly at 18 knots blowing us in. As I write this at 4:30 p.m., we are cheering that we have broken the 1000 NM to go barrier! An extra round of chocolate for all hands!

Today has seemed to be an endless series of small, difficult repairs. Our gas shut off solenoid stuck partially open, which was tough to diagnose. It seems to be fixed now, but the T-junction valve also failed, and we had great difficulty putting together the parts to plumb it all back together. Now we are using gas from a little Brazilian bottle, which should get us to Fremantle.

*"... A perfect fit! It is now getting epoxied into position in a fresh fuel filter and we will know tomorrow morning if we have a functioning engine."*

The diesel was hard to start this morning, and when I went over it, I found a small diesel leak from the bottom of the fuel filter. A small drain valve in a plastic water-in-the-fuel sensor had come free and was dripping fuel. We took that apart and used epoxy to seal the drain hole. Four hours later, with the epoxy set, we reinstalled the sensor, only to have it break when it was tightened. OK, we don't need the sensor, let's just plug up the hole. Easier said than done…large metric hole. We searched the whole boat top to bottom and couldn't find anything that fit. Then, finally going through a jar of junk, I found the discarded, failed, salinity probe from the watermaker, which we had replaced in the Seychelles. A perfect fit! It is now getting epoxied into position in a fresh fuel filter and we will know tomorrow morning if we have a functioning engine.

Hannah made a delicious little chicken for lunch. Roasted with lots of onions, olives, curry and garlic. Perhaps "puttanesca" if it were italian, but we christened it Roast Chicken, Indian Ocean. Marvelous! We were able to have a civilized meal, eating on deck as we rush along almost at hull speed.

We should have a favorable breeze, 20 knots from either our port or starboard quarter for the next three days. The next gale is headed our way on the 16th, as we close the Australian Coast. We will be very careful to keep our options open.

## 13 February 2007

We are headed 104 degrees magnetic, right for Fremantle, at 10.2 knots, hull speed. We have one reef in both the main and the fore. The wind is relatively steady from the northwest at 18–25 knots. This is perfect sailing conditions for the *Maggie B*. We have occasional long swells of perhaps 10 feet that push us forward, with occasional surfing. The boat is perfectly balanced with zero rudder angle and Jorge only needs a few degrees one way or the other to handle our surfing.

We did 219 NM in the last 24 hours.

We are 819 NM from Fremantle and have come 3820 NM from the Seychelles. At this speed, we will be in Fremantle in four days.

We need to get to Fremantle pretty soon because critical supplies are getting low. We are OK on garlic, coffee and Tabasco sauce, but chocolate is getting critical. We have only two more bars of dark chocolate! And Hannah has claimed one of them for the Valentine's Day cake she is making for tomorrow. Our Twix bars and Kit-Kats are all gone!!

We are still seeing dusky shearwaters, but we seem to have gotten out of range of the albatross. Yesterday we saw a solitary stormy petrel, who seemed a bit out of place 1,000 miles at sea.

Those who know the sea and sea shanties know that the words that sailors actually sang to the tunes were pretty rough and occasionally gross. Most modern shanties seem to be sung by choirs who have never tasted salt water, let alone rum with a dose of lime juice, such as the Mormon Tabernacle Choir or Robert Shaw Chorale. For those who want a taste of the real thing, get a copy of *Rogue's Gallery*, produced by Hal Willner. It's great.

One of my favorite songs is from an album called *Scotland the Real,* where a marvelous singer named Adam McNaughtan sings *a cappella* a song called *Oor Hamlet*, which tells the whole Hamlet story, seemingly in one breath. Well worth it.

Our Yanmar main engine is functioning perfectly now with the salinity probe epoxied into the opening at the bottom of the fuel filter. Whew!

## 14 FEBRUARY 2007

Happy Valentine's Day! We are all thinking of friends and family distant in space but close in our hearts.

We are back on starboard tack, making 8 knots straight for Fremantle, which is 625 NM away—three days at this speed. The wind is from the southwest at 22 knots.

The waves are playing with us a bit, but rarely get to more than 15 feet. We had a cold front pass at about 8:30 this morning—some rain and wind, but not much of a fuss. We jibed with the wind shift from northwest to southwest—opposite from the Northern Hemisphere.

I forget to mention earlier one little indication of the conditions we had last week. In all the photos of someone at the wheel, one can see the old-fashioned Danforth steering compass mounted on the binnacle. During the blow, one wave came over the side, took off the top cap of the compass and kept going right over the side. People used to say that Neptune/Poseidon takes presents from sailors, if not properly gifted. We gave him a nice dollop of Madagascar rum at the start of this leg, but perhaps that wasn't enough. I think that he is wearing our brass compass cap as an earring now.

We have two powerful navigation systems on the boat. Furuno's NavNet2 and MaxSEA 12.5. Japanese and French. Neither country has much of any army any more, so they seem to get their hostilities out through technology. Furuno and MaxSEA get along like two bulls in a boxcar. Last night I got up to find that our principal Furuno system was completely frozen and would not restart and the MaxSEA on my laptop had crashed Windows. It was two boxers who had been going at it until neither could rise. MaxSEA eventually restarted, but was taken offline from the ethernet—"Go to your room!"—but the Furuno multifunction display will have to go to the hospital (French 1; Japanese 0). We have redundant Furuno systems, so Owen and I removed the old primary display and brought in the slave, which had been set up at the helm station. The understudy finally got to come on when

Hannah's Valentine's Day cake.

the Star broke her leg! But, of course, Owen and I had to hack into the code to persuade #2 that it was #1 now. But all is now working well. Hopefully there is a great Furuno dealer in Fremantle.

The "to do" list for Fremantle is up to 25 items. The merchants will be glad to see us.

Hannah made a marvelous chocolate layer cake for Valentine's Day—chocolate with chocolate frosting on top and jam and yogurt inner frosting. Total pig out! It will probably not live to see sunset. We decorated the crew mess with cut-out red and silver hearts. Hannah had Valentine pencils for all of us. Owen burned a CD of all our best love songs. It was perfect, except for being absent from friends and family.

QUOTE OF THE DAY: "You only live once, but if you work it right, once is enough." Joe E. Lewis (1902–1971).

## 15 FEBRUARY 2007

We are headed right for Fremantle at 9.6 knots, with the speed varying from 7.5 to 12.5 knots with gusts and surfing swells. We have made good 800 NM in the last four days and have 430 NM to go to Fremantle. The wind has been from the southwest at 20–25, but we are expecting frontal passage soon when it will switch to northwest 20–25. We are continuing with both main and fore with one reef.

Freo for Saturday night! Hooray!

Supplies are getting low for fresh food, being 2 1/2 weeks out of Mauritius. But we continue to be inventive for our communal noon meal. Today, with the help of the *All Around the World Cookbook* by Sheila Lukins, I made Irish Soda Bread, which came out pretty well. We then had butternut squash soup and a horizontal *pissaladiere*. We have lots of onions for the onion tart, and olives, but sardines instead of anchovies, and the soda bread instead of puff pastry. It was delicious!

Waves at sea are endlessly interesting. The ocean here is a steel grey when it is cloudy, bright sapphire blue when sunny. But not necessarily a nice blue—very hard. White caps out here are totally different than watching a wave break onshore. On shore the froth leads the wave and is the main action and attraction. At sea, a breaking wave can be spectacular—you can see why they are called "white horses"— but immediately as it breaks, the wave leaves it behind. It is as if the wave has places to go, things to do, and isn't interested at all in something frothy and frivolous. Occasionally a wave will peak up near you, and if you are lucky, you see the light through it and it is a bright, light, shiny blue that reminds you of beaches in the tropics. Then it breaks over you and beach thoughts are forgotten as the bright, shiny blue water finds every tiny opening in your foul weather gear and fills your sea boots.

*"At sea, a breaking wave can be spectacular—you can see why they are called "white horses"—but immediately as it breaks, the wave leaves it behind. It is as if the wave has places to go, things to do, and isn't interested at all in something frothy and frivolous."*

## 16 FEBRUARY 2007

We are headed directly for Fremantle at 10 knots (hull speed). The wind is perfect for us, 300 degrees magnetic at 22–30 knots. We have a long swell behind us that occasionally lets us surf up to 16 KNOTS! This is for a 35-ton wooden gaff-rigged schooner!

This morning I noticed that the forepeak gaff topping lift halyard had managed to tie itself up in a knot on the pin rail. It was under quite a bit of pressure and couldn't be loosened because of the way it was tangled. I went to the cockpit and asked Bori and Owen for the Tweaker and the Prusik line, which they handed me from the lockers. As I sorted out the tangle, I though of how specialized language can become on a ship. A Tweaker is a Canadian term for a light block and tackle with a whip rope on either end that can be used for a variety of temporary purposes. Others would call it a Handy Billy, a Purchase, or a Come-along. Dr. Karl Prusik was an Austrian mountaineer and invented a climber's knot that can grab and hold a line under strain, but easily release and slide when the Prusik is released. With a Prusik line and the Tweaker, I was able to take up tension on the halyard enough to release the messy knot it had made on the pin rail.

In the same way, on a gaff sail, there are many round metal pieces sewn into the sail, to take different pieces of line to hold and control the sail. If those round pieces of metal are at the bottom (foot) of the sail, in the corners, they are cringles (tack or clew), if they are in the top, head, corners, they are thimbles (throat or head/peak), if they are along the boom or gaff, they are grommets or eyes (head or luff). Of course, if they at the reef, they are cringles, except in the middle of the sail, where they are points.

*National Lampoon* has a hysterical short audio on their site called "Rigging a Ship" where a man with a thick accent just recites accurate historical ship's parts. It would surely get you a drink on the house if recited in any yacht club bar in the world.

As I write this, we have only 190 NM to go to Fremantle, I am conscious that we have the hard part of the trip ahead of us. Finding our way through the reefs behind Rottnest Island, landing at the Quarantine Dock, making Customs happy, and finding a spot for the night. Much harder than Blue Water sailing!


## 17 FEBRUARY 2007

*Maggie B* docked at the Fremantle Sailing Club at 4:30 in the afternoon. Striped Dolphin escorted us in the last few miles. We cleared Customs, Quarantine and Immigration in about an hour and a half with only the loss of all our remaining fresh provisions.

We did 4545 NM in 24 days from the Seychelles, an average 189 NM per day, 7.9 knots average speed. Top wind speed, 52 knots. Top boat speed 17.4 knots. Fast cruising, just what I asked Nigel for!

Hot showers, restaurant meals, and cold Australian wine next.

Fremantle market.

*"In the old days,*
*if you got into trouble in England,*
*you were shipped to Sydney.*
*If you got into trouble in Sydney,*
*you were shipped to Tasmania*
*(then called Van Diemen's Land).*
*If you got into trouble in Tasmania,*
*they sent you to Port Davey to die."*

## 9

# FREMANTLE TO HOBART

**21 FEBRUARY 2007**

*Maggie B* is at the Fremantle Sailing Club, and they have moved us to the VIP berth right in front of the clubhouse, where we get a constant stream of visitors.

We will be here for at least a week or two. Lots of boat work to do, plus we have to sightsee. We haven't even gotten into Perth yet.

For boat work, the sails are off at a loft getting touched up; we have done lots of sanding for varnishing; the stove gas system was overhauled; the main Furuno box is in the shop to get its circuits tested; the toilet was overhauled (again!); new blocks are on order; new Yanmar fuel filter sensors are coming; parrell beads are being made from jarra wood; a new top for our steering compass is being turned, also from jarra, with an old Australian penny in the top; the bilge is cleaned; interior and exterior paint has been touched up; we replaced some worn halyards and furling lines; etc.

Fremantle is wonderful. The weather is bright and hot, but with a nice sea breeze. It is part of the western desert, so the air is dry, more like Colorado than the humidity of the Seychelles. Freo, as it is called, is strongly Italian in background. Certainly all the restaurants are Italian. The Fisherman's Memorial in town lists all the names of fishermen lost at sea and the names are almost 100% Italian. The local small "quick" supermarket has 20 different kinds of olive oil and 40 different kinds of salami. The big club in the middle of the park is the Italian Club.

We have noticed the number of very tough cars here: the big Land Rovers or Toyotas with four-wheel drive, extra road clearance, roof racks

The Captain giving the tour in Fremantle.

with three spare tires and two jerry cans of fuel, six special lights on the front, two shovels strapped on and big 'roo bar protection for the grill—ready for the worst that the desert roads can dish out.

Hannah has had a continuing saga with the African drum that Willis left on board for her. It has springbok leather and Australian Customs has, after much toing and froing, confiscated it and sent it to Willis in the States because it was illegal to import the skin to Australia.

One Customs issue that made us very nervous was that part of their checklist asked: "What anti-fouling do you have on your bottom and when was it put on?" We were hauled and repainted in the Seychelles in December, but I could not remember the name of the paint and they did not press it. Certainly there has been a change away from the toxic stuff that everyone used to use. I suspect that the paint we used in the Seychelles may now be something that is outlawed in Australia. Could they kick you out or force you to be hauled, scraped and painted? I just didn't know and didn't want to find out.

Later we found that the real story was worse. Australia is concerned that boats arriving might carry some pests that will infect Australian waters. In fact, the bilge water of some of the big freighters did bring in some invasive species. But now there is a proposal to mandate that all arriving boats have to be recently hauled with new anti-fouling applied, then be hauled and cleaned AGAIN within a week of arriving in Australian waters! It seems a little mad, as it won't apply to all the huge container ships that caused the original trouble, so why pick on the little boats? Perhaps because they can, whereas they can't with a Japanese or Korean freighter?

## 26 FEBRUARY 2007

Last night the Cruising Section of the Sailing Club had a barbecue, where the *Maggie B* was the treat. We had perhaps 50 visitors on board. She is looking her best, even after 16,500 miles.

We are still in Fremantle, but working hard and playing only a bit. Yesterday was the Perth Zoo and the day before was two Maritime Museums in Fremantle, plus a tour of a submarine. Today is work—painting, plumbing, sanding, varnishing, sealing, organizing. Tomorrow we work on our sails at the loft, to help speed their return, and enable the Furuno technician to reassemble our system and improve our Furuno vs. MaxSEA contention.

We hope to head off to Hobart next Monday, March 5th. Depending on how we go, it is about 2,000 miles. We believe that we will have to do our usual trick of heading south until we get cold, and then turn left until we run into land. This time we will have to go a bit further south to 43 degrees, 40 minutes, the latitude of Whale Head on the southern side of Tasmania, well into the Roaring Forties.

We have done a lot of work in Fremantle. Getting the three sails off, repaired and back on again was a huge job. Rips, wears, and tears were fixed up plus five battens replaced and sewn into their pockets—they won't be able to get out now! Sailmakers Western Australia did a great job and provided lots of good advice. We just about lived at Wilson Marine, a chandlery, getting some new Australian blocks from them, which we hope will last better than the Lewmars. The Chart and Map Shop is one of those stores I shouldn't be allowed into. Every sailing and adventure book, map, chart or poster one could imagine. John Mason of Creations Wood Gallery made our lovely compass piece. We polish the kangaroo penny daily. Ian Duperouzel at

Our new compass cap out of jarra wood with an Australian penny.

Yanmar Diesel had everything we needed, or found it, if it wasn't already in stock. Taylor Marine took in our Furuno gear, tested everything, and reinstalled it so that it now works fine. Finally, Yacht Grot supplied us with lots of new rope so that all our running gear can be wear-free. While they had just what we needed, at a fair price, the colors are such that we have had to learn new names—"Haul on the fuchsia reefing line!"

All four of us found Fremantle such a nice place that we could imagine living here.

We have developed a few impressions of Australia, or at least Fremantle: 1) this is just about as car oriented as America; 2) obesity is almost as endemic as in the States, a big change from the poorer countries we have recently seen; 3) lots of dogs; 4) Fremantle's weather is very dry, so lots of great outside restaurants; 5) very friendly and open, at least superficially; 6) huge beer focus, even though this is one of the top wine producing areas; 7) seems egalitarian—while there are a few BMWs and an occasional Rolls—it generally appears to be a very level society, with similar dress and one class of service; 8) no apparent incoming "underclass" who trim the lawns, work as dishwashers, street sweepers, though immigration is a hot political issue; and 9) Western Australia is the end of their supply chain—many say WA means "Wait Awhile" not Western Australia.

The Fremantle Sailing Club is by far the best Yacht Club we have been to. Great showers! Hannah and Bori took so many hot showers that they should be clean through the end of April. Free wireless internet in the bar, which has 12 different beers on tap—very good food in the restaurant. Lovely people. We were totally impressed by one of the big varnished boards up on the wall which has a listing of all the club members who had sailed around the world. Sixteen of them!

*"Each has a one-way valve. That valve, after a year and 16,500 miles and a bit of saltwater corrosion, can change from a one-way valve to a no-way valve."*

We managed to embarrass ourselves when we went to fill up on diesel at the Club. We have high-tech vents air/fuel separators on each of the fuel tanks. Each has a one-way valve. That valve, after a year and 16,500 miles and a bit of saltwater corrosion, can change from a one-way valve to a no-way valve. If that happens, and you fill your tank fairly fast, your diesel filler becomes like the man in the restaurant in Monty Python's *The Meaning of Life* after "one last wafer-thin mint." Not nice for anybody around to have it burp back a half gallon of diesel on the deck and into the water. Of course, the air/fuel separator, once found and disassembled, fills its compartment— the Captain's closet—with a fine mist of diesel. Sigh. But all fixed now.

We also found and fixed a problem we didn't know we had. Our boom is carbon fiber and hollow. The main outhaul line was not lead straight down the boom, but rather over and under some cross-members hidden in the middle. So as the sail worked, the Spectra line sawed into the cross members and the cross members sawed into the Spectra line. The line is now reversed and cleared with no great damage to the boom.

## 5 MARCH 2007

*Maggie B* is at sea again. We left the charming Fremantle Sailing Club at about 4:30 on March 5th, underway for Tasmania.

We hope to be in Hobart for the start of their bi-annual "Ten Days on the Island" Festival, which starts March 22.

If we have the time, we hope to explore the wild southwest coast of Tasmania, especially a place called Port Davey. Not only are there no buildings, there are no roads. It takes six days to walk in from the nearest trailhead. It is supposed to be lovely, even though the history is hard. In the old days, if you got into trouble in England, you were shipped to Sydney. If you got into trouble in Sydney, you were shipped to Tasmania (then called Van Diemen's Land). If you got into trouble in Tasmania, they sent you to Port Davey to die.

## 6 MARCH 2007

We are making 4.4 knots on a heading of 160, as the southeasterly is dying out, getting ready for the land breeze. We are off the Marguerite River, and will pass the corner of southwest Australia this afternoon. We have come 138 NM from Fremantle in the last 20 hours, and have 1563 NM to go to Tasmania.

Last night at 2 a.m. we were under full sail, close hauled and had a medium-sized ship approach us from our port side at 15 knots. They didn't reply to VHF calls nor seem to notice us in any way. Both eyeball and computer said that we were going to get very close, so even though we had right of way, we tacked away, which allowed the ship to pass safely less than a mile from us.

We have great weather conditions now, but a front with a fair bit of power is headed our way towards the end of the week, which should make our life in the Great Australian Bight interesting. Not sure yet how we'll play the pressure, but we'll take it carefully and respectfully.

Owen made a great Fritatta for breakfast with a pile of our fresh veggies. Perfect way to start out, for those few of us who were interested in solid food.

## 7 MARCH 2007

The skies are clear and the temperature is perfect for t-shirt and shorts, though the bright sun can burn quickly. We had a nice lunch in the cockpit: shrimp in garlic and a big mixed salad with fresh avocado and tomatoes. We are cleaning the Fremantle

## HOBART, TASMANIA

Hobart was my favorite port. Big enough to have movie theaters and two good ship fitters, small enough that they quickly knew how you liked your coffee in the coffee house. Safe from the weather, natives very friendly, not too expensive, a happy drinking culture, and great wild sailing.

Tasmanian Memorial.

All of Tasmania is about a half a million people, half of which reside in the Hobart area. It was founded by the English as a penal colony in 1804. After the American Revolution, Australia became the primary destination for transportation of convicts from Great Britain. If you got in trouble in mainland Australia, you were sent to Hobart in what was then called Van Dieman's Land. If you got in trouble in Hobart, you were sent to the southwest side, Port Davic, where you died.

Van Dieman's Land was rebranded as Tasmania and the settlers turned to making it a beautiful, successful island. Fully 45% of the island is dedicated to nature reserves of one sort or another. The D'Entrecasteaux Channel coming into Hobart is as beautiful as anywhere I have seen, full of pear and apple orchards and towns with names like Snug and Flowerpot.

In the 1950's to the 1970's, the farming and mining industries weakened and land and housing prices fell. This provided good, inexpensive housing and land for Australia's new hippie population, who moved to Tasmania to invigorate the culture at every level.

Salamanca Place is a lovely precinct of 19th Century sandstone buildings, only a few short blocks from our lovely dockage at the Elizabeth Street Pier. A market is held there every Saturday, full of hundreds of local vendors and buskers. A grandmother and her friend sell sweaters where they have raised the sheep, sheared them, carded the wool, spun the yarn and knit the sweaters. Nearby there is a family of ten – mother, father and many sizes of kids, all with different instruments, singing and playing for donations.

Errol Flynn and Mary, The Crown Princess of Denmark, were both born in Tasmania. We found that the Tasmanians we met were fully as handsome, vivacious and interesting as those two stars.

We sang and played and fixed the boat, enjoyed the great restaurants, saw plays, heard marvelous bands in hot spots, and went sightseeing. I would go back and stay in a heartbeat.

dirt off and finishing all the thousand little rigging jobs.

Books we are reading: Hannah is reading *Pride and Prejudice,* Bori: *The Soul in Tibet*; Owen: a Fremantle Historical Society publication called *The Globalization of Containerization*; and Frank: *Mayflower–Courage, Community and War.*

The moon is three days after full and gives us a beautiful moonrise just as Venus is setting in the west. Jupiter is climbing into Scorpio and gives the midnight watch a perfect steering star.

Being back at sea is great on our feet. We are barefoot most of the time on board and our feet spread out somewhat. Getting squished back into shoes ashore (Hannah even has high heels!) is, literally, a pain.

We have been puzzling over the mystery of what happens to the big ships during the day. At night, they seem to be all around us—last night perhaps a dozen within ten miles. During the day, we keep just as good a watch but there are no ships. Perhaps they hide under water during the day like in *Pirates of the Caribbean II*?

We are very focused on a front that is developing to the west of us. We are just beginning to see the barometer fall and some faint high clouds. The GRIB files call for winds up to 55 knots, developing once it is past us as the front concentrates its low in the middle of the Bight. We will stay clear of that area, probably by running off to the south.

## 8 MARCH 2007

We are headed 140 degrees at 6 knots. The wind has come around to the southwest at 14 knots. It is overcast with some breaks to the west. The barometer is steady at 1007 mb.

We've had the first front come through, with the windshift from north to southwest. We have perfect sailing conditions for Tasmania, with a fresh south-southwest breeze. But we have a problem. This nice little front that just passed becomes something nasty by the time it wraps itself up a bit in the middle of the Bight. Winds of 50 knots with higher gusts! Yikes!! Our job right now is a tough one for *Maggie B*—go slow and don't overrun the front as it slows down. So we've double reefed the main and will double reef the fore by sunset, but we are still going over eight knots.

This storm is a bit unusual in that there is less wind to the south. Also the Bight is best known for light or no winds, though the Bass Straights at the Eastern end has a nasty reputation. We'll keep a careful eye out.

Between our love for Fremantle and our attraction to Tasmania, we have

*"But we have a problem. This nice little front that just passed becomes something nasty by the time it wraps itself up a bit in the middle of the Bight. Winds of 50 knots with higher gusts! Yikes!!"*

bypassed much of Australia's southwest and southern coast. Some of the names that we have missed are fascinating: Quindabelup, Mooringa, Moulyinning, Jerramungup, Warrawoona, and Ivy Tank Motel. Less interesting for sailors is: Windy Harbor and Foul Bay.

## 9 MARCH 2007

We are headed straight for Davey Sound in southwest Tasmania, 110 degrees magnetic at 1136 NM. We have come 642 NM since Fremantle. We are doing 8.5 knots with the wind at 180 at 25 knots. The seas are lumpy, with fair wave chop and swells from both northeast and southeast. The sky is overcast with promise of more showers. The barometer is continuing to drop and is at 1002 mb. We have the full jib up, the foresail down and furled and the main with two reefs. The boat is comfortable and dry—at least below decks!

QUOTE FROM THE FUTURE: One of the crew with his/her granddaughter: "Grandfather (grandmother), how windy was it when you first crossed the Southern Ocean to come to Tasmania?" Answer: "Aaaarggg, Maggie, it was so windy that there were whitecaps in me cocoa!"

We are learning Aussie Talk. Some of it rather resembles English, though we do not want to be associated with any Pommie Bastard sneering about Territorials. My favorite is "Good Onya" which is "good for you," or "well done!" The everyday greeting is: "How ya gong," as in "How are you going." A basic cup of coffee with milk is a "flat white." "Bugs" on the menu of a top restaurant are medium-sized crayfish. So much to learn!

I realize that some of these reports have made it sound as if the systems on *Maggie B* are a basket case. Certainly we have had things to fix. But I wanted to take the time to highlight the systems that have worked great for the last year and 17,500 miles. The first that comes to mind is the Onan diesel generator. It ate one impeller a bit early, but it spat back all the pieces and the change was easy and it shut itself down as soon as it noticed the problem. It has worked 642 hours for us so far with essentially no maintenance other than changing oil. Another is the Spectra Watermaker. It has produced 1800 gallons of fresh water for us with barely a hiccup. Bravo!

We are driving for Tasmania with a careful eye on one low ahead of us. It is supposed to exit southeasterly fairly fast, so we should have an easy time after it. Perhaps six days to Davey Sound.


## 10 MARCH 2007

We are in a proper southwesterly Southern Ocean gale. It is more wind and weather than predicted and we are getting a bit thrashed. At noon the wind was at 220 degrees at 30 knots, but during the night it was sustained 40 knots with higher gusts. The barometer is now up to 1008 mb, from a low of 999 last night. The seas have made up quite a bit and are generally about 20 feet, with occasional higher. These Southern Ocean waves seem to have more tricks than their more northern colleagues. We are getting water into the boat and into our foul weather gear in all sorts of new places. We are reefed down, with the main as small as it gets, the fore furled up and the jib partially rolled up.

*Maggie B* is handling it well, showing a few extra moves as the waves and swells push her around.

*"We have been used to big waves, but here in the Great Australian Bight, they seem to build up fast and come down on you from steep peaks."*

We have the usual sort of heavy weather boat issues. Every drop of water or gunk in the fuel tanks has headed straight for the Yanmar main engine and the Onan Genset. But all have been heroically filtered out by our twin RCI vortex fuel purifiers. These little gems work perfectly, clearing out water and debris without the use of filter media, so that when its insistent alarm goes off, all you have to do is drain it and get going again. No need for new filters! We had to drain it seven or eight times since midnight, as well as draining the low point in each fuel tank. We seem to be OK now, with the Yanmar purring along, charging the batteries, heating hot water for showers and circulating warm air through heat registers in the cabin to dry things out.

We got a little salt water of unknown origin in the mid-section and a fair amount in the engine compartment. Both our mid- and engine room bilge pumps are inoperative. We manually pumped out the mid-section and ran our BIG pump (100 gal/minute) to clear out the engine room. We also have another portable bilge pump that can be used anywhere.

We were appalled to see all the water in the engine room. This was a big deal. On a boat you have to be sure to defend your engine room from flooding more than any other part of the boat. No engine or generator can mean: no hope. We got the water out and got both the engine and generator going, but we had to search and solve what was wrong.

We fixed the bilge pump, which was inoperative because the float-switch cover had come off, which meant it would not work when it was underwater, nor when its master switch was on. But the real puzzle was how the water got in. I guessed that it was through the engine blower outlets. We puzzled and puzzled, pulling everything out of lockers and crawling around to look for hidden openings. In the end the answer was painful. We have a big 100-gallons per minute emergency pump that can double as a fire hose or to pump out a nearby boat. The deck fittings are two inches across and can have a variety of hoses that can snap on, ready for any emergency. The two deck fittings also worked to drain all the cockpit water right into the engine room when the cockpit partially filled while we were on starboard tack. They are now closed off.

We were in pretty big water and a fair blow and perhaps I had too much sail up. We have been used to big waves, but here in the Great Australian Bight, they seem to build up fast and come down on you from steep peaks. We were making good time towards Tasmania and probably should have reefed down earlier than we did. Water was coming into the cabin through the front deckhouse breather, maybe a pint or quart a wave, in spite of the canvas cover.

Today we had another first! The sat phone rang—our first incoming call ever! I picked it up and there was my son, Alden, in Chicago. While thrilled to hear from him, I was perhaps a bit short: "What's up? We're getting a bit thrashed here." He and I had been emailing about sat phones and I thought he was testing the link. Alden says, "I know you're getting thrashed, I just had a call from the Australian Coast Guard!" Captain/Dad: Speechless. Alden: "Your Emergency Locator went off for a second and only gave your ID, but no location, they looked you up and called the house." Captain/Dad: Speechless. Alden: "What's your position and are you OK, I have to call them back." I replied that we were OK and gave the Lat/Long and got the Australian's phone number to check in.

We have our high-tech EPIRB locator in our liferaft and other rescue gear. The EPIRB gives out our unique identifier and can, within 30 seconds, give our position from GPS, accurate to within 100 feet, if activated. The unit I have is sealed, watertight and NOT automatically activated when in the water. You have to lift a cover and throw a switch. Then everyone on the planet knows you are in trouble. Somehow a lot of water got in the compartment and jostled the EPIRB just enough that it let out a tiny message, and that was enough to alert the world. Reassuring, somewhat. The Australian Coast Guard guy, who called us just after Alden, was very understanding.

We had been thinking of exploring the wild southwest coast of Tasmania before going the last 80–100 miles to Hobart. Right now we are more eager to meet in a cozy pub in Hobart. Actually, we are up for meeting in a cozy pub anywhere.

But *Maggie B* is handling all this with total class. The sails are perfect, the hull is sound, the motion is generally easy, the autopilot is doing an excellent job of steering and…all is well.

Sea boots drying in the cabin blower.

A meeting of the Chocoholics Anonymous.

## 11 MARCH 2007

We are out of the bad weather, shaking ourselves off like wet dogs, headed directly for Tasmania at 8 knots under all plain sail. The wind is from the south-southwest at 12–15 knots. We have come 1068 NM from Fremantle and have 716 to go to the corner of Tasmania.

The skies have mostly cleared and we have carpets, towels, boots, and socks hung out to dry. We are running the Yanmar to keep it healthy, but also to circulate some heat in the cabin and make hot water for showers. We had lunch on deck for the first time in a while. Hannah made hamburgers with a mushroom, onion, olive and corn hot chutney dressing. We had fresh steamed celery and cauliflower. Hannah found a hundred tiny green worms in the cauliflower when preparing the dish and threw them all overboard. It is awful seeing them wiggling their way after us, squeaking for help, chased by every bird and fish in the ocean.

As you know by now, chocolate is a regular issue on board. One of Fremantle's many charms is the Chocolate Factory, which is two blocks from where we were docked at the Fremantle Sailing Club. We stocked up there. We also have received lots of chocolate bars in the mail. Today, at lunch, we laid out all our chocolate, just for quality control and to inventory. We had: Mango Crush, Dark Chocolate with

Rosemary, Macadamia Nut Dark Chocolate medallions, Hazelnut medallions, Chili Chocolate, Raspberries in Dark Chocolate, Ginger crystallized in Dark Chocolate, 55% Dark Chocolate, Lavender Dark Chocolate, Cadbury Thins milk chocolate, Mint Organic Chocolate, Lavender Organic chocolate, Dark Chocolate Ginger, and Dark Chocolate coated plums. So much chocolate, so little time....

We are slowing down a bit, only 197 NM yesterday. There is a new high filling in behind us, which will position fairly far south, so we may have light, unfavorable, or no wind tomorrow. We are heading south of the rhumb line to minimize our adverse winds.

## 12 MARCH 2007

We are motoring with only the main up to help stabilize us. The wind is 110 degrees magnetic at 7–8 knots and there is a fair sea running, so no chance of sailing, even if the wind wasn't right in our face on our course to Tasmania.

We have tentatively decided to call the Yanmar engine Nane, after the great sea dog we met in Mauritius. Of course, we will seek Didier and Celine's permission. Nane is good in water, hardworking, loyal and only needs a bit of care and feeding. Just like a good engine? The inspiration came to Owen when he was in the engine compartment after we pumped out all the water after the storm. When I started up the engine, it shook the water off onto him like a wet dog.

We seem to have finally gotten all the water out of our fuel tanks. It must have forced its way into the tanks during the storm, possibly through the deck vents. Maybe those damned one-way valves that acted up in Fremantle have gone to two-way valves! Our latest addition to our planned boat work in Hobart is that our mainsail boom outhaul pulley is delaminating from the inside of the boom end. We have rigged a strop to decrease the chance of a major failure.

We haven't decided what to do when we arrive at the southwest corner of Tasmania in about three days—whether to explore the wild area of Davey Straight or to continue the 100 NM to Hobart and find a good spot on the wharf. We'll take a vote, depending on wind, weather, and attitude, and then after the vote, the Captain will decide.

Lunch was Australian steaks with baked potatoes, steamed cauliflower and peas, with a nice lettuce and tomato salad, and King Island cheddar cheese. South African Shiraz washed it down perfectly.

## 13 MARCH 2007

We are motoring towards Tasmania in essentially no wind as the latest high is right over us. We should have some wind from the north tomorrow as the high moves east past us. It is overcast but with good visibility, there is a long swell from the southwest but no waves or chop.

One of our more interesting recent failures is with our Danforth steering compass. It locks up from time to time and is no longer dependable. It appears as if the part below the card has come loose in some fashion. This comes as quite a surprise as one would think that it would be about the last thing on the boat to fail. We'll have to drink the alcohol in it and rely on the GPS.

Today was rather boring. If you are sailing, you are always working to optimize all the elements, to take advantage of the free energy. Motoring, you put the autopilot on and rumble along.

We celebrated the quiet day by first cleaning the boat and then having a movie party. After lunch (ginger and garlic shrimp with rice and salad with basil vinaigrette dressing), we set out a plate of apples, cheeses and chocolate, strapped the computer to the bulkhead, and watched *My Fair Lady*. The nice addition was that we were able to connect the computer to the Bose sound system, so it was almost Surround Sound. Yo-Ho for the Life of the Sailor!


## 14 MARCH 2007

We are motorsailing at 7.1 knots, headed due east for the southern tip of Tasmania. The wind is beginning to fill in from the north as the high continues its way east. It is a surprise for all of us to be essentially becalmed in the Roaring Forties—not that we want another gale!

We have come 1558 NM from Fremantle and have about 326 to go to Hobart.

We should see Tasmania about dusk tomorrow. Our thoughts are to continue to Hobart, arriving perhaps before noon on the 16th. A friend from Chicago, Jim Lasko, is running the opening night show for the Tasmania Festival, and we hope to help him however we can.

We have regular albatrosses on patrol around us. We are pretty sure that one is young black-browed and another is a yellow-nosed albatross. Our bird guide tells us to differentiate between the Northern and Southern Black-browed by the color of the eye's iris. Good luck with that!

The D'Entrecasteaux Channel, Tasmania.

## 15 MARCH 2007

Our wind is petering out and it is overcast and raining lightly. I guess that it has to rain a lot to make the rain forest. The computer says we will arrive at about noon tomorrow, Hobart summer time, which is +11 from Greenwich.

We will pass Whale Head, which is the southeast cape of Tasmania at about dawn tomorrow. Being daylight, we have the confidence to go inside on our way to Hobart, taking the D'Entrecasteaux Channel, which runs between Tasmania and the Bruny Islands. It is about 40 miles long and less than a mile wide in some places. One cove is described as "the prettiest anchorage in the Southern Hemisphere." We have seen some pretty ones, so it will be interesting to compare.

This southeast part of Tasmania is the apple and berry growing part of the country. They grow almost 400 different kinds of apples. As it is just coming into fall here, perhaps we could get jobs as pickers?

Commanders' Weather sent a quick note to say that things should be quiet for the next 24–36 hours. They say that they had to route Ellen MacArthur, on her non-stop solo around the world sailing record attempt, south to 54-55 South to get clear of a high in the Great Australian Bight. Glad we're not down there where she is!

We passed Whale Head about midnight. Off to the south were a bunch of squid boats with huge lights to attract the prey. It looked like a big town where there was only deep water on the charts.

## 16 MARCH 2007

The Schooner *Maggie B* is safely docked in Hobart, Tasmania, at Elizabeth Street Pier. The city looks marvelous and is sure to be our favorite spot, so far.

The Captain on watch, coming into Hobart.

*Maggie B* docked at the Elizabeth Street pier, Hobart.

*"This is such a wonderful place we all might desert ship ... I may have to use our famous Nova Scotia ice mallet to keep some of the crew from hanging onto the pier to prevent our departure."*

# 10

# HOBART TO WELLINGTON

## 23 MARCH 2007

*Maggie B* continues happily tied up at Elizabeth Street Pier in Hobart. Tonight is *Dream Masons*, the opening show for the Ten Days on the Island Festival, run by my Chicago friend. We are proud that Hannah and Bori have parts, as theatrical unrollers of the series of banners that frame each scene. Owen and Frank have been working hard as riggers, helping finish last minute details.

We haven't done much boat work as our attention is on *Dream Masons*. Nevertheless, we have replaced two bilge pumps, drained and refilled the hydraulic steering system, ordered new cockpit cushions, ordered new paper charts for the South Pacific, got electronic charts for the same region, replaced some broken electronic systems, etc.

We are all marvelously happy to be in such a great town as Hobart. A gem. Some observations: less obesity than in Fremantle—lots of bush walkers; very boatie/yachtie, a high proportion of people know what they are doing on the water and appreciate wooden boats; in respects to Fremantle, more people here have kids and fewer have dogs; warm days, cool nights equals perfect weather; very artsy, hippie, down-to-earth, organic; a great outdoors cafe society where in a block you can get a perfect Guinness and a perfect macchiato, with excellent fresh organic food everywhere. In other towns we ended up quickly with a few favorite restaurants and pubs, here we still have a dozen of each and new ones continue to be discovered.

The Salamanca Saturday market must be experienced. Yes, there may be some silly wooden toys and strange t-shirts, but mostly it is

Street buskers, Salamanca market, Hobart.

marvelous people who tend sheep, card, spin and knit during the week and sell lovely hats and sweaters each Saturday. We are happy to be here this time of year as there are many growers with their best apples, raspberries or flowers. There are bands and buskers on every corner. We all are quite taken with it.

## 2 APRIL 2007

We had a real scare today. I was wandering down the dock to get a parking permit for our rental car when two friends came running down towards *Maggie B* with the dread word "tsunami" on their lips. A major earthquake had sparked all sorts of alarms along Eastern Australia, and Queensland in the north was expecting a surge. Hobart is much further south and well protected, but we were untied and heading out to sea in less than sixty seconds. The time of expected tsunami arrival came and went with calm seas. We returned to our same spot on the pier, but the rental car was issued a parking ticket.

Later I wrote the Hobart Municipal government about the circumstances and the parking ticket was rescinded. A cute municipal employee said that my excuse letter had won first prize for originality from the Department!

One day we watched a little proa get underway for the 1200 NM trip to New Zealand. We had met the crew of two young men, and are appalled at their planned trip. The Australian Coast Guard is appalled also, as the last people who tried the trip in a small traditional boat disappeared at sea. Our acquaintances were given a formal warning from the Coast Guard, and told that if a rescue should become necessary, that they, or their families, will bear all costs. These young men wisely gave up after two days at sea.

Australians take Easter seriously, though not necessarily religiously. They get Good Friday off from work, plus Easter Monday AND Easter Tuesday. We may head out to find little coves, but we hear there will be a series of great bands coming to clubs in town. Decisions, decisions.

Over the weekend I drove up to Launceston, on the north side of Tasmania. Going up on the main highway I was appalled to see how degraded the countryside was, with most of the trees cut down and the pastures "sheeped," which takes up everything else. Coming back I took a longer scenic road through a lake district that was lovely. I'm glad that I wasn't on the road at night, though, because the amount of roadkill was horrific, with the carrion crows seeming to be the big winners. There was easily one recent kill every kilometer. Even though it was daytime, I had two wallabies make a fair effort to see if they could dive under my car.

## 13 APRIL 2007

This is such a wonderful place we all might desert ship, just like the stories of the ships that got to San Francisco in 1849, and all, from Captain to Cabin Boy, took off for the gold fields. But we are planning to get underway this Monday. I may have to use our famous Nova Scotia ice mallet to keep some of the crew from hanging onto the pier to prevent our departure.

What have we been doing? *Dream Masons* was a marvelous way to start. Since then we have driven all over the island, seeing beautiful spots and horribly degraded areas. We have camped out on the Bruni Peninsula, we have sailed on the brigantine *Windward Bound*, we have rowed single sculls, we have been up Mount Wellington, gone to Opera, ballet, plays and movies, been to cabaret shows and many music sets, swam in the ocean, toured wineries and distilleries, seen where the convicts were kept, enjoyed wonderful food, went out sailing on the *Maggie B* with friends and we kept making new friends.

A world's worth of charts for the Furuno.

The weather has been perfect, like the fall in Maine: cool at night (two blankets!) and t-shirts during the day.

There has been lots of boat work. When we arrived in Hobart we had a list of 21 "to do's" and as we went over the boat it grew to 34 items. We are now down to seven items and the *Maggie B* is stronger, safer and more efficient than ever.

On the boat, we have fixed and replaced 2 bilge pumps and re-routed the drain lines so, hopefully, they don't ever fill up the bilges by draining IN instead of OUT. We have changed and cleaned all 7 of our fuel and water filters, we have again rebuilt the wash-down pump, we have replaced our deck cushions, we have rebuilt our boom outhaul sheave, we have replaced several shackles which were worn, we have worked out a method to drain the shower when we are on the starboard tack, we got new electronic and paper charts that covers from here to Chile, and we have gone over the rigging top to bottom. New hose pieces to extend our bilge systems seem to be cleverly designed to be just a tiny bit too small or too big to fit together. Must be a metric/English fight.

We discovered "dip." Basically, a compass that is perfect in Nova Scotia doesn't work in Tasmania. The magnetic fields are different. Big ships have vertical magnets that are flipped for the northern or southern hemisphere. Not so little ships. Our compass can be taken apart and rebalanced for the southern hemisphere, but then it wouldn't work when we go back north. I have purchased a second "southern" one that will be cheaper that getting our current one fixed twice.

We are thinking of going around to Port Davey on the southwest coast of Tasmania. But we are watching a very intense low—970 mb!—that is working its way here. We might just end have to stay a little longer. No hardship!

*Maggie B* anchored in Port Davey, Tasmania.

### 17 APRIL 2007

We left Hobart at last, but just for a side, backtracking trip to Port Davey, which had so fascinated us on the trip around from Fremantle.

We sailed and motored last night, passing through the lovely D'Entrecasteaux Channel. It is only about 100 miles around, but through some complex water. We were passed from lighthouse to lighthouse like a partner being passed from hand to hand in a contra dance. We saw some incredible phosphorescence where the creatures were joined together in rectangular blocks the size of a large loaf of bread. In some places there were perhaps 100–200 "blocks" glowing well before being stimulated by our passage.

The entrance to Port Davey is invisible from the sea and guarded by some very scary broken tooth-like islands. Once inside there is every sort of cove and harbor. Some are just big enough to anchor across with bow and stern to trees, others have room for a fleet. Some places have romantic names like Black Swan Island; others less so, like Starvation Cove. There is no development, no roads, no buildings and only one very rough path. Where we are anchored in Swan Cove of Bathurst Harbor, we can see ten miles in most every direction, and there is not a single light or dwelling. The water is the color of strong tea from the tannin in the run-off. We went swimming when we arrived: 16C or 63F, brisk!

We rowed ashore in the *Reep* and climbed a small hill along the shore, which is unnamed. We christened it "Mount Maggie."

Matthew Flinders, the first to circumnavigate Tasmania, described the Southwest: "The mountains are the most dismal that can be imagined. The eye ranges over these peaks with astonishment and horror." We find it much nicer. The landscape reminds us of wilder parts of Scotland or Newfoundland.

Onboard we are six. The four regular crew, Hannah, Bori and Owen, plus the Captain. Joining us as crew is Theresa Chapman, a 24-year-old Australian. Along for the fun of the trip is Claus Heinrich, a 22-year-old German friend of Theresa's, and now of us all.

Today is Hannah's birthday. Owen baked her a chocolate cake with chocolate icing and sparkles.


## 18 APRIL 2007

We got started early this morning as a 30-knot blow came on us from the one direction where we were exposed and the anchor started to drag in the soft mud. We were being blown ashore! We hustled to get the anchor up and motored in moderate rain to a more protected spot. We had a nice hike ashore after the rain mostly cleared.

Now we are tied up to the bank of Melaleuca Inlet. We are about two miles up stream from anything resembling open water. *Maggie B* is as far inland as she has ever been, and may ever be. Coming up this inlet was a bit anxious-making as the passage was often narrower than we are long, though we did carry more than 10 feet under our keel most all the way. We ran aground once, but fortunately the bottom is very soft mud and we just plowed through.

At the end of the inlet there are a few posts along the bank, called, rather grandly, King's Landing, and—to our surprise—we found another sailboat already there. We had to put our nose into the bank on one side to spin her around, and I never worked out a proper plan. The wind was blowing one-way and current pushing the other. We made a complete thrash of it, to my great embarrassment. My lame excuse to the skipper of the other boat was "we're more used to Blue Water...." His wife looked at us with horror.

We saw two marvelous birds today. First was a big flock of black swans. While all black when they are on the water, they show lots of white on their wings when they fly. We had a big flock fly near us this morning. I had always thought that black swans were just a convention from the ballet *Swan Lake*.... The other delight was a wedge-tailed eagle, which looked quite surprised and irritated as we squeezed our way into the Melaleuca Inlet.

A Black Swan in Port Davey, Tasmania.

Entering the Melaleuca Inlet, Port Davey.

We had movie night last night, watching *South Pacific*. We choose movies from our collection of about 50 by pulling numbers 1 to 6 out of a hat. The person who gets the 6 pulls the six movies he/she would most like to watch, "5" reduces the number to 5 by returning one, etc. until "1" chooses between the two finalists.

The trip up this narrow inlet was made much easier by our Probe forward-looking sonar, from Interphase. It does a good job of imaging what is coming, though it can only look ahead four to five times whatever depth you are in (50 feet ahead if you are in 10 feet of water), but still that is a lot better than waiting until you hit something.

## 19 APRIL 2007

Rainy day today. We are happy for Tasmania, which has been dry. The scene on *Maggie B* was very domestic: Hannah sewed up her trousers and then made tea muffins; Bori wrote in her journal; Claus studied the walking map to decide on hikes he is going to take; Owen worked on our SSB radio to tease weather reports out of the air; Theresa stitched a sheath for her new marlinspike; and Frank wrote postcards.

When Hannah's muffins were done, we had tea and ate them with jam and butter while we watched the excellent video: *The Last Cape Horners*. Every sailor should see it.

We then motored most of the way out of Davey Sound to Wombat Cove, near the mouth. It is a tight anchorage and well protected from the northwest and westerlies, which we expect tonight. After some boat cleaning chores, most of us plan to go ashore for a hike, possibly up the nearby Mt. Misery (catchy name!).

## 20 APRIL 2007

Last night in Wombat Cove, Port Davey, Tasmania was marvelous. It was clear at night, with no moon. Since it was dead still, all the thousands of stars overhead could be seen reflected in the dark water.

After dinner, we read poetry to one another for perhaps two hours (or two bottles of Tasmanian Pinot Noir). We found that we had 15 books of poetry on board. Something for everyone! I read Tennyson's *Ulysses*: "'T'is not too late to seek a newer world. Push off and sitting well in order smite the sounding furrows…."

We set out for Hobart at 6 a.m., a little before sunrise. For the first part of the route we had a good northwester, but it died out at about 1 p.m. and it looks as if we will have to motor the rest of the way in.

Theresa in Wombat Cove, Port Davey.

Today coming around, we had two seals playing around us for 10 minutes, jumping most of the way out of water. Perhaps they were hunting fish that our passage had stirred up, or perhaps they were just doing it for the fun of it.

I have continued to have some issues with the Lewmar blocks we have on board: six have broken! I got a nice letter from the Lewmar Product Manager for Blocks, concerned about my troubles, or perhaps concerned about my blistering negative reports. I think that perhaps Nigel Irens, our boat designer, burned his program outside their booth at the Paris Boat Show as a protest. In any case, I wrote the Product Manager a detailed report on our problems and he supposedly is having their research group do some tests on my specific areas of concern, to improve their next generation of blocks. So perhaps some good will come of our problems.

On our return from Port Davey we saw one of the most marvelous sights I have ever experienced. As we came in to Storm Bay approaching Hobart, it was completely dark and the water was full of phosphorescence. Four or five dolphins joined us. As the dolphin rode our bow wave it seemed as if they were illuminated from inside and when they jumped or came up to breathe, it was like fireworks going off.

Maatsuker lighthouse behind offshore dangers, Tasmania.

## 23 APRIL 2007

*Maggie B* is back at Elizabeth Street Pier in Hobart, Tasmania. We are sorry to lose Claus to the Overland Trail. He left this morning in a discouraging drizzle.

Our main compass now is a handsome Plath that is set up for southern latitudes. We will store away the Northern Hemisphere Danforth compass until we once again cross the Line.

While we are ready, more of less, to leave Hobart and head for New Zealand, the weather isn't ready for us. A high has settled in to the south of us, which is spinning off strong easterlies. Not good for the route east to Nelson, NZ. However, there is a nice tight low coming that should bring big northwesterly winds, so we'll wait the 3–5 days, with no hardship in Hobart, for the wind to shift.

We're still learning. Customs duties and VAT/GST (Value Added Tax and Goods and Services Tax) taxes can add up to real money. Many countries, including Australia, have mechanisms for "Boats in Transit" to avoid or recoup those taxes, but just try to actually make it happen! Australian GST is 11%. In theory, it is refundable when you leave, but the rules make it essentially impossible. First you have to sign into a "scheme" (yes, that's what they call it) that, besides paperwork, requires you to pay

$38 for each crewmember. That $190 for us would mean that we would have to have spent more than $1727 before we would save any money. But on goods, not services. Goods and services mixed in a bill? Sorry, not deductible. Then if it is just goods, you must be able to prove it is being exported. Paint, painted on already? Sorry, can't tell. Rope made up into halyards? Sorry. Did you know it also has to be exported within 30 days of purchase? Sorry. And you don't get 100% of what you spent due to unspecified charges. I talked to three Customs officers and a "question line" at the Capitol, and got the impression that it had never, ever, actually been refunded.

Supposedly New Zealand is sufficiently enlightened that when you arrive you can get a certificate that, if presented to a supplier, can enable you to avoid VAT/GST. We'll see.

## 28 APRIL 2007

The route across the Tasman Sea, between Tasmania and New Zealand, is famous for big weather. As we were preparing to set off, we got the following complex email from Commanders' Weather:

SUMMARY

1) A bit of a knee-knocker, but it may be doable—Hobart to Nelson. Certainly nothing better over the next 6-10 days.

2) Dual lows, one south of Melbourne and the other in the Tasman Sea will combine into a large gale near 39-40S/156-157E by 00UTC Monday. This low will move slowly ENE and thru the Cook Strait on Thursday, May 3rd.

3) A little concerned about the S-SE wind coming out of Hobart, but looks fairly light, so should be okay. Once out of Hobart, I have you aiming for 41 30S/152E. It would be nice to get some of the strong south winds behind the Tasman gale, but may only touch 20 kts. for a time late Mon night/Tue am

4) I have you running out of wind during Tue. When this occurs, I just have you motoring straight at Cape Farewell. I think it will be important to get east and we will have some northing in, so just motor at the Cape when light on Tue

5) Likely gale coming southeast out of the Great Australian Bight—it will be near 44-45S/141-142E at 00UTC Wed. First wind from the gale will be a moderate northeasterly wind late Tue night/Wed morning—don't want

237

to get slowed too much and forced too far south, but winds will back into the north Wed night with wind speeds up to 25-35 knots and higher gusts—could be pressed here and should be okay to point south of rhumb line. The cold front will arrive during Thu with winds backing to westerlies and this will allow us to come back to rhumb line for Nelson.

Wed night will be a rough night!

6) Will have another cold front to deal with Fri night/Sat with more NNW gales possible

Provided the headwinds/NE winds are not too strong Tue night/Wed morning, we should be okay

Please advise on your plans—if it is a go, we will update tomorrow

END

The Tasman Sea in fall is rather like a fast revolving door with a continuing series of gales. If you jump in just right, it is OK. If your timing is off….

I also very much appreciated Commanders' phrasing "we should be okay, " where the "we" is five people on board the *Maggie B* and one at his desk in New Hampshire.

## 30 APRIL 2007

*Maggie B* has finally hoisted the Blue Peter. The Blue Peter is code flag "Papa" which is white in the center and blue outside. It means, "outward bound" and was a warning to crew that a ship was ready to sail. We are off for Nelson, New Zealand, after clearing Customs and finishing all the last-minute errands.

There is a deep gale out in front of us in the Tasman Sea. This is good news, as it will throw off southerlies behind it, which we should pick up tonight. More interesting is a monster late fall gale with pressure to 960 mb south of Tasmania, coming this way. We should be timed right that we will have the help of this first one, then a day of motoring and then pick up the northerlies of the next one, and tuck ourselves into Nelson well before it gets too big. Our usual rule is to motor when the wind gets light enough that we slow to 4 knots. This trip the engine will be on if we are under 6 knots. I don't want to hang out in the Tasman Sea and get the full brunt of this second low.

Tasman Island, with sunset behind.

## 1 MAY 2007

We are motorsailing at 7.2 knots northeast for a recommended turn point for weather, where we will head for Cape Farewell at the northern tip of the southern island of New Zealand. We should hit the turn point at about midnight tonight. The wind has been essentially non-existent since we left Hobart, but there is a long easterly swell reminding us that there is some weather out there.

Things are quiet on board with everyone finding or remembering the pacing of a Blue Water Passage.

## 2 MAY 2007

We are finally sailing with all plain sail, doing 7.8 knots for Cape Farewell, in 13 knots of wind from the north-northwest. The swell is somewhat confused and the skies thinly overcast with a few bands of rain showers about. We have come 349 NM from Hobart and have 843 NM to Nelson.

Last night there was a huge halo around the almost full moon. Old salts say that a ring around the moon tells that bad weather is coming. The timing can be

Grey-Headed Albatross.

determined by holding your fist up at arm's length. Each fist width is a day. Tonight the ring was three fists away, or three days away. That seems to roughly check with Commanders' latest forecast.

We have a large flock of grey-headed albatrosses (*Thalassarche chrysostoma*) following us. Their wingspan is up to 6 feet. One reference book says that those nesting on Macquarie Island are so mellow that they have been known to preen the hair of researchers as they allow their leg bands to be read at their nests. Looking at the hair of the crew of *Maggie B*, probably they are following us not for food scraps, but to help out with our coiffeur. More recently some black-browed have joined the squadron. I love that their scientific name, *Thalassarche*, means: "Lord of the Sea."

We will probably take the main down one reef before nightfall if the wind continues to freshen. The prediction is for about 20 knots from the northwest, which would give us a lovely beam reach for Nelson.

If you're thinking about reefing, it's already too late.


## 4 MAY 2007

We are making 9 knots on the rhumb line for Cape Farewell. We have come 785 NM from Hobart and have 431 to go to Nelson. We have come 214 NM in the last 24 hours, and 611 in the last three days.

The wind has been steady at 25–30 knots from 330–340 degrees, or 70 degrees off our port side. We took in the foresail before lunch and now are under full jib and the main with one reef. The *Maggie B* loves these conditions! The waves have made up a bit to 3–5 meters, but although they are fairly short and sharp, they are on the beam, so she shrugs them off with aplomb. Every now and then, though, she throws up a fair heap of water off her hip into the cockpit, as if to remind the watch that this is real stuff.

We are anticipating frontal passage sometime fairly soon. Bands of rain showers, 12–15 NM wide and 3–4 NM thick have been marching past behind us, but we haven't been in one yet. We expect some more wind with the passage of the front, and then it should back to the northwest and west and lighten up a bit. We don't think that the actual front will be too severe because the barometer has stayed fairly steady

*"The prediction is for about 20 knots from the northwest, which would give us a lovely beam reach for Nelson. If you're thinking about reefing, it's already too late."*

at 1010 mb the last 12 hours.

Shy albatrosses (*Thalassarche cauta*) have joined the aerial circus following us.

One marvelous sight is a little pocket rainbow that appears in our bow spray as we plunge along. When the sun is just right, it is bright, though just a few feet long.

Our Furuno autopilot is doing a marvelous job. We are charging along at about hull speed in somewhat confused seas and it keeps us on track to Cape Farewell, with an occasional one degree starboard or port "touch." The autopilot is "adaptive," which means it learns the performance of its vessel. It has figured us out.

Two nights to Nelson, if the elements are willing.

### 5 MAY 2007

The first front has passed and we have hoisted the foresail and shook out the furl on the main and are under all plain sail. The wind is 300 degrees magnetic at 15 knots right on our port beam. We are making 8.5 knots in a sloppy sea with a thin overcast and occasional mist and drizzle passing over us. We did 196 NM in the last 24 hours.

Port or starboard tack would seem not to make much difference, but most of us prefer port tack because most bunks are on starboard, and port tack means we can nicely snuggle into the "V" between the bunk and the hull side. On port, however, Hannah has to hang on against her lee strap. Greater good for the greater number....

New Zealand requires at least 48-hour warning of arrival (Australia was 96 hours!). We are in contact by email with Nelson Customs and have filled out their Arrival form. But at this speed, we would arrive at about 10 p.m. Sunday, which is not a great time to come into a tight, unfamiliar port. Nor is it a desirable time to get Customs officers out of their bed for an inspection. We are therefore trying to slow *Maggie B* down. We expect the wind to fall off tonight, so we haven't taken sails in or streamed drogues, but we may have to take a wander around Tasman Bay to allow for a more civilized arrival on Monday morning.

The Yanmar engine has been using more oil than expected, and on inspection we found that the T-joint installed in Mauritius, to allow for an additional oil sensor, had cracked slightly. Fortunately, we had a plug to seal off the whole fitting, and we will fix it in Nelson or Auckland.

The ship's time is now +12 from GMT, but on the east side of the Date Line. We're getting closer to home!

What we are reading: Frank: *Cochrane—Britannia's Sea Wolf* by Donald Thomas; Owen: *The Fatal Shore* by Robert Hughes; Theresa: *The Odyssey* by Homer, the Fagles translation; Hannah: *The Last Grain Race* by Eric Newby; Bori: *For Esme with Love and Squalor* by J.D. Salinger

Theresa reading the *Odyssey* on watch.

## 6 MAY 2007

At noon, we were under power, making turns for 6 knots, so as to arrive at Nelson at 8 a.m., as arranged with NZ Customs. The wind is 3 to 5 knots from the west and the skies clear. We have come 1131 NM from Hobart and have about 120 to go to Nelson.

We are drying out gear, enjoying the sun, and having lunch in the cockpit. We need to eat up all our fresh provisions, as NZ Quarantine will surely seize everything.

Right after lunch we had the huge pleasure to see our first Snowy Albatross—an adult with a wingspan of at least eight feet!

Then we heard the NZ weather report, which changed everything. It is hard to listen to radio weather reports in a new area because one generally doesn't know the demarcations: "From Cape Seggatiania to Port Whammational, the wind will be...." But we did hear clearly that "Cook" will have a gale to 45 knots tonight. While technically we are entering Tasman Bay when we round Cape Farewell, and pass Farewell Spit, where we will spit, Cook Strait is around the corner. The barometer fell three millibars from noon to 3 p.m., though just from 1018 to 1015. We don't need any more clues! The engine is now to full cruising speed, and if we arrive Nelson early for Customs, we'll just sort it out.

Tasman Bay, with Nelson at the bottom faces north. Not a nice place to be in a northerly gale, but Nelson harbor should be the best harbor of refuge anywhere around as the entrance is north/south, closing to 200 meters, then with a dogleg to the west, where one is immediately protected by a "Boulder Bank" with lots of room behind it to anchor, if no suitable quays are available. Should be interesting. ETA at Nelson is 4 a.m. at this speed.

## 7 MAY 2007

*Maggie B* arrived in Nelson, New Zealand at 7 a.m. this morning. We are safely tied up in the Nelson Marina.

The gale last night was about 50 miles east of us in the Cook Strait, where the wind tends to funnel. We got very little of the weather, which was fine with us.

The crossing of the Tasman Sea was routine, with not much more than 30 knots of wind. We thought that the area was rather over-hyped until we saw the large sloop moored near us when we arrived, which had been dismasted two weeks ago coming from Australia. We heard the story of another sloop that had been rolled over three times after it had set out for Tasmania, and returned rather chastened.

Nelson looks lovely and we look forward to discovering it.

## SCHOONERS

Books say that Andrew Robinson built the first true schooner in Gloucester, Massachusetts in 1713. When this ship was launched, a bystander exclaimed "Oh how she scoons," *scoon* being a Scots word meaning to skip or skim a stone over the water. Robinson replied, "A schooner let her be."

The *Lady Nelson*.

Other possible origins are the Icelandic *skunda* or *skynda*, meaning to make haste or hurry, which certainly fits. "Schoon" in Dutch means "clean" and "beautiful."

Regardless of the etymological origin, a schooner is a ship with predominately fore and aft sails, with two or more masts, with the main mast towards the stern. More common these days are sailboats with only a single mast - sloops or cutters - or two masts where the main mast is forward - yawls or ketches.

Schooners were a revolution because of their ease of handling compared to the square-riggers of the time. When I worked the big German sail training brig *Roald Amundsen*, the captain joked that "schooner" meant "lazy man" in Dutch, because they were so easy to handle that they could be run by "a man and a dog."

Most current sailors think of gaff schooners as heavy, slow and picturesque, because that represents the boats they know, which are generally early 20th century fishing boats.

Too many sailors confuse speed around marks in a sheltered bay with an optimized boat. Blue Water sailors respect the incredible attributes of the America's Cup boats, but tend to be a bit smug when those races are called off when the wind is stronger than 22 knots or when boats break in half on encountering a wave. Any automobile fan can admire a racing Ferrari, but would never drive one on the Paris-Dakar rally.

Even the incredible modern Blue Water racing boats, like the open 60's, are very hard on their crews and the list of boats that have lost their keels or broached, putting them out of action and often killing crew, is way too long for any sensible sailor to accept. In the 2008-2009 Vendee Globe Around-the-World race, only 11 out of 30 boats finished.

So what is it about schooners that has me so convinced that they are the most "fit and able" design for a world cruise? First and most obvious is the fact that compared to a similar sized sloop with the same sail area, more smaller sails are easier to handle than fewer bigger ones.

The second point is that schooners get their power out of their main sail while modern sloops get it from their jibs. When the wind blows up, it is much easier and safer to reduce your main than to go up on the foredeck to change jibs.

Finally, in big water the greatest danger for ships is broaching. This is when a ship loses directional control and twists sideways to the full force of the wind and is knocked over by the force of wind and water. By their very design, schooners resist broaching more than cutters and sloops.

All well-designed sailboats have their center of pressure and center of resistance balanced. The center of pressure is the sum of the force on all the sails, how the boat would be pushed sideways by the wind. The center of resistance is how the hull would take the sideward push of the wind on the sails. If they are balanced, the boat goes straight sideways. If the center of pressure is ahead of the center of resistance, the bow will go away from the wind. If the center of pressure is behind the center of resistance, the bow will want to come up into the wind.

You can change the center of pressure by changing the sails, but generally the center of resistance stays as designed.

*Blizzard.*

Sloops usually reduce their jibs first when the wind freshens. That moves the center of pressure back behind the center of resistance. Conversely, the schooner captain will reef his main first, moving the center of pressure forward. Reaching or running before very big winds, the sloop will want to turn up or broadside and get the full force of the wind, where the schooner will want to turn away.

It is also essential to understand the impact of the different hull shapes. If the center of resistance is forward to match the center of pressure, the boat is harder to steer and keep straight. If the center of resistance is aft, as with the schooner, there is greater directional stability. The schooner will want to go straight, just like an arrow or a dart. Racing boats value low directional stability so that they can maneuver quickly to tack or turn a mark. It is also handy when entering and leaving tight marinas. But low directional stability can kill you in the Southern Ocean.

The gaff rig is also seen as eccentric, scenic and antiquated. But that ignores the reason for gaffs. Simply put, gaffs allow you to put more sail on the same mast than you can with a triangular Bermuda rig. A gaff-rigged schooner simply makes better use of the area of a boat.

A sloop or Bermuda rig enthusiast would say "But a gaff rigged schooner can't go to windward as well as an optimized sloop." That is true to an extent, but not as true as it used to be. Modern stiff sails, full battens and carbon fiber yards greatly reduce the former advantage. In any case, *Maggie B* wasn't optimized to go to windward; she was made to live her life on a broad reach, making the best speed over the great ocean routes.

One famous short-handed schooner the 109' schooner *Donald II*. She was manned only by Capt. Trenholm and his daughter Ann, on trips between Nova Scotia and the Caribbean, carrying wood south and salt back north. On a trip in north in 1937, Captain Trenholm died and Ann brought in the schooner alone. Not a big deal today, perhaps, with modern gear, but it must have been a handful in the years before efficient winches, radar, autopilot, GPS, radios and engines.

Today one thinks of workboats as slow; racing boats as fast. Truck versus Maserati, perhaps. But when sailing boats were working for a living, fast was often an essential attribute. Fast meant getting more money for your fish. Fast meant getting the pilot's job of guiding a foreign ship into your harbor. Fast meant getting the best money for the first load of the New Year's tea. Fast meant getting the news of a great victory home to your country. Often a working boat's most important attribute was to be fast.

*Esmerelda.*

Schooners remained the fastest open water racing boats well into the 20th Century. What knocked them out of competition wasn't new designs or new material; it was new racing rules. Schooners were the fastest design around, so they were given extra handicaps to make it "even" and "fair" with slower designs. Racing rules over the years have caused some nautical architects to produce ugly, awkward boats to get an extra second a mile due to a rule-beating quirk in the details. I didn't want to race, I just wanted to go fast, safe and comfortable around the world.

The fastest current monohull is the *Mari-Cha IV*. A schooner.

Another ship's experience with the Tasman Sea.

## 9 MAY 2007

The crew of the *Maggie B* is settling in well in New Zealand. We are already finding favorite restaurants, laundromats, bookstores, cafes, and bars. The Nelson marina has more interesting boats than anywhere we have been, with the exception of Antigua during Classic Race Week.

We are in the midst of the usual series of little fixes, adjustments and preventative work. Owen and Theresa are making new pendants for the mainsheet attachment to the boom, Bori and Hannah are re-sewing a protective strip on the mainsail batten pockets. We have taken *Strika*, the kayak, to get a nose fitting so we can tie her alongside. The boat cover for the *Reep* is getting patched. Our T-joint for the dual oil pressure sensors on the Yanmar is being replaced by something more permanent, because the Mauritian one failed after two months. Our new steering compass will be swung tomorrow. Theresa finally found a pesky leak in the vent for the diesel space heater. Tomorrow I overhaul the toilet—whee!

Theresa and Owen splicing up new main boom bridles.

New Zealand is very enlightened in many ways. One amusing area is that they have legalized prostitution and made it subject to "standard workplace regulation." We don't know nor will we find out just what that means. We did see a marvelous article in the local paper. The headline is "Fire sparks bed appeal." It goes on to say: "A Napier brothel is soliciting donations of old beds so that it can resume operations after a fire.... Manager Paul Hale said: 'Club 100 has been giving out to Hawkes Bay for more than 25 years, now it is time for Hawkes Bay to give back to Club 100.'"

## 17 MAY 2007
*Maggie B* is happily tied up at the Tasman Cruising Club marina in Nelson, NZ, waiting out a classic Kiwi southwester. It is blowing 25–30 knots in this sheltered port, and lots more off shore.

Tawhirimatea.

Our exciting news is that we have acquired a guardian for the boat. Tim Wraight, a famous local carver, has made a boom end cap of Tawhirimatea, the Maori wind deity. Tim left the tongue blank instead of the gale-like swirl that is traditionally seen on it, so that we won't get too much wind. It is made of Totara wood and paua shell.

We're still learning. One new Nelson friend, Adrian Faulkner fell in love with the *Maggie B.* He was shocked, however, about our main anchor, which is an 80-pound CQR plow. He had come to know the French inventor of the Spade anchor, which is quite different in design. I said, well, everybody has a favorite anchor. The next day he brought a thick package on all sorts of careful tests by several independent organizations, which proved that the traditional plow anchor was pathetic and the Spade was terrific. That caused me to recall that *Maggie B* did drag in Barbados, the Seychelles and twice in Tasmania. Yes, all were in notoriously bad holding grounds,

*" The Spade has 50% of its weight in the tip and supposedly digs in so hard and fast that new owners think that they have snagged an underwater cable. We'll see."*

but then I thought of the anchoring challenges ahead of us in the Marquesas, the coast of Chile and Patagonia, and all of a sudden a top rated anchor seemed much more attractive. While the Spade anchors are excellent, their availability isn't. The company is run by Frenchmen in Tunisia and the New Zealand importer's last order is five months overdue.

Adrian is off to Southeast Asia for five months and has loaned us his Spade anchor with the understanding that we either get it back to him by his return or get him a new one. I'm hoping that the overdue shipment will arrive in Auckland by the time we get there. Meanwhile we'll try it out in Marlborough Sound and the Bay of Plenty.

The essential difference is that the plow anchors plow up the bottom. I have seen it happen in Barbados. The Spade digs in. Also the plow anchors have a big proportion of their weight in the shank and not much in the tip, which needs to dig in. The Spade has 50% of its weight in the tip and supposedly digs in so hard and fast that new owners think that they have snagged an underwater cable. We'll see.

Last Sunday we had a lovely road trip from Nelson to Blemheim, in the heart of the Marlborough wine country. We went first to my long-time favorite New Zealand

Happiness at Cloudy Bay winery.

winery, Cloudy Bay, where we loved their Sauvignon Blanc and Pinot Noir, and bought a case of each. Then on to a marvelous lunch at Vintner's Retreat. Tapas all around—marvelous. Then two more wineries and a few more cases. We tasted everything, though we tried to spit out most. Our final stop was the stunning Nautilus Winery.

The *Maggie B* used to be "sitting back" with the bow a bit high on the painted waterline. Not a problem anymore! Nigel must have planned it that way—for us to fill up the forepeak with 5 months' worth of wine. How fine it will be to be sitting inside the reef at T'ahaa, waiting for the sunset with the perfect Marlborough Sound Sauvignon Blanc?

Nelson, and probably every other major NZ port, is well set up for boat refits. We used a great outfit called Dickson Marine for two projects, and they were quick, accurate and reasonable. The stainless steel forming shop was just down the street; "Boat Bits" and three other ship chandleries were within three blocks; hydraulic specialist around the corner, etc.

## 19 MAY 2007

*Maggie B* got underway from Nelson, NZ at 11 a.m.. Tonight we are anchored in Greville Harbor, D'Urville Island, also known as Rangitoto Ki. D'Urville Island is the western wall of Marlborough Sound. It is only 40 NM from Nelson, but quite wild. New Zealand's Southern Island is only another 40 NM from the Northern Island, but across the Cook Strait, which seems to attract weather from everywhere.

We ran aground on our way in. We had to cross a "boulder bar" and it was just at low tide. We had 15–20 feet of depth in the channel, but I didn't have enough speed and the last of the ebb spun us out of the channel and onto a ledge, where we sat for about an hour until the tide came in. We will check the bottom when we next haul out.

It is completely calm tonight but tomorrow there are forecasts of gales up to 50 knots for our area and especially Cook Strait between the Northern and Southern Islands. We plan to find nice spots in Marlborough Sound for Sunday and Monday and then catch the brief opening between gales to jump across Cook Strait for Wellington.

Today in our motoring up to D'Urville, the calm waters produced at least 30 dolphin playing around our bow. We have never seen them so thick—they were like kids fighting in a playground.


## 20 MAY 2007

The clouds are streaming by overhead, working their way down the hills. We will probably be pretty closed in by tonight with rain and more wind. Tomorrow we may work our way around the corner more into the middle of Marlborough Sound, or we may just hide out here and start a Marathon Team Scrabble game. We are happy to be on a mooring.

Earlier I mentioned the endless complications that every country seems to impose when you try to get back GST/VAT taxes. New Zealand has a system that recognizes Ships in Transit, so that you can avoid paying the taxes to begin with. It works! Purchasing major items for *Maggie B* can easily be done without the 12% GST. Sometimes just by saying you are In Transit, sometimes by showing the Customs Form and your passport. What a pleasure! I suppose that it helps that the Kiwi's current tax problem is that they have huge surpluses and are mostly arguing over how to spend them. But in any case I'm wearing my All Blacks rugby shirt in appreciation.

We went ashore during the afternoon to fight our way through the thick forest

> *"In the morning, we found that we had dragged the 3-ton mooring about 300 meters southwest, thankfully clear of the land."*

to the ridge. It was an interesting walk, though rather difficult. But the real joy of going ashore was that Theresa discovered wild oysters and mussels along the shore. We played caveman, hacked a few dozen oysters off the rocks and ate them on the spot. Delicious! We gathered mussels for the others, which were cooked that night in garlic and onions.

The night at D'Urville Island was very bad. We were well protected all around by hills, but the 50 knots outside would hit the anchorage in blasts from time to time, and spin us around. We were moored to a Tasman Bay Cruising Club Mooring, 3 tons worth, with a huge new cable attached. Thank goodness! The wind would hit us from north to east to south to west and then back again. We would lurch back and forth. It was strong enough that we would take a 10–15 degree heel from one side and then the other. It was strong enough to knock the boom out of the boom gallows even with the mainsheet tight! We couldn't make out all of what was going on because it was very dark in driving rain. In the morning, we found that we had dragged the 3-ton mooring about 300 meters southwest, thankfully clear of the land. I will write the TBCC Commodore and pay to have it returned to its proper spot.

Fresh oysters on D'Urville Island, Marlborough, NZ.

New main boom bridles.

### 21 MAY 2007

We have only come perhaps 20 NM as the crow or the black oystercatcher flies from Nelson. But we covered more like 50 NM as we came around the north end of D'Urville Island and then outside Stephens Island (Takapourewa) and its wild lighthouse. The wind was variable from 10–35 knots and we sailed with the main with two reefs and the jib. The seas west of D'Urville were rough with the swell from the old storm, wind waves from the new blow and 2–3 knots of tidal current kicking in from time to time.

We are moored in Homestead Bay, Port Ligur, in Pelorus Bay. Port Ligur is a grand name for a place that has three houses and one boat. There are oyster farms all around, so maybe there is more action than it appears. The wind has petered out, at least where we are, surrounded by mountains. The sky is clear with the new moon bright in the west. The town has just a single light on.

This is a serious weather area. Thank goodness that *Maggie B* is a big, strong ship. Today the forecast for the Cook Straits between the north and south islands was for 55 knots north, easing tonight to 45 knots north. Easing to 45 knots! But tomorrow it is supposed to be just a light 15–25 northwest breeze. We plan to cross the 46 NM to Wellington tomorrow.

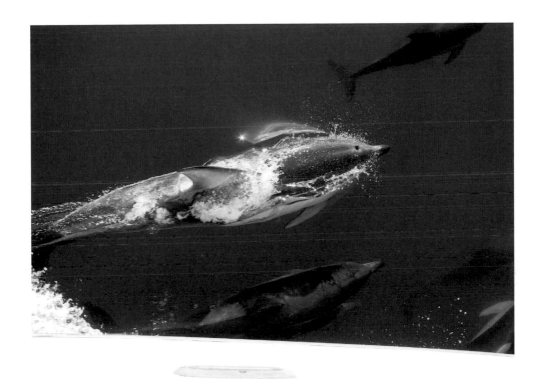

In the Cook Straits, New Zealand.

## 22 MAY 2007

*Maggie B* is safely tied up at Chaffers Marina in Wellington, NZ. We had an easy crossing of the Cook Straits with not much more than 25 knots wind, in clear weather with favorable tide. Tomorrow the Straits are due to get another front with 45 knots. Whew!

Matauwhi, NZ.

*"In the old days Russell was a magnet
for rough elements such as fleeing convicts,
whalers, prostitutes and drunk sailors."*

## 11

# WELLINGTON TO RAIVAVAE

**26 MAY 2007**

The wind has stopped blowing in Wellington and it is as if we are deaf in the silence. The first 3–4 days we were here, the wind was steady at 30 knots in the inner harbor. Blows the head right off your shoulders!

We are getting to know Wellington and really like what we are finding. It is complex, artistic, scenic, walkable, and creative. We all love the Te Papa, the new national museum that is only 100 meters from our spot in the marina.

As part of our crew-training program we all went off to the Opening Night of the latest of the *Pirates of the Caribbean* movies. It was shown in the glorious Embassy Theater, a true movie palace, built in the 1920s but completely restored in 2003 for the opening of the Lords of the Ring series. We should have been in costume, as many were. The movie was fun, one of the highlights being Keith Richards as Pirate King (he didn't need any make-up.....).

Last night we went to the yacht club to get information and pointers from local yachties. However, it was Rock and Roll Night, and if we got any pointers, they were forgotten. The crew mutinied, declaring it "Too Old," but the Captain knew the words to all the songs, and had a fine time.

We have made a beachhead at the Welsh Dragon, which declares itself to be the only welsh bar in the Southern Hemisphere. Music and singing every night and the barkeeper is very welsh, full of stories and song. Pushed only a little by her comrades, Theresa sang "Waltzing Matilda" to the crowd, which produced the expected Aussie/Kiwi

A new marae at the Te Papa Museum, Wellington.

"banter." We barely escaped with our lives.

Bori is off tomorrow to return to Hungary, a big step for her and us. She has been with the *Maggie B* since before launch day, all the way except for the Brazil to Cape Town leg. She will be missed and we hope the best for whatever will be her next "ship."

The *Maggie B* hauled, with the Te Papa Museum in the background.

## 30 MAY 2007

We got underway this morning and are making 9 knots power sailing. We are headed up the east coast of the northern island, hoping to get to Gisborne tomorrow afternoon. We are going as fast as we can as there is a real blow coming in towards the end of the week. The plan is a long weekend in Gisborne and then on towards Auckland, which is about 400 NM away, with perhaps some exploring in the Bay of Plenty.

Lunch today was smoked salmon and avocado sandwiches on sourdough bread, with fresh local apples and aged cheddar for dessert.

We hauled out in Wellington yesterday. They have a very interesting "travel lift." It

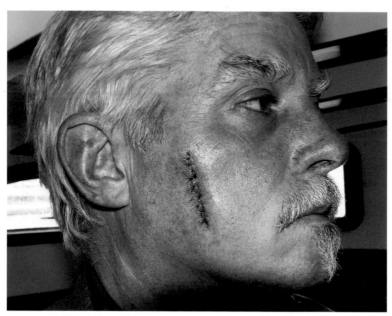

Blue Water skippers get new scars in New Zealand.

doesn't travel. They lift you out vertically and then slide the "floor" underneath the boat. Only NZ$200 (@US$150), including the use of a pressure washer! We cleaned off the hull, replaced the prop anode, and checked for damage, which was minimal.

Some people get a souvenir tattoo in New Zealand. Real Blue Water skippers get a new facial scar. I went to see a dermatologist about one suspicious piece of skin on the top on my ear, but he zoomed in on a dark spot on my cheek. "Premalignant!" he cried, "It should come out." I asked for a suggestion of a doc in Auckland and he said, "Oh, I have some time now and we'll get it right out—do you want local anesthetic or a shot of rum and a wooden stick to hold in your teeth?" I hate surgeons with a sense of humor, and chose the local. Now 10 stitches later, I look even more like Keith Richards as the Pirate King.

### 31 MAY 2007

We are still motorsailing in about 10 knots of wind, making our best time for Gisborne, where we should arrive today at about sunset. We are safely ahead of the gale. Castle Point, where one turns north after leaving Wellington, had 41 knots of

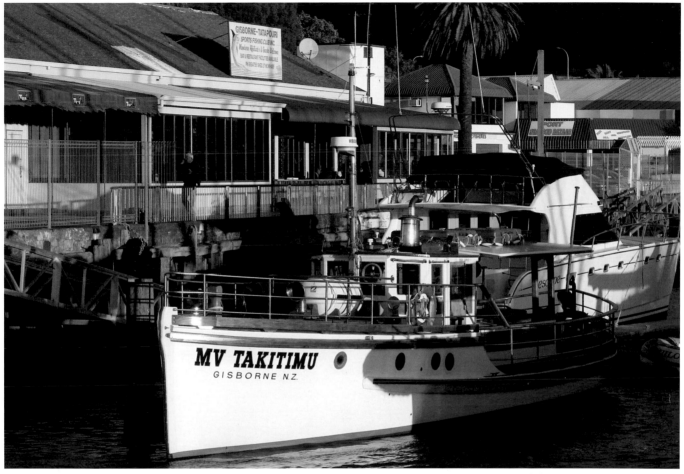

The MV *Takitimu*, Gisborne, NZ.

wind at noon today. Whew!

Today is the first time we have been north of the Roaring Forties, 40 degrees South, in a long time—March 10th, to be exact. We are headed north, seeking the sun as winter settles in to the south!

As we left Wellington yesterday, we passed the Chilean Sail Training Ship *Esmerelda*; a four-masted square rigger—just magnificent—though somewhat in need of a paint job. She was there for a port visit and surely will have lots of fun. She does carry some baggage, though, as she was used for terrible purposes years ago under Pinochet. For many, a trip on the *Esmerelda* was one way.

We passed Young Nick Head, named after Captain Cook's Cabin Boy, who was the first to spot New Zealand. Gisborne is the place where the marvelous movie *Whale Rider* was filmed.

In Gisborne there are lots of Captain Cook memorials. The best of all has to be up the hill at Titirangi at Cook Plaza, where, due to some historical screw-up, the statue isn't in British naval uniform, nor is there any facial resemblance to Cook. The plaque reads: "Who was he? We have no idea."

There is an Irish bar that we will no doubt seek out: the Irish Rover. It supposedly has a sign, "No hats, no undesirable tattoos." I'm not sure that all the crew will be able to get in.

Lunch today was fettuccini with roasted garlic and New Zealand Green Lip mussels, chased down by a Nautilus Sauvignon Blanc.

We arrived at the Gisborne Inner Harbour Marina late at night. We were a bit delayed in entering by a huge grain carrier that required us to stand by outside. Once inside, after dark but with a full moon, the chicane to find the inner harbor was less than obvious. We've got to stop arriving in strange harbors at night, especially as the wind starts up! Nonetheless, we are snugly tied up and ready for the blow, which is just starting as the barometer is falling rapidly. Hannah is ashore checking out the showers and Owen and Frank are sampling South Island wines. Theresa is helping to finish off our Tassie Beers.

Theresa making fettuccini with green lip mussels.

*Maggie B* cast off from the Gisborne Marina exactly at noon today. We are headed north for the Bay of Plenty, running up the East Coast at 9–10 knots in a nice big southerly. A nor'westerly gale is due Tuesday, so we hope to be safely around East Point and across the Bay by then. Depending on our speed and the speed of advance of the gale, we should be in either Tauranga in the Bay of Plenty or Whitianga on the Coromandel Peninsula. From Whitianga it is just a half-day to Auckland.

We hope to go by White Island—Whakaari—in the middle of the Bay of Plenty, which is New Zealand's most active volcano, last erupting a few years ago and still actively steaming.

We are 70 NM from the International Date Line, which makes some of our electronic charts act as if it is the end of the world. We have seen the latest *Pirates of the Caribbean* too recently to laugh too hard! It is tempting to cross over and back to spend the shortest day ever!

## 4 JUNE 2007

We are power sailing towards Whitianga, where we hope to be tied up tonight at their little marina. We will be there for the next gale, which is due tomorrow.

Whitianga is small with only 3500 people, but interesting. We will rent a car to see some of the sights in the area, including Hot Bath Beach, where one shovels out a hole in the beach near low tide, which produces your own hot tub from thermal water bubbling up.

There is also a man in Whitianga who will teach you how to make your own Maori bone carving. He must have bought up all the used dentist drills from miles around.

Once this next blow is over, we will slide around the corner of the Coromandel Peninsula into the Hauraki Gulf. It is a complicated route into Auckland and we are headed all the way into the center of the city to the Viaduct Marina, so we will be sure to arrive in daylight, for a change.

## 6 JUNE 2007

*Maggie B* is safely docked at the Viaduct Marina in downtown Auckland. We are surrounded by condos, office buildings, great bars and restaurants. When we were in Cape Town, we though that we were right in the middle of things, but here it is astonishing, especially after being in smaller places for a bit. We are like Midwest farmers staring at the tall buildings in Manhattan.

Coming across the Hauraki Gulf was relatively easy. Easy, that is, for the Hauraki Gulf with only 20 knots right on the nose. But it blew 40 here yesterday and is due to blow again tomorrow. Coming in the channel at night and docking—back in, of course—wasn't much tougher than a night carrier landing. There were more lights of every color than at O'Hare Airport, and we had to dodge two big container ships outbound, four or five ferries, three pilot boats, and some odds and ends.

*Maggie B* in the Lighter Basin, Auckland.

## 16 JUNE 2007

The days are getting pretty cold, so it is time to head for the Tropics!

We have been enjoying the town and also getting a lot of routine work done. Our liferaft is checked and repacked, as is the MOM8, our Man Overboard Module, and all the life jackets. The 406 EPIRB, our rescue beacon, is overhauled. We have a huge new anchor, a 100-pound Manson Supreme, which should keep us safe in the tricky anchoring challenges of the Marquesas and the coast of Chile and Patagonia.

Theresa overhauled our diesel cabin heater and Owen has our stove propane system fixed up. The remote propane sensors in the bilge seem to have a mind of their own. We are fitting some additional heavy weather ventilation systems so that we can get closer to the impossible goal of keeping below decks dry and well ventilated even when it is splashy on deck.

We have carefully been through our engineering spares, such as fuel filters and spare impellers, because it will be a long time before we will be in a place as well supplied as the Viaduct in Auckland. We purchased a 30-pound "Kiwi Anchor Buddy." They are also known as an "angel," kellet, sentinel, or anchor weight. It will ride part way down the anchor chain, to help keep the pull and surge against the anchor parallel to the bottom, rather than prying up the anchor. With the new anchor and the kellet, we should be able to sleep well at night most anywhere.

*"Sailors, when they land in a marina, immediately ask the whereabouts of 1. toilets, 2. showers, 3. Laundromat, and 4. bars, though not necessarily in that order. "*

Auckland is a marvelous town, heaven for sailors. There isn't just a single good chandlery; there are half a dozen, all fighting for your business. One near us is called Nelsons and it has been in the business more than 100 years. On the other side of us is Sailor's Corner, which has one of everything, or can get it in a minute. They have deeply discounted Musto wet weather gear and we added another suit to the ship's inventory—just Owen's size.

The Maritime Museum here is excellent. It is huge and has fascinating exhibits on everything from the earliest Polynesian voyages to yesterday's America's Cup Race. Up the hill is the War Memorial Museum that is an amazing resource on Maori history and artifacts.

But Boats! Auckland is all about boats. Across the way is Team New Zealand's base and near it is a spare hull for BMW Oracle. In the basin near us are the America's Cup racers NZ 40 and 41, which can be hired for day trips. Or you can hire both and race against yourself! Around the next corner is the square-rigger, *Pride*

Touching history, Auckland.

*of New Zealand*. The next way you look there is an Alden schooner that used to belong to General Patton, or a marvelous little 80-year-old steam launch called *Puke* (pronounced poo-kay, which means a low hill in Maori).

Sailors, when they land in a marina, immediately ask the whereabouts of 1. toilets, 2. showers, 3. Laundromat, and 4. bars, though not necessarily in that order. Most marinas have 1, 2 and 3 near the gates, marvelously called Ablution Facilities in Cape Town. Here things are a bit different. Viaduct Marina is more for working (tourist) boats or plastic monstrosities belonging to someone in a nearby office or condo. So for #1, we use a public facility 20 feet away. For #2, we have joined a nearby YMCA that has taken over the historic "Tepid Baths" facility and has steam, sauna, hot tubs and two big lap pools. For #3 it is a bit of a hike, as we are in an area too fancy to have anything like our favorite cafe/laundromat in Salamanca Square in Hobart.

For #4, there are 100 great bars within a 10-minute walk. A favorite is a nearby Irish bar, which has a comfy fireplace as well as live music every night. A recent note from T'weez speaks for it:

The *Spirit of New Zealand*, tied up in downtown Auckland.

Danny Doolen's is a tidy pub,
Where Weeza's gone to dwell.
She hopes that you will see her there,
Before she starts to smell.
(Last word hard to read, could be "swell")

One important purchase is red socks for the crew. They are a symbol of the New Zealand America's Cup boat. Peter Blake, the legendary Kiwi sailor, used the sale of red socks to help finance his original challenge. We wish them the best in the finals this month against the Swiss boat, which is also full of Kiwi sailors. Tonight may be a bit more difficult as the All Blacks are playing Canada in rugby. Hannah is insisting that we all have to wear Canadian flags on our faces when we go out to the sports bar to watch the match. We may not live to see Sunday.

Off to root for the Kiwis at the America's Cup.

## 22 JUNE 2007

*Maggie B* is still in the Viaduct Marina waiting out a big blow. The forecast for the route between here and Opua in the Bay of Islands is northwest 35 winds gusting to 45 knots. We will be heading northwest, right into it. No hardship to sit things out here. After frontal passage, it is due to freshen to 40 with gusts to 50 knots from the southwest, then reduce to 25 by Sunday. Our plan is to stay up late Saturday night for the first race of the America's Cup, cheering the Kiwi boat.

We had hoped to watch The Race at the Royal New Zealand Yacht Squadron, which is having a supper with big screens all around, but they decided that it should be Members Only and guest yachtsmen weren't welcome. Too bad.

One area of critical interest for every Blue Water sailor is "man overboard." The best strategy, of course, is not to go overboard to begin with. We have purchased two new miniature waterproof VHF radios and four day/night flares. We are having pouches made to integrate the radios and flares into the life vest/harness system, which the Watch will wear. We always listen to Channel 16 at sea and if someone went over, they could immediately call the *Maggie B* to alert shipmates. The flares would be used to locate the person. We have the advantage of keeping a continuous ship's track on the course plotter, so it is easy to go back over our course and know that we are within 30 feet of where we had passed before.

This assumes that the person in the water is conscious. Unfortunately we all know that an unconscious person in the water has very little chance of survival. So all our efforts are focused around keeping people on board, and in rescuing a shipmate promptly.

## 27 JUNE 2007

*Maggie B* arrived in Russell, NZ, yesterday. We are at the town dock. We made an easy trip up from Auckland overnight, despite rather dire weather forecasts. The trip was enlivened by dolphin playing around us at midnight, and a large, mysterious sailboat, traveling slowly with no lights on.

Once into the Bay of Islands, we were surprised to see about a dozen tourist boats rushing around and a big gaff-rigged topsail schooner *R. Tucker Thompson*. Several of the tourist boats came by to look and one small motorboat came alongside to welcome us.

In the old days, Russell had quite a reputation. Quoting from the *Lonely Planet* guide: "Russell was a magnet for rough elements such as fleeing convicts, whalers, prostitutes and drunk sailors." Charles Darwin described it in 1835 as full of 'the refuse of society' and it also picked up the chirpy nickname 'Hellhole of the Pacific.'" Russell is a marvelous little community, now a bastion of cafes, gift shops and B&B's.

There is essentially only one good docking space at the Russell pier. It is a narrow "U" facing outwards, with big posts all around. We backed into it with some difficulty due to the 15-knot cross wind. With good crew coordination and some acrobatic work from Theresa, all worked well despite many onlookers at the pier. We are now trussed up like a moth in a spider's web.

Owen had to leave us to return to the States for work. We will miss him.

We are planning to explore the surrounding area, which includes Tane Mahuta, The

Historic Note, Russell, NZ.

Lord of the Forest, a 2,000-year-old kauri tree that is 51 meters high and has a girth of 13 meters.

In Opua, there is a man who specializes in solar power and we are going to see if we can get some panels fitted to help with our electrical consumption. Our big batteries seem to be holding their charge less well. We end up running the generator for about two hours a day if we are at sea and the Yanmar main engine is off. The biggest energy users seem to be the radar/GPS and the autopilot, not the refrigerator and the watermaker, as I had suspected.

We are organizing supplies and beginning to track weather for the run north to French Polynesia. We will leave early next week, weather permitting. There are a series of gales forecast for the end of this week.

We are a bit groggy, not from grog but from staying up late to watch the America's Cup—thrilling to have the Kiwis up 2–1. Last night's race was a real cliffhanger with the Kiwi's ahead 400 meters, a huge distance, only to have the Swiss catch and pass them by the last windward mark, and then to have the Kiwi's slip past on the last downwind leg and win by 20 seconds. That doesn't happen often in match racing.

Matauwhi, NZ.

## 5 JULY 2007

*Maggie B* has moved a bit to Opua, in The Bay of Islands, only a few miles from Russell. We are getting a 220V shore power connection. We have a great 110V system, but it is useless outside of the US and Canada. We are also getting solar panels.

The solar panels can potentially give us 15 amps per hour, which could meet most of our 100-amp daily energy appetite.

We had a little party last night for the Fourth of July. It was a fun evening. I was able to find some other Americans! We had all the local boaties, including lots of Germans, some English, an older French woman, a Brazilian, a Canadian, some Kiwis and an Aussie or two. We quickly forgot the glorious Fourth and got well into Jamaican rum, Scotch whiskey, Tasmanian wine and Belgian beer. A very international night!

One German couple had spent two years along the coast of Chile and they had some good advice, and annotated our Chilean cruising guides. My favorite piece of advice from them was about anchoring in unknown Chilean harbors:

1. If no trees along the shore in the harbor, leave at once.
2. If there are trees, anchor near where the taller ones are.
3. When anchoring near the taller trees, see which way they are leaning, and set your (multiple) anchors accordingly.

## 9 JULY 2007

*Maggie B* is back in Russell, NZ, tied up securely to the pier. The forecast for tomorrow is for an easterly gale with winds up to 65 knots, and 10 inches of rain. We are nose first, headed easterly, into a "U" shaped part of the Russell pier with nine dock lines mooring us in tight as a nut.

We had a marvelous sail yesterday with Bill and Claudie Sellers. Bill is famous even among the many famous Kiwi sailors. He has traveled the world by sail, often single-handed and has great stories about every port. He is also one of the best scrimshaw artists in the world. His watercolors of nautical themes are very successful, and now his "Cook's *Endeavour* in a Calm" is the centerpiece of our crew mess. He has built his own boats, as well as his house, which looks like a medieval Norse church. With piercing blue eyes and a full white beard, he looks, and is, the archetypal clipper captain.

Bill and Claudie took us to Roberton Island to see their friends Jim and Terri Cotter. Jim is the Master of the *Soren Larsen*, a very successful and well-traveled

Captain Bill Sellers, Bay of Islands, NZ.

square-rigger. His great book is *Soren Larsen - Homeward around the Horn.* Terri is a highly experienced Blue Water Master. One of the best stories about Terri was when she was captain of a transatlantic training ship. One of her nine adult male students became stuck on the vacuum toilet. Always bring a wooden spoon when you sail with Terri!

Bill, Jim and Terri gave us lots of valuable tips about our next few legs. Hannah got scrimshaw advice and some more tools and material to work with. We hope she will have delightful objects for us all soon.

We made our first anchoring and departure from an anchorage under sail, under the eyes of very experienced skippers. All the crew worked seamlessly together.

When we were in Opua we got great support from S.J. Ashby Boatbuilders. They helped install our Helios solar panels. But more importantly, they overhauled our Groco toilet. Some people have questioned the *Maggie B* design in that we have only one toilet. I answer that one toilet is enough, if it is a good one. The Groco has been working less well recently. It had been overhauled by amateurs, Willis and me, but it needed professional help. Fortunately we had an overhaul kit with all the rings and seals, and Ashby had the professionals. The real surprise was that the system was messed up by a NZ$0.20 coin, stuck in the middle of things. I'm keeping my eye on the crew now, to see who is swallowing coins.

At the boat yard, there was a sign next to the crane for launching boats: *No Cash, No Splash.*

Last Saturday was the First Annual Russell Birdman Festival. A birdman festival basically means people dressing up in funny costumes, often with wings, and hurtling themselves off a pier, into very cold water, to see who is funniest and flies furthest. Russell is a town of perhaps 900 in the winter and 8,000 in the summer! The festival had beach digs, kayak races, spaghetti eating contests, barbeque cook-offs, and the Birdman Competition.

Just about exactly at 10 a.m., as things started, the sun came out and it was hot enough to think about sunscreen. The day was perfect and perhaps 4,000 people showed up.

I am very proud that our new shipmate, Ben Carpenter, led the "Super Liquor" sponsored Birdman entry, which won the "Master of Ceremonies Favorite" prize, NZ$100. Plus two cases of beer from his sponsor! Right after the final prize giving, at exactly 4 p.m., the rain and cold returned. A perfect day!

Ben Carpenter of Bristol, England has joined the crew. He is 27 and has been working in New Zealand as a carpenter, looking for a chance to crew

Birdman about to crash, Russell.

on a sailboat for the Islands. He has had previous Blue Water experience sailing around Australia.

Ben Carpenter celebrating
his Birdman crash.

Experienced advice is that to get to Tahiti from here, one needs to head straight east, however far you need to go to get a westerly, from between 32 and 40 South, until you get to about 155 West, then you turn left for the islands. The joke is that if you turn too early, you end up in the Cooks, and never, ever, get to Tahiti. Our latest forecasts say it may be until July 21–22 before a chance of a nice southerly. We are ready whenever it comes.

### 12 JULY 2007

We are still tied up to the Russell pier, now with 12 lines out in every direction. The storm on Tuesday was a real dilly; it reached cyclone strength. Near Russell one rain gauge recorded 274 mm of rain (11 inches) and a regional weather station recorded a 180 km/h gust (100 mph). We saw 51 knots on our wind gauge, but felt stronger gusts.

All around the area, many boats dragged, broke their moorings, hit other ships, blew ashore, sank or were damaged on piers. The Coast Guard was scurrying around, Channel 16 was full of Maydays and flares were shot off. Ashore, roofs blew off, trees fell and closed roads and took down power lines, low areas were flooded and some bridges were washed out. Russell was without power for a day. *Maggie B* danced a bit amid all her lines, but rode things out fine. We kept the diesel stove burning, the deck lights on as a guide for others, and bailed the *Reep* every hour.

We helped rescue one boat, *Figment* from Florida. She had broken free from her mooring, gotten holed when she hit another boat, and sunk her two dinghies. She had quite a struggle in the wind to make the lee of Russell. Her owner had a broken ankle from putting his foot between two ships, and both on board were in early stages of hyperthermia. We guided them into a safe berth, handled their lines, got them on board and gave them warm, dry clothes and hot tea with a big dose of rum.

Commanders' Weather says that we may be able to get an opening for a nice southwesterly to take us to Tahiti by next Monday, July 16th. We are ready.

Porto Beach, Fernando de Noronha.

## THE PERFECT ISLAND

Raivavae is the perfect Polynesian island, or so you might think. It is about six square miles in size, is home to about 1000 people and lies 450 NM south of Papeete. The anchorage is well protected once you get inside the reef, the beaches are lovely and the natives are friendly though cautious.

We had arrived in the Austral Islands from New Zealand. They were discovered by the Spanish but later annexed by the French. Fletcher Christian and his mutineers considered a nearby one, Tubuai, as their refuge after the Bounty mutiny but were discouraged both by internal discord as well as hostility from the inhabitants. The Bounty took off after two months to return to Tahiti and then to sail on to Pitcairn.

We didn't find the locals on Raivavae hostile, but they were not really interested in us either. The island had a bakery but no real shops. Even the baker insisted that you had to reserve your bread a day in advance and be at a street corner at the appointed time with your money ready. The police station and administrative headquarters for the French Republic had been closed for some years.

We fished, climbed all over the island, motored around to find the perfect beach, bought fresh fruit ($5 for a whole stalk of bananas) swam, sunned, read books, and fixed the boat. But soon we were ready to sail on to Tahiti.

When I titled this sidebar "The Perfect Island" I meant it somewhat facetiously. We Westerners, like Gauguin perhaps, imagine the perfect Polynesian island. But we bring too much baggage with us. When we find the Perfect Island, it doesn't have Internet or mail or pizza or movies or a bar or an oil filter for the engine or diesel that you can buy. We didn't want the fleshpots of Tahiti, but we couldn't drop back fifty or a hundred years either.

Hokianga Harbor, NZ

*"... one rain gauge recorded 274 mm of rain (11 inches) and a regional weather station recorded a 180 km/h gust (100 mph)."*

## 17 JULY 2007

We are finally underway from Opua for Tahiti. We had been waiting for the right low pressure system, to jump on its shoulder and ride it east to about 155 degrees West, heading along the 35 South parallel. At least that is what all the old salts tell us to do. Waiting got old, so we jumped on the back of a little low, and right now have a nice 15 knots westerly blowing us along direct to Tahiti at about 8 knots. Tahiti is about 2200 NM, or perhaps two weeks. We may stop in the Australs, about 200 NM south of Tahiti, if the weather permits.

Unlike the big South Atlantic High or the high in the Southern Indian Ocean, the South Pacific—east of New Zealand—responds to many different influences, rather than one dominant weather maker. We will have to play them as they come.

It was very hard for all of us to leave New Zealand. The people have been so friendly, it is a very yachtie environment, world-class boat support, lovely towns, tons of fun things to do ashore, excellent food—oysters, baby lamb, seafood—and superb wines. We won't forget our new friends, and hope that we see them again.

## 18 JULY 2007

We are headed directly towards Tahiti, on the Great Circle Route. We have come 146 NM in the last 22.5 hours and have 2082 to go to Tahiti. We are slipping along at 6.3 knots with the G2 gennaker up in 9–10 knots of wind on our beam. It is a lovely day with just a few rain showers marching along in the southerly, spreading more rainbows than rain. It is sunny enough for Ben to have already burnt his fair Albion skin.

A pintado petrel rolling in.

We are again shadowed by our "air cover" of seabirds. The marvelous new addition is the black and white spotted cape or pintado petrel, also known as the cape pigeon.

This Opua to Tahiti route has been sailed many times in the last 1,000 years, and we feel the spirit of the big sailing wakas on the water. We are glad to have our carving of Tawhirimatea on the boom end to accompany us. The weather looks favorable for this next week. We are positioned just right for the next low, expected Friday to bring a 25-knot northwesterly.

Ben is a little stunned by the level of cuisine on the *Maggie B*. On his last boat,

*"We are now on GMT +12, where yesterday it was GMT –12. I haven't yet been able to persuade the Furuno operating system that today is yesterday, so it may be time to break out the manual."*

they lived mostly on cheese sandwiches and cold corned beef. Hannah baked a chocolate cake for tea, gilding it with fresh cream and raspberry jam.

## 19 JULY 2007

Our wind has pooped out and we are headed northeast at 5 knots. We have traveled 271 NM from Opua and have 1962 to go to Tahiti. It is a lovely day as the high fills in and the sky clears.

It appears that we have about half a day of light wind before the next low sets us up with a nice northwesterly. Right now we are headed directly for Papeete, but we are being careful not to get too far north and miss out on the westerlies. One low at a time!

We are in an area of wonderful phosphorescence. Having dolphin alongside was Theresa's delight last night and Hannah brought a bucket of seawater on board to light things up. I turned out the running lights (the stern light is very bright) for a while to admire the lighting in our wake.

We are now standing three 4-hour watches, and Ben is taking a watch with everyone, to learn the ropes—literally! Soon we all will be comfortable and he'll be able to stand his own, and we will return to the luxury of three hours on and nine off.

We have a ritual aboard when we set sail on long legs. We gather in the cockpit and pour a glass of rum. The first drink goes as a libation into the sea, then I say a short quote or poem, then all drink and make a toast. Setting out for Tahiti I read from Joshua Slocum's *Sailing Alone Around the World*: "I had penetrated a mystery, and, by the way, sailed through a fog. I had met Neptune in his wrath, but he found that I had not treated him with contempt, and so he suffered me to go on and explore." We hope that the *Maggie B* will be "suffered…to go on and explore."


## 19 JULY 2007 – Again!

*Maggie B* has now crossed the Date Line, so it is again the 19th of July. We are now on GMT +12, where yesterday it was GMT –12. I haven't yet been able to persuade the Furuno operating system that today is yesterday, so it may be time to break out the manual. The MaxSEA software refused to cross the Date Line and had to head all the way back west, around the globe, to work. But we crossed the line last night about 2000 and broke out a bottle of Tasmanian sparkling wine.

Many people have told me that we are going the wrong way around. Hard to fully understand how anybody could argue with today's sail: doing 6 to 7 knots in 10 to12 knots of wind on our beam, all in t-shirts and shorts and barefoot. We did the usual make/fix jobs, including new leather jackets for some blocks, repairing running lights, and adjusting the bolts for the centerboard hydraulic "foot." One bolt broke and we didn't have a spare long enough. Thanks to Bart Gabriel's advice, who was on the Southern Atlantic Crossing, we had a length of 8 mm threaded rod, which we cut to length.

Shipwork: Theresa renewing the leather on a block.

We are setting a course right along 33 degrees South rather than straight for Papeete. I expect we'll get more easterly winds after this next low, and it gives some "northing" to draw on, when we need to. Theresa complained at lunch that it wouldn't get any warmer if we stayed at 33 degrees South, but I said that we'd get to Tahiti faster and not have to beat our brains out to get there, which made it OK.

Over the last few nights, when I came on watch at midnight, I had been intrigued by one star. It was just rising in the south-southeast, and appeared to be pulsing red and green when it was low to the horizon. It turned out to be Canopus, an orange-white super giant, the second brightest star in the sky after Sirius, the Dog Star. It is 100 light years away and 2,000 times brighter than our sun. It is the principal star in Carina, the Keel. But, most important to sailors, it was the focus of the huge Chinese multiple-fleet circumnavigation so well described in the book *1421* by Gavin Menzies. They were plotting the position of Canopus to improve their navigation expertise in the Southern Hemisphere.

## 20 JULY 2007

We are making 7 knots essentially right along the 33 South latitude. The wind has piped up a bit to a perfect 12–14 knots from the West, as the barometer is beginning to fall. The next front is also being indicated by the progression of clouds from high cirrus mares tails last night to altostratus this morning, to lower cumulus and stratus showing up on the horizon at dusk.

We started fishing today, and have our wasabi ready. Our Fishing Stations are 1) Whoever is on watch sets the hook, 2) Hannah takes over handling the boat and slowing her down, 3) Ben takes over handling the rod, 4) Theresa gets the saltwater wash down hose going and gets the gaff, 5) Frank gets the killing gear—hammer, ice pick and sharp knife, 6) Ben brings the fish in close enough for Theresa to gaff, and she lands it, 7) Frank kills the fish with the ice pick, stunning it first with the hammer, 8) Frank slits the arteries in the gills and tail and ropes up the fish, which is then dragged to bleed out, but not so long that the sharks arrive. It is cleaned, washed down and sashimi within minutes. Yum.

We had a big fish hit about sundown, but it spat out the hook before it could be set. Tomorrow is another day.

Our overhauled C. Plath Southern Hemisphere steering compass is leaking out its fluid. I accused the crew of drinking it, but it was pointed out that A) it contained oil, not alcohol like in the old days, and B) we have better alcohol on board. It appears to need a new expansion seal at the base plus some more fluid.

Much of today was taken up by overhauling docking lines from the beating they took in the storms in Russell. All protective leathers came off, and two were shortened and respliced where chafe was severe. We also made up 2 new lines from 50 meters of rope purchased in Opua. All the books about the coast of Chile emphasize how much line you'll need to carry.

## 21 JULY 2007

We are booming along at hull speed, 10 knots, on a beam reach with 25–30 knots of wind from the west-northwest. The sky is overcast with occasional rain showers. The wind waves are only 2–3 meters from the northwest, but the southwest swell is making up 2–4 meters also, making for occasional good surfing. The max GPS speed this afternoon was 14.2 knots. We have reefed down both the main and foresail one reef.

We made 205 NM in the last 24 hours, and 53 in the last five hours.

Different suntan solutions during rope work.

Reefing down the main and fore, but leaving the jib full moves the center of pressure forward, as the *Maggie B* is more pulled than pushed. We also have the centerboard down about one-third, which reduces rolling. Both the centerboard and moving the center of pressure forward increases directional stability, which makes Jorge, the autopilot, happier. In about the same conditions, with full sail and no centerboard, Jorge took 2 degrees port and 8 to starboard (we are on port tack) to keep us straight as the waves and gusts push us around. With the reefs in and 1/3 centerboard, Jorge takes 2 degrees port and 2 degrees starboard. It makes it less likely that Jorge will throw up its hands and turn us towards Tonga or the Antarctic, as it did a few times last night.

*"It is such a pleasure to watch the petrels do aerial maneuvers that this former fighter pilot wholly envies. What is more amazing is to see an albatross doing much the same, like a 747 in an air show."*

The plan of staying south of the rhumb line seems to be working out. We are in the right place, for this low. We are easing north a bit, aiming for a point at 32S/155W, due to Commanders' heads-up about a "Big Dog" gale possibly developing in Fiji/Tonga early next week. We are in the traditional storm track, which is where we want to be, but it makes sense to slide a bit north so that we don't get too much of a good thing.

When I was growing up racing in Maine, I was taught to "tack on a header," which means if the wind shifts to push your nose away from your goal, it is time to go over on the other tack to take advantage of the shift. In Maine, it was a question of going a couple of hundred feet to get a shift, in the America's Cup, they go perhaps 300 meters to grab one. We are planning three days or 600 NM ahead for our easterly header, which should hit us about when we get to our 32S/155W turn point. We'll tack there and head north for the Islands. That's the plan, anyway.

We started fishing again this morning, though we were really going too fast for good trolling speed. The speed made it very difficult to keep the lures underwater. We were horrified when a pintado petrel briefly became tangled on one lure, and fishing quickly ended for the day.

The rain, waves and wind have attracted a whole mixed squadron of Blue Water birds around the boat. It is such a pleasure to watch the petrels do aerial maneuvers that this former fighter pilot wholly envies. What is more amazing is to see an albatross doing much the same, like a 747 in an air show.

I have a neat new gadget. A striking Brazilian woman in a Paihia shop effortlessly sold me a "2C Light.com" ball cap. It is the size of a normal ball cap, but the top of the visor has solar cells and under the visor are two LED's, which give good light. You wear it during the day and charge up, you use it at night to read on watch. My shipmates think it is dorky, but I'm sure I'll have the last laugh.

## 22 JULY 2007

We are still in the right place, riding the shoulder of the gale. We jibed at dawn this morning with the wind shift, and now have 25–30 knots from the south-southwest, which has us on a starboard broad reach, speeding along to our turn point at 32S/155W. We have about 1/2 to 1 knot help from the Southern Ocean Current. We did 217 NM in the last 24 hours and 30 NM in the last three. The barometer reached its lowest point, a relatively modest 1008 mb at 0400 this morning and is slowly working its way back up. The rain, which had been heavy at times, has cleared and our new solar panels are back working for us.

The southwest swells are 3–5 meters and of a period that gets us surfing, while causing heading excursions of 20–30 degrees port and starboard. But the basic ride is more comfortable than last night and seems to be calming down gradually. Our speed is 9–10 knots, speeding up to 12–13 while surfing.

We have come 985 NM from Opua, and have 1332 to go to Papeete.

We have at least one grey-headed albatross *(Diomedea chrysostoma)* flying with us, plus a cloud of pintado petrels and sooty shearwaters. Theresa and Hannah were all the way on the stern, behind the boom-gallows, harnessed in, surfing the boat and dangling their toes in the foam of the waves rushing up on us. It seemed sometimes that the birds were almost in their hair.

The Force 10 stove, which is central to our happiness, has been acting up a bit. The burners' auto-igniters weren't working anymore and the burners didn't want to stay lit after lighting. After pulling it all apart, I discovered a simple AA battery well hidden that had lost most of its charge. Now that it is replaced, the stove is running as good as new.

I'm pleased to report that Ben has passed his initial apprenticeship, where he stood watches with all of us. He will start standing his own watch tonight on the 2100–midnight. I'm on the midnight–0300; Hannah the 0300–0600; Theresa the 0600–0900.

## 23 JULY 2007

We are booming along at 10 knots in a nice 20–25 knot south-southwesterly. The waves have made themselves up into proper swells, nice and regular, 4 a minute, and are 7–9 meters, somewhere between "Wow" and "Oh, #@$%&*!" The day has cleared with only occasional little rain showers marching by, leaving more rainbows than freshwater washdowns. We did 227 NM in the last 24 hours, or 804 in the last four days. We are still riding the shoulder of the storm, keeping between 32 and 33 South, racing for our left turn for the islands, which is perhaps a day and a half away.

One of *Maggie B's* truly lovely characteristics is that even as we are hurtling along like this in big water and doing hull speed, we were able to have a pleasant lunch in the sun on deck. Steaks with roasted potatoes, beets and garlic; salad with avocado, apple and macadamia nuts. We only occasionally had to grab the HP sauce bottle as it hurtled across the table.

This morning Ben was tripped up by one of our system's booby traps. Our shower's control lever, if bumped, sprays the victim. It can be neutralized by turning off an additional valve on the showerhead, but that doesn't always happen. This morning, while getting ready for watch, Ben got an unexpected and unwanted shower below. He went on deck, drenched, to complain to Theresa. Just as his head appeared from the hatch to voice his irritation, the *Maggie B* finished the job with a perfectly aimed bucket full of salt water. He got no sympathy from Theresa on watch.

One skill that is important for long-distance cruising, but is not taught in sea schools, is being a good librarian. Ships have endless systems: liferafts, watermakers, fuel pumps, portable VHF's, EPIRB's, roller furling, stove gas shut-offs, transformers, etc. Everything comes with installation manuals, parts catalogs and operating instructions. If you have the paperwork and reasonable spares, you can fix most everything. Without the manuals you have to be a plumber, electrician, diesel mechanic, rigging superman, or wait for the next port. The *Maggie B* has a shelf about 3 feet long of manuals.

What we are reading: Ben: *Stella Rimington's* (ex-Head of MI-5) "At Risk;"
Theresa: George Orwell's *Down and Out in London and Paris;*

284

Hannah: James Herriot's *All Creatures Great and Small;*
Frank: Nicholas Shakespeare's *In Tasmania.*

Sailing in the dark of night on the shoulder of a storm can be a marvelous experience. Last night was mostly overcast, but with stars shining through gaps here and there. The sea was large and boisterous, but only throwing occasional mists of spray on board. The rain had ended. White caps were faintly visible in the light of the red and green riding lights. The wake could be seen briefly lit with the white stern light, rushing into the night at 10 knots. Black-on-black waves intermittently blocked the faint horizon like 2-D cutouts moved back and forth in a school play's seascape scene. At the setting of the half moon, a small gap opened in the clouds to light the scene:

The setting half moon
Seen through a break in the rain:
A last kind gesture.

*"Sailing in the dark of night on the shoulder of a storm can be a marvelous experience. Last night was mostly overcast, but with stars shining through gaps here and there. The sea was large and boisterous, but only throwing occasional mists of spray on board. The rain had ended."*

### 24 JULY 2007

We are headed for our turn point at 32S/155W at hull speed, 10 knots. The weather continues to favor us, as predicted, and we have a nice, steady 25-knot Southerly to drive us along. The wind is slowly backing to keep us on a beam reach as we make our gradual turn for the Islands. It is overcast again with light rain showers, presumably signaling the outer reaches of this next front. The swell has steadied down to 7–10 meters from the southwest, with 1-meter southerly wind waves on top. *Maggie B* is riding comfortably with only occasional dollops of spray. We are still getting occasional 13–14 knot surfs.

We did 219 NM in the last 24 hours, and 1023 NM in the last five days.

We have come 1431 NM from Opua and have 1054 to go to Tahiti. We are currently anticipating stopping at Raivavai in the Australs, which is about 830 NM from our current position. Besides being well spoken of by many sailors, it will also give a chance to sit out what may be a big northeasterly coming in the end of the week.

The bird life continues to amaze us. Sometimes there are 100 close by, and you think that they should have an air traffic controller to keep order, and then the skies are empty. Today's crew included a juvenile wandering albatross *(Diomedea exulans)* and an adult black-browed *(Thalassarche melanophris)*. Excitement was provided by several broad-billed prions *(Pachyptila vittata)*, which can out-fly our numerous pintado petrels, which is saying something. One of the prion's common names is whalebird, and the black-browed albatross's common name is mollymawk.

Theresa delighted us today by making whole-wheat bread from a recipe from my father's cook. It was absolutely delicious, especially spread with NZ Manuka honey. We got the honey when we drove around the north of the Northern Island to see the Lord of the Forest. The honey came from a crossroad called Waiotemarama, which isn't on many maps. We never met the beekeeper as it was just out on a shelf, with an "honor box" nearby: NZ$15 for a kilo! (US$5 a pound). Manuka honey has a great reputation for being especially healthy. It sells for up to US$20 an ounce in the US. From another grower and honor box (with the cash out so you could make change), we bought a huge pile of avocados, NZ$4 for four kilos (US$0.35 per pound).

Just to continue on the gastronomic theme, lunch today was venison sausages, in a tomato/mushroom/onion/garlic sauce on top of whole-wheat fettuccine. It was washed down with a nice Central Otago Pinot Noir called Carrick Unravelled. I wonder if Carrick was the wine maker?

Everyone on board knows when we hit 10 knots with the centerboard down. The centerboard sets up a deep, strong hum just above the threshold of hearing, like the sound of someone blowing across the top of a big jug. Having the centerboard down significantly helps our stability in the more complex wave patterns.


## 25 JULY 2007

We have started our slow turn north for the Islands, and were headed 030 degrees at seven knots in a 13–18 knot breeze from 170 degrees magnetic. The sea remains fairly large so we bang around a bit. We have shaken out the reefs and are under all plain sail. We have come 1644 NM from Opua, and have 897 to go to Tahiti.

We have come 213 NM in the last 24 hours and 1236 in the last six days.

Splendid sailing!

Some patterns in the watches are beginning to take shape: Hannah's watch always get the rain; Ben's watch get the buckets of salt water in the face; Teresa's watch is slower; and the Captain's watch gets all three!

We passed a 100-foot fishing boat yesterday, going the opposite direction. It was only 2 miles away and was only intermittently visible due to the swells. They didn't have their radar on, so we got no alert from the Sea-Me, and it was very difficult to pick them out on radar with the big swells and rain squalls. A sharp lookout spotted them, gray on gray.

Last night on a routine scan of the horizon at about 0100, I saw, to my horror, a big red riding light seemingly right on top of us, like what your view of a container ship might be. Right after my heart jumped out of my mouth, I perceived that it was a glimpse of the 2/3 moon, made red by the atmosphere as it set. Whew.

Going through stores, we found lots of lentil beans, loaded aboard in Canada. What were we thinking? We have a number of jars out in sunnier spots to sprout them. We haven't perfected the system yet. Last night's boisterous sea spread damp lentil beans all over the galley.

Sailing measurement continues to puzzle and inspire. One guide to the Pacific Islands refers to anchoring areas defined as so many cables from this or that. So we go to our reference books and find that a cable is 120 fathoms or 720 feet, though sometimes shortened to 600 feet so that it would be 1/10 of a nautical mile. Why 120 fathoms? That used to be the length of a standard anchor warp. What's a fathom, anyway? Six feet. Why 6 feet? About the spread of arms, the easiest way to measure rope on board a vessel. Fathom's probable origin is "favn," Norse for "armful." But the Bible mentions fathoms in Acts 27, Paul's great description of his shipwreck. Did the early Christians speak Norse, or is it a translation or recalibration? Posidonius apparently wrote in the 2nd century BC of a depth of 1,000 fathoms. Makes you appreciate the metric system.

While we are only five days from Tahiti, we are three days from Raivavae in the Austral Islands, where we will probably call, depending on the weather.

## 26 JULY 2007

We have 8–15 knot breeze from the southeast to move us along on our course of about 030 to Raivavac at 6 or 7 knots. The seas have calmed down nicely and the 2/3 moon is guiding us along. We have about 440 NM to go to Raivavae.

*"We had big following waves pushing the water in. Isn't there anything you can do? Yes, run the engine every day to keep up the backpressure to help the air/water separator keep the South Pacific out. I forgot to do it."*

Much of the day was spent mostly stopped, or going the wrong way, due to problems. We hooked a fish at about 10 o'clock this morning and went to Fishing Stations. When we tried to start the engine to be ready to maneuver, it wouldn't start. It wouldn't even turn over. The fish spat out the hook and we got to diagnosing our problem. Hmmm—plenty of battery power, and it's trying to turn over and it's not going anywhere? Oh, my God—waterlock!

Waterlock is when water gets in the engine, all the way to the cylinders. A diesel can compress air, but not water. If a cylinder is full of water, it isn't going anywhere, unless the starter is strong enough to break things. How does water get in? Through the exhaust. Why don't you have something to stop it? We do, a nice Vetus Air/water separator. But it must have been overwhelmed by six days of going hull speed and submerging the engine exhaust. We had big following waves pushing the water in. Isn't there anything you can do? Yes, run the engine every day to keep up the backpressure to help the air/water separator keep the South Pacific out. I forgot to do it.

So, how do you recover? First thing is to stop the water coming in. When I pulled off one of the injectors, lots of water came gurgling out….lots, an open tap to the sea. So we tacked over to port tack because the engine exhaust is on the port side, and slowed the boat down. Then I cracked the low point in the exhaust system and let out perhaps 10 gallons into the bilge. Then off come the four fuel injectors, which are shaped sort of like spark plugs, but more complicated to remove. That opened up the cylinders. We turned over the engine a few revolutions with the starter, which blew out the water from the cylinders. So the diesel fuel and water was nicely spread all over the engine room and those within it. Then reinstalled the injectors. Then changed the oil. Then prayed that nothing was bent or broken. Then started it! After a splutter or two, it started right up. Yea! We ran it for a few minutes and shut down to change the oil again and tighten up the injectors. Now it is running fine. We will change the oil a third time tomorrow morning. This took about six hours.

Happily, we were able to call the Service Manager at Yanmar in Nelson, NZ and John Steele at Covey Island in Nova Scotia for advice. And we had all the maintenance manuals.

In the midst of all this, Ben was able to cook a tasty lunch, which was perhaps underappreciated in the stress, Hannah kept the boat in control and safe, and Theresa became expert at extracting and re-filling the oil system, which requires both strength and flexibility.

But the weather is good, we all learned lots of lessons and Raivavae is only a few days away. Maybe we'll land that fish tomorrow.

## 27 JULY 2007

We are continuing to make good time to Raivavae, making 6.9 knots on a heading of 030 with the wind at 150 degrees at 12 knots. Our life on a broad reach!

We have come 1998 NM from Opua and have 275 to go to Raivavae and 620 to Papeete. We should be at Raivavae about midnight tomorrow, and will stand off until dawn to enter the complicated pass.

Our main engine is purring along fine now, after Theresa did a third oil change to remove all the water from the crankcase.

John Steele, and everyone at Covey Island have been a great support for us, all around the world. I suppose that the boats that a yard builds are like children: you mostly hear from them when something is wrong.

We have a hymnal in our library. It was published in 1893 and belonged to my great grandmother. I was looking in it for tunes to be adapted for a *Maggie B* song. I found 2 hymns for "Travellers by Sea", one written in 1845 and one in 1887. One called: "While o'er the deep Thy servants sail" says "Send Thou, O Lord, the prosp'rous gale." The other hymn, called "Safe upon the billowy deep" has "Mid the dark, send fav'ring gales." We have just had a favoring gale, which has blown us from New Zealand to the Islands. But I suspect that no modern congregations raise their voices to pray for a gale.

At night we are happy to see the return of well-known constellations, including Orion, the Swan, the Dolphin, and the Pleiades. It is a function of being further north, and the time of the year. For the Maori, the first view of the Pleiades was the signal for the winter celebration. It was one of their central sailing stars. A tattoo of the Pleiades decorates my shoulder.

## 28 JULY 2007

We have tried to slow down to arrive at Raivavae at dawn, but *Maggie B* is still too fast. With the foresail furled up and the main and jib luffing lightly, we still did 194 NM in the last 24 hours. The wind is from the east at 20 knots and we are headed north for the sheltered side of the island. We should arrive about midnight. We'll decide when we get there whether to range up and back or to anchor outside the reef until dawn.

The waves are messy with the new 2–3 meter wind waves from the east mixing up with the old southerly swell. The deck is wet even though Ben isn't on deck.

*"I thought I was well prepared ... But, when I began plotting out the Admiralty Directions on the chart, there were glaring errors in the Lat/Long descriptions. I'll trust Theresa's eyes."*

Raivavae in the Australs has an interesting approach, with a dogleg right in the middle. Fortunately the pass is on the north side of the island, so our current big southerly swell won't be breaking across the opening in the protective reef, as happens sometimes in other weather. We'll hoist Theresa up the main mast with a radio to talk us in. I thought that I was well prepared with 1) the *Pacific Crossing Guide* with detailed charts of the approach; 2) the *Admiralty Sailing Directions, Pacific Ocean Pilot, 2006*; 3) the latest electronic charts, and even 4) a 1944 USN chart done from French soundings of 1901. But, when I began plotting out the *Admiralty Directions* on the chart, there were glaring errors in the Lat/Long descriptions. I'll trust Theresa's eyes.

The Spaniard Tomas Gayanos discovered the island in February 1775. It has a population of about 1,000, two stores, a post office, a Gendarmerie and a bakery, which supposedly does great petit pain au chocolate. There are a number of standing stone tiki, so the missionaries may not have been as thorough as on bigger islands. The seawater has warmed up to 72F/22C from 60F/15C in Opua.

*Maggie B* Bora Bora.

## 29 JULY 2007

*Maggie B* arrived at Raivavae Island, Australs, at about midnight, 28 July, and anchored outside the main pass until dawn. We proceeded in Passe Mahananatoa to Rairura Harbor without incident. We are currently anchored in about 40 feet of water. The water is warm, the sky is clear and the beaches beckon.

We have come 2287 NM from Opua. Papeete is 392 NM NNW of us. It took us about 12.5 days to make the passage, or averaging 183 NM per day or 7.6 knots, including the half day we had to go the wrong way when we had engine problems.

There are 3 other boats in the harbor. It looks quiet ashore, but then it is Sunday morning. Theresa jumped in the water the minute the anchor was set, and we will follow her soon. Hannah made pancakes for breakfast, so we might need to take a minute for things to settle. We have spotted the Mairie, so the Gendarmarie shouldn't be too far away. Though they aren't open, I'll leave a crew list and report to keep good relations. We have our yellow "Q" flag flying as well as the French Tricolor.

*"Papeete is full of hard truths and fragile promises."*

## 12

# RAIVAVAE AND AROUND
# FRENCH POLYNESIA

**2 AUGUST 2007**

This morning started poorly—we are out of cooking gas. We left Opua low in one bottle and the other full one, apparently short-filled somewhere. No coffee this morning made us all slow starters and a bit cranky. I went into the village to see the lady who has gas cylinders in her yard and asked if I could get ours filled. Alas, this was not the routine and thus was not done. She had cylinders for sale or exchange. They were filled in Tahiti and shipped out and back on the supply boat. She wasn't there to fill little ones for boats.

I went back to the boat and got my assortment of fittings and tubes and came back to the lady to try to decant some. I would have to buy a cylinder, take what gas I could out of the cylinder and then sell it back to her empty. An additional problem was that I only had US dollars. She wasn't interested in dollars and didn't know of anybody who might be. "Maybe the shopkeepers in the next village would exchange as they had some American family, perhaps." Credit cards also had no interest. A wonderful older ex-pat Frenchman, who had happened by, said that we could get gas on his account, if we were able to hook it up. Stunned by his lovely gesture, I offered some wine or whiskey from our locker, but he said that he had never drunk alcohol. It was moot in any case: we were unable to get any gas because the only connector she had that fit the French bottle had a built-in step-down valve.

Back at the boat, we set about going to rescue our kayak, *Strika*, which had pulled out her bow attachment and escaped downwind, ending up on some coral just before the barrier reef and deep ocean.

We upped anchor and motored down as close as we could get in *Maggie B*, a few hundred yards away. Hannah and Theresa set out in *Reepicheep* for the rescue. Ben's wrist is sore so he couldn't row, and I had to stay on *Maggie B* to maneuver in the narrow channel. When they were about halfway there, the wind rose from 15 knots to 25 knots and the *Strika* rescue soon became a Hannah and Theresa rescue. They were able to get down to *Strika*, but were unable to make any headway back out of the coral field with the wind up. Friends from two other boats, who had been over at *Maggie B* the previous evening for movie night, hopped in their rubber inflatable outboards and pulled everyone out. It was a sobering, trying time.

We motored along the island to the other store, anchored off, and rowed ashore. They also refused to have anything to do with our gas bottles, but showed some interest in the US dollars and were happy to sell us a huge French butane bottle, including deposit and attachment fitting, plus some supplies for a small fistful of US$50s. We now have our coffee! Our gas bottle assortment includes bottles from Canada, South Africa, Brazil and France, plus a variety of connectors and fittings.

> *"When they were about halfway there, the wind rose from 15 knots to 25 knots and the Strika rescue soon became a Hannah and Theresa rescue."*

We moved around the main island to anchor near a small island called Motu Vaiamanu. Others call it La Piscine, the swimming pool. It is just lovely. We ended up at this lovely place about 3 p.m., made some scrambled eggs, toast and bacon and collapsed. We plan to explore lots tomorrow.

It looks as if we will have favorable wind for the 400 NM run to Tahiti by this Sunday, the 5th. A little weather system is due through here Friday and Saturday, with a nice southerly following it.

Theresa with beach fire, Motu Vaiamanu, French Polynesia.

## 4 AUGUST 2007

At dawn 35 knots of wind came in from the northwest. This was more or less as expected, maybe 10 knots more and more northerly. We were in a lovely spot for a quiet evening, but not for a blow. We raised anchor, with some difficulty due to coral heads entangling the chain and anchor, but we did it with grace using tight teamwork and early attention of divers.

We motored over to Vaiuru, where we had seen a big marae, laid out in a series of gigantic steps towards the water, and found what seemed to be a nice spot. The day began calm but then started to blow again at 25–35 knots, and the bottom proved, on inspection, to be bits of sand and coral shingle—not great holding. We headed off for the end of the island, Isle Hotuahua. This proved to be a brief respite. We anchored in 20 feet of water, dried out a bit, and had a cup of tea. The wind switched from 35 knots from the north-northeast to 35 knots from the south—in about 10 minutes! Much of the time it was raining at about one inch each 15 minutes.

We continued along around Raivavae to Rairua Harbor. The hills looked incredible with waterfalls falling 200 meters off the cliffs, blown away by the wind, while all of the wetness whipped around us as we dodged the coral outcroppings to find our way back to a safe anchorage.

In Rairua, our Norwegian friends were still there. We woke them up as we arrived, by passing close by and giving them a big blast of our marvelously loud Kallenberg horn.

That evening, after a celebratory round of Hot Toddies, we fixed a comfort dinner of baked potatoes and "garbage" soup. While dinner was fixing, it HAILED! a shock to us in French Polynesia. We tried to gather enough ice for our rum and Cokes, but it was too transient. Movie night that night was *Whale Rider*, which brought us closer to Maori culture.

## 6 AUGUST 2007

We are making 6 knots with full main and foresail and the G2 gennaker. The wind is 8–10 knots from the southeast, on our starboard quarter. The sky is full of small puffy clouds and we are all barefoot and in shorts and t-shirts.

We have come 2451 NM from Opua and have 264 to go to Papeete.

When we set "the Bird" this morning I noticed a small rip by the clew; we had it down and Hannah had it patched within 20 minutes. Ben fixed the bow of the tender *Reepicheep*, hurt in the blow at Raivavae, and I patched a hole in my favorite

shorts. All in all, a productive
morning.

## 7 AUGUST 2007

We are 72 NM from Tahiti.
We have come 2633 NM from
Opua, NZ. We are booming
along at 9 knots in a 15-knot
southeasterly trade wind.

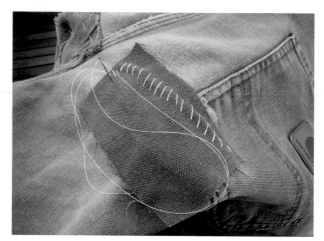

Fixing favorite shorts at sea.

We should come up to Tahiti
at an hour or so after sunset, not
a great time to work our way
into an unknown harbor full of
coral reefs. Our plan is to anchor for the night at Baie de Popoti, a small bay that
makes an opening in the barrier reef. It should be protected from the breeze, but the
*Admiralty Guide* says that the swell can work its way in. If it isn't a suitable anchorage,
we'll just stay clear and stand off until morning. Popoti is about 10 NM South of
Passe Taapuni, the complex entrance that we will use to get into downtown Papeete.

I think of Papeete as an un-Polynesian metropolis full of noise, cheap tourist
shops, dirt, gangs, and shiny office buildings. But it is impossible not also to think
of it as the goal of so many dreamers, many of whom got here (Fletcher Christian,
Sterling Hayden, Paul Gauguin) and the millions who never made it. We will find
our own Tahiti.

*Maggie B* was safely tied up, Mediterranean-style—anchor out and stern in—in
Papeete at the Quai Bounty, AKA Quai Bir-Hakeim, AKA Quai des Yachts, at 11
p.m. Celebrations included opening our last bottle of Laphroaig. Technical paperwork tomorrow, and then off to the Marina Tahina.

The *Lonely Planet* guide describes Papeete well as "full of hard truths and fragile
promises." The reason why no one stays in town once they have cleared Customs, is
that there are no services and it has much of the ambiance of any big city anywhere—
hot, sirens, rush hour, and concrete. As quick as we could, we moved around to
Marina Taina, a few kilometers past the airport. It is new, clean, well run, full of
interesting boats, and with all the services. On the other side of town is the Yacht
Club de Tahiti, but it is separate from the rest of things and is crowded, with limited
facilities.

We have enjoyed the marina, and made friends among the other boaties. We met skippers from all over in the Dinghy Bar in the Casa Blanca restaurant. Germans, Chileans, Argentineans, English, French, Irish, Norwegians, and many of inscrutable mix. But, it was a marina and the real islands beckon us. From my father's visits over the years, we have a number of friends in Tahiti, Moorea, Tahaa, and, especially Bora Bora.

In Tahiti, we rented a car and had a nice drive around the island. Lunch was at the Botanic Garden, enlivened by a birthday party of about 400 people from an extended family. The nearby Gauguin museum lays out the artist's life very well, but is spoiled by terrible reproductions of his work—old photographs that have sat in the sun too many years. The last room is both fascinating and pathetic. It has postcard-sized copies of all his paintings, bunched together by location: Chicago, St. Petersburg, private. The diaspora is astonishing.

*"The reason why no one stays in town once they have cleared Customs, is that there are no services and it has much of the ambiance of any big city anywhere—hot, sirens, rush hour, and concrete."*

There is also a good museum called "Tahiti and the Islands," that was well worth it. To plug into real history, we stopped at the rebuilt Marae Arahurahu. It is tranquil, beautifully maintained and has amazing energy radiating from it.

We shopped at the huge Carrefour supermarket and refilled the boat with tons of food. It will be a while until we plug into a supermarket again. Many of the foods are French, of course, and, marvelously, subsidized by the French taxpayer! Merci!

The epic, however, was dealing with customs. The basic issue was "Cautions." They are bonds costing a one-way return plane ticket to your home of record. If you are non-EU, you go to a bank and pay for a full fare ticket, plus the usual charges. When you check out, you take a paper from customs and the bank gives you your money back, in Polynesian Francs, just what you need when you are going to Chile or New Zealand. Of course, you can change the Polynesian Francs into "real" money, for a fee....

All that is good and well, but Theresa, alas, is switching to another boat, *TeTega*, that we met in the Australs. *TeTega's* Captain John is happy to pay the Caution, but there is no bank in the Gambiers, nor the Australs, for that matter. So no bank, no Caution, but she has one now, so how to "close" it? In theory, an affidavit from the Gendarmerie in the Gambiers will let me get the money back. We'll see.

Did I mention how expensive French Polynesia is? A simple dinner for seven at the Dinghy Bar—4 pizzas, 2 bottles of wine, 3 big salads? US$245! Anchoring stern to at marina Taina? US$110 a night. Catch fish, eat coconut and grapefruit, and drink rainwater....

Hannah is the only strong one of us as I have a broken rib due to a fall down the hatch when dropping the main, and Ben has a strained wrist from a "sand surfing" incident. We'll do our best.

It will be nice to sleep out in the breeze tonight as Marina Taina got a bit hot in the lee of the island.

## 15 AUGUST 2007

*Maggie B* is anchored inside the reef in Moorea, just outside Cook Bay. It was a lovely sunset with a two-day-old moon peeking above. We motored across the 13 NM and are anchored out in the perfect temperature easterly trade wind. We are in a hole that is very narrow, but 60 feet deep, reportedly with good holding. There are two other boats in this perfect anchorage, a French sloop with a older couple aboard, and a Polish catamaran named *Gdansk Spirit*, with all the style and attractiveness of a 1920s boxcar.

We had two marvelous days in Moorea. One high point was to have a drink with a long-time friend, Moana Suchard, who is chief designer for Tapu, a Tahitian surf clothing firm. It was fascinating to hear how he got the inspirations for next year's successes, as well as the dynamics of leading the creative work for an international clothing company from a house on the beach in Moorea.

On returning from Moorea to Tahiti, we had the pleasure of watching a mother and tiny humpback whale calf play around at the edge of the reef.

In Marina Taina, we had gotten to know the crew of some of the super yachts. Friday night is BBQ night, and last night was a lovely one. We have persuaded the crew of at least one of the yachts to bring it to Bora Bora for "training" while her owner is away, so we'll have some pals to play with....

Kath and Hannah, Bora Bora.

## 18 AUGUST 2007

At 1400 today we departed the Marina Taina for Bora Bora. The day is overcast with rain and no wind. It is about 135 NM to Bora Bora, so we should enter the pass at about 1000 tomorrow morning. I have flown to Bora Bora from the States 15 times since my first visit in 1972. But this will be my first time by boat. It is going to be interesting and emotional to sail in through the pass.

We are greatly regretting Theresa's departure this morning for the Gambier Islands, to join *TeTega*. We all hope that she has a safe journey and we will do our best to keep a sense of her joie de vivre on board.

Kath Moore will join us in Bora Bora and we hope Willis Sautter will be able to return. Willis was with us from Cape Town to the Seychelles and we met Kath in Hobart, where she was Mate of the brigantine, *Windward Bound*.

## 19 AUGUST 2007

*Maggie B* sailed through the Pass in Bora Bora at about 0945 Sunday morning. For the first time in a long time, the GPS and the charts didn't match up. The difference is only 300 meters, but then the Pass is only 200 meters wide. It certainly is a good reminder to keep one's eyes open. I did hand-bearing compass sights to nail down our position, but they came out crazy—then I saw the note on the paper chart "Magnetic Anomalies" and then "Differences in Latitude and Longitude may exist between this chart and others." So, anyway, we are in a marvelous spot, led in by our friend Richard Postma of *Taravana* with his son Kahai and his granddaughter.

We had a quiet motorsail from Papeete. We dodged Huahine, Tahaa and Raiatea, which was easy. We also dodged perhaps half a dozen cruise ships rushing back to Papeete for the next changeover.

We have had a lovely welcome from Bora Bora and our dance card is filling up fast. We are near the famous Hotel Bora Bora, where my father has been going for 45 years. Dad was made the First Honorary Citizen of French Polynesia when he was here last. Bora Bora will be great fun even before our yachtie friends from Papeete arrive! We hope to work out the opportunity to do a traditional pig roast, with underground oven, cook for a day, etc., with all our new and old friends.


## 27 AUGUST 2007

For the weekend in Bora Bora, we went on a little road trip to Taha'a, an island that is just 20 miles across the channel. Older romantics may remember the movie *South Pacific* where there was the big US Navy base on one island, but across the way, close but remote, was Bali Hai. The base that Michener was writing about was Bora Bora and Bali Hai was Taha'a and Raitatea—they share a lagoon. In the Second World War, most of the girls were sent across to Taha'a to be out of the reach of the Americans.

Taha'a isn't like that today. It is the sleepy garden island. Currently we are at the Tara Vana Yacht Club, on one of their moorings. It is a perfect quiet spot just at the south end of the island. We went touring around today and couldn't help but notice that the roads were the best we've seen in all of French Polynesia. The answer seems to be that no one uses them. No big trucks, no tearing up everything for new sewers, just bicycles from time to time on the smooth macadam.

We had a great sail across to Taha'a with Erwin Christian. For those who might want to see more of this lovely area, get some of Erwin's books: *Tuamotu Islands* (with Dominique Charnay), *Moorea* (with Claude Robineau), *Marquesas: Images from the Land of Men*, *Light in the Lagoon* and, my favorite, *Tahiti, au gre du vent* (Tahitian Glimpses). The last one is all black and white photos, and I think has Christian's favorites.

*Maggie B* near the Hotel Bora Bora.

We were fortunate that Christian, before he sailed with us, got a speedboat and photographed *Maggie B* in the lagoon of Bora Bora and just along the reef outside. As everyone know, *Maggie B* is beautiful, but Christian's photos make her exquisite.

### 4 SEPTEMBER 2007
We have returned to our spot off of Hotel Bora Bora. Communication from *Maggie B* will be erratic for a while. A few nights ago, I fell in the water when returning to the boat, unfortunately carrying a briefcase with the primary computer, camera, and cell phone. None swam well. Even though the briefcase was in the water for only a few seconds, everything was ruined. In 2,000 departures and arrivals on the *Maggie B*, this was the only time I fell in the water—and I was carrying all the good stuff! All ship's papers, passports, etc., as well.

After passing up the briefcase, I swam around to the ladder to get on the boat, losing my wallet in the process.

The next day at first light I went looking for the wallet and there it was 50 meters behind the boat, in 30 feet of water. At least I didn't have the hassle of obtaining new credit cards and license.

A new phone was easy and the SIM card worked fine. The computer was backed up and the hard drive seems fine. The camera's SIM chip seems fine. And we have the #2 computer, all paralleled, right? Wrong. The #2's power connection failed and the power supply chip shorted out the first morning it was called on. But I've saved its hard drive and will download everything, as soon as I can get a new computer in a few days. There is a helpful team of computer wizards on the island, so we are well supported.

## 9 SEPTEMBER 2007

We are on a lovely sand platform in about 20 feet of water. The area is about 200 meters by 300 meters, without any coral. We have an excellent anchoring system out, 120 feet of half-inch chain, a 100-pound Manson Supreme anchor on the end, and a 30-pound "Anchor Buddy" about 17 feet down the chain from the bow.

As the *Maggie B* works back and forth, the chain rakes the bottom. The other night we had a bit of a weather system go through with 20–25 knots of wind from all around the compass. The Manson Supreme reset perfectly and didn't move more than a few feet in any direction. In the morning when I swam to check the anchor, the bottom looked like a Japanese Zen garden that had been raked in a perfect 100-foot circle.

The local rays seem to like the anchor chain's raking of the bottom. They search for goodies just under the surface and then suck them up, ejecting the sand out of their gills. The depressions that they leave are the size of large soup plates. The spotted leopard rays spread out their normally narrow nose to something that looks like a sapper's mine detector as they swim along close to the sand hunting their prey.

There are many flounders along our sand platform. Normally they are invisible, but they can't effectively hide where the movement of the chain has raked the sand because, though they have the color right, they can't match the ridges.

We are near the famous Hotel Bora Bora. Their over-water bungalows are the most expensive on the island. We, however, have the perfect over-water bungalow in the *Maggie B*, though the beds aren't king-sized and romantically draped with mosquito netting.

It is interesting to see the current dance program at the Hotel Bora Bora. All of it is quite authentic as different troupes compete for the Bastille Day festival. Ten years ago, it was mostly girls dancing, with just a few guys taking part. Now there is lots of emphasis on the traditional male exploits, including fire dancing, spear throwing, and rock lifting. They even do a "haka" imported, perhaps, from the Maori.

## 24 SEPTEMBER 2007

The Schooner *Maggie B* is still in Bora Bora. No, we haven't swallowed the anchor, though it is getting a bit of marine growth on it. We are still waiting to get a new computer and camera, which have made it to Tahiti, but are caught in customs. Each day they say tomorrow, and then ask for more documentation.

Ceremonial dancer, Maupiti.

After Bora Bora we are headed over to Taha'a and Raiatea, then off to Rangiroa in the Tuamotus. We have spent a lot of time looking at the charts of the South Pacific and it seems we will have to skip the Marquesas this lap. The general plan is to be in Montevideo, Uruguay, about the second week of December, which would mean passing the Horn about the first of December, which would mean hitting Puerto Montt, Chile, about the first of November.

It is about 4200 NM from Rangiroa to Puerto Montt, or perhaps a month, allowing for a stop at Easter Island. That means leaving Rangiroa about the first of October. Not that far away.

We had a lovely trip to Maupiti in a friend's little game fishing boat, the *LunaSea*, named after his daughter Luna. We went over in the speedboat because the pass at Maupiti is famous for its danger and difficulty. Even with *LunaSea*, it took 2 boats coming out of the Pass to guide us in. The swell breaks fully across the opening, and the outflow is about 8 knots, with a 90-degree turn right in the middle. You have to wait for a break in the wave sets to rush in. Fortunately, our captain was a surfer and good at reading waves. Even so, we would have gone back to Bora Bora if it hadn't been for the locals helping us to time the wave sets.

We went for a historic occasion: the people of Maupiti were choosing a new king. They had delegations from Hawaii, New Zealand, Tonga, and Easter Island to support the occasion, which was held on Monday the 10th, the new moon, at their restored *marae,* the traditional temple. On the following day, they had a *pêche au*

*"The rest of the fish are speared or grabbed, making for a reasonable catch, though not worth all the effort in a narrow cost/benefit analysis. But for community building, invaluable."*

*caillou* (literally, "pebble fishing"). The pebbles are stones about as big around as two fists together, tied to a 2- or 3-meter rope.

The whole community comes out, including every boat. One man to steer and one man to scare the fish by smashing the water with the stone. The goal was a strip of beach perhaps 200 meters wide. At either side of the target were wings of people with palm fronds tied together, extending out into the lagoon perhaps 200 meters. At the signal—a smoky fire lit on a spot of beach visible to all—the two wings of boats close in from left and right, perhaps 30 boats to a side, smashing the water and creating maximum fuss. Behind the boats are little speedy boats with tall flags, zipping up and down like samurai warriors on horseback with their signal flags, keeping the lines straight.

The boat wings meet those standing in the water—including your Captain—and more palm fronds are rushed out to close gaps. Much shouting and thrashing. The trap is closed with the usual confusion of too many chiefs giving too many orders, but all good humored with singing and insults and encouragement shouted up and down the line. Everyone is dressed in *pareus* (sarongs) and flowers, some combinations being amazing. The biggest, baddest guy has his tiny granddaughter on his shoulders, teenage boys tease teenage girls, westerners shoulder the line and

New King of Maupiti.

learn the latest variation of hand-slap greetings. Brave fish jump the line, occasionally hitting people in the head, to great amusement. Once the circle is pushed all the way in, dignitaries are given fish spears to get the first fish. The Hawaiian representative, a state senator from Maui, went first, looking very uncomfortable, but handily spearing a nice three-foot jack. The rest of the fish are speared or grabbed, making for a reasonable catch, though not worth all the effort in a narrow cost/benefit analysis. But for community building, invaluable.

Jack London, in *The Cruise of the Snark*, reports on a *pêche* au *caillou* held in his honor in 1907 in Bora Bora, where they got zero fish. He reported that one out of five were complete failures, and that they did it monthly. In Maupiti, this was the first *pêche* au *caillou* in seven years. It isn't done any more in Bora Bora.

## 27 SEPTEMBER 2007

The Schooner *Maggie B* is on the move again. We left Bora Bora on Tuesday, September 25th and had a lovely sail across to Taha'a, as the wind had come a little south. We moored at the Taravana Yacht Club.

All positions in this part of French Polynesia are approximate as the charts and

Band and Chorus, Taha'a.

GPS disagree by about two-tenths of a mile. In any case, no prudent captain would trust his GPS to take him closer than two-tenths of a mile in French Polynesia, or perhaps anywhere else, until setting local error rates.

Tuesday night at the Taravana Yacht Club is buffet and dance night. The yacht club is ably run by Maui Postma, the son of our friend Richard. The buffet was delicious and included many of my favorites: chicken fafa, poisson cru with coconut milk, and plates of sashimi—all improved by a rum punch, whose mixture had had the afternoon to steep. The dance was very good for a little, quiet island, with a great fire-dancer to finish it off. As always, one fascinating element was how many locals showed to watch from the shadows. While the show was officially for us tourists at the yacht club (we were perhaps 30 in number), the real audience was the aunties and uncles and kids and boyfriends and girlfriends, who outnumbered us.

We motored on Wednesday, September 26th to Uturoa, the second biggest town in French Polynesia—three-story buildings! We fueled up and shopped the stores for provisions for the long leg to Chile. The town was quite different from Vaitape in Bora Bora. Vaitape is all about tourists and selling them pearls, or at least a t-shirt. Uturoa is the regional market town. Stores sell crates of things, not individual items. The ferries are loaded with food and packages more than people. There are even a few chic cafes, where overseas French pass a few hours over lunch, with cigarettes hanging from their lower lips.

Wednesday night we anchored near the Pass Teavamoa. It was lovely, with the hills and valleys west of us and the rollers pounding the coral reef to the east. But the bottom went from 130 feet to 4 feet in about 50 yards, a tough anchorage. We nosed in and dropped the anchor on the edge of the "hill" and hoped that the wind wouldn't change. Fortunately, it didn't.

Today, Thursday, we went to one of the most fabulous spots in French Polynesia, the Marae Taputapuatea. This is the Vatican, the Jerusalem, the Mecca, of Polynesian culture. All other maraes had to have a stone from Taputapuatea to be consecrated. Voyages of exploration and conquest departed from here and went out through the pass Teavamoa, the holy pass. New Zealand is 2216 NM, Hawaii is 2381, and the big canoes, the waka hourua, came from here. The site is well restored, used regularly, and quite impressive. The delegations that came to Maupiti to invest the new king came here for ceremonies afterwards, including fire walking.

We are reminded of the international cultural connections tonight because 200 meters away is a dinner with a visiting Maori group and their Raietean hosts. The music, dancing, and drums over the last three hours makes *Maggie B* shake.

We were met here by a new friend, Charlie Gomph, who sailed here 35 years ago from Hawaii with Richard Postma. Charlie has a lovely Raietean wife and lives in the hills above Taputapuatea, growing vanilla, noni *(Morinda citrifolla, which makes a popular health food drink)*, coconuts, bananas, breadfruit, avocados, papaya, taro, and much more. He recently got electricity and a telephone, which he considers a bit decadent. He is passionate about his island and is helping it to a clean, green, not a tourist-over-run future. We had a fascinating day with him covering history, ecology, gardening, politics and the future. He loaded us down with so much fruit and vegetables that we had to beg him to stop. We are baffled what to get him to thank him as he has everything, though not much by most standards. He asked for some tubes of Neosporin, which isn't available here. Charlie uses it regularly as he is also the bush doctor for his valley. Our new crewmember, Robert Farrar, will be able to bring some out to Rangiroa, which we can mail back to Charlie.

Tomorrow we plan to go back by Uturoa to get a few things that we forgot, then

Charlie at marae Taputapuatea.

on back to Taravana Yacht Club for the night. We are hoping that the next weather system, with a nice southeasterly, comes through on Saturday. Rangiroa is about 260 NM to the NE from here, so anything south of east would be a blessing.

In Rangiroa, at Hotel Kia Ora, on October 3rd, we should rendezvous with Robert Farrar, who will be our fourth crew member. Robert is an experienced sailor from Atlanta, which we will not hold against him as he can more or less speak standard American. He will join me, Hannah Jordrey, and Kath Moore. Ben has left the ship to stay in the islands.

## 29 SEPTEMBER 2007

We are finally underway for Rangiroa. We have about 235 NM to go, and, wind and weather permitting, should be there Monday, October 1st.

We are doing 6 knots, headed for our target, and we have a 10–14 knot southeasterly, though things may change as we work our way out of Huahine's wind shadow. It is a clear day, with only a few clouds, which serve as punctuation in the blue sky.

Huahine is about 20 NM off our starboard beam, the twin islands of Raietea and Taha'a are 20 NM behind us, and Bora Bora punctures the horizon about 35 NM away on our port quarter.

## 30 SEPTEMBER 2007

We have about 106 NM to go to Rangiroa. The weather is changeable. We had been more or less close hauled on the starboard tack, generally heading for Rangiroa from noon yesterday to noon today. Light winds, 10–12 knots from the southeast, but adequate to move the *Maggie B* at 4–6 knots. Lovely sailing. At noon today we got a little frontal passage, and now we are close hauled on the port tack, a 120-degree wind shift. There are small rainsqualls all around, so we are ready for anything.

Lunch today was our friend Livio's avocados from Bora Bora with four-clove garlic vinaigrette dressing, along with french brie cheese, small, hot pork sausages, and Arnold's Ship Biscuits. Dessert was Charlie's perfect papayas with lime juice. Washed down by the Schooner *Maggie B*'s finest desalinated water.

Most sailors know the term marlinspike. It is an essential tool for splicing lines and opening difficult knots. Few realize that marlinspikes were, in fact, marlin spikes, that is, the beak of marlin fish. Hannah and I are fortunate to have been given nice marlinspikes by Richard Postma. They have dried out for a year. Now they need to be sanded and polished and appropriately decorated with fancy work.

At current speed, we will arrive at Rangiroa during the night. We will either slow down as we get close or find a nice spot to heave to, well off the reef. The *Pacific Islands Pilot* says that we can expect slack water in the pass "five hours after moonrise; four hours before moonset; five hours after moonset; and three hours before moonrise."

## 1 OCTOBER 2007

*Maggie B* anchored off the Kia Ora Hotel in Rangiroa at noon on October 1st.

We sailed in the little pass at Rangiroa, Passe d'Avatoru. This pass gets going at up to 8 knots outflow, but we entered only an hour and a half after theoretical slack. We had only about 4 knots of current, enlivened by 4–6 foot dropping waves caused by the 20-knot wind in against the current. The turn into the pass was made more interesting by a dive boat in the middle of the channel picking up eight divers, all scattered about. We were doing 8 knots, jumping from wave to wave. Once inside it was a short sail to the "Schooner Cove" near the hotel and the main pass, Tiputa.

We weren't too encouraged by the helpful advice concerning entering passes in the Tuamotus as described in the *Admiralty Sailing Directions*: "Low powered, shallow draught, strong wooden vessels such as schooners, should keep close to the east side of the pass. If too close, a counter-flow may be experienced, but rates are much reduced close to the sides of a pass. A vessel grounding at low speed will generally be driven off again by the flow of water through the pass without damage." Perhaps that is why we saw a nice sloop high and dry on the west side of the Avatoru Pass.

We look forward to rendezvousing with Robert Farrar on October 3rd. We will be off for Chile not too long afterwards.


## 7 OCTOBER 2007

We are making 6 knots, closed hauled, headed southeast. The wind is from the east at between 12–20 knots, with an occasional 35 knots in rainsqualls. The weather is mostly clear.

We had a super ride yesterday coming out of the main pass in Rangiroa. The current was perhaps 6 knots, flowing into a 20 knots opposing wind. We hit the pass at 1600, just as the outflow was beginning to crank, under full main and jib. *Maggie B* rose marvelously to the occasion, giving spectacular leaps from wave to wave. We blew our very loud horn as we entered and the dive boats scattered and watched us with awe.

The waves are now settling down somewhat. Last night it was rough and not all members of the crew were fully active.

Days of departure are always hectic. Yesterday seemed a bit worse than usual. Routine engine checks gave the Onan generator a bad case of the air locks and we had to rig a temporary header fuel tank to solve it. Final rig checks found a badly frayed main throat halyard, which was replaced. The joy of having a simple rig, both engine and aloft, ample supplies, and a fit, skilled crew, was that these two major problems were solved in little over an hour.

We are making our way south and east, sliding outside the main mass of the Tuamotus. Kaukura, Arutua, Tupana are behind us. The only one still on our way is Anaa, which is about 60 miles ahead. We should be well outside the restricted zone around Mururoa, where the French used to test nuclear weapons.

Easter Island is about 2150 NM away, a little south of east. The coast of Chile

Sunset at sea en route to Rangiroa.

is about 4000 NM.

We are starting crash courses in Spanish.

## 8 OCTOBER 2007

We are making about 165 degrees magnetic doing 6 knots. The wind has stayed at about 100 degrees magnetic at 18–25 knots. We are somewhat off close hauled because the seas have made up a bit and if we are hard on the wind; we beat our brains out and make little headway.

We have come 265 NM from Rangiroa and Easter Island is 2075 NM away.

We are headed south instead of east for three reasons: 1) the wind is from south of east, and would be directly on our nose if we pointed towards Easter Island, 2) there is a whole mess of Tuamotus between us and Easter Island, and 3) we're after a favorable breeze. In about 2–3 days, a nice, fat 300-mile-wide band of a fresh southerly breeze should work its way east past 145 West longitude. But we'll have to be south of about 25 degrees to catch it. The timing should be right. It will take us about two days to get another 6 degrees—360 NM—south. Then we'll put our thumb out, tack over to starboard tack, and hope to ride that southerly most all the way, 2000 NM or 10 days, to Easter Island, which is about 27 degrees South and 109 West. That's the plan, anyway.

We are passing the last of the Tuamotus on our course. It has the engaging name of Hereheretue. Here means "beautiful." Herehere means really beautiful. Not sure about "tue," but would suspect it means "spot or place." Must be an early form of marketing to call a tiny out-of-the-way place "really beautiful," like the Vikings calling that rough, icy island "Greenland."

We have fitted our Fremantle-made gaiters around the skylights to help keep the salt water out. *Reepicheep* has additional lashings to keep it from roaming. And Robert has discovered a little leak through the deck by the foot of his pilot berth, which we won't be able to track down and fix until we get on the other tack. Fortunately, it can drip straight into the bilge.

All hands are back, mostly functional, and the Blue Water routine is beginning to settle in.

## 9 OCTOBER 2007

This has been a bad day. A little before 0900, our main throat halyard block failed. It was a heavy duty Antal triple. We noticed serious wear on the brand new halyard we put up three days ago. It has been three days of close-hauled sailing in a 20-knot breeze, with occasional gusts to 35, but nothing serious. As we were securing the main, and not more than five minutes from the first failure, the fore throat halyard block failed. It was a Lewmar triple.

Robert experiencing quality time aboard.

We were in fairly rough seas, too rough to send anyone aloft with our spares, so we made for the nearest atoll, Hereheretue, to find a spot in the lee to make repairs. We got to the atoll at about sunset, and Kath, with a great effort, got the main throat halyard up. But by then it had become clear to us that we weren't in a position to press on to Chile. We need more rigging work, especially to find and eliminate the source of wear on the main throat halyard. We need more blocks. We need to clean up the mess in the lazyjacks made by the emergency lowering of the sails. We need to raise the fore throat halyard with the new block. Did I mention that the GPS receiver antenna also failed last night? The spare works satisfactorily, but has to be properly installed.

It also looks as if the hoped-for big southerly isn't going to happen and we would be facing more strong headwinds.

So now we are headed back to Marina Taina in Papeete, a trip of a little more than a day. It is a lovely place, but rather discouraging to retreat. I am not at all sure what this means for timing for Easter Island, the Horn, or Montevideo. I hope that the prospect of Big City Bright Lights will dispel some of the gloom.

Heaven knows what the French Border Police will make of our return. Perhaps we can sneak in and out? Nah.

## 14 OCTOBER 2007

The Schooner *Maggie B* is safe in Marina Taina in Papeete. We are pretty much fully recovered from the equipment problems of last week. We have re-rigged and fixed our major problems. Minor things still need to be done like attaching more protection to the masts and properly routing the wires for the replacement GPS antenna. The mast protection is flexible plastic that we glue on in the positions where the gaff saddles ride. It reduces or eliminates wear on our strong, expensive carbon masts.

It looks as if a nice weather system is going to go through Tahiti Sunday night, which might have a nice broad shoulder of a northerly that we can ride down the line. We hope to be off Monday, though now Tuesday seems more probable. We have a rather complex report from Commanders' Weather for our possibilities on the leg to Chile.

In fixing the block failures, we found out two things: first, that in Papeete no one stocks the big triple blocks we use for the throat halyards; second, it was not the wheels in the blocks that broke, it was the connection to the mast. So instead of non-existent "triples," I bought a pile of big single blocks that we can secure to the mast with ultra-strong line, rather than with the metal connectors that kept breaking.

It is now Sunday, October 14 in Papeete, my birthday. It looks as if it is going to rain all day. But all is well.

*"When we get to 9–10 knots speed in the Maggie B, a faint hum develops. Technically it is probably some interface with the centerboard, but we all think that it is just the hum of happiness."*

## 13

# PAPEETE TO
# PUERTO MONTT, CHILE

### 16 OCTOBER 2007

We are just outside Tepuhaonu Pass, a few miles from Marina Taina, finally underway for Chile, with a hoped-for stopover in Easter Island. We are full of diesel, water, food, and good will from the Polynesians and our fellow yachties, who gave us a nice send off from the marina. Puerto Montt is about 4115 NM away. If we are able to match our speed from Mauritius to Fremantle, 7.9 knots, it will take us 22 days.

This last visit was a "technical," meaning that we didn't want to be there, but we had to fix up the boat. We sorted through Customs, gear, supplies and fix-up in a professional fashion—in a place of dreams and imagination and the cherished ideal of millions. Tahiti! One thinks of sunsets, of swimming in turquoise waters with the perfect partner. Our goals were more practical, like finding a big halyard block in the back of a cluttered warehouse in the tough part of town. We have been in French Polynesia since July 29th. Two and a half months. Cape Horn and our third great passage beckon us out of the harbor!

Yesterday we had rain of biblical proportions. It was as if a thunderstorm sat right overhead the marina for 4 hours. Besides the rain, we saw one serious waterspout that did no damage, but did organize the 20–30 boats at anchor off the marina into a perfect circle, perhaps 500 meters across. It was like a movie of a wagon train circling under attack.

But today, Tuesday, is clear, with a fickle northwesterly wind tumbling over the mountains. We have the promise of a northerly wind until we get west to about 140–141 degrees West, when we will hit the usual easterly, which will force us south. Our general plan is to work our way east as best we can on this little northerly, until we have to turn south or southeast. We hope to settle in along 27 degrees South and run along to Easter Island, which is about 109 degrees West, right at 28 degrees South. But much depends on the positioning of the next high, which we will have to get south of, in order to get decent winds. That may be a ways south. *La Niña* conditions are setting in, which traditionally means the highs go further south.

When I started writing this report at about 1600, I had barely entered the addresses when the main throat halyard came down again. Our hearts just hit rock bottom as we took in sails and headed to the nearest port. But then I was just thrilled to see that nothing had broken, just the knot in the halyard attaching the bitter end to the jigger had come untied. We motored into Port du Phaeton, rehung the halyard with a proper whipping (the halyard, not the bosun) and slipped out of the unlit, complex Passe de Teputo just at full dark. Onwards!

Then the toilet plugged up, but that was fixed in an hour. Whee! I want one day with no problems....

## 17 OCTOBER 2007

We are making 8.3 knots, headed on a rhumb line course for Puerto Montt. The wind is a nice 15-knot northeasterly and the seas, while somewhat confused, are settling down.

We are doing what *Maggie B* does best, making good time on a broad reach on a long passage. We are all settling in to the Blue Water routine, though a little warily after all the former alarms. I'm still on the midnight/0300, noon/1500 watches; Hannah is on 0300/0600 and 1500/1800; Kath is on 0600/0900 and 1800/2100; and Robert is on the 0900/noon and 2100/midnight.

The next big challenge is to update our iPods, so that we can enjoy downloads from when we were in Tahiti, rip off some of Robert's music, and generally update. Our onboard computers have about 5,000 songs. Something for everyone! Listening to old favorites makes night watches pass easily and happily.

In the civilian world, this is a big effort—3 to 4 weeks away from land, covering 4,000 NM. But we have light duty compared to the old days of sail. We stand two 3-hour watches a day, instead of the traditional four hours on and four hours off. We each have our own comfy bunk rather than a hammock and 14 inches to swing it in. Radar, autopilots, and GPS keep us safer. But we are still going over the horizon to a distant, unknown destination, as so many of our heroes did in the old days.

## 18 OCTOBER 2007

We are making 7.2 knots to the east-southeast in a punishing, confused sea. The wind is from the northeast at 20 knots and it is overcast with occasional light rain showers.

We have about 3/4 of a knot current with us, which is probably the reason for the difficult sea.

We are sailing a course to stay clear, to the south and west, of the French nuclear test sites, where we expect we would be unwelcome.

*"In the civilian world, this is a big effort—3 to 4 weeks away from land, covering 4,000 NM. But we have light duty compared to the old days of sail."*

## 19 OCTOBER 2007

We are making 7.4 knots to the southeast in an 18–22 knot northeasterly. We did 165 NM in the last 24 hours, close hauled. Our course made good is only about 10 degrees south of the Great Circle Course to Puerto Montt. We are still taking a bit of a beating from a choppy 3-meter swell, accentuated by having the current against the wind.

In about two days we will have to start positioning for the next system. We will have to make the decision either to stay up around 27 degrees South and work for an Easter Island visit, or continue south to assure ourselves of a good westerly to blow us to Puerto Montt.

Now three days into the leg, life is settling into the Blue Water routine. We had our first meal all four together today and everyone is fully able to stand watch. We have been trading around a little cold that goes from throat to sinuses to head to stomach.

Yesterday's disaster was losing the little mid-filter piece of our espresso maker overboard. I was emptying the used coffee grounds and Neptune sent a wave and took it for a new ornament. We have an emergency supply of a product called "Java Juice" which will give us enough time to experiment with cowboy coffee and cold-brewed extract.

Other than the coffee crisis, all is well.

## 21 OCTOBER 2007

We are making 8.2 knots close hauled to the southeast, on our Great Circle for Puerto Montt. The wind is 15 knots from the east-northeast. The weather is lovely with little scattered clouds.

There was no noon report yesterday because our Captain and Chief Plumber were making a heroic but unsuccessful 15-hour attempt to fix our toilet. It was disassembled and reassembled. Joker valves were replaced. Hoses were switched and decalcified. The black water tank was plumbed. Seacocks were checked to be clear. Nothing helped.

Today Deputy Chief Plumber Robert Farrar is attacking. Pressures are being applied and we all hope for success. The problem was finally solved by shoving a stick up the underwater exit pipe. Not nice, but a great relief for all.

## 22 OCTOBER 2007

We are making 8.7 knots on the route to Puerto Montt. The wind is a very pleasant 15 knots on our beam. Just another pitch about how wonderful *Maggie B* is—we are doing almost 9 knots in 15 knots of wind, and with our main at one reef!

Things are looking up—we found an old French Press coffee maker, hidden away for just such an emergency, such as the Captain losing part of the espresso maker overboard.

Robert made lunch: chicken with a sauce of shallots and garlic in a court bouillon reduction, finished with morel mushrooms rejuvenated in red wine, assorted vegetables and saffron rice on the side. In the midst of this delicious meal, the strap holding the main peak block to the top of the mast parted. Having our priorities right, we lowered the main, took in the jib, and proceeded under fore alone while we went back to lunch. The triple Spectra strap was an experiment, to reduce metal-to-metal wear between the masthead fitting and the block's shackle. The experiment was unsuccessful as the strap only lasted 2000 NM.

Our world is getting colder as we make our way south. It seems like just yesterday that we would wake with sweat-soaked pillows in Bora Bora, and now we are digging out blankets and wearing shoes on night watch!

Today we made the tough decision to bypass Easter Island. The reality is the wind. We are right on the island's latitude and only 1300 NM away. But a high pressure is filling in over us and if we keep on due east, we will have little wind and what there is would be right on our nose. We have about 1100 NM of diesel left for motoring and 3000 NM to go to Chile. There is usually no fuel available at Easter

Island. So, it isn't a choice, it is reality.

Following our instincts, the indications from the GRIB weather files, and guidance from Commanders' Weather, we are now headed aggressively south to 35S/125W, which should set us up for favorable wind from this next front, without dipping too deep into the Southern Ocean before we have to. Puerto Montt is at 42 South, the Horn at 55 South.

## 23 OCTOBER 2007

We are just barely sailing at 3.7 knots in an 8–10 knot breeze from the northwest, which put it on our port quarter. We had "the Bird" up with full main and the fore-sail doused, to give more of the breeze to the gennaker. All our tricks were of no use as the breeze died out to 6–8 knots and we started the engine, at long-range cruising speed, using about one gallon per hour to get 6 knots at 1800 RPM.

Our basic rule is that if we can see any white caps anywhere, we can sail. Sailors will recognize this as Beaufort Force Three.

We have come 2007 NM from Rangiroa and have 2910 to go to Puerto Montt. We shifted to GMT –9 when we crossed Latitude 135.5. Papeete was –10, the same as Hawaii, and Chile is GMT –4, the same as Halifax.

Furuno USA has been a huge help with technical advice on our radar/GPS/autopilot system. Some might say that a really good system shouldn't need technical advice after a year and a half at sea, but ours is sophisticated and complex and takes some care and feeding. It is so great to be able to reach a knowledgeable person on the first try by email, from 10000 NM away, and get an answer that solves our problems. If Jorge is happy, the crew is happy.

Every season, passage, and watch has its celestial delights. Right now, my midnight watch is blessed by having moonset, followed not long after by Arcturus, the Bear Keeper, rising in the east-northeast, bright like a ship's steaming light. Orion and the Pleiades stick with me the whole watch. The Pleiades have fascinated me since I was small. The Greeks considered them "the sailing stars," as their rise in the old days was considered the start of the safe sailing season. The Maori called them Matariki or Makalei'i, and they heralded the start of the New Year. They are tattooed on my right shoulder.

## 24 OCTOBER 2007

We are motorsailing at 1800 RPM towards our next decision point at 35 S/ 125 W. The wind, as expected, is 8–10 knots from the northwest, which is just not enough to keep us going above out arbitrary motoring point of 4 knots. We have been able to sail only about half of the last 24 hours, though the sails have always helped. We expect to have a few days of light or no wind, by which time we will be at the decision point, where we will choose how far south our track to Puerto Montt should be, balancing favorable wind against the chance of getting way too much.

After a week at sea, life is settling in for the long leg, as it should. We are doing the usual sailor's make/mend work: new sheaths for knives, leather wallets for shore, and patches for clothes. We wash our laundry, chase leaks in the head, and go over the rigging. Hannah baked a "Lady Baltimore" cake, and Kath, Hannah, and Robert went for a quick dip/drag when we were ghosting along. Tonight's entertainment is a poetry slam with everyone bringing a favorite to read aloud from our many books of poems.

In all the discussions about things that break or are poorly made, I want to recognize systems that do their duty day in and day out without a problem. Today's star goes to our Spectra Watermaker, which has run with no problems for 532 hours over the last year and a half, making about 3200 gallons of fresh water to sustain us.

## 25 OCTOBER 2007

We are motorsailing at 6 knots towards our turn point at 35 S/ 125 W. The wind has stayed light from the northwest at 8 knots, or about directly behind us. The weather is clear, though a big swell is beginning to make up from the southwest, foretelling a serious low.

We are rather out in the middle of things, with Pitcairn Island being 500 NM away to the north, Easter 1000 to the northeast, and Papeete 1500 behind us to the northwest. The ocean seems empty. We haven't seen a ship since Papeete, and only get faint "cheeps" on our Sea-Me radar detector. There have been no birds for the last several days, and alas, no fish have taken our lures.

Beside the full moon tonight, Sirius and the Big Dog, followed by the Ship Stern, fill our skies.

The long swell from the southwest is an obvious clue together with our GRIB weather report, that we will have some wind in a day or so, maybe a lot of wind. With the frontal passage, they are predicting at least 30 knots. With Commanders' help, we will focus tomorrow on just how to best catch a ride with this next system, hoping for wind, but not too much. If we time it right, we might get a ride most of the way to Chile on this low.

Movie night tonight is *A Prairie Home Companion*.

We have a series of podcasts of Garrison Keillor's *News from Lake Wobegon* on our iPods, which make great night watch listening. I was shocked that in his September 8th report on the funeral for Miss Lewis, Garrison butchered the Shakespeare Sonnet #116:

> *"We are rather out in the middle of things, with Pitcairn Island being 500 NM away to the north, Easter 1000 to the northeast, and Papeete 1500 behind us to the northwest. The ocean seems empty."*

"Let me not to the marriage of true minds admit impediments." For the line "[Love] is the star to every wand'ring barque, whose worth's unknown although his height be taken," Garrison replaced "height" with "depth."

Speaking for wandering barques, or at least for wandering schooners, we take our celestial navigation seriously. And this line seems to clearly indicate that the writer, Shakespeare, was knowledgeable about sailing. In it I can so clearly see the master of a barque, far from land with position unknown, spotting a star through the scudding clouds and taking its height with his octant, but not knowing its value until he gets other clues. Certainly, the writer was comparing how stars help guide ships to safe harbor as love guides people. Garrison should know better. I sent a concerned email. Probably the only one *A Prairie Home Companion* gets this week from the Southern Ocean.

## 26 OCTOBER 2007

We are sailing at 6.7 knots with full main and fore and "the Bird" up. The wind is from the northwest at 11–14 knots. A long swell is making up from the southwest and there is a high overcast filling in. We are headed about 100 degrees magnetic

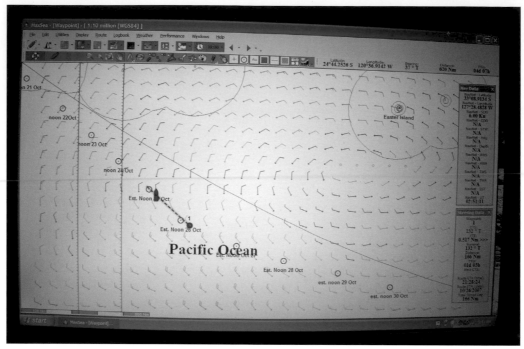

Our wind and routing information showing empty parts of the South Atlantic.

along the Great Circle course for Puerto Montt.

We are just skirting the southwest side of the building high, which will remain a factor for the next several days. The big low to the southwest is too far away and too far south to affect us, but a front off of it should bring us a good breeze early next week. Commanders' Weather sent us this interesting information:

"I would not oppose going down to 40s if you were game for NNW 25-40 knots in the Tue-Wed period, but point out that details of the guidance 4–5 days out may be less than precise. Also, in this remote part of the ocean, we cannot find detailed model output on pressure and wind field from US Navy or other models that we often use to sanity check the workhorse GFS model – i.e. no second opinion. We suggest we take another look in a few days."

We will be down at 37–39 South by Tuesday and will certainly keep our eyes open and consult with Commanders' again. Earlier I described catching a low is like catching a bus. It is more like catching a ride on a freight train, because getting your timing or positioning wrong can be serious.

Analyzing the halyard block problem…

We have received a very interesting analysis of our throat halyard block problem from Nigel Irens, the ship's designer. It is a bit over my head. The essence of the analysis is that the peak halyard INCREASES the load on the throat halyard, not decreases it. Conventional thought was that the throat tightens the luff and carries part of the strain of the sail, with the peak halyard carrying the other share. Nigel's analysis is that our very vertical gaff has a significant downward force vector that increases the load on the throat. Looking at it now, it seems obvious. His analysis also emphasizes that a single triple block is getting pulled at least three different ways at the same time, which would further reduce an otherwise "pure" breaking load.

About two weeks to go to Puerto Montt.

## 27 OCTOBER 2007

We are motorsailing, or mostly motoring, at 6.2 knots towards Puerto Montt. The wind is 290 degrees at 8 knots, or dead astern. There is still a long swell from the SW and the sky is now overcast with mid-altitude clouds.

We have come 2609 NM from Rangiroa and have 2321 NM to go to Chile.

We are getting into the Southern Ocean. The water temperature is now down to 62 F, where it was 82 F in Rangiroa. And finally, we are seeing some birds—petrels and albatrosses.

Last night there was a big ring around the almost full moon. It was "three fists" wide, meaning that the weather was three days away. It is strange that we are using pre-industrial weather forecasting together with modern information—the barometer with satellite analysis—to gauge our weather and the prospects.

I had a waking dream yesterday that I was in a big kitchen or bar and had a huge pile of limes that I was squeezing in a sparkling juicer. I don't remember seeing any rum or tequila. When I woke up I took it as a direct signal from my body and went and make limeade for all hands. No scurvy on the *Maggie B*!

By the weather charts, it looks as if we have one more day of motoring and then this front will catch up with us and we will have all the wind we should want, which will blow us most of the way to Chile. We are ready for it. We ran our first, little, fuel tank dry this morning—meaning we have used 120 gallons and have 200 remaining, with an additional 10 in jerry cans. It appears we are getting about 5–6 NM per gallon, so we should have at least 1000 NM of steaming remaining, plus the emergency 50 NM. It should be fine.

## 28 OCTOBER 2007

We are back under all plain sail, slipping along at 5 knots in 8 knots of wind on our beam. We have a series of complex mid-level overcast clouds with occasional light rain. The barometer is just barely beginning to fall from a high of 1020 mb. The waves are relatively flat with just a long period SW swell to give definition to the wide waters.

Today was clean the boat day, and Robert showed off his beginner's luck by pulling "head and shower" out of the hat. We also started securing for a blow, putting extra baffles on the ventilation system, installing the heavy windows on the aft side of the pilot house, and tightening all deck equipment's lashings, especially *Reep*'s. We practiced setting "Cathy," our storm main staysail between the main and the fore masts.

We are beginning to see albatrosses and petrels. My favorite, the pintado petrel, showed up yesterday. We haven't been able to identify the albatrosses because as soon as they see Robert's camera with the 300 mm lens, they take off for Antarctica.

## 29 OCTOBER 2007

We are rushing along at 9 knots directly towards Puerto Montt. The wind is NW at 17–19 knots, essentially right on our port beam. There is a medium level thin overcast, but the sun is still fairly warm.

It looks as if we will have a marvelous ride the next five days. We have a big high—1034 mb—centered about 700 NM in front of us and a deep low—950 mb—about 1100 NM south of us. We should keep a Northerly 15–30 knot breeze right on our beam for the next five days, which should move us half the remaining way to Chile. We reefed the main down one reef after lunch and will consider doing the same to the fore before dark.

When we get to 9–10 knots speed in the *Maggie B*, a faint hum develops. Technically it is probably some interface with the centerboard, but we all think that it is just the hum of happiness.

As Captain, I felt my first responsibility was for our basic safety. The second was to put the schooner in the right place to move us fastest and safest towards Chile. We needed wind from the right direction to move us. But not too much wind. Meteorology is a science of probabilities. We could cover up to 1000 NM in the scope of a five-day forecast. The job was always where to put the boat in the swirl of the probabilities.

## NIGHT WATCH

Very few modern Americans spend much time outdoors at night. Most sailboats, if they are traveling, find a nice anchorage before cocktail time. However, on a Blue Water passage, you are underway 24/7 and night watch is just another part of your day. Night watch is central to your responsibilities – it is also one of the most novel and memorable experiences.

At night we would switch almost all the lights to a soft red to avoid damage to night vision. Sometimes you could see the whole universe all laid out for you; sometimes you couldn't see an inch beyond the bow or the green and red navigation lights splashing in the waves.

If the weather was steady and once you got used to getting your eight hours of sleep in separate snatches, you were well rested to be up at night. Still, no one really wants to be awakened in the middle of the night, but once you got your cup of coffee, night watch was often the loveliest time on the boat. My clearest memory on the passage from Mauritius to Australia was watching and anticipating Jupiter's progress through the constellation Scorpio. I always knew just when the moon would join my watch, or leave me with starlight to help guide the way. Also, somehow things seemed a bit safer in big weather when you couldn't actually see the waves all around you.

Still, no matter how nice the night watch was, you treasured the shipmate who was ready early to take over from you.

Conrad in "The Secret Sharer" talks of the warm, wonderful strength of comradeship when he was on night watch and could hear the snore or quiet breathing of shipmates asleep in their bunks, off duty, as the ship sailed on in the dark.

On night watch sometimes I would read with my little headlamp, doing the rounds every fifteen minutes – look out all around; check the radar; check the sails; walk below to the bow to make sure all was secure; walk up on deck to check all lashings. Perhaps some exercise – sit-ups, ballet at the barre, and dance to music on headphones. I would try to figure out a new planet or an obscure constellation. And then it was 2:45 am and time to wake my relief.

A regular scare was Venus rising in the morning. All would be quiet and you would look over your shoulder and yow! There was the bow light of a huge ship about to cut you in half! Oh, no, OK, it is just Venus poking her head over the horizon. All is well.

## 30 OCTOBER 2007

We are rushing along at 8.3 knots with full jib, one reef in the main and the fore furled up. The wind has been pretty steady at 310–320 degrees at 20–25 knots with gusts to 32. There is a medium high overcast but no rain, only occasional spray on the boat.

We have come 3119 NM since Rangiroa and have 1812 to go to Puerto Montt. We did 209 NM in the last 24 hours. It looks as if we will keep this ride through November 2nd. We should be within 1,000 miles by then.

Last night at midnight we took in the foresail. What was special about it was… that there wasn't anything special about it. The wind was steady at 25 knots with gusts to 32. *Maggie B* was going hull speed and then some and though still pretty dry with the scuppers clear of the water, she felt over-pressed. All hands were called at midnight, gear and harnesses went on quickly, over jammies, and we did a quick brief in the galley. Deck lights on, a dose of chocolate, and everyone went to his or her stations. One, two, three and down came the foresail into the Lazy Jacks, to be tightly furled up and lashed down. The off watch was back in their bunks by 0030.

## 31 OCTOBER 2007

We are still blasting along at 8.9 knots with 20–25 knots of wind on our beam. We are right on the Great Circle Route to Puerto Montt. We made 217 NM in the last 24 hours. The skies are clearing and the waves are settling in a bit more regularly, though still with a southwest swell against northerly wind-generated waves.

It looks as if we will have two more days of this great breeze. Our high is steadying into place ahead of us and we are running into it—our barometer is up to 1022 mb. Another high looks to develop behind and below us, but we may slip through the gap between the two before it overlays us and stops our progress. We'll have some tactical decisions to make on November 2nd, at which time we'll have only a little more than 1000 NM to go.

We are now on GMT –8, the same as California. While we are sliding waaaaay south, it is amazing to us that if we were at the same longitude in the US, we would be crossing the Utah/Colorado border now. Puerto Montt is at about the same longitude as New York City. A usually successful "bar bet" is asking which South American city is directly south of Miami. The answer is: none—they are all to the east. When we go around the Horn, we will be about as far east as Halifax.

Robert is earning a new name: Splash Gordon. He seems to have unerring

Schoonering at sunset, South Pacific.

ability to arrive on deck just as the biggest splash within hours zeros in on him. This morning he went out for his watch at 0900, having been informed by Kath that there had been no spray for an hour. On emerging in his foulie bottoms, to put on his top and harness on deck, he got the Three Bucket Special square on his head.

## 1 NOVEMBER 2007

We are making 9.1 knots with 20 knots of wind on our port beam. The seas have settled down a bit and the skies are clearing. We are catching up to the high—the barometer is up to 1027 mb—so we may not have this marvelous sailing much longer. In the Roaring Forties, this is as good as it gets. But for the chill in the air, all is perfect.

We have covered 410 NM in the last two days. We are about 800 NM south-southeast of Easter Island.

I've previously mentioned how international *Maggie B* is: Japanese radar, French navigation software, English blocks, Danish riding lights, American Watermaker, New Zealand anchor, etc. I've also been noticing how international our food is: Thai rice, Guatemalan molasses, New Zealand beef, Argentinean chicken, French cheeses, Australian anchovies, American mayonnaise, Danish bacon, Canadian maple syrup, Brazilian sardines, Dutch salt, Mexican hot sauce, Swiss beef stock, South African chutney, Laotian mango slices, Chinese sesame oil, Japanese teriyaki sauce, Scotch whiskey, Barbados rum and French Polynesian beer!

## 2 NOVEMBER 2007

We are making great time, going 7.9 knots in a wind from the northwest of 13–17 knots. The sky has a thin high overcast and there is a long southwesterly swell of perhaps four meters. The air is chilly and we are living in our thermal underwear, under our other gear.

We have come 208 NM in the last 24 hours and 823 NM in the last four days. We have 1208 to go to Puerto Montt.

We're now doing our homework on the arrival in Chile. The channel into Golfo de Ancud, Canal Chacao, between the mainland and Isla Chiloe, runs at up to 10 knots of tidal current. The channel is about 30 NM from Puerto Montt, which is at the top of the Gulfo de Ancud, or four hours steaming/sailing from the channel. Since we will want to do it all in daylight, we'll have to be very attentive to the timing of the flood.

We are all on crash courses to learn Spanish. We are accustomed to "Island Time" from French Polynesia, but it was still a surprise to get introduced to "Manana Time" from the Spanish course, where it is advertised as "Speak Spanish in a Week," although the CD's and workbooks cover four weeks.

Insurance is always an interesting issue. Smart insurance policies are crafted to match a boats strengths and weaknesses, and against known dangers, like the huge seas and strong winds in the Southern Ocean. I paid extra to be allowed to sail south of 50S, but we can't go that far south until after November 30th, considered to be the relatively quietest time of year. Sailors call the area from 40 degrees south to 50 degrees south the "Roaring Forties." South of 50, it is the "Furious Fifties." On inquiry, the insurance company will allow us to head south for Cape Horn a week earlier, for an additional $450. Why $450? Just because.

We have switched to GMT −7. This is particularly exciting to me because it is the same time zone as Chicago, my home. If we were coming east from Denver in a prairie schooner, we would be coming up on the longitude of Kearney, Nebraska.

## 3 NOVEMBER 2007

We are still making good time: 7 knots on a heading of 075 degrees magnetic, holding only a little north of the route to Puerto Montt as we sharpen up to obey the wind as it backs around to the west.

We were disappointed that with the lightening, backing winds we were only able to go 166 NM in the last 24 hours, so our five-day run was 990 NM. So close to the darling 1,000!

We are expecting the winds to fall off further and back around to the southwest, and do at least one full 360 in the next 36 hours. A little high is coming through and we expect tomorrow to be motorsailing, washing and cleaning. Following the high should be a nice breeze from the south-southwest, starting at 25–30 and then tapering off to a fine 15–20 knot southerly to blow us all the way in.

## 4 NOVEMBER 2007

We are motorsailing on the heading to Puerto Montt at 7.8 knots. The wind has backed around to the south at 7–9 knots. We are on the starboard tack for the first time in three weeks!

There is essentially no wind. Fog and a low overcast have come in with a moderate drizzle and cold. The water temperature is down to 54 degrees F. The watch is largely kept in the "Winter Porch," fueled by cups of tea, coffee and cocoa with Hannah's molasses cookies.

We are about 41 degrees South, just in the Roaring Forties. This is about the latitude of Puerto Montt, our destination in Chile. On the globe, north to south, Cape Town is further north at 34 degrees and Cape Horn is 56 degrees south.

In the northern hemisphere, a wind from the south usually means "warm and wet." Here, in the southern half, a wind from the south comes from the Antarctic, and means "cold." The watch reported snow showers during the night. And this is "May" for the Southern Hemisphere.

## 5 NOVEMBER 2007

This morning brought a new surprise. On his watch, Robert collected about a dozen inch long pea green round tubes off the after deck, and asked me what they might be. My first thought was some strange sort of chewing gum pieces. On inspection they proved to be the inner rollers of one of our Lewmar mainsheet blocks, which was spitting them out. We rigged a replacement block and were able to replace all the rollers in the original. Situation solved? Nope. Two other similar Lewmar blocks proved to have far less than their full complement of rollers. Hopefully Lewmar will sell us some replacements and we can get them to Chile with our crew change at Puerto Montt.

We are making good time, 8.1 knots more or less directly for Puerto Montt. The wind is from the northwest at 13–16. It is overcast with fog. Visibility is up and down from 100 meters to 1/2 mile.

This has been a fairly mixed period, with the wind going up and down in strength and all around in direction. I wish that I could say that we are following a clever strategy with carefully defined tactics for dealing with this little high sliding out and the strength of the low coming to bear, but we aren't. We are just taking the wind and waves as they come and doing our best to keep the boat going as much towards Puerto Montt as we can. In the last three weeks we have been completely on the port tack with the sheets almost nailed down. In the last day have jibed 3 times and even now Hannah, on watch, is eager to go back to starboard. It should steady in from the south, but the wind hasn't gotten the message as yet.

## 6 NOVEMBER 2007

We are motorsailing downwind towards Puerto Montt at 6.5 knots. The wind is from the west at 10–12 knots. *Maggie B* doesn't do well going directly downwind, and, after about 4,000 miles, we are more in "delivery mode" for the last little bit, rather than extracting every last knot out of whatever wind we have.

We are focusing on arriving at Canal Chacao at the start of the flood, which is one hour before low tide. Low tide on November 10th is at 0830 local, GMT –3, so we are shooting to be there at 0630 local—better early than late. The math is Fourth or Fifth Grade, but still so often done wrong. Ship's noon now is GMT 1800. We want to arrive at 1130 GMT in @3 1/2 days, or 90.5 hours. 597 divide by 90.5 equals 6.6 knots average speed. Could we arrive by the end of the Friday flood? It starts at 0940 GMT, it would end at @1530 GMT or 69.5 hours equals 8.6 knots.

Hmmm. Could do it, but not with 10 knots of wind on our stern and tight on diesel. We have fuel for 6 knots for 600 NM, but not 8.5 knots—which would require approximately twice the fuel flow for the 40% more speed. So Saturday morning it is.

It was lovely at noontime today. We had lunch at the table in the cockpit. It is so strange to go from snow flurries two nights ago to lunch on deck.

No one on board speaks Spanish, but we are all trying to learn. The Armada, the Chilean Navy keeps a tight track on shipping. One must report to each lighthouse or Naval Station one passes. But what to say? Probably not *buenas dias* or *mas cervezas, por favor*, the Spanish we are learning. So catchy phrases like "*A que hora es el corriente de creciente en el canal Chacao?*" are the order of the day ("When does the flood start in the Chacao Channel?"). But will we understand the answer? We'll know Saturday. I wish my daughter Alexandra were on board with her fluent Spanish!

I am pleased to report that we seem to have shopped successfully for this leg. It appears that we will have sufficient supplies of coffee, garlic and chocolate.

## 7 NOVEMBER 2007

We are still motorsailing with about 10 knots of wind directly behind us. We have 428 NM to go to Canal Chacao. The sky is partly cloudy but visibility is good. It is nice on deck in the sun, but the cabin is chilly with the hatches open to air out. We are seeing lots of birds again—albatrosses and petrels—but we are still skunked on catching fish.

We are hoping for a wind shift to a nice fresh southerly. Probably more wind than we need now because our target speed is 6.5 knots to get us to the mouth of the channel at about daybreak on Saturday, an hour or two before tide change.

Looking at charts, one way to grasp our position is that we are exactly on the longitude of Columbus, Ohio. The 4513 NM that we have come from Rangiroa is just about the distance from where we are to Atlanta, Georgia, or by plane from San Francisco to London.

Work on board is now all about landfall: checking brightness of riding lights (we haven't seen a boat, even on radar, since Tahiti); cleaning; printing out crew lists; cleaning; reorganizing stores; cleaning; preparing Spanish standard phrases; cleaning; studying charts.

## 8 NOVEMBER 2007

We are thrashing along more or less close hauled in 25–30 knots of wind from the southeast. A nice Roaring Forties Spring Event, with occasional sleet in the rain showers. Waves making up into a nice chop, but not too serious yet. It is supposed to blow through pretty fast, which would be good. We are under one reef in the main and the jib rolled up about half way. *Maggie B* is handling well, but we'll take the main in to the second reef if things don't abate by sunset.

We are on schedule to arrive at the mouth of the channel at sunrise Saturday, which is two hours before low water or one hour before the flood starts. If we get there really early, we will anchor nearby at Puerto Ingles, if we get there as late as noon, we would catch the tail of the flood. We should be in Marina del Sur by noon on Saturday.

The storm seems to bring out the pintado petrels. There are at least a dozen working close in our wake and they fly within arm's length of the stern. Albatrosses are around also, and a 5–6 foot juvenile wandering albatross came almost close enough to touch the boat with a wing.

The boat is moving a lot, as if to remind us that we are in the Roaring Forties. We are only able to eat a soup/stew for lunch out of mugs and dinner will be baked potatoes with a bit more of the same soup.

*It was a tough night, lots of tide swirling around, big, peaky, rough waves coming from every direction, lots of wind and dangerous land close at hand. We ran back out to sea, which we knew and where we felt safer; we WERE safer."*

## 9 NOVEMBER 2007

We are taking a bit of a beating. The wind is from the south at 25–30, which puts us on a broad reach, but the southerly waves and swell make for a short sea that is putting a lot of water on board, and giving the boat an occasional abrupt motion. We still have the main up with one reef and the jib rolled up to a bit less than 50%. The foresail is stowed.

Church in Rargua, Chile, on the reach to Puerto Montt.

We have 117 NM to go to the mouth of the channel into Puerto Montt. We seem to be right on time to arrive at about daybreak tomorrow. If we need to wait for the start of the flood, there is a protected bay where we hope we can hang out.

We have 15–20 pintado petrels doing their aerial ballet in our wake. Hannah saw them doing a "walk on water" technique to attract food. It is behavior that I only associate with stormy petrels.

As with most boats that get themselves in a churn, our fuel tanks produced a big load of water and junk for the engine fuel filters. Fortunately, the filters are instrumented and warned of the junk, which we removed before any trouble. What a great way to start the day—getting coated in diesel fuel before breakfast!

One more day! It seems impossible.

## 10 NOVEMBER 2007

We made landfall last night at about 0100, sighting the Faro Corona through the mist and squalls. We hoped to get into Puerto Ingles, past the light, to anchor, but we didn't have enough power to make it against the tide into the quiet harbor. It was a tough night, lots of tide swirling around, big, peaky, rough waves coming from every direction, lots of wind and dangerous land close at hand. We ran back out to sea, which we knew and where we felt safer; we WERE safer. It was strange to have been fully at sea for 3 ½ weeks, finally in sight of land, but rejected, scared away, and head back out to sea. We knew how to handle dark, black, empty Blue Water, and we shied from the danger of the shore.

After three or four hours off shore, we hit the flood perfectly a bit after dawn. We had up to 5 knots favorable current to help us up the channel to dock at Puerto Montt at 1630. Every lighthouse, all of which are run by the Armada, quizzed us as we came in. Fortunately their English was good as our Spanish was lacking.

We covered a total of 5036 NM from Rangiroa, or 4252 from Papeete. From Papeete to Puerto Montt took us 25 days, or an average of 170 NM per day.

One of the amazing experiences of arriving here is the bird life. We went from wandering albatross to pelicans in five miles. We also had the good fortune to set a new record for clearing Immigration and the Armada. We arrived at 1630 and were cleared by 1900. Another boat took four days. Apparently we still have Health and Customs, but we are told to call on them at their offices on Monday, so that hardly counts.

All is well.

Marina del Sur, Puerto Montt, haulout.

*"But it is probably the wildest stretch of water in the world.
All within sight of land, but what a land—Patagonia!"*

# PUERTO MONTT
# TO CAPE HORN

### 18 NOVEMBER 2007

The Schooner *Maggie B* is at the Marina del Sur in Puerto Montt, Chile. We are mostly ready for the trip south to the Horn.

This next leg is very exciting for us all. It is the last step to the Horn! It isn't too far, only about 1,000 NM and we have just done more than 4,000. But it is probably the wildest stretch of water in the world. All within sight of land, but what a land—Patagonia! The Andes! Much of it is uncharted and subject to powerful and unpredictable winds and currents. There are few lighthouses and few buoys; no 911, no hardware stores, no fuel docks and few other boats. We will anchor almost every night because navigation at night in these waters would be reckless. I'm setting a goal of 80–100 NM a day, half our Blue Water average. We have a strong, well-stocked boat and a great crew.

The crew for the trip south is Hannah Joudrey, Alden Blair, Freddie Kellogg, Curtis Weinrich and Frank Blair. Hannah has been with us since Cape Town and is Bosun. She will whip the new recruits into knowing their ropes! Alden is my 25-year-old son, fresh from Africa, Freddie is an experienced sailor whom I have known for fifty years and Curtis is the fix-it man from my brother-in-law's farm and an Alaska commercial fisherman.

It has been hard work this week to fix things. We have re-varnished the cockpit table; renewed the protections on the mast where the boom jaws rub; rebuilt blocks; changed the engines' oil, fuel and oil filters; cleaned out both fuel tanks; rebuilt the toilet again; restocked food, water and fuel; and replaced the injectors on the Yanmar. We are "re-" tired.

We have two fuel tanks, a smaller one at 120 gallons and a bigger one at 200 gallons. I, mistakenly, generally used the smaller one to "save" the bigger. Because it was not used regularly, the big one built up water, biological fouling and sediment. Our engine problems in the last few days were from the bigger tank getting stirred up, bringing sediment and water into the engine feed in amounts that overwhelmed the two filters. To help fix things, we purchased the last four Yanmar injectors in Chile. The new injectors, together with new filters and burnished fuel and clean tanks, seem to have solved our problems.

We also purchased six more five-gallon jerry cans for diesel, to give us a little extra margin and also make it easier to resupply in the towns to the south, where you fill up ashore and lug the fuel to the boat.

Sadly, we are going to leave *Strika*, our South African surf kayak, here in Chile. In the last storm, the jib sheet got tangled around the tip of her bow. When the sail filled, the sheet bent the bow up almost 90 degrees, cracking the fiberglass all around. She is repairable with time, skill and plenty of space—not available on the *Maggie B*. She will make a fine project for someone.

The Chilean Navy, the Armada, have issued our Zarpe. The Zarpe is a formal itinerary with specific places and times that we are required to follow all the way south 1000 NM to Puerto Williams. You are expected to check in twice a day with your position, direction, speed and ETA to the next point. It isn't that big a deal in the north. But in the south, closer to "differences" with the Argentineans and more extreme climate, the Armada keeps you closely monitored. One must check in with every reporting lighthouse and with any Armada boat that passes.

Chile has been fascinating. We explored Puerto Varas to the north, a beautiful lakeside town, and Chiloe Island to the south. Economically things seem pretty good, streets clean, people well dressed and active shoppers. People work hard, six days a week not being unusual. Our repaired sail was finished and returned today, Sunday. The Armada issued the Zarpe at 1700 on Saturday. Puerto Montt is a tough fishing port, and not necessarily a fun place. Perhaps it is livelier in the summer season. There are not many English speakers, however everybody has been kind and helpful.

*"The mechanics took US dollars, the marina insisted on piles of pesos and the gas dock loved my Visa card. We are full of fuel, water, food and good cheer."*

## 19 NOVEMBER 2007

The Schooner *Maggie B* got underway from Puerto Montt at about 5 p.m., headed south through the Chilean Channels for the Horn. It is clear and lovely, with the snow-capped Andes as backdrop to the east. The wind is light from the south and we are motoring at 7 knots. The tide is playing with us—sometimes our GPS speed is 8 knots and sometimes 5 knots.

Monday, today, was like Mondays anywhere. We had the diesel mechanic come back one more time to help us change the impellers that pump the engine cooling water. He was a few hours late, but then worked very hard. It was fortunate we changed the impellers as the Onan generator's had already lost one of its vanes. Now both engines are running smoothly and all our fuel is perfectly clean. The mechanics took US dollars, the marina insisted on piles of pesos and the gas dock loved my Visa card.

We are full of fuel, water, food and good cheer.

We have doubled the watches, with Hannah and Alden on one and Freddie and Curtis on the other. I have taken myself out of the rotation and will be up with both watches, especially Freddie and Curtis on their first few shifts, to do the necessary training in our systems. The channels, here close to port, are full of boats—we probably passed or were passed by 40 in the first two hours out of Puerto Montt, including little wooden fishing boats and oceangoing tugs towing big barges.

We have an open stretch in front of us, about 250 NM across the Gulf of Corcovado and down the Canal Moraleja, which we hope to do in a day and a half. This will give us some time to play in the Canal Errazuriz, where they make a great Sauvignon Blanc, before we pick up a nice northwesterly breeze to make a big run down the coast.

Note: "Canal" in these parts means straits, a reach or a channel. They are the folds between the mountains that have been filled by the sea.

The view from Puerto Lucas.

## 20 NOVEMBER 2007

We are powering at 6.8 knots, headed south. The wind is from the south at 18 knots. We plan to spend tonight at anchor in the Bahia Anihue, main anchor out and a line to a tree on shore.

We have come 105 NM since leaving Puerto Montt. We have 796 NM (as the condor flies) to the Horn.

The Chonos Archipelago protects this area from the ocean. Hundreds and hundreds of islands run from about 44 degrees south to 46 south. Canal Moraleda is a deep channel separating the Chonos from the mainland.

Between now and Sunday, the wind is forecast to be from the south, at speeds up to 40 knots—a good time to hunker down.

Tomorrow we plan to deviate from our Zarpe a bit to the east, to the Canal Puyaguapi, to visit a five star hotel and hot springs called Bahia Dorada.

You can only deviate from your Zarpe in an emergency or "by necessity." Surely a five star meal and country club showers are a necessity?

Today is lovely and clear, even with the unfavorable wind. The excitement after lunch was a new and not nice sound from the rear of the engine compartment. On inspection, it turned out that the stuffing box had lost its lubrication and was almost ready to ignite. We stopped the engine, tightened bolts, blew out the water supply line (it is a "dripless" system), and, after a while to cool, all is well.

East, towards the high mountains, is a series of National Parks. There is one stunning snow-capped mountain after another. This morning the perfectly shaped pyramid of Mt. Nevado in Parque Nacional Corcovado emerged first out of the low morning fog like a Japanese dream of Mt. Fuji. It looks as if tonight we will be anchored under Mt. Melimoyo.

Alden fleecing Kath.

## 21 NOVEMBER 2007

We are navigating out of the incredibly beautiful Canal Refugio, where a ship called *Anna* took refuge in 1741 after having been dismasted off the Horn. She was properly called a "pink," so the bay ahead is called Bahia Anna Pink. The wind has been from the north, west, south and east, and calm. The sun is bright and the sky is clear. The barometer has fallen 15 millibars since we set out on Monday.

We spent last night in a nice spot called Bahia Anihue or Bahia Islas, in an unnamed harbor. Our anchor was out ahead in 8–9 meters of water and astern we tied to a tree with about 100 meters of dock line. We had no swinging room to starboard and a small island was about 10 meters in front of our anchor. Despite some current (3–4 meters tide) through the harbor, we spent a perfect night. A small pod of active dolphin met us and played close around the boat. They were small in size, like a US harbor porpoise, but had a quite different dorsal fin, rounded and relatively soft.

We are briefly out in the big Canal Moraleda, in a maze of fishing buoys, and then we tucked into the narrow Canal Jacaf. Next is Canal Puguguapi, then Seno Ventisquero and finally Bahia Dorita.

Our new Spanish dictionary includes:
Seno=sound;
Canal=channel;
bahia=bay;
cabo=cape;
boca=mouth;
caleta=cove;

goleta=schooner;

punta=point or cape;

faro=lighthouse;

racha=williwaw;

velero=sailing yacht;

zarpe=permit to navigate.

It is hard to describe how beautiful it is here with the deserted green shore and the snow-capped Andes as backdrop. Those of us who know and love Maine, Tasmania, Newfoundland and New Zealand are still searching for new superlatives.

Hannah and Alden are both knitters. We bought some yarn in Puerto Montt. Alden can only knit hats and Hannah can only knit scarves. The rest of us are looking forward to hat and scarves and we are also wondering if they get together, perhaps there'll be a sweater in it somewhere.

This area is a bit of a nightmare for the navigator. While it is always exciting to discover, the charts are very sketchy. Every bay, channel, sound, or cove has a different name on each chart, if it is named at all. Depths are infrequently recorded, and will have 45 feet right next to 774. The general rule is to look out for kelp, which marks 30 feet, or zero. On top of all this, the Armada has changed the position of things on the official charts, presumably to make invading Argentineans run aground.

Hot baths and great food tonight!


## 22 NOVEMBER 2007

The wind is light and variable, the sky overcast with occasional drizzle and rain. At noon we are headed down Canal Puyuguapi under motor.

Yesterday was marvelous with the views of the snow-capped mountains. Today we can't always see the sides of the channel in the fog, but somehow it is more personal. Motorboats, large and small, bustle about, tending the endless salmon farms or fishing. One boat came alongside to offer us a conger eel, but we passed on it.

Our current plan is to anchor tonight on Islas Las Huichas in Caleta Poza, near to Puerto Aguirre. We should arrive at about 6 p.m. Then tomorrow morning we will tie up at the pier in the village (population 1200) and fill up on diesel and buy a little fresh food.

The weather reports still look good for a big northwesterly on Sunday and Monday to blow us south out of Bahia Anna Pink, across Golfo Penas and well down

Puyuhuapi Lodge and Spa.

towards the Straits. The Armada wants us to go "inside" after Golfo Penas, but if we get a few days of good northwesterly, we may stay outside and put a big piece of our southing under our belts.

Yesterday we did get a nice fresh 35 knots at one point during the afternoon—needless to say just when we were threading our way through a very tight spot.

Last night we arrived at Bahia Dorita and picked up a mooring right off the marvelous Puyuhuapi Lodge and Spa. I'm afraid that anyone who looks at photos of the lodge will feel no sympathy for us poor sailors. It is a well-run five star hotel and restaurant, sited right next to a series of hot springs. Pisco Sours and a world-class dinner with Chilean wines.

In the morning we had a test. The engine wouldn't start. Just crank and crank. I immediately suspected sabotage, as there certainly are few nicer places on the planet to be stuck. But all the crew claimed innocence. Here are the clues: 1) we had had extensive fuel problems in Puerto Montt, with new injectors and lots of fuel drained and polished, taking out more than a liter of water and gunk. 2) But we had motored successfully for 38 hours after the engine work. 3) On inspection there was another

Curtis and Alden jumping in.

cup of dirty water in the primary filter, but none in the secondary. 4) The oil level was down a fair ways. 5) We suspected a blocked secondary fuel filter and changed it. Still wouldn't start. 6) When the fuel supply lines to the injectors were opened, proper amounts of fuel came out. 7) The engine had been working perfectly coming in to the anchorage, but was totally dead. Hmmmmm. The answer is: the "Off" button had corroded and was stuck in. Once lubed up, it was fine.

Alden, Curtis, and Freddie want credit recorded for their dips in the cold ocean when we were anchored in Bahia Anihue. Hannah and I watched.

With email help from my brother Ed, and his dolphin and porpoise contacts, we have identified the dolphins we saw two days ago as *Cephalorhynchus eutropia*, the Chilean dolphin, a relatively rare species.

## 23 NOVEMBER 2007

Happy Thanksgiving! No turkeys in Chile, but Curtis made us a seafood stew with fresh salmon and abalone. The wind is calm and the sky is clear. It isn't quite warm enough for shirtsleeves, but jackets are left hung up. A lovely early spring day…in the Roaring Forties.

We have come 287 NM from Puerto Montt and have 695 NM to go to the Horn.

We spent last night in a delightful cove just next to the town of Puerto Aguirre. We were totally comfortable with land all around us, and anchored in 10 meters of mud with a line ashore to a huge tree root. It was overkill for the calm conditions, but if we perfect the routine of anchoring and lines ashore now, we will be skilled when we need it.

We arrived at the pier at about 9 a.m. Curtis had walked the half-mile into town to aid our docking. It was a new cultural experience. No one had any English and our Spanish is progressing only slowly. A lieutenant from the Armada greeted us as we tied up and took me up to the Capitaneria. It was manned by the lieutenant and a secretary. My Zarpe covers us from Puerto Montt to the Horn, but the lieutenant insisted on issuing another updated one. It was painful. First the secretary had to copy out by hand all the information on the Zarpe into a huge book. Then she typed out the same information into her computer, with some updates and minor clarifications of the route. Then she tried to print it, but it had to be on different paper stock than what was in her printer. She hand fed the special Zarpe paper into the printer, one page at a time, having to restart the "print" on the computer between each page. Only then would the lieutenant read it. Each mistake he found was marked and the Zarpe had to be reprinted before he would read further. Then the next mistake would be found, reprinted, etc. You can imagine the effort I had to put into being the cheerful American. Of course, once it was presented to me to sign, I found that they had laid out a geographically impossible route, and offered changes, back to what was on the original Zarpe. Three hours for what could have been done within 60 seconds: "Let me look at your Zarpe. Any changes? All OK? Have a nice trip!"

We left at noon from the dock, which was 20 meters from the Capitaneria. At 1 p.m. we got a call on the radio asking for our ETD from Puerto Aguirre. We were told to report to them when and where we anchor tonight. I think that part of the problem was that we have been making our morning and evening reports of our position and intentions by email to the Armada Headquarters, but I did not also radio the base at Puerto Aguirre that we were anchored in one of "his" coves.

We bought some minor supplies at the store in Puerto Aguirre. We were mostly interested in filling up on diesel. No diesel in town. There was a service station just 10 meters from the dock, but they had no diesel, only gasoline and kero. We were incredulous because there were many boats around that clearly had diesel engines. After a bit, a fisherman sidled up to us and said that he had diesel that he would sell at 500 pesos a liter (mainland prices!). We immediately emptied all our new jerry cans into our fuel tank and hopped in his truck with a fistful of dollars and pesos and got an additional 150 liters (enough for 150 miles) of clean fuel.

According to the Armada Lieutenant in Puerto Aguirre, there is no reliable diesel between there and Puerto Willams, all the way to the Horn. Puerto Eden sometimes has some, though generally at high prices and infrequent availability due to delivery every 4 months. But I suspect that if we are friendly with fishermen, we'll find lots at reasonable prices. Reasonable given the situation and the compensation, possibly assisted by cigarettes or rum bottles. Curtis and Alden are quite entrepreneurial in this way.

Tonight we will be in a tight little caleta called Jacqueline, named by a French yacht called *Maris Stella*. It is on Isla Humos. The Royal Cruising Club guide has the following engaging advice: "Many of the names used in this guide have been coined by yachtsmen and have no official status whatsoever. Hopefully some of the more historical ones will become recognized, as appears to be the tradition in Chile (Mischief Narrows and Tilman Island are excellent examples). The present editor has bestowed many names on anchorages: usually they have been called after vessels or people who provided information. Any users who are aware of a local name or official name for such anchorages are urged to report these for inclusion in future editions." Perhaps we'll discover a Caleta *Maggie B*?

Curtis gooping a plumbing part.

## 24 NOVEMBER 2007

We are motoring west towards our anchorage for tonight, Puerto Millabu, on Isla Clemente. We should arrive at 3 to 4 p.m., in time for a shore expedition.

It is overcast, somewhat cold with occasional drizzle. The wind is light out of the west. We have come 336 NM since Puerto Montt and have 668 NM to go to the Horn.

Nautical twilight at dawn is now 5:40 a.m. and twilight at sunset is 9:58 p.m., or more than 16 hours of daylight. At the Horn, in a week, there will be about 18 hours.

Currently we are threading our way through the Islas Canquenes. We have seen two concrete markers in the 20 NM since setting out this morning. Otherwise, no boats, no houses, no nothing. It is wild and beautiful. The water is getting cold—50F or 10C—and there has been no more talk of morning dips.

Freddie cleaning the starboard fuel tank.

Puerto Millabu is described as: "an inlet, around two miles long....surrounded by beautiful high mountains. The anchorage lies deep into the west side, facing a small beach with large round boulders, in 10 meters of water. The Rio Casma flows into the head of the inlet creating shoals and a nice white beach. The beautiful Cascada Salmon falls down the NW slope. Follow its course to the higher lakes for a great excursion. The highest hill is Monte Haddington, at 982 meters. The anchorage is subject to strong gusts in NW and SW winds."

(Rolfo & Ardrizzi, the authors of our best guide, *Patagonia and Tierra del Fuego Nautical Guide*, by Imray.)

Last night we spotted several dark weasels. One stunned us by diving into the water from a rock, and going underwater far enough so that we never saw it surface. We know that there are otters around, so perhaps we were mistaken.

Alden chose the perfect wake-up music this morning: *The New World Symphony*.

The weather still looks just right for a big sail south starting tomorrow morning. It looks like a 3–4 day northwesterly, so we will have the chance to put some big miles in. The Armada wants us back inside at about 48 South, to go down the Messier Canal. Commanders' Weather has been advising us to tuck back in there as the southwest swell is supposed to come up to perhaps 20 feet, which might be a handful if the wind is from the northwest. The winds are supposed to start at 15 and crank up to 35 knots. We'll reef early and be cautious. We plan to get lots of sleep tonight.

*Reep* ashore in Patagonia.

### 25 NOVEMBER 2007

We are on the south side of Bahia Anna Pink, making for open water. We finally have our sails up, but are still motoring, as the northwesterly hasn't come in yet.

The skies are clear, and it is warm and sunny, at least for 46 degrees South in Chilean Patagonia.

We expect to reach south at good speed, passing Cape Rapier at sundown and crossing the Gulf of Penas during the night to arrive at the mouth of the Messier Canal (Bahia Tarn) at about dawn. We plan to push on to the Seno Glacier for the night of the 26th, which should be spectacular.

But we are running out of adjectives. We came into Puerto Millabu about 5 p.m. yesterday and were all just gob-smacked. The hills are steep on either side, perhaps 300–500 meters, with the inlet fairly narrow. The fjord is about two miles long and has a wide sand beach at the end. The end of the fjord is highlighted by the Salmon River, which cascades down the hill in a series of stair-step waterfalls from lakes up the side of the 1,000-meter mountain.

Our arrival was further highlighted by a swarm of 3-inch, red crustaceans that rushed about under the boat. They looked like crayfish and traveled by snapping their tails, but the red color surprised us—as if they were miniature lobsters that had already been boiled. If we had had a dip net, we would have had a feast. As it was we ate marvelously: carrot ginger soup with a garnish of cream, balsamic vinegar and spicy pepper; chicken marinated in garlic, morel mushrooms, heavy cream and red wine (Chicken Millabu?); potato pancakes with lemon zest. Dessert was "After Eight Mints."

The generator isn't working. There is a problem with the fuel supply. Curtis is on the hunt. We suspect a physical break or kink in the supply hose. There's always something to be deviling us.

> *"We made the famous light at San Pedro at a little after dawn, and we were as happy to see it as the lighthouse keepers were astonished to see us."*

### 26 NOVEMBER 2007

We are proceeding south-southeast down Canal Messier at 8.2 knots under reduced sail and engine, pushed along by a favorable tide. We hope to make Glacier Seno by about 5 p.m. We have come 567 NM from Puerto Montt and have 540 NM to go to the Horn.

Last night we got what is apparently a typical Gulfo de Penas spanking. There was a proper northwesterly gale with sustained winds above 40 knots. We sailed with three reefs in the main, the fore down and the jib up. The *Maggie B* handled it well. The waves were large and confused, breaking all around us, but not often on the boat. All watches got wet and cold but no stomachs were unsettled. We made the famous light at San Pedro at a little after dawn, and we were as happy to see it as the lighthouse keepers were astonished to see us. We found, or caused, a one-foot rip in the main between second and third reef, which seems contained and fixable on board (Hannah!). During one of our reefing evolutions, one of the lines looped around the helm station Furuno display and ripped it free of its mounting. The electronics are fine, but the balance arm is finished.

The Seno glacier, Patagonia.

As the wind petered out, we started the engine and the Newport Stove. We are beginning to dry out and warm up.

We ended up motoring to the Seno Glacier. It was stunning, with incredible fractures and the deepest, lapis lazuli blues. We stopped the engine for a half hour just outside the bergy bits field and listened to the glacier crack, groan and explode. It threw off Volkswagen bus-sized pieces every few minutes. The experience was only slightly diminished by the intermittent rain and sleet.

As we circled around after the glacier, we went by a small prefab house with one resident glacier scientist. He was the first human we had seen since Bahia Dorata, several days ago. He called us on the radio and said, "come my house" but unfortunately, there was no safe anchorage.

After the glacier we motored out to Caleta Ivonne. It was a spot so tight we could have tied up on all four corners with 100 meters of line and had rope left over. It was marvelous. We had captured one bergy bit at the glacier: perfect ice for our various Mt. Gay and Laphroaig drinks.

## 27 NOVEMBER 2007

At noon we were at the Angostura Inglesa. I used to think that Angostura was a secret brew that my parents put in special alcoholic drinks. In fact, it means "narrows" in Spanish. This narrows is transited by very large ships. It must be wild at times. There is a tight 90-degree turn in the middle and currents run at up to 8 knots. The small island at the tight turn has a statue of the Virgin. After the narrows, we stopped at Puerto Eden to check in with the Armada (obligatory!) and to buy whatever supplies we could. That consisted of 3 kilos of potatoes (US$3) and 60 liters of diesel (pesos 650/liter or about US$1.25). Sixty liters isn't much, but that is 60 NM of steaming.

The lieutenant at this Armada office didn't have a secretary, and I escaped with only a long entry in a big book. He was enthusiastic and helpful. He had no English, so I had my first full, successful, technical conversation in Spanish. He also had a big iron stove with a wood fire, which was most welcome.

We anchored at Puerto Riofrio, named after Lieutenant Riofrio of the Chilean Schooner *Covadonga*, which sailed these waters in 1872.

Outside, according to the GRIB files, it is blowing 35–40 knots from the northwest. We are SO happy to be safe in the canales with two lines ashore and the anchor out with a 6 to 1 ratio of chain. The clouds are streaming by overhead but we rarely

*Maggie B* anchored in Puerto Millebu.

Alden, Curtis and Freddie hauling away on a rainy day.

have more than 20 knots in the anchorage, which is picture-postcard pretty.

Alden, with help from many sous-chefs, made a stunning dinner of onions, carrots and sausages, chopped fine, wrapped in spring roll wrappers with ship-made mango sweet-and-spicy salsa.

We have come 664 NM from Puerto Montt and have 483 NM to go to the Horn. Perhaps we will knock off another 100 NM tomorrow?

## 28 NOVEMBER 2007

We are off the northern tip of Isla Saumarez, in the Paso Abismo (no translation necessary). We are heading south under power, making 8–9 knots with the current. The wind is northerly at 15, blowing in fits and spurts out of the different intersecting fjords. It is overcast with rare bright intervals. Rain with occasional sleet. This northerly breeze is due to continue for the next several days. The barometer is down to 1008 mb and continuing to fall.

### MAGGIE B WORK SONG

We have developed a schooner *Maggie B* work song to help us raise the sail and do any "haul" work. Traditionally, sea shanties were both work songs (Way, hay, up she rises) as well as "fo'c'stle" songs, which were more for straight enjoyment (Shenandoah). Here's our work song:

The *Maggie B*'s around the Horn,
Homeward Bound, Hooray!
What care we for wind and weather,
When we get our pay?
The Pisco Sour is our drink,
Which we learned in Chile.
Williwaw's do blow us around,
Glaciers make our day.
Reef her up and reef her down, boys,
It's our time to play.
The *Maggie B*'s around the Horn,
Homeward Bound, Hooray!

The landscape is definitely changing. Now, on the high hills, there aren't just occasional waterfalls, often the whole hillside is awash. All the hills have snow on the top, not just the distant Andes. Trees hide along the shore and in gullies, and the low tundra is spread across the open slopes. The water is cold and choppy. Winds alternate from northeast and northwest, making sailing essentially impossible as we would be jibing every minute. If only Nigel would have let me have a proper yard!

Hannah is making good progress on sewing up the rip in the main. Curtis and I believe that we have traced the Onan generator problem to some feed restriction from the port tank. Freddie is working on the verses and score to Barrett's Privateers and painting the scenery; Alden is reading *1421: The Year the Chinese Discovered the World.*

We are getting good at setting up and clearing from three-point anchorages, improving every time. Tonight we are planning to be in Bahia Hugh, tucked behind Isla Bun on Isla Figueroa. Rolfo & Ardrizzi describe the entrance as "delicate and difficult to find," being encumbered with islets and submerged rocks, but once inside, "a hurricane-proof cove of great beauty."


## 29 NOVEMBER 2007

We were making our way through the Angostura Guia in-between Canal Inocentes and Canal Sarmiento. It is still blowing out of the northwest with an average speed of 15–20 knots. It is overcast, raining occasionally and not too cold. We have the foresail up alone, with the engine helping a bit. There is plenty of wind to sail, but it is generally funneling straight down the channel, which tends to make the jib useless and the main dangerous.

We have come 779 NM from Puerto Montt and have 407 to go to the Horn. The barometer is at 995 mb and continues to fall.

Last night we tucked behind the Isla Bun (it looks, indeed, like a small bread roll) in Bahia Hugh. The cove was perhaps 200 meters by 200 meters, with 10 meters in good mud for the anchor in the middle. I could have dropped off our shore party with their lines from the bow, as almost all the shores were steep-to. The entrance carried 10 meters of water all the way, though the trees on either side almost brushed the gunwales. The wind whistled overhead, but we barely moved all night. We toasted the Italian authors, Rolfo & Ardrizzi, for finding this lovely spot for us.

Since the marvelous spot last night, our trip has been spiced with dolphin playing around our bow and jumping out of the waves. We believe that they are *Lagenorhyn-*

*chus australis*, known as the blackchin dolphin. But the usual name in literature is Peale's porpoise as they were first classified by Titian Peale, who was naturalist on the USS *Vincennes* on the 1838–42 expedition to Patagonia. Peale is an ancestor of mine on my mother's side.

We hope to spend tonight in the marvelously named Caleta Moonlight Shadow. It is a two-mile long inlet in Isla Piazzi. The isla was named by Fitzroy in 1830 in honor of Guiseppe Piazzi, the astronomer in the observatory of Palermo. At the end there is a tiny caleta, just 25 meters wide by 100 meters long.

*"The wind increased to 62 knots (the highest that I noticed on the wind gauge), and shifted in an instant 40 degrees to starboard, jibing the foresail. The* **Maggie B** *took a knockdown, burying the port rail and more ..."*

Today we have had our first knockdown. We were carrying just the foresail, with the wind at about 20 knots, on the port side at 140–150 degrees relative. We had been watching a black cloud catch up to us, certainly full of rain, and we expected some more wind. We didn't realize how much. The wind jumped to 40 knots and everything was obscured by the rain and flying spume. The crew was on deck in an instant, in full foulies, ready for anything. And it was something. The wind increased to 62 knots (the highest that I noticed on the wind gauge), and shifted in an instant 40 degrees to starboard, jibing the foresail. The *Maggie B* took a knockdown, burying the port rail and more, but Hannah, cool as a cucumber, eased the starboard, windward, sheet as Freddie trimmed the port sheet. The *Maggie B* sat right up, responded to her Captain at the helm and took off downwind like a shot.

With steady 40–50 knots, the *Maggie B* was surfing at 10–12 knots, in zero visibility. We functioned perfectly as a crew. Hannah went forward as bow watch, Curtis was on the radar to help keep us in the channel, and Alden and Freddie stood by the sheets. It was wild but safe. Great credit goes to North Sails for building the foresail to take such a blow.

## 30 NOVEMBER 2007

At noon we are motorsailing with just the foresail up, in a 15–20 knot northerly, which is right on our stern as we continue south. We have come 851 NM from Puerto Montt and have 344 to go to the Horn. The day is overcast with occasional light rain. While the wind baffles back and forth down the channels, there have not been any significant gusts. The barometer is up a bit to 997 mb. According to the weather maps, offshore it is continuing to blow 40 knots from the northwest.

The day has been peaceful.

Last night we were in a marvelous spot up the end of a two-mile reach. We carried 15 meters of water almost the whole way in, with the width sometimes being barely 20 meters. There were many wild ducks and geese, with some of the ducks in molt so they couldn't fly, and they would splash away from us in a tizzy. Our anchorage was about 15 meters wide and 35 meters long—lines from the stern to shore and the anchor outside the notch in 10 meters of water, dug into thick mud. Nothing could have moved us.

Tonight we hope to be down near the end of Canal Smyth, just before it opens up into the Boca Ocidental of the Estrecho de Magallanes. It will be very exciting to see the Straits. Still no sign of the southwesterly wind shift.

It has been wonderful to have lots of Arctic terns in the channels. We see—literally—the same birds in Maine in the northern summer. They travel 10000 NM from the Bay of Fundy to Patagonia, an astonishing distance for what seems to be a very delicate bird.

In making the watch lists, Alden is using new nicknames like "blushiest" and "lawyeriest." I wonder why he calls me "Dear Leader?"


## 1 DECEMBER 2007

Happy December! At noon we were rounding Isla Falgate where Canal Smyth meets the Straits of Magellan. We have come 930 NM from Puerto Montt and have 294 NM to go to the Horn. Those reading carefully will note that the total distance from Puerto Montt to the Horn has changed as we have progressed. It is because the real miles traveled down these canales are quite different from a straight line.

The weather continues to be poor. Outside, in the Pacific, the wind has shifted to the north at 40–45. Inside that means steady 35 knots with gusts to 45. It hailed on Curtis's watch, coating the cockpit with pea-sized pellets. Rain showers come and go, and we get occasional glimpses of sun.

Paso del Abismo.

Yesterday's trip down Canal Smyth was fairly uneventful. Alden won first prize for spotting interesting sights, detecting the wreck of *Santa Leono* (USA), a huge rusting hulk of a 100-meter steamer, which had missed the turn at Paso Shoal. The steamer *Hazel Branch* was also wrecked in almost the same spot in 1904, but only a few ribs were left of her. Alden also spotted a school of Peale's dolphins, which included two mother/baby pairs.

Our anchorage last night was great, tucked in a little narrow caleta called Teokita. It was so narrow coming in that we wouldn't have fitted if we had been towing our tender *Reepicheep* alongside. We had fenders ready. We carried at least 7 meters of depth the half mile in. Because of the wind direction, we set shorelines first, and then slid out to set the anchor. That probably was a mistake, as we didn't dig in the anchor with 50% throttle astern, as we usually do. We set three shorelines in trees, including attaching one to a line on a perfectly positioned tree on top of a steep bank, thought-

The *Santa Leonor*, Paso Shoal, Chile.

fully left by another boat. The night was quiet and mostly snug.

In the morning the wind was working its way right down the narrow caleta, blowing 35 knots in the anchorage. The anchor was slipping us back towards shore bit by bit, despite having 40 meters of chain in 7 meters of water. We had been thinking of a "layover day" but the prospect of being blown ashore quickly dismissed that. Going out was wild. We had to keep a fair bit of speed as the wind was throwing the boat around and there was no room to spare. All hands had either fenders or poles to fend off. A 2-meter swell was breaking across the mouth of the cove. Curtis on the bow made the steering calls and the *Maggie B* responded to every turn and twist, fair jumping out of the mouth like a champagne cork.

Now we are scudding down the Straits of Magellan under bare poles in a fresh gale with 2–3 knots of current with us. Thank God we are not trying to go west! We have come through Paso Roughwater and Bahia Corkscrew—ah, these English with their subtle sense of humor!

We hope to make Bahia Borja tonight, which is on Isla Riesco, just before Paso Tortuoso, where the Straits tighten up a bit. This is a well-known historic cove because it has an *arbol con tableros* (trees with boards bearing ship's names). This tradition is very old and was mentioned by Slocum in *Sailing Alone Around the World* in 1895. We will add a *Maggie B* board if we make it.

## 2 DECEMBER 2007

We are motoring down the Straits of Magellan with just the jib helping us along. The wind is dead behind us at 20–35 knots. The day has mostly cleared up with only occasional rainsqualls. Some sun even! And the barometer is all the way up to 1001 mb!

Last night was quiet and pleasant in Bahia Borja though initially we pulled out a substantial tree with our shore line during a racha (williwaw). It is a historic cove, a logical stop before or after Paso Tortuoso in the Straits. Slocum anchored there 111 years ago. We didn't see his board, but there were many others. Slocum found the place depressing; we found it an excellent, safe spot for a night's rest.

The oldest board that we saw was from 1958. We added one from the *Maggie B*, and took lots of photos. I was particularly delighted to see a board with *Jolie Brise* on it. She is a famous French pilot cutter. I have a drawing of her in our house at home, done when she was in the inner harbor in Honfleur, France. While the *Maggie B* is nothing like the *Jolie Brise*, she was in some ways the inspiration for the look and feel

of our schooner. I am as thrilled and honored to have been in the harbor with her as with the *Spray*, Captain Slocum's boat.

Alden is making bread for us tonight!

We hope to spend the night in Caleta Cluedo or Caleta Luis, both on Isla Clarence, near Canal Cockburn. We plan to be in Puerto Williams by December 4th, and hopefully pass the Horn, en route to Buenos Aires on the 6th.

Alden making fresh bread.

The crew ashore in Bahia Borja with nameboards.

## 3 DECEMBER 2007

At noon we are just making our way through Canal Cockburn. The weather continues to be poor. The wind is from the southwest, occasionally 10–15 knots, but with gusts to 40 knots. The sky is overcast with williwaws full of rain, snow, ice pellets and hail. The fresh snow level on all the mountains and hills is down to about 150 meters. Welcome to late spring in Patagonia!

We intend to press on late tonight, making it to an anchorage in Caleta Emilita. From there we will have about 100 NM to go to Puerto Williams, which should be possible in one more long day.

Last night we had trouble getting the anchor to set in Caleta Cluedo, a spot described as having only fair anchoring. Alden and Curtis were able to haul the anchor ashore on a rocky peninsula, and they wedged it in and covered it with stones. We added two shore lines to be sure of a quiet night.

It was a huge effort on Alden and Curtis's part. They were trying to tow a 100-pound anchor and half-inch chain in our tender, rowing double to shore in a stiff breeze while the 63-foot schooner on the other end of the chain skittered with the wind shifts. I also had an awful time controlling *Maggie B*. If it were not so serious a feat, it would have been hilarious. Alden ended up carrying the anchor waist-deep in 40-degree water, which he feared might have curtailed his fertility (but the birth of my granddaughter has proved him wrong). It worked out great, but was a tough spot.

In the morning as we got underway, a small fishing boat came by and sold us 3 king crab (centello), about 5 kilos worth. We traded for a bottle of scotch and a pack of cigarettes. The crab were boiled up immediately with a garlic-butter dipping sauce; it was better than the best lobster I have ever had. We have enough for several days—hooray!


## 4 DECEMBER 2007

At noon the Schooner *Maggie B* was passing Isla del Diablo in the Beagle Straits. The wind continues to be 10–35 knots directly behind us, whistling down the channel, bringing rain, sleet and snow with it.

We have come 1199 NM from Puerto Montt and have 48 NM to go to Puerto Williams and 84 NM to the Horn. We should be tied up at Micalvi Yacht Club in Puerto Williams by dinnertime tonight. The Yacht Club is run by the Armada and consists of a former ammunition ship, sunk in place on purpose to be a base.

We are setting plans to do all our tasks tomorrow: refuel diesel and propane, restock food, mail letters, do laundry, refresh our Zarpe with the Armada, and clear Customs and Immigration.

The weather might let us go on the 6th. Light winds—only 15–20 knots are forecast. Maybe even clear. The problem is the 7th, when the next front is due, with winds of 30–40 knots. Our choices are 3: wait in Puerto Williams for the prospect of two good days together; leave on the 6th and either keep going after the Horn, or tuck in one of the two safe anchorages nearby after passing the Horn, and wait out the blow.

At the end of the day we arrived in Puerto Williams and moored up near the *Micalvi*. The raft of boats around the *Micalvi* didn't have room for us to join the pile. Many promised to be off early the next day to make space for us, so we went out to a huge Armada mooring buoy, scaring off a nesting gull. Alden did an upside-down trapeze stunt while trying to set lines, and somehow managed to stay out of the water.

So we went out drinking that night, planning to decide tomorrow with the day's weather news, together with our success in provisioning and getting clearance from the Armada.

## 5 DECEMBER 2007

We are moored safely in Puerto Williams at the Club Naval de Yates Micalvi, only 80 miles from Cape Horn. *Micalvi* has a variety of boats scattered around it like a sow with piglets. The ship looks as if it would have sunk by now, even if it hadn't been sunk on purpose. There is a little bar that opens occasionally in the old wheelhouse. Last week the electricity to the boat blew up so there are no lights, no washing machines, no showers.

We cleared in with the Armada on arrival, and applied for a zarpe to pass the Horn and continue to Buenos Aires. Our plan is to watch the weather, load up on supplies, and wander the town a bit. Puerto Williams is a depressing naval base with only a little civilian dressing on it. I suspect that they look across the Beagle Channel at Ushuaia, Argentina and envy their neighbor's success at being a tourist destination. We were astounded to see a half a dozen tourist boats skittering around the Beagle Channel in the snow, showing hearty visitors a seal, a porpoise, and an albatross.

There were grey Naval vessels from both Chile and Argentina patrolling the channel. Ushuaia and Puerto Williams are close to each other, but clearing out from one and clearing into the other is tortuous.

## 6 DECEMBER 2007

We had a marvelous evening at the bar on the *Micalvi*. Even before you had your first drink, you were already listing at 10 degrees, due to the way the boat had settled into the mud. The bar was full of fascinating boat folks and their equally fascinating scientific passengers. As best I recall, they made great Pisco Sours.

By noon, we had come 45 NM from Puerto Williams and have 33 NM to go to the Horn. The Horn! We estimate to pass it at 4 p.m.

The weather is nice! We have a light 15-knot northwest wind and the overcast is midlevel. It isn't raining or snowing or sleeting! There are even "bright intervals." But this is literally the calm before the storm. The barometer was at 1000 mb at noon and it has dropped another millibar an hour later. Some very significant pressure is

The crew rounding Cape Horn.

coming in from the west. The Horn should have 30–40 knots tomorrow.

We hope to stay ahead of the storm, at least for a while. If we pass the Horn at 4 p.m., we should be at the Straits of Le Maire (between Terra del Fuego and Staten Island) at about 4 a.m. tomorrow, which would be perfect as that would be first light and the end of the vicious north-going flood tide. The Straits have a terrible reputation: 10-meter standing waves are regularly reported when the strong northerly flood is opposed by a strong northerly (opposite) wind.

As always, we are keeping our options open. There are 2 good anchorages in the vicinity of the Horn—we'll tuck in one if we get jumped early. Also, right after the Straits of Le Maire there is an excellent anchorage on Staten Island, which we will use if the wind is too much for us to head north right away. This is about as good a window as one can get for the Horn in spring.

Getting resupplied in Puerto Williams yesterday required huge teamwork. With

Cape Horn on a good day.

no real supermarket, we got food from 3 different stores. Propane took several hours and some good luck. For diesel, we had to move to the main Armada pier, after getting official permission and persuading the gas station to send out their truck. Laundry took a long walk, some cajoling, a lot of money, and wasn't delivered back to the boat until 11 p.m. The Post Office was friendly but complicated. And the Armada/Customs/Immigration was…bureaucratic. We did not get our Zarpe issued and passports back until 1:30 a.m. this morning. We left at 6 a.m.

Going around the Cape Horn is reaching, perhaps over-reaching, for something totally special. From Puerto Williams to the Straits, to the Atlantic, is not too far, almost directly east. Just go! But, to go past Cape Horn is an extra 60 or so miles. Not far, unless you are in 55 degrees south and it means going further south. But it was not any real question for us. The navigation isn't hard, around the corner from Puerto Williams, south 10 hours, around a few islands, and there you are! Easy, at least in good weather.

Alden as pirate, rounding Cape Horn.

We passed the Horn about 5 p.m. It is hard to write about it—the end of the Americas—most southern Patagonia—the wildest Terra del Fuego. I had read about it for 50 years. On another trip, I had seen hundreds of ships in the Falkland Islands broken by the passage. I knew of endless expeditions turned back or destroyed off these forlorn rocks. We had come tens of thousands of miles. And we had an easy passage.

Richard Henry Dana, Jr. in *Two Years before the Mast* described the Horn as "an end to all our fine prospects." Charles Darwin on the *Beagle* describes it as "this notorious promontory in its proper form—veiled in a mist, and its dim outline surrounded by a storm of wind and water." Perhaps best, the famous yachtsman Bernard Moitessier, said, "I can hardly believe it. So small and so huge. A hillock, pale and tender in the moonlight; a colossal rock, hard as diamond."

This was our Everest. But after climbing it we had to come down. Ahead of us was the Straits of Le Maire, one of the roughest passages in the world. Past that was the 100 degrees of latitude up to Lunenburg, almost straight north and more than 6000 NM distant. Our situation was hugely pressured by the next big low, barreling towards us from the west with serious winds and waves.

There was another strange sensation: we were finally out of the Chilean channels, where there was usually rock on all sides and depths unknown. Here at the Horn we had running room—Blue Water—safety at sea. We are open ocean sailors and happy to be fully back at sea, moving away from the dangers of the land.

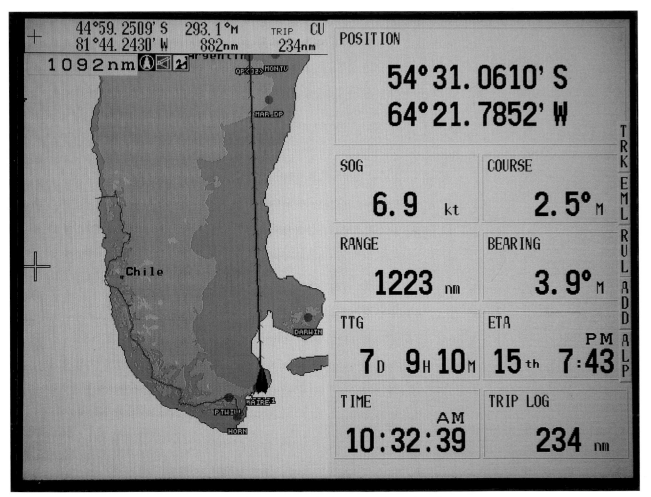

Around the Horn, with the route clear ahead.

## 7 DECEMBER 2007

At 11:00 a.m., the Schooner *Maggie B* was safely anchored in Puerto Hoppner, on the NW side of Isla de los Estados (Staten Island), Argentina. It is raining and blowing about 30 knots in the anchorage. But we have three lines ashore and the anchor is in mud with 50 meters of half-inch chain in 7 meters of water. If we are not safe here, we will never be.

After passing the Horn yesterday, we continued for the Straits of Le Maire. That's the place where for half the day the Atlantic tries to fill up the Pacific and half the day it is the other way around. We had light winds between the Horn and the Straits. In fact, it was essentially calm and we hit it at highwater, slack tide. Even with no wind and no tide, the waves bursting through the 14 NM gap were sharp enough to regularly send green water over the boat. I can't imagine what it must be like on a bad day.

We decided to tuck into this tight cove because we all felt that we had about used up our luck, and should sit out this next gale. Having an effortless passage around the Horn and across the Straits of Le Maire is about all the luck a sailor could hope for. We didn't want the sea and wind gods to think that we assumed good treatment.

The entrance to the inner harbor is very narrow. We made it through at just about low tide. There was still about a 3–4 knot current coming out as the basin emptied. We had only a meter to the rocks on either side. Alden's kayak experience helped him as bow watch to read the water and current. We had to gun it going through, and fully commit, as we needed the power and velocity for control. We had crew on both sides with our big fenders, to be ready for the worst. From the helm I could only see rock on either side. Those on the starboard would yell "Come Port!" and those on the port side would yell "Come Starboard!" but I only listened to Alden. There was all of 2 meters under the keel. We didn't touch.

When we got into the little caleta, we were happy to see shore lines tied to a prominent, useful tree, at the top of a 4-meter cliff. Alden selected the heaviest rope to use as an aide to climb the cliff so that we could place ours. About two-thirds of the way up the line parted and Alden ejected into 46-degree water. He was out of the water and into the *Reep* so fast there was hardly time for a splash.

We expect to continue tomorrow to Buenos Aires, which is about 1200 NM away.

All is well.

*"Hooray for the Atlantic!*
*It is so great to be back in our ocean again*
*after a year of the Indian and the Pacific!*
*No more barriers between us and home, though surely*
*there will be more adventures in this last 7600 NM."*

## 15

# CAPE HORN NORTH

**8 DECEMBER 2007**

We are headed north at 8 knots! Clouds behind us, clear ahead. The forecast from Commanders' and the GRIB files make things look pretty good, promising 15–25 knot westerlies for the next five days.

We have come 244 NM from Puerto Williams and have 1212 NM to go to Buenos Aires. At this speed, we should make Buenos Aires on December 15th, which assumes an extra day to go upriver.

Last night was very tough in Puerto Hoppner. We were relieved not to be at sea. We had our anchor out with 120 feet of chain in 20 feet of water, a line from our bow to shore and two lines from our stern to each shore. Thanks goodness, because the night was full of williwaw/rachas. Gusts of 40 knots or more would hit from all directions, including vertically. One moment, a line to shore would be as tight as steel, then an instant later it would be completely slack and the line on the other side would tighten up. We had made a rough door to the companionway with a heavy wooden crosspiece and strips of thick plastic hanging down to keep the warmth in. It had been jammed into the top of the hatch, but a gust pulled it out and flew it somewhere ashore. We were briefed where the nearest Argentinean Navy outpost was, in case we had to abandon ship, and had "go bags" ready for an escape. It was a very wild night.

We are now sailing with three reefs in the main and one in the fore. I would have preferred two reefs in the main, but the tear with Hannah's patch is near the second reef cringle, and I don't want to stress it. Hannah's patch is in blue material and makes it look as if we have a big #1 on the white sail. Why not?

Hooray for the Atlantic! It is so great to be back in our ocean again after a year of the Indian and the Pacific! No more barriers between us and home, though surely there will be more adventures in this last 7600 NM.

## 9 DECEMBER 2007

We are running north at 8–12 knots before a southerly gale. The skies are clearing up and the rain has mostly stopped. It is a little warmer, which isn't very warm. We have the main up with 3 reefs, the foresail up full, and the jib about half reefed. The wind waves are developing into small swells that we surf from time to time. Jorge, the autopilot, is doing a great job.

At noon the wind was only 15 knots and some might have been tempted to shake out our triple-reefed main, but the barometer was down at 984 mb, and we know to be ready for the next blow. Rather than heading straight for Buenos Aires, we are edging in towards the Argentinean coast to reduce the height of the waves and to avoid, we hope, a predicted northerly that may come in with the next front.

We are all looking forward to leaving the Furious Fifties behind for the relative calm of the Roaring Forties.

### EMAIL FROM COMMANDERS' WEATHER
Summary

The current weather map features a very deep gale center just east of the Antarctic Peninsula with a pressure near 956mb!

A strong cold front extends northward from this gale to near the Falklands.

A very strong area of high pressure is centered well to the northwest of the area in the southeast Pacific with a pressure near 1040mb! (An 84 mb difference is about 2.5 inches of mercury.)

There is a significant pressure gradient between the gale to the southeast and the high to the northwest with your area currently caught in the worst of it.

Expect south-southwest to southwest winds to continue on the strong side through today with speeds of 30–40 knots, coming down a bit by this evening to around 20–30 knots.

Later Saturday night into Sunday will be a rough period behind this cold front as yet another low spins up along the front to the east of your route with southwest winds increasing to 30–40 knots!

A period of headwinds is possible on Monday ahead of the next trough with winds clocking to north-northwest with speeds around 15–25 knots.

Yet another trough will approach Monday night with another period of headwinds possible before winds again back to southwest behind it and, not to sound like a broken record, but there may be another trough approaching late Tuesday.

Seas may reach as high as 10–15 feet later Sunday into Monday.


## 10 DECEMBER 2007

Despite the scary weather forecast, we are making 10.5 knots northbound, including a knot of favorable current—the Falklands current. In the last 24 hours we did 204 NM. The wind is a steady 25-knot southwester and the seas are only 2–3 meters. The *Maggie B* loves this kind of weather—we are often going hull speed, 10.2 knots—and below decks it is comfortable for me typing at the keyboard, Curtis is watching a movie on the other computer and Alden and Hannah are napping. Freddie is on watch on deck. We have the main up with one reef, full foresail and full jib. The centerboard gives off a happy hum when we are going more than 9 knots, and we are hearing it almost constantly.

A betting pool has formed regarding our arrival time in Buenos Aires. Current guess is between noon on the 14th and end-of-day on the 15th.

Our port diesel fuel tank has been giving us fits, acting like it is out of fuel when plenty is left. We had blown out the fuel vent, but discovered yesterday that the one-way valve that was supposed to stop water from coming in was also stopping air from coming in. After an hour or so of running, a vacuum developed to reduce the fuel flow—always new riddles!


## 11 DECEMBER 2007

We are making 9 knots headed north, with one reef in the main, full foresail and jib. After a night of a 20-knot northwesterly, we are basking, literally, in a 20-knot sunny westerly.

We have come 813 NM from Puerto Williams and have 672 NM to go to Buenos Aires. We are angling in to close the Argentinean coast where it runs east and west between Bahia Blanca and Mar del Playa because we are expecting a stiff north to northwesterly on the 13th, so we will have some protection and some westing to give up.

Temporary new crew, asleep.

Our beloved Jorge (the Furuno autopilot that has guided us most all the way for the last 28000 NM) has given up, or at least it is refusing to talk to the rudder motor, or the motor is no longer following instructions. Furuno technical support advises it is probably a blown circuit board in their control unit and they will send us a new one directly, though obviously not before we make Buenos Aires. So, we have to hand steer, not a hardship with five skilled helmsmen (helmspersons) on board. We are doing 2-hour shifts during the day and one hour at night. Last night Freddie was able to find the "sweet spot" when we were close hauled and *Maggie B* sailed herself. I didn't have to touch the wheel for my entire 2-hour shift, as she balanced between jib and main.

The weather is startlingly different from just a few days ago. Today was the first time I've stood a watch without full foul-weather gear in a month. We are searching for suntan lotion! Wool hats are exchanged for ball caps. But the wandering albatrosses are still with us as are the Peales dolphins jumping around the bow.

## 12 DECEMBER 2007

We are motorsailing at 7 knots more or less due north, still making for the coast of Argentina between Bahia Blanca and Mar del Playa. The weather is clear and sunny and the sea is mostly calm, at least calm for Blue Water. We are now in the lee of the Argentinean coast, which is only 150 NM away to the west, so rollers don't have much fetch to make up.

We are expecting a fresh northerly to start about midnight tonight and our course should both give us some protection from the build up of the seas as well as having "banked" a lot of westing that we can give up as we run along the coast towards Mar del Playa. If we time it right, about when we get to Mar del Playa, the "corner," at dawn on the 14th, the wind will shift to a strong southwesterly which will blow us up the Rio Plata to Buenos Aires.

The waters here must be very rich. Before we would generally see only a few albatrosses, here there are hundreds. The fishing boats (draggers) are out, and we have seen two pods of southern right whales. We had a line out to catch fish for dinner, but had to pull it in as it was attracting albatrosses.


## 13 DECEMBER 2007

We are motoring at 6 knots northeast into a 15-knot northeasterly. A clear day, but with short chop that slows us down. We are all in boat delivery mode rather than "trim the jib to squeeze the last 1/100 of a knot out of the sails" mode.

We still have to get around the headland that makes the south shore of the Rio de la Plata estuary. We are as sheltered as we can reasonably be from the northerly, but there aren't a lot of tactics you can do when your course is 035 and the wind is from 035. Once past Mar del Playa we will gradually turn north, then northwest up the historic estuary.

We are waiting for the next system to go through, which won't be until dawn tomorrow. It will bring in the southwesterly, which will power us along. Our target speed to make Buenos Aires by 6 p.m. on Saturday is 7.6 knots. Certainly that is something the *Maggie B* can do. But currently at cruising RPM, we are making 5.7 knots into the wind and waves.

We were about 100 NM off the coastline this afternoon. To our great annoyance, a huge number of houseflies made it out to the boat, presumably helped by the wind. Then a special visitor arrived! A yellow/green parakeet with blue cheek patches flew into the Crew Mess, reported for duty and promptly fell asleep, perched on the

Watch Schedule. After a nap, it indulged in a snack (sesame seeds), some water, sat on Hannah and Curtis's fingers, checked out its assigned bunk—a straw basket with paper towel strips for bedding, and promptly deserted for a more stable perch. It must be mating season.

## 14 DECEMBER 2007

We are under full sail, making 8.9 knots in a nice 20-knot southerly breeze. Buenos Aires is 187 NM away and we have come 1394 NM from Puerto Williams. The sky has a high overcast, but no rain as yet. We should arrive in Buenos Aires tomorrow afternoon. The computer says we will be at the Antipuerto Norte—northern outer harbor—at 1423 on Saturday.

Last night when we were 25 NM offshore, we had thousands of dragonflies come aboard, perching everywhere. And lots of other bugs. Must have been a mating dance as all the bugs are gone or dead today. A flycatcher has been hanging out on our shrouds, probably having heard about our abundance.

We are on a broad reach running up the Rio Plata estuary. Our entrance into this historic body of water was immeasurably improved by the accompaniment of a pod of false killer whales (*Pseudorca crassidens*). They average about 18-feet long and were a bit of a shock after seeing much smaller dolphin. They played in the bow wave, wake and right alongside. Only the appearance of cameras on deck made them leave us....

As sailors making landfall after a long, successful voyage, we are getting ready in traditional ways: braiding hair, Curtis; shaving, Alden; reading the history of the place, Freddie; studying the charts of the complicated channel, the Captain; and airing out the Little Black Dress, Bosun Hannah.

## 15 DECEMBER 2007

We are at the corner of Canal Punte Indio and Canal Intermedio, in the Rio Plata estuary, about 75 NM from Buenos Aires. The wind is from the south at 15 knots, and we are sailing with one reef in the main and our G2 gennaker up.

The bay or estuary here has us all astounded. We have been sailing for a day, mostly outside of sight of land, in water between 20 and 50 feet deep. This is after being in the Chilean canals, where you can be in 500 feet of water while only 200 feet from land. Here there is a main ship channel that is dredged all the way to...27

*"... we ran the main tanks dry 125 NM from port. Thank goodness we are a sailboat. Why don't you have fuel gauges, you ask? We do, Acu-gage Ultra-8, and it says both fuel tanks are full. "*

feet. The chart shows dozens and dozens of shipwrecks, most annotated with the name of the sunken ship. We go by the *Astarso, Carumbe, Roco, Pingo, Calipso, Hierro Belgiano, Rio Santiago, Barcozo*, and many more.

We are running later than I hoped—we may not get into Buenos Aires until 11 p.m. or midnight. We are late for two reasons. One is that I underestimated the current of the Rio Plata. Right now we have full flood favoring us, and the tide about balances the outgoing dark brown river current. When the tide was ebbing, we had a total of a knot and a half against us.

The more serious reason for being late is that we are out of diesel in the main tanks. We are down to our fuel reserves, the 10 gallons in jerry cans. We are saving that until we get close, perhaps the last 30 NM (10 gallons = 40 liters = 60 NM at 6 knots). I made the mistake of forgetting to write down the engine hours when we refueled in Puerto Williams, so I don't know how long we have run it. I also underestimated the distance we would end up covering from Puerto Williams, which will end up being 1600 NM. We used the engine a lot coming up the coast, more than we needed to, to help keep warm and to speed our arrival. All in all, we ran the main tanks dry 125 NM from port. Thank goodness we are a sailboat. Why don't you have fuel gauges, you ask? We do, Acu-gage Ultra-8, and it says both fuel tanks are full. I'm sure that my loving, faithful crew, especially my son, Alden, will never, ever, let me forget this.

We think, and are hoping, that Buenos Aires is a "late" town.


## 16 DECEMBER 2007

*Maggie B* docked safely in the Puerto Madero Yacht Club in the heart of Buenos Aires at midnight, December 15th. The arrival was very, very difficult. I had talked to the marina on the radio, but the instructions were limited, and my Spanish is poor. Which is the outer or inner harbor, was that left or right? Where is the opening? Oh, my God, is that huge high-speed ferry going to run us down?? Finally the marina sent

The *Maggie B* docked at the Puerto Madero Yacht Club, Buenos Aires.

a boat out to guide us into the intricate, well-hidden passage. Now we are right in the heart of waterfront Buenos Aires. It is 1 a.m. and there are about ten restaurants within sight that are still serving dinner. Perhaps we will find a steak and a glass (or two) of nice Argentinean wine. We have come 1625 NM from Puerto Williams. It is a lovely, warm, dry, spring night.

## 18 DECEMBER 2007

*Maggie B* remains tied up at the Yacht Club Puerto Madero. The YCPM isn't really a yacht club, it is a floating function room (weddings, corporate meetings, etc.) with a small marina. The facilities are fine and the administration is eager and helpful, but there is no members-bar where you can find fellow seafarers. I suspect that the YC Argentino, out the harbor, is the place for all that.

In many ways, Buenos Aires isn't really a seafaring town. It is on a historic estuary, but there is about 100 NM of dirty brown 20-foot deep water before you get anything really like the open ocean. One clear sign is that even the biggest boat here in the marina has only a 30-pound Danforth anchor. Clearly they never go anywhere.

Buenos Aires is cosmopolitan, very European. Most all the faces are Spanish, English or Italian. This Puerto Madero area is the old dockyards, built about 1890 and rebuilt in 1930. The area languished from 1930s until 10 years ago when the City and Federal governments got together and developed what is now the hottest area in Buenos Aires. Our walkway to the boat is illuminated by the AON, ABN-AMRO and NORTEL signs, not by floodlights or the half moon. The restaurants are great and varied, but it is a bit unsettling to be only a week away from Cape Horn and have a TGI Fridays, Bice and Hooters nearby. But, with help, we have found the Argentinean ones. There is really only one acceptable thing to order in restaurants here, *carne* (beef). I was in an Italian restaurant and ordered a Caprese salad, and a seafood risotto, with a nice bottle of Sauvignon blanc. The waiter and then the Captain, tried to talk me into a steak and a bottle of Malbec. What was I thinking??

It is interesting to compare Chile and Argentina. Not fair, as Buenos Aires is the Washington and New York City of Argentina, where Puerto Montt is the… Oakland or Jacksonville of Chile. But you get a sense. In Chile you saw signs of permanence and stability. Modern progress was going to get better, gradually. In Argentina, it seems more fragile. Maybe it will work; maybe there will be the next crisis—tomorrow, next week or next year, but coming, for sure. Argentina has a "make hay while the sun shines" sensibility, Chile seems more…Lutheran.

Dinner in Buenos Aires.

North Sails Argentina is going to check out all our patches tomorrow and we need a diesel mechanic to solve the Onan generator problems, but generally we are in good shape.

Hannah, Alden and I leave tomorrow for our homes for the holidays, Freddy left today. Curtis is going to stay with the boat and roam Argentina a bit. The next big challenge is to decide where we should have *Maggie B* for Carnival!

Squall line.

"*And then in less than a boat length, we went from
20 feet on the depth sounder to 3 feet and an awful crunch.
We spun around and after two more ugly crunches,
were lifted off by a swell and returned to deep water.*"

## 16

# BUENOS AIRES NORTH
# TO BAHIA

THIS LEG WAS VERY DIFFERENT from all the others in 3 big ways. First, we all knew there were no more great capes like Cape Horn, no more three-week-long passages, no more cold weather or big storms. Secondly, we were "smelling the stables" and ready to finish. Finally, there just wasn't a lot of wind and having to motor is a letdown for sailors.

We had lots of stops on this stretch, and life became more about the land than the sea.

### 25 JANUARY 2008

*Maggie B* left Buenos Aires today, motorsailing across the Rio de la Plata to Colonia del Sacramento, Uruguay. The estuary was as brown as ever, and littered with shipwrecks. The passage was made more interesting by high-speed ferries zipping past at 40 knots on their way to or from Buenos Aires. On the 25 NM crossing, other than the two dredged channels, the deepest depth we saw was 18 feet.

Colonia del Sacramento is a small, old-fashioned town of about 20,000, founded by the Portuguese in 1680 to smuggle goods across the river to Spanish Buenos Aires. It changed hands many times over the years as the Spanish and Portuguese fought along their borders. This lovely town is a relief after the scale, dirtiness and bustle of Buenos Aires. We are anchored off the yacht club. There are about 100 boats on moorings, many of them Argentinean, here for the holidays. The boats, almost all sailboats, (*veleros*), are generally about 30 feet long and shallow-draft. We are at the outside of the pack, only partially protected by the breakwater with 5 feet of water under our keel.

The *Maggie B* is in pretty good shape. The mainsail and "the Bird," have been patched by North Sails Buenos Aires. The autopilot was overhauled by Furuno USA, and they gave us a new Rudder Reference Unit, all of which seems to be working well.

The generator is still bedeviling us, having some sort of fuel supply problems. Our chief suspect is that the electric fuel pump has lost its pull after working so hard these two years. We are getting a new fuel pump shipped to us in Piriapolis, just down the line, where we plan to haul out next week. The Buenos Aires Onan distributor said that they knew the pump, they had it in inventory, but that it was out-of-stock, yet would be in "in 10 days to 2 weeks," which means "never" in South America.

The crew for this leg is Curtis Weinrich and Hannah Joudrey continuing—Hannah all the way from Cape Town! New shipmates are Thomas Didier from Quebec, Canada and Janet Gibb from Wellington, New Zealand. Thomas is a former shipmate of Hannah's from her time on the *Eye of the Wind*. He has been in Montevideo for a year's apprenticeship at the Canadian Embassy. His fluent Spanish has been a huge help for us. His Portuguese will help in Brazil. Janet has been sailing and racing for many years, like every Kiwi! Her day job as manager for a high-end Wellington provider should help us nail the finest food and supplies.

Our current plan is to spend this weekend in Colonia, leaving Sunday afternoon for Piriapolis, which is about 160 NM east. We hope to arrive there on Monday and get hauled out either Monday or Tuesday. We will clean and scrape the hull, and repaint the bottom. We have to change one through-hull fitting, where the handle was broken off, fortunately in the open position.

After hauling and painting in Piriapolis, we plan to reward ourselves by spending several days in Punta del Este, the very chic Uruguayan summer resort. While we are the biggest boat in Colonia, we will probably be the smallest one in Punta del Este. After Punta del Este, we plan to make for Florianopolis, a large island in Brazil, a summer resort for those fleeing the big cities.

It is good to be underway again, and heading north.

A close pass by the *Atlantic III*.

## 27 JANUARY 2008

We left Colonia about noon today. We are headed east-southeast at 7.5 knots, motor-sailing, for Piriapolis. We should be there a little after dawn tomorrow. It is warm and hazy, with a 10–12 knot east-northeasterly breeze.

We put the main up for the first time since it was repaired in Buenos Aires. We had also replaced the topping lifts and lazy jacks. It was a mess with seemingly everything on the wrong side or upside down or backwards.

The weekend in Colonia was a delight. Old buildings, cobblestone streets, lots of great restaurants and bars and some very interesting stores, including a Musto store, our favorite for high-end sailing gear. We even found some restaurants that served something besides beef! Our research on wines continues, and we found some Uruguayan whites and rosés.

Curtis supervising the haul out in Piriapolis.

## 28 JANUARY 2008

We are tied up at the pier in Piriapolis, Uruguay. Passing Montevideo at midnight was complicated—lots of wrecks scattered around, a zigzag dredged channel full of a variety of boats coming and going, tugs with long tows moving our direction and draggers head to head. All topped by a huge ferry doing two 360s in front of us as we tried to avoid everybody. We were passed by another ferry doing 44 knots!

Piriapolis is a nice beach community just before Punta del Este. There is a tight little harbor, which is very friendly. The harbor is run by the Uruguayan Navy. The Volvo Ocean Race stopped at Montevideo some years ago and they brought a huge Travelift to work on their boats. After the race, the Travelift was donated to the People of Uruguay, and it was moved here to Piriapolis. It is rated for 80 tons and has lifted 70, so the *Maggie B* at 35 tons should be no problem.

## 30 JANUARY 2008

Yesterday we were plucked from the water by the Travelift and placed delicately in the yard. We worked like dogs, sanding the whole hull in the morning, getting completely covered with the red dust from the old paint. In the afternoon we painted, getting a coat on the hull by 5 p.m. She looks lovely! Tomorrow we will put a second coat on, and cover the spots where the supports prevented us sanding and painting the first pass. The *Maggie B* now has two coats of expensive bottom paint that will make us fast all the way home, as well as poisoning every barnacle within 100 feet.

Curtis did a quick job of replacing the through-hull fitting, after making a call to Covey Island and talking to the very person who installed it in 2006—great support from Nova Scotia!

We had a reception on our last night in Piriapolis aboard the *Maggie B*, as we often do in harbors with a nice crowd of yachties. This was the first time we had done it when hauled out. I was concerned later in the evening that we might lose a guest overboard—concrete 15 feet down instead of water 3 feet away. Aboard were four French, one Irish, one Scandinavian, two Canadians, one Uruguayan, the crew of the *Maggie B* and probably some others.

## 1 FEBRUARY 2008

We motored the short distance from Piriapolis to Punta del Este in a 10–15 knot headwind. We are now tied up Med-moor right next to the Prefectura crash boat, which has a helpful crew.

Punta del Este is very different from Colonia and Piriapolis—lots of motorboats in the 40- to 60-foot range. We are not seeing any superyachts, but that is OK—they are probably already north for Carnival or the Caribbean. It is a well-protected harbor with perhaps 1,000 boats tied up or at anchor. Ashore there is a mix of some lovely old buildings and super-flashy condos and hotels. Most of the boats seem to be Argentinean.

Essentially everything on the *Maggie B* seems in top shape for this last leg, with the exception of the Onan generator. We are waiting for a new fuel pump to be shipped from Canada, which we hope will solve our problem. It is due here "any day."

This time of year the South Atlantic High sits out at about 30–35 degrees South. In 2006, we went south of it to get from Salvador, Brazil, to Cape Town. Having it sitting there, however, means that the wind along the coast of Uruguay and southern

Brazil is from the northeast, or right on your nose. But if you wait for a nice juicy low to come by from the south, the wind starts from the northwest and then shifts to the southeast afterwards, both of which are just right for us. Right now it looks as if the next southerly is due February 3rd, to help us make the 600–700 NM run to Florianopolis, Brazil. It will be nice to have a proper sail after way too much motoring recently.

One afternoon I was sitting at the desk in the ship's office and heard the sound of crackling and popping from behind the main switch panel. When I opened the panel, there was some smoke coming from the AC sensor panel. I turned off the power and disassembled the paneling to get at the main sensor. It had burnt out and melted one of the coils. It is all detached and disassembled now—we will just have to trust on proper polarity from shore power.

One of the restaurants in Punta del Este had a charmingly fractured English-language menu. Fortunately their chef made better paella than their translator wrote menus. Some of our favorites were: Padded Codfish; Sprout her Special; Pan of mud, bound in her own sauce; Stewed lamb with blow, onion and potato; and Prawns to the Iron.

In Punta del Este we had our first and only experience in being solicited for a bribe by an official for doing his job. The Immigration Official on departure claimed that we didn't have the proper papers with our passports. We explained that when we checked in at Colonia the immigration person didn't issue them to us and said we didn't need them. Oh, no says our man, it is about US$100 fine for trying to check out without the proper paperwork. We said that we did everything that they told us. Well, says he, there might not be a fine, but he would have to check with Montevideo, which might take a few days. But if we paid the fine, he could clear us immediately. I said we would have to have a receipt. Oh, no, says he, to give a receipt, he would have to check with Montevideo, which…would take a few days. And tomorrow his colleague was on duty and she was much tougher than he. I say, "no receipt, no money." We go back and forth (this is all being translated by Thomas). Finally, when Thomas says, "I'm sorry but the Captain insists," he gave us our stamped passports, which he had been waving at us and said, "Get out of here." I shook his hand, which he almost refused.

Optimist fleet in Punta del Este, with Sea Lion observing.

### 3 FEBRUARY 2008

We left Punta del Este about noon today and are making 8.5 knots motorsailing more or less due east. We are only about 20 NM from the end of the Rio de la Plata estuary, where we will turn left and head northeast for Florianopolis, Brazil. The headland where we start our turn is called La Paloma, the dove.

The weather is overcast with rain showers marching past and over us. Right now the wind is light from the south, but we expect it to pick up to 15–20 knots from the southwest as we get further along. There is a big southerly swell. We have about 1.5 knots of current with us, which is probably partially tide and partially a back eddy of the usually southwest bound, unfavorable, Brazilian current. As we go northeast to Florianopolis, we will do our best to play the current, staying inshore enough to catch a bit of a counter current, without getting tangled up in drilling platforms, inshore fisheries or other complications.

## 4 FEBRUARY 2008

We are under all plain sail, making 6.5 knots northeastward in 12–15 knots of wind from the west-northwest. It is a lovely day. We are about 15 NM off the coast of Brazil, carrying about a knot of favorable current.

This morning there was a beautiful astronomical sight just before dawn: the moon was on its last day, only a fingernail slice, and Venus and Jupiter were right nearby. It was like silver and diamonds on a velvet cloth.

To our frustration, the Furuno autopilot is out again. I have emailed for help from their US headquarters, where we have always gotten good support. Because we are hand-steering, we now have a fairly complicated watch system as we are five and have decided to have one hour solo watches during the day and 2-person, 3 hour, overlapping "sociable" watches at night—sociable meaning that you spend part of your watch with one person and part with another.

There has been a lot of traffic. Perhaps one very large ship every 4 hours, generally not too far from our track, especially if northbound. There are groups of fishing boats around. A small tanker came up from behind us, seemingly oblivious of the need to stay clear of the sailboat (us) that they were overtaking. Keeping out of their way almost drove us into two fishing boats, which were working a big net between them.

It is great to be sailing again in perfect schooner conditions.


## 5 FEBRUARY 2008

We are schoonering along the Brazilian coast, making 7.3 knots in 12 knots of wind on our beam. It is clear, bright and warm. The sun is getting higher every day, and is now heading north, like us. It is about 15 degrees south of the equator, and we are 15 degrees south of it.

We still have about one-third of a knot of favorable current. We expect to be motoring again soon, as the wind is beginning to fade, as forecast. We expect to arrive at Florianopolis at about sundown tomorrow. Today is Mardi Gras, so we will arrive on the very somber Ash Wednesday.


## 8 FEBRUARY 2008

The schooner *Maggie B* is at the Yacht Club of Santa Catarina in Florianopolis, Brazil, a beautiful big island a bit more than half way from Montevideo, Uruguay to Rio de Janeiro.

After Mardi Gras in Florianopolis.

Yesterday did have its victories—our bar bill at the yacht club turned out to be only 12 reals, or about US$6 and the security guard at the gate of the marina let us back in. Otherwise it was not a great day.

We knew that Canadians and US citizens needed visas for Brazil. When we were in Buenos Aires at the Brazilian Consulate, there was a huge crowd and weird requests for two months of bank statements from each petitioner to prove financial independence. I had the good idea to call the Federal Police in Florianopolis to see if a visa could be issued to yachties on arrival. No problem they said to Thomas in Portuguese—come on along to our lovely island and all will be well!

Yesterday we all trooped over to the big new Federal Police building to check in. All was well at first: we got to see a charming officer who spoke good English, we had the right documents, he filled out the right forms, we signed everything, then he looked at the passports. Where were our visas? We said that we were told that we should come on and they would be issued in Florianopolis. No, no, no, he says, against the law. America makes it hard for us Brazilians to enter the US, so we

387

make it hard for Americans to enter Brazil. We have our pride, etc. Papers were taken back, and torn up and thrown away. We were issued a "Termo de Notificacao No. 34/2008" ordering us to leave Brazil within eight days. When we protested, he said that we were fortunate he had made it for eight days—that it was usually only three.

His suggestion was that we should go to Uruguay or Paraguay and get our visas and come back, though there might be a problem since we had entered illegally. All of a sudden the thought of flying to Buenos Aires or Montevideo seemed less attractive. A real disaster would be to leave the country to get the visas and then not get them and have the boat stuck in Florianopolis, and us certified undesirable aliens.

Our plan now is to rent a car and drive the 1,000 kilometers to Iguazu Falls on the border with Brazil and Argentina. We'll cross over into Argentina, get our Brazilian visas, and return as legals!


## 16 FEBRUARY 2008

We had the great fortune to have two days to explore the Iguazu Falls. Up, down and around some of the most stunning views on the planet. The volume of the water is astonishing, but the variety of falls is the real romance of the place. When Eleanor Roosevelt saw the Falls, she said "Poor Niagara." Poor Niagara, indeed. It makes other waterfalls seem insignificant.

How to describe the Iguazu Falls? The remorseless power is stunning. A 10-meter Southern Ocean wave has some of the same sense of total force. Same for the tides in the Straits of Le Maire. You know that you can't resist the power of the water, and that you have to be lucky and skillful not to be hurt if you get in the flow.

The Brazilian side view of the Falls was stunning in the sunset and then illuminated by a half moon. After a nice dinner buffet, Curtis and Thomas led us down to the catwalk in the Devil's Throat. It was about 2:00 a.m. The moon had set and we had only the light of

Toucan, Bird Recovery Sanctuary,
Puerto Iguazu, Argentina

The Devil's Throat, Iguazu Falls.

stars to find our way. The stars were our old friends—the Twins, Orion, Alpha and Beta Centuri, the Southern Cross. We got soaked but had the stunning experience of being almost under the Falls under the starlight.

## 20 FEBRUARY 2008

We spent last night anchored off a lovely beach, the Praia Magalhaes. We were visiting Alain and Fabienne Poiraud. Alain is the inventor of the Spade and Sword anchors, and is the author of the book, *The Complete Anchoring Handbook*, (McGraw-Hill, 2008) which every sailor should read!

We had a perfect evening. We rowed in to their house for a round of excellent Caipirinhas, then off to a local restaurant for piles of local seafood—oysters, squid, little fish, big fish, washed down with some white wine. We were happy that we didn't

Missed the turn, Sao Francisco do Sul.

drag that night, in front of his house!

Now the *Maggie B* is finally moving again. We are motoring north in about a 10-knot northerly, which is due to die out this afternoon. We are 390 NM south of Rio and 2750 from Antigua.

After leaving our friends just north of Florianopolis, we made for the town of Sao Francisco do Sul to clear customs. We didn't want to arrive in a complicated port at night, so we stopped at Ilha da Paz, just offshore, which seemed to afford a protected anchorage. The chart showed a buoy for pilot ships, but we only saw a few plastic jugs floating as mooring markers. At about 1:00 a.m. the wind shifted and we swung around and hit the mostly submerged mooring buoy, which was made of steel and about six feet in diameter. Only the ring was visible above water. The plastic jugs we had spotted were supporting the thick mooring pendant. We got only cosmetic damage, though it sounded at first as if a giant was using a battering ram to break through the hull. We moved our anchor to another spot and stood anchor watches through the rest of the night.

In the morning we motored into Sao Francisco do Sul. We were stunned to see a 500-foot coastal freighter partially sunk, upside down, just off a turn in the entrance channel. It was surrounded by perhaps 40 boats, all scampering at different tasks, mostly oil clean up. In town, we were told that the wreck had taken place two weeks previously. The ship was loaded high with fairly heavy cargo; it was poorly secured and it shifted as they made the corner in the channel, and the ship turned turtle, just like that.

The site of the town of Sao Francisco do Sul was discovered by the Frenchman de Gonneville in 1504, and the Portuguese developed it in the early 1600s. It is the third oldest city in Brazil. We were able to clear Customs quickly, pleasantly and with good wishes for our travels. No one cared that we had been in Brazil for two weeks and could have unloaded Chinese stowaways, smuggled cigarettes or whatever. But now we have all the right papers and stamps!

*"The ship was loaded high with fairly heavy cargo; it was poorly secured and it shifted as they made the corner in the channel, and the ship turned turtle, just like that."*

## 21 FEBRUARY 2008

We spent two nights at Ilha do Mel, Honey Island.

We ran aground getting into the anchorage. It was horrible. We arrived just at dark, having spent too much time in Sao Francisco do Sul, and the full moon was hidden behind a cloud. We were trying to stay clear of a fishing boat, which was motoring in the same direction with only one faint white light showing. We were coming up to the Farol das Concas point in what the chart showed as 22 feet of water. And then in less than a boat length, we went from 20 feet on the depth sounder to 3 feet and an awful crunch. We spun around and after two more ugly crunches, were lifted off by a swell and returned to deep water. Amazingly, two fishing boats were following close behind us and almost hit us when we were spun around. We anchored at the far edge of perhaps 40 small fishing boats. We think that the fishing co-op is building an informal breakwater to protect the harbor. Certainly there was nothing on the charts.

In the morning, a careful inspection of the hull and rudder using our hookah— an air compressor with 20 meters of tubing to a diving mouthpiece—showed only

Fisherman on the cliff, Brazil.

missing paint and a slight crack in the very bottom flat piece of the keel, and no damage to the rudder. Whew!

We spent the days off the beautiful Praia da Fortaleza, guarded at one end by the Fortaleza de NS dos Prazeres (Fort of Our Lady of the Pleasures!) dating to 1760, and at the other end by the Farol das Concas, a lighthouse which was ordered up by King Dom Pedro II from Scotland and shipped out and assembled in 1872.

Ilha do Mel has remained marvelously undeveloped. No cars, motorcycles, streetlights, horses or donkeys are allowed on the island. Accommodations on the island range from rustic to extremely rustic. The surf is good on two of the beaches and it is very much of a surfer/beach/shacks culture.

## 2 MARCH 2008

We are motoring due east at 7.7 knots for Cabo Frio. The wind is calm, the skies clear and the swell 2–3 meters from the southeast. The barometer is down to 1000, which is about 10 mb below what we have been seeing.

Good surf, Ilha do Mel, Brazil.

Cabo Frio, where we turn north, is 112 NM away, Salvador 687 and Antigua 2614. We have come 1301 NM from Buenos Aires.

John Steele, the owner of Covey Island that built *Maggie B*, our shipmate, friend and ever ready at "mission control," has suggested that we might consider entering a contest in Antigua that he won with his former boat, *Marguerite*. It is not the "Concors d'Elegance" but the "Concors de Negligence." I was just a little hurt as we have not been at all negligent about taking care of *Maggie*—she has added some… character. I consider the imperfections akin, perhaps, to the face of a Prussian major of old with honorable dueling scars here and there, and a tale about each one.

### 3 MARCH 2008

We are motoring in light or no wind, on a calm sea with only residual rollers. The sky is clear but with cumulus clouds over the land to the west. We passed Cabo Frio at dawn this morning and are heading northeast, more or less straight for Salvador.

Commanders' Weather says: "we are getting in the part of the world where not much [meteorologically] goes on."

> *"About noon today we stopped for a swim in mid-ocean. Curtis was super eager and jumped in before the boat was stopped, which he quickly found to be a mistake."*

The coast from Rio to Salvador contains dozens of beach resorts and our tough job is to choose where and when to stop. We have already passed Buzios, the beach resort made famous by Brigitte Bardot. Ahead lie Porto Seguro, the site of the first Portuguese landfall in the 16th Century; Ilheus, the hometown of Jorge Amado, Brazil's best-known novelist; Caravelas; Barra Grande; Itacare; Valencia; and many more wonderful stops.

Our current goal is some islands that make up the Parque Nacional Marinho de Abrolhos, Brazil's first national marine park. It is about half way between our current position and Salvador. The name comes from the sailor's warning *abre os olhos* (open your eyes).

About noon today we stopped for a swim in mid-ocean. Curtis was super eager and jumped in before the boat was stopped, which he quickly found to be a mistake. He was shocked at how fast he was left behind. In a minute, we covered about 100 meters, faster than even an Olympic swimmer could swim.

Moqueca con tutto dentro.

## BAHIA or SALVADOR, BRAZIL

The joke is that the bay is called Baia de Todos os Santos – The Bay of All Saints – because the principal town, Salvador, Brazil, is the city of all sins. In fact, it was discovered on All Saint's Day – November 1st – in 1500 by the Portuguese explorer Pedro Alvares Cabral.

The bay is a real gem. It is deep and safe with the endlessly enjoyable town of Salvador on one side and the enchanting island of Itaparica on the other. Salvador has two good world-class marinas that are well protected both from storms and unwanted visitors.

The city is split into the lower town and the upper town by a tall dividing escarpment. Some roads connect the two, but everyone takes the amazing Elevator Lacedera, built originally in 1873 that lifts you up the 85 meters.

Island Church.

The lower town is rough at night; the upper town is a World Heritage Site, the Pelourinho. The Pelo was the first slave market in the Americas and is full of 17th and 18th century architectural gems. There are churches, museums, restaurants, theaters, universities, bars, nightclubs, hotels and every sort of shop. The streets are full of tourists, natives, students, elderly, pickpockets, fortunetellers, girls of the night, boys of the night, buskers, beggars, artists, and vendors for absolutely everything.

Something is always going on in the Pelo, especially at night. Music is everywhere. And if things slow down, a fifty-person samba-drumming troupe may march past, rattling the old bricks and dancing the glass off your table.

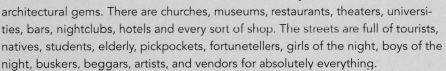

Thunderstorm.

Our favorite restaurant was on the second floor of an old building. We would sit at tables along the street and wait salivating for the food to be lowered in a basket from the front window on the second floor. The scene was managed by an enormously friendly, huge black man who would run off the beggars and generally keep order. I noticed that he would save the scraps from the plates to feed some of the younger, thinner street kids.

Deciding to leave Salvador for Cape Town was one of the toughest decisions I made during the circumnavigation.

*"The Navy and the Environmental Service (IBAMA)
told us on the radio that we were welcome to the mooring,
but would be boarded and inspected directly.
That was 3 hours ago, so maybe
it will happen tomorrow, or, more likely, never."*

This morning's sunrise was heightened by having Venus and Mars rise close together just before dawn.

### 4 MARCH 2008

We are motoring northeast in very light or calm winds. It is hot and sunny, and quite humid. If we weren't making our own breeze and didn't have the full sunshade up, we would perish. Our only sail handling is tacking up and down the sides of the awning from morning to evening. We have even put the sail covers on the foresail and main with no prospect for wind. We all can imagine the crews of square-riggers going mad.

We have been stopping around noon each day to take a brief dip in mid-ocean. Recently we have been seeing Portuguese man-of-war, (*Physalia physalis*), which are also known as blue bottles as they resemble plastic trash more than anything. Physalia are really interesting beyond offering swimmers very serious, possibly fatal stings. They are not a single organism, but a colony of different individuals, one being the float, another the mouth and stomach, another the sexual organs. The colony doesn't just float, it has a sail. Marvelously, there are two basic types, one with a left-handed and one with a right-handed sail, set so that they "sail out" and scatter in different directions, depending on the winds and current.

The man-of-war fish (*Nomeus gronovii*) lives unharmed among Physalia's tentacles. Physalia are eaten by violet bubble raft snails (*Janthina janthina*). Really!

We have been motoring about 20 miles offshore and have had the unusual nighttime view of vast oil fields even farther out to sea. It looks as if there are towns twenty miles away on each side of us, which is sort of true. During one regular radar check we discovered a target moving swiftly towards us, perhaps 70 knots. After a short period of panic about military action, we realized that it was the return of a low-flying helicopter servicing the oil fields. I had not known that basic ship navigation radar would pick up low-flying aircraft.

Paraty Bay, Brazil.

## 5 MARCH 2008

The Schooner *Maggie B* is moored off of Santa Barbara lighthouse in the Parque Nacional Marinho do Abrolhos. Santa Barbara and nearby islands give us a 220-degree embrace against the prevailing winds. We are moored on an enormous buoy that should be able to hold a small tanker in a moderate gale. I think we will have a quiet, safe night.

The island has lots of huge posted signs saying that no one can land. It looks like a James Bond island, with strange mechanical objects in caves and big ramps coming out of the water. The Navy and the Environmental Service (IBAMA) told us on the radio that we were welcome to the mooring, but would be boarded and inspected directly. That was 3 hours ago, so maybe it will happen tomorrow, or, more likely, never.

The islands were discovered by Amerigo Vespucci in 1503 and visited by Darwin in the *Beagle* in 1832. Dozens and dozens of white-tailed tropicbirds (*Phaethon lepturus*) swarm around the boat and scream at us. On shore there are piles of nesting masked boobies (*Sula dactylatra*), who have been diving into the water to catch fish. They are clumsy on shore, but loving—entwining necks before the seafaring partner regurgitates morsels for the nesting one.

Snorkeling shows a fine variety of coral, including one new to me that seems a cross between fan coral and elkhorn. Many beautiful fish are around and they seem completely oblivious to humans.

We are happy to have the engine off for a while. There is faint promise of a favorable easterly tomorrow. Sailing? It has been a long time since we have had a sail. We have come 1784 NM from Buenos Aires; we have 303 to go to Salvador and 2493 to Antigua.

We were surprised to see a nice sloop sail in. We haven't seen a lot of real travelers along the coast of Brazil. Aboard were three Frenchmen and a dog, Hugo. They have been out a little more than a year, and were working their way down the coast, headed for the Horn and Chile. I passed them our big book of Chilean Navy Charts that we had gotten from an Irish boat in Fremantle, in trade for a case of beer. I am so much happier to have that book out and helping sailors than sitting on a shelf somewhere. They promised that when they were finished that they would pass it along to someone else. I wish that I had written in the book its provenance.


## 6 MARCH 2008

We are motoring north at 6.5 knots. The skies are clear, the wind is a light northerly and the seas are mostly calm. We are currently headed to Ilhéus, former center of cocoa production and home to Jorge Amato, the famous author. It is 184 NM away.

We got a huge laugh in our email this morning. It came at the expense of the "Mail Marshal" system at a New Zealand company called Munro Benge. In my last entry, I mentioned the bird *Sula dactylatra*, known as the masked booby. It just was too hot a topic for the Mail Marshal. See below:

"The following email message was blocked by Mail Marshal:
From:FrankBlair@uuplus.comTo:    XXXXXXX    Subject:Schooner Maggie B in the Abrolhos

Because it may contain unacceptable language, or inappropriate material.

If you believe the message is business related, please send a message to call4help@infinity.co.nz and request that the message be released, or remove any inappropriate language and send it again. If no contact is made within 5 days the message will be automatically deleted.

MailMarshal Rule: Content Security (Inbound): Block Unacceptable Language Script Offensive Language (Basic) Triggered in Body Expression: b00bies Triggered 1 times weighting 5."

So the word booby has a 5 weighting. I wonder at the scale. Do you get a degree of difficulty like at the Olympics?

Side street, Ilhéus, Brazil.

120-liter resupply, Ilhéus.

## 8 MARCH 2008

The Schooner *Maggie B* spent the night of March 7th anchored off the Ilhéus Iate Clube.

The town of Ilhéus itself was pleasant and quirky, with few straight streets and no tourists. Just to be sure after our embarrassment in Buenos Aires, we got 120 more liters of diesel. Curtis and I rowed about a half mile to a beach near a gas station, carried up our six spare 20-liter jugs, filled them, and rowed back. It was a relatively easy stunt except that the beach was filthy and we both needed two showers to feel clean again.

The Ilhéus Yacht Club has a great bar and restaurant, three swimming pools and excellent showers but… almost no boats. There were three boats moored off the Club and perhaps 20 more in dry storage.

We have 114 NM to go to Salvador.

Squall line, Bahia de Totos Santos.

**9 MARCH 2008**

The Schooner *Maggie B* is tied up in the Centro Nautico do Bahia in Salvador. Since Buenos Aires we have come 2099 NM and used the engine for 276 hours, or about 90% of the miles.

We celebrated our arrival here with a bottle of Tasmanian Sparkling that Hannah deftly opened with a machete. Champagne for breakfast!

We were last here on August 1, 2006, when we left for Cape Town. We have traveled around the world, covering about 28,860 NM.

We—have—circumnavigated!

*"It all would be perfect except for a gale about 3000 NM away, off the coast of Newfoundland. It has sent a reminder of home in the form of 7–8 meter swells. The effect here at the island is enormous."*

17

# BAHIA TO MARTINIQUE

**19 MARCH 2008**

Spit Shine and ready for Blue Water, the Schooner *Maggie B* cast off from the fuel dock in Salvador at 1300 today. Finally, we have a decent breeze and should be sailing. We really haven't had a good, long sail since before Buenos Aires.

When we start out on long legs I usually read a poem or quote to set our minds to the task ahead. Today I read *The Sea Gypsy* by Richard Hovey:

> I am fevered with the sunset,
> I am fretful with the bay,
> For the wonder-thirst is on me
> And my soul is in Cathay.
> There's a schooner in the offing
> With her topsails shot with fire
> And my heart has gone aboard her
> For the Islands of Desire'
> I must forth again to-morrow!
> With the sunset I must be
> Hull down on the trail of rapture
> In the wonder of the sea.

Right now the *Maggie B* and her systems are in great shape. The long-standing problem with the genset appears to have been a fuel clog in the switch panel, which Marcello's boys found (Marcello is the master problem solver at the Centro Maritimo). The autopilot is now working and its problem seems to have been the electric motor in the hydraulic steering pump, which needed to be disassembled and cleaned. The Yanmar main engine was not charging after our trip to Itaparica, and that turned out to be a blown 200-amp fuse, which apparently blew because the electric capstan was abused when we pulled the anchor up when it was well set in deep mud.

The amazing story here is not how tricky we were in fixing all these problems, it is how much great support we were able to get. Marcello at Centro Maritimo is a wizard who also has lots of practical experience and can sniff out solutions like a police dog going after doughnuts. More amazing, though, is how well we were able to tap into expertise around the planet. Only a phone call away was the technical support at the alternator regulator company, the hydraulic steering manufacturer, Furuno USA, and, always, John Steele at Covey Island. I am not a plumbing/hydraulic/electrical/ diesel whiz. I am a patient plodder who keeps all the technical manuals handy and doesn't hesitate to call for advice. It is marvelous to work with skilled diagnosticians who are sitting at their desks 10,000 miles away.

We are now carefully counting the days and distances to Antigua via Fernando de Noronha, so that we arrive punctually on April 12th for registration for the Antigua Classic. It is 669 NM to Fernando de Noronha, or about four days, and 2135 NM from Fernando de Noronha to Antigua, or about two weeks. So we have about 18 days of sailing and 11 days ashore. We hope to spend a few days in Fernando de Noronha—*Lonely Planet* says that it is "one of the most stunning places in Brazil, if not the entire world"—and perhaps some more in Tous Saintes in Guadeloupe, one of my favorites.

On our last night in the marina there was a newly arrived French boat with a husband and wife and three girls on board. The girls were about 11, 9, and 4, polite and nautical. I lent them our copy of the *Maggie B* book to read at bedtime. It was a great success and I was very flattered that this morning the two older girls brought back the *Maggie B* book and then lent me THEIR favorite two books for me to read. It was charming. I told them that if they worked hard and learned all the nautical skills, they could come and crew on the *Maggie B* when they got big.

We are full of water, food, and diesel. We have a fair wind, a strong, fast boat and good experienced crew. We will be in Antigua on April 12th for Antigua Classic registration, and we'll do our best to have fun getting there.

Thomas on watch along the Brazil coast.

## 20 MARCH 2008

We are under full sail, making 8.2 knots for Fernando de Noronha. We have come 183 NM in 23 hours from Salvador and have 487 to go to Fernando de Noronha. Antigua is 2243 NM away. We have a nice 15–25 southeasterly that lets us make the rhumb line for Fernando de Noronha, as we slip along about 20 NM off the Brazilian coast. It seems to us as if it has been a long time since we had a full day's sail under a fair wind.

The weather is overcast with occasional rain showers marching past, messing with our wind. We should continue to have a more or less favorable wind to Fernando de Noronha, possibly dying out tonight.

All systems are working well, with almost nothing for the crew to do other than getting everything back in place after an extended shore period.

I have been doing the math on how much we had to motor from Puerto Montt, Chile to Salvador. From Halifax to Puerto Montt was 28,833 NM. We used the engine 1,527 hours, including some before we left Nova Scotia. That is, we traveled

18.9 miles for each hour the engine was run; 12 miles sailed; 6.9 miles powered. From Puerto Montt to Salvador is 4977 NM and we used the engine 615 hours, or 8.1 miles traveled for each engine hour; 6.9 miles powered; 1.1 miles sailed. We hope to sail much of the rest of the way home.

We were saddened today to hear of the death of Capt Svend Friis Hansen, skipper the *Eye Of The Wind*, the tall ship that was home to Hannah and Thomas at one time. I am sure we will see him again as an albatross in our wake.


## 21 MARCH 2008

We are motorsailing in a light southeasterly. The skies are mostly clear with scattered rain showers all around in the distance.

We have been catching a series of little tuna, about the size of a big trout, each big enough for a nice lunch for two people. They go from the hook to the fire with a little garlic, butter and lime juice—all within 10 minutes! Delicious! We think that perhaps we have a school of juvenile tuna following us for the flying fish and whatever else that our passage kicks up. The predators become the prey.

We are almost out of the Southern Hemisphere for the North Atlantic. Soon after we leave Fernando de Noronha, we will cross the Equator northbound. One minor ritual will be switching our steering compass to the northern hemisphere one. A major ritual will be the 2 shellbacks on board, Frank and Hannah, introducing the two pollywogs, Curtis and Thomas, to King Neptune and his court, and suitably initiating them to the mysteries of the Equator.


## 23 MARCH 2008—Easter Sunday

We are anchored off Fernando de Noronha. The prevailing wind here is from the southeast and we are tucked in a broad cove with another 70–80 working boats on the northeast corner. Most of the island is a marine park and we are anchored in the only legal area. The breeze is light and the skies mostly clear.

The sail last night was as nice as any of the whole trip. We were doing 6 knots in a 10–12 knot close reach, with a full moon and little wave chop, and clear skies. It all would be perfect except for a gale about 3000 NM away, off the coast of Newfoundland. It has sent a reminder of home in the form of 7–8 meter swells. The effect here at the island is enormous. There is a very hefty 20-foot high breakwater sheltering a small boat harbor. The waves are breaking over the top and full across the entrance.

Praia do Leao, Fernando de Noronha.

Trying the passage in the *Reep* or any other boat would be death. The Maritime Police have closed the port. Some moored fishing boats are tossed almost vertical in the waves. We are told, "Tomorrow may be better."

The surf hitting the shore is spectacular. We have seen a few surfers, and no one has taken a second ride. We are relatively comfortable outside the surf line, in 50 feet of water with 200 feet of chain out. Just after we set the anchor, though, one of the swells jumped us and tore the pawl off the capstan. One more thing to fix when we get back to Nova Scotia.

The next day the seas calmed down a bit and we were able to get ashore with a local sailor using his knowledge and skill.

We all fell in love with Fernando de Noronha. On one side of the island the beaches had surf, on the other—great snorkeling. After our boat jobs, we would share the rest of the day between the two sides of the island. One marvelous beach on the quiet side was full of sea turtle nests, all carefully staked out and managed by Project TAMAR, a Brazilian sea turtle rescue, recovery and education group. Even this late in the season, we were thrilled to see fresh track of mother turtles making their way up the beach to lay their eggs. The beaches are closed to the public from 6 p.m. to dawn to allow TAMAR to follow, research, record and assist the hatchlings. They say that they assist 600,000 hatchlings a year.

## 27 MARCH 2008

The Schooner *Maggie B* hoisted anchor, set sail and headed for the Caribbean a little after noon today. We have about 2143 NM to go to Antigua, which should take us about 12 days. The sky is mostly clear with occasional rain showers. The wind is 5–7 knots from the southeast. There is a gentle remaining swell from the northeast. We are motorsailing at our efficiency cruise RPM (1600) for maximum range.

With a few *Reep* trips, we added 280 liters of diesel to our tanks, which should give us plenty of steaming range. We should hit the northeast trades in a few days as we pass north of about 2 degrees North. In the Caribbean, we will probably land first at Martinique, to clear in with the French before heading to Iles des Saintes, to see if it really is as pretty as Fernando de Noronha. Certainly, Fernando de Noronha, Iles des Saintes and Bora Bora are all in very much the same category, right up there with La Digue in the Seychelles.

## 28 MARCH 2008

The wind is calm and there are gentle, long rollers, and the sky is partially cloudy with small cumulus. The barometer is steady at 1003 mb.

It is easy to see how, in the old days, men must have gone crazy when they were caught in these calms. This area, the Inner Tropical Convergence Zone, ITCZ, is also known as the Doldrums.

North of this area, at 30 degrees to 38 degrees North (and also in the Southern Hemisphere) is another area of high pressure and low winds. It is called the Horse Latitudes. Some books say that the expression refers to ships getting caught here and running short on supplies; they threw their horses overboard to save drinking water.

We think that is ridiculous. Why would any sailor waste fresh horsemeat? A more likely explanation is that this was the area where sailors from Europe had worked off their advance pay. That point was called "finishing the dead horse," and sometimes was attended with a ritual which included throwing over a horse effigy.

We are used to having porpoises, dolphin and pilot whales play in our bow wave. Today Thomas spotted a small school, 10–20 fish, of young tuna working our bow in the clear, calm water. Each was about 2 feet long and had a bright green/yellow iridescent spot just at the top base of the tail. The side and top fins were yellow. They stuck with us for at least an hour.

We are doing our laundry Blue Water style: saltwater soaping and three saltwater rinses, then a final, long, freshwater rinse. We are also starting on varnishing and oiling the deck. All to make us presentable in Antigua!

## 29 MARCH 2008

We have come 1025 NM from Salvador and have 1810 NM to go to Antigua. We are just a few miles short of the Equator, which we expect to cross at about sunset today.

It is typical ITCZ weather: rainy and no wind. Thomas maximized his 9 a.m. to noon watch by taking a shower on deck in moderate rain. Can't get cleaner! Our GRIB files and Commanders' Weather, our weather router, say that we should get into steady northeast trades tomorrow. We are ready for it!

Thomas flambé.

The shellbacks on board, Frank and Hannah, are feverishly preparing for the visit of King Neptune, Iemanja, and their courts. The pollywogs are hoping to be passed without too many complications. Little do they know….

Long Blue Water passages are great for reading and the *Maggie B's* library is rich and eclectic. I have been recently through: Jorge Amado's *Gabriela, Clove and Cinnamon*; *Harry Potter and the Deathly Hallows;* Carl Hiaasen's *Stormy Weather*; and now started on Robert Fagles's translation of Virgil's *Aeneid*. Thomas has started *1421*; Curtis is reading Mark Helprin's short story collection, *The Pacific*; and Hannah is reading *Thirteen Moons* by Charles Frazier.

**3 APRIL 2008**

We are making 10 knots for Martinique. We have come 2061 NM from Salvador and have 655 NM to go to Martinique. We expect to arrive in Martinique the morning of April 6th. The skies remain a thin overcast with occasional small rain showers. The wind has been very steady from the northeast at 15–20 knots.

We are excited to have gone 242 NM since noon yesterday. Our best 24-hour run ever was 245 NM. Thomas did our best watch with 33 NM in 3 hours. In the last three days we have covered 675 NM, or averaging 225 NM per day—schoonering along in the trades!

The crew of square-rigged ships looked down on schooners, because the simpler sails were so efficient. When I worked on the *Roald Amundsen*, a 165-foot German sail training brig with two masts of six square-sails each, my captain remarked that "schooner" was a Dutch word meaning "lazy man" because even a big schooner could be worked by a man and a dog. Hmmmm, some dog!

*"We set our clocks to Caribbean Time, —4 Zulu, same time as the eastern US. It is the first time in two years we have moved the clocks back."*

**4 APRIL 2008**

We are making 8.6 knots for Martinique. The wind has veered a bit to the east, and increased to a steady 20 knots. We have reefed the foresail down to one reef, like the main. We have come 228 NM in the last day, 470 in the last two days, 701 in the last three days, and 903 in the last four days, giving an average of 226 NM.

The seas have come up a bit. In the Southern Ocean, the swells helped us along, with *Maggie B* surfing down their long sides. Here, they really don't help as they are from a little behind the beam, and throw us around a fair amount. Our trusty Furuno autopilot is working very hard and effectively. The general sensation is that of a skier doing a long traverse on a very steep hill with endless 3- to 4-meter moguls to cross or negotiate. Most of the time it is a marvelous rhythm that keeps us hanging in the windward shrouds to watch. Occasionally there is a big guy, a shoulder-to-shoulder hit, with the wave wanting us in one place and the *Maggie B* wanting something else.

Schoonering along.

We are earning our fresh croissants and French government subsidized pinot noir!

We set our clocks to Caribbean Time, −4 Zulu, same time as the eastern US. It is the first time in two years we have moved the clocks back.

### 5 APRIL 2008
We are making 8.4 knots for Martinique, which is only 189 NM away. It is mostly clear weather with an occasional rain shower marching through with a bit more wind. Mostly we have 15–20 knots at a relative angle of 120 degrees on our starboard side.

## THE *MAGGIE B* AT SEA

When Nigel and I met in Paris to shake hands to have him design the *Maggie B*, I told him that she would have to be safe, fast and comfortable. He laughed and said that usually you get only one of the three. The *Maggie B* was fast – averaging 7.9 knots for three weeks from Mauritius to Chile and had a 246 NM day. The *Maggie B* was safe – surviving a 72 knot uncontrolled jibe with no gear failures. But perhaps her best quality was her comfort at sea.

We noticed first what a pleasure she was when we crossed the Gulf Stream southbound from Lunenburg the end of March, traveling at ten knots, hull speed. The watch below never missed a hot meal and was able to sleep soundly in comfort.

A more amazing display of her seaworthiness was in the Southern Ocean. Even when we had a big breeze, 25-30 knots just aft the beam, and 30 foot long rollers, we all were comfortable with single person watches and autopilot steering. Hannah was on watch when we hit our top speed, 17.6 knots on the GPS. Many other boats have hit that speed surfing in the Roaring Forties, but what deeply impressed me was that the autopilot, the excellent adaptive Furuno, only needed a degree or two of rudder, port or starboard, to steer her in those conditions.

Pizza tonight.

Many things come together to make an excellent offshore boat. If she is too steady; she plows through waves, if too light; she bounces off every little thing. The *Maggie B*'s earlier "cousins" from Nigel's pencil were the *Rozanne* and *Romily*. They were made stiff also, but were designed for shallow English rivers so the keel was long fore and aft rather than deep. *Maggie B* inherited these design characteristics. With a 140 degree righting angle and 39% of her 77,000# in her lead keel, she was stiff. But with a 6 foot draft for her 62 foot length (centerboard up), she was shallow. So her 30,000# keel was much more fore and aft rather than stuck deep, as is the current fashion.

With her stem almost plumb, a shallow forefoot, the weight of her keel fore and aft, and a fore volume relatively "under-inflated," the *Maggie B* would handle ever wave with respect, but rarely, crash, splash, or make a fuss.

We still have a reef in the main and in the foresail, which is essentially like taking in topsails in a traditional schooner. The long swells are 3–4 meters and rather unruly and splashy, but *Maggie* isn't paying them much attention.

We made 224 NM in the last 24 hours. We have come 1127 NM in the last five days, or an average of 225 NM per day. We expect that when we post these marvelous times on our story board at the Antigua Classic, the Race Committee will increase our handicap.

We are in the midst of flying fish grounds. This morning there were a dozen on deck, which Curtis collected and gutted. They were delicious for breakfast, quickly cooked in a hot pan with garlic and butter. Hannah made raisin tea biscuits—a perfect breakfast with black, black, black Brazilian coffee! We have been out for two weeks but are having no hardships.

The wind has lessened a bit and veered (Thomas says from the French *virer*—to turn) more to the east. The sailor's expression for wind shifting in an expected direction is to veer, the unexpected way is to back, which can bring bad weather. In the Northern Hemisphere, veering is shifting clockwise, in the Southern, counterclockwise. As an example, in Maine, if the wind shifts, backs, from south to east, trouble is coming. Conversely, veering from southwest to northwest is clearing for good weather.

*Reep* snug aboard, northbound.

We are about 60 NM from Barbados and are already seeing some light sport-fishing boats that are essentially invisible on radar in these swells. The watch is shifting to inshore levels of attention.

We expect to be in Cul de Sac de Marins, Martinique tomorrow morning. Just in time for church, or croissants and *chocolate chaud*.

*"We were primed for the landing, but after we committed to the turn, it became apparent we had no reverse. We were just able to bail out, missing a lot of expensive maritime real estate by a few hair's breadth. "*

## 6 APRIL 2008

The Schooner *Maggie B* was safely anchored in Cul de Sac des Marins, Martinique at approximately 11:30 a.m., April 6th. The trip from Salvador was 2732 NM. We covered the 2046 NM from Fernando de Noronha to des Marins in 10 days. Ten days for 2046 miles! Antigua is about 160 NM away.

Yesterday was very eventful. At approximately 2130 last night, when we were about 25 NM off of Barbados, Thomas saw a distress flare, rising from the surface to the base of the clouds at a 45-degree angle. Color unknown as he had his tinted sunglasses on, having lost his regular glasses. He called me and we checked the radar for any targets. We were going about 10 knots in moderate seas. We watched for another flare for a while and then called the Barbados Coast Guard on VHF. They answered, but were impossible to understand, so we gave the report as best we could.

The clearest communications equipment we have on board is the Iridium Satellite Phone. The question was: "who to call?" Despite having lots of reference material on board, we only had the number of the Barbados Port Captain, which didn't answer. But New Zealand is really well organized for this sort of stuff and I had their Rescue Center number handy, and they answered immediately. After only a bit of explaining, they gave me the Barbados Rescue Center number, which went right through. I gave the report and suggested a helicopter search. The weather was wind 20–25 with perhaps five meter breaking swells. About an hour later I got a call from a Barbados Government boat called the *Lady D*, which had been dispatched. About four hours after we saw the flare, I got a call from a rescue helicopter doing a sector sweep in the estimated area.

I called the Barbados Rescue Central today and the news is that the searches turned up nothing. You never know. It would have been a very tough night to be in the water.

We arrived in the safety of Cul de Sac in very sloppy seas—big and unkempt—and 20–25 knots of wind. The marina said that they could find a space for us, though they were full and we hadn't reserved. The engine had behaved a bit strangely on start up, but motored us in OK. Our berth required a tight turn and then backing between tightly packed buoys—with very big, shiny boats all around. We were primed for the landing, but after we committed to the turn, it became apparent we had no reverse. We were just able to bail out, missing a lot of expensive maritime real estate by a few hair's breadth. When there was a clue that something might be wrong with the engine, I should have considered the problem more before committing to tight quarters!

After a few tries, we found a good spot to anchor. A dive on the prop showed that the feathering J-Prop would almost go into the right setting for forward, but reverse left the blades at zero pitch. Something screwed up in the gears. We took it off and dismantled it, finding that the reversing gears were totally trashed. This is the same type of prop that came off two years ago somewhere between Barbados and Brazil. Perhaps there is something in the water here? We carry a spare non-feathering prop, which we will install.

As marvelous as this last passage was, we all are delighted to be safe at anchor and to not have the boat bouncing around.

Photo credit: Irwin Christian

*"We had the "little gale" last night. It didn't seem so little.*
*Winds to 46 knots, with about eight hours of 35+ knots.*
*We had the foresail down and the main with two reefs.*
*Maggie B did fine and all were relatively comfortable."*

## 18

# MARTINIQUE
# TO HOME

### 9 APRIL 2008

We got to work in Martinique to remove the failed J-Prop, which took only an hour using the Hookah underwater gear. Then we installed the spare fixed prop, which took only half an hour. It fit perfectly on the shaft. Unfortunately it did not fit in the opening, having a shorter shank than the J-Prop. Our prop shaft was made in two sections, with a massive coupling. It took an hour to get the four nuts off the coupling. But the shaft had long since fused to the housing and no amount of force, lubrication or heat guns could persuade it to slide.

It took another hour in the water to saw enough room in the hull for the prop to turn so that we can motor as necessary.

When we put the mainsail up this morning, we found a 2-foot rip just below the second reef luff cringle. So we set the main only to the second reef. Hannah will have busy fingers tomorrow!

Cul de Sac des Marins is a lovely little harbor. Only slightly marred by 1000 rental catamarans. The restaurants are great—fresh vegetables! —even the little supermarket had 200 different cheeses. But everything was very expensive, a combination of the weak dollar against the Euro, and the generally high living costs in Martinique. The gear stores are well stocked and have knowledgeable staff, something we haven't experienced since New Zealand.

Now we are sailing on a close reach in 15–20 northeasterly trades along the Caribbean coast of Martinique, protected from any Atlantic swell. At noon we were just about directly off Fort de France, the capitol and main port. It is sunny with only a few rain showers around.

We are headed to Les Saintes, which is an island group just south of Guadeloupe, and have about 80 NM to go. Antigua is only another 75 NM from Les Saintes. We should arrive tonight about 10 p.m.

Iles des Saintes was discovered by Christopher Columbus on his second voyage, on November 4, 1493. It is largely populated by fishermen from Brittany and Normandy, and never had the scourge of slave plantations due to the weak soil. The islands changed hands endlessly between the French and British during their wars, and were a hotbed of resistance to the French Vichy regime during the Second World War.

Iles des Saintes will be a welcome break for a day or two and then we jump into the craziness of Antigua Classic Race Week.

*We raced with the fixed prop on the first day and it was awful. Having a fixed prop in place is like towing a bucket, in comparison to a feathering prop. In a decent breeze it makes a difference of 3/4 of a knot, if not a full knot in boat speed."*

**23 APRIL 2008**

We arrived in the historic Nelson's Dockyard on Antigua right on schedule for the April 12 Classic Race Week Registration.

It was also a reunion. Nigel Irens, the boat designer, came over from England; Sandy MacMillan, President of North Sails Atlantic and our sail designer, came from Halifax, and John Steele, President of Covey Island Boatworks, where *Maggie B* was built, came from Lunenburg.

We got a lot of press attention. Our friend Aaron Porter of *Professional Boat-Builder* magazine sailed with us. One day we had the official Antigua Classics film crew on board, on other days there were writers and photographers from *Wooden-Boat*, *Boat International* and *Classic Yachts*. Many fellow sailors came by at other times. I think that we were the only boat ever to race in the Classic, circumnavigate in the Southern Hemisphere, and race again on the way home.

During the Classic Race Week, what stunning boats to sail with! *Juno, Adela, Altair, Eleonora, Ticonderoga, Wild Horses, Ranger,* and many more.

Two years ago there was a big yacht at the 2006 Classic whose cockpit light was a Chambered Nautilus shell with an internal bulb. *Maggie B* has an old-fashioned brass oil-fired lamp we use as a cockpit lamp. But when we were in Cape Town in 2006, one store specialized in ostrich eggs that had been cut and carved with designs. One was drilled with constellations and the Milky Way—I was unable to resist it. It got packed away and mostly forgotten. Arriving back in Antigua for our second Classic, I got John Steele to wire it up and now we have a beautiful cockpit light that is lovely to look at directly, and casts a light show of the galaxy around the cockpit like in a planetarium.

We raced with the fixed prop on the first day and it was awful. Having a fixed prop in place is like towing a bucket, in comparison to a feathering prop. In a decent breeze it makes a difference of 3/4 of a knot, if not a full knot in boat speed. I was faced with a mutiny. Nigel Irens was ready to get back on an airplane, John Steele had a very long-suffering face, Sandy MacMillan was ready to go to the Chinese Olympics. It wasn't nice. I've sailed the boat enough to know what to expect with her performance.

I said that I'd take the fixed prop off if we talked to the skippers of the boats we were closest to, and got approval from the Race Committee. We did that, talking especially to the Head of the Race Committee and got his approval. The morning of the second race we motored out to a safe spot, anchored, and I jumped over with our Hookah breathing apparatus to remove the fixed prop. Every boat going racing could see everything we were doing. One boat even stopped to videotape the operation.

We smoked that race and there were smiles all around, at least on the *Maggie B*. After the race, the skipper of one boat came to visit and inquire about the prop and asked what we were rated for—the answer being a folding prop. He had the video, and had taken it to the Ratings Committee. We told him the whole story—who we talked to and when. His boat was slow and uncompetitive, and I hadn't mentioned it to him beforehand because I couldn't imagine why it could be important. But the Ratings Committee decided that I should have written them a letter asking to be re-rated and not done anything until I had a written response. Talking to the Head of the Race Committee and what he said was not relevant. I could withdraw or be successfully protested. We withdrew.

We raced the next two days without the prop. We would motor out, anchor, take it off, up the anchor under sail, race without the prop, sail in, anchor, put the prop

Winning the start, Antigua. Photo credit: Tim Wright, Photoaction.com

back on and motor back to the dock.

We all had great fun, probably a bit too much rum at night, but the work and heat of the racing sweated each night's excesses out. Lovely parties and a kind reception for our circumnavigation everywhere. I single-handed *Maggie B* on the fifth day of racing and I'm pleased to report that we came in second, despite our new, very high, "propless" rating. After the morning single-handed race there was gig racing in the afternoon, and the *Reepicheep* was well admired and much borrowed by different rowers. It was a fun day and *Reep* won in the Woman's Singles and the Family Race.

We are looking forward to a nice peaceful Blue Water passage.

When we went to fill up with diesel for the leg to Bermuda, we had formally checked out of Antigua, which normally allows you to buy fuel duty free. I enquired if Duty Free was available at the Cat Club and the nice lady in charge said, "Yes, Dear, but you don't want it." I inquired why not, and she replied that it was more expensive than non-duty free. I asked why and she answered, "The election is coming up." Apparently the politicians had drastically reduced the price of fuel for the locals, so as to be re-elected. Not being able to argue with logic, I happily bought 199 gallons of non-duty free.

*"It is great to be back in Blue Water. It will probably take us most of the way to Bermuda to recover from the frenzy of Antigua Classic Race Week."*

We are more or less ready for the 930 NM run to Bermuda tomorrow morning. The weather going north should be interesting. We hope to be in St. Georges Harbor by the end of April.

### 24 APRIL 2008

We are a few miles off the coast of Antigua at Curtain Bluff. We are underway for Bermuda, motorsailing in a light southeasterly. The sky is clear and the air is hot and humid. We will be happy for a little cooler weather.

The weather forecast is not particularly favorable. Commanders' Weather comment was: "light winds to start and then upwind to Bermuda followed by a possible gale the middle and end of next week. Welcome home, I guess!"

We hope to be into Bermuda before the gale.

Onboard for this leg is Frank Blair, Hannah Joudrey, Curtis Weinrich (aboard since Puerto Montt, Chile), Danette Eden and her partner Rik Hansen. Danette was our landlady when we lived in Lunenburg for the completion of *Maggie B* and Rik spends part of the year in Russia or Northern Canada working oil exploration, and the rest of the time messing about in boats. Danette has a marvelous business in Lunenburg converting worn-out sails into very imaginative high-end purses, packs and bags.

It is great to be back in Blue Water. It will probably take us most of the way to Bermuda to recover from the frenzy of Antigua Classic Race Week.

### 25 APRIL 2008

We are making 7.2 knots due north, motorsailing in a light southwesterly. We are flying "the Bird," the G2 gennaker. It is 4562 NM from here to Cape Horn and only 1469 to Halifax.

The weather is clearly changing. Last night at sunset there were high cirrus mare's tails. Today at noon the high clouds were mostly obscured by altostratus, with some lower cumulus working their way in. Rain showers are on the horizon to the southwest. The barometer is still mostly steady at 1006 mb, but the wind has shifted around from the southeast to the southwest and increased a bit.

It would be lovely to have a few days of a nice southwesterly blow, but Commanders' says that a weak low is coming through, with northwest and north behind it. We'll take it as it comes.

We must be trailing a big school of fish from the Caribbean. There has been a very aggressive juvenile masked booby following us and diving regularly, apparently successfully. Perhaps it is time to get the lines out to share in the ocean's bounty.

We are all beginning to settle into the watch routine for passages. But being such a short leg, we will be there before we fully get our inner clocks readjusted.

## 26 APRIL 2008

We are motorsailing directly towards Bermuda, helped a little by a 10-knot northeast breeze. The sky is mostly clear and the humidity is significantly lower. On night watch last night we had to dig out jackets. Blankets are beginning to make their way back from the linen closet to the bunks.

## 27 APRIL 2008

We are motoring directly north towards Bermuda in a 5–8 knot headwind. The skies are clear, the barometer is up to 1011 mb and there are long swells from the north. We have come 513 NM from Antigua and have 430 NM to go to St. Georges.

We have been trying to fish, but we have been more successful catching lots of sargassum weed. Most seaweed varieties are attached to rocks in shallow water but not sargassum weed. It lives in the center of a giant gyre called the Sargasso Sea. This is an area east of the Bahamas Islands roughly between 25 and 30 degrees north, 40 to 60 degrees west. The name comes from the Portuguese word *sargaco*, meaning grapes. This is a unique habitat that includes the sargassum anglerfish which has the same coloring as the weed, and bodies that are covered with protuberances resembling the seaweed's grapelike fronds. It is also the main breeding ground of the eels whose elvers swim to Europe in the Gulf Stream.

With Curtis's encouragement, we broke out the sextant today. Following a short discussion on celestial navigation, we took the sun's altitude to get an afternoon line of position. With total beginner's luck, it came out within 1/10 of a mile of our

Curtis and his Mahi-mahi.

actual position. I confess that we used a computer program to do the math, but still it was an excellent introduction. We'll try for a 3 star fix tonight, and probably plot ourselves in the middle of North Africa.

Last night the moonrise was just after midnight. The half moon seemed to be cradling Jupiter, which was bright as a diamond. It was hard not to think of ancient stories of the stars and the gods.

## 28 APRIL 2008

We are motoring north towards St. Georges at 7.5 knots in a 3–5 knot northerly. There are long swells from the north, courtesy of a gale off Newfoundland. The skies are clear and the barometer is rising.

We are still hoping to get some sailing in on this leg. There is a new low coming off of the American continent which should give us a nice southwesterly, starting perhaps noon tomorrow. We are slowing our speed a bit so as not to arrive earlier than dawn on the 30th. I know Town Cut into St. Georges Harbor, and I know not to try it at night.

Two more sleeps to Bermuda!


## 29 APRIL 2008

We are finally under all plain sail with "the Bird" up. We are making 6.2 knots in a 10–12 knot southwesterly, straight for St. Georges. We have 113 NM to go to Bermuda and have come 833 from Antigua. It looks as if we will arrive, assuming that the wind freshens a bit, after dawn on the 30th. That should get us tucked into Captain Smokes Marina in St. Georges Harbor before the cold front arrives with fresher winds.

We are at that perfect point of sailing with the wind about on our beam, with long swell and no wave chop. It is a relief to have the engine off. The big prop is stopped with a short lasso about the fitting on the shaft in the engine room. It is still like towing a bucket, but *Maggie* seems so happy to be under sail, she is not complaining. Yesterday Curtis caught a large mahi-mahi after a bit of a struggle. It is the biggest fish we have ever landed on the *Maggie B*. How big? Curtis is 6′ 3″ and it came up to his shoulder. We should get six meals for 5 out of it. It was delicious in garlic and butter, flash-fried in a hot pan and even more so the next day in a thick fish soup concocted by Rik.

Last night, or actually this morning, Curtis and I did our star sights once the moon rose enough to give us a satisfactory horizon. We shot the moon, Jupiter and Arcturus and were delighted that of six observations, none were more than 7 NM from our actual GPS position. We might even be able to find Bermuda without GPS!

Bermuda tomorrow!

Bermuda decorations.

## 30 APRIL 2008

The Schooner *Maggie B* is safely docked in St. Georges, Bermuda, at Captain Smokes Marina. Our last day coming in gave us a lovely sail, though it did end in a rather heavy downpour this morning as we danced around a huge Norwegian cruise ship while we waited for dawn to break before entering Town Cut.

## 7 MAY 2008

The week in Bermuda passed quickly. St. Georges is always a pleasure to visit and we all enjoyed the town. But we had our eyes looking north for this last leg. It is just a bit more than 700 NM, and after the circumnavigation, we feel we could almost spit that far. Nevertheless, it is early May in the North Atlantic and we have the Gulf Stream to cross. Four days! Commanders' Weather is working to find us a spot in the weather, and we spend lots of time looking at the clear, professional forecasts from Bermuda Weather.

Commanders' Weather has us primed for 3 gales, which is a lot for a 4-day

427

## THIRTEEN THINGS I LEARNED CIRCUMNAVIGATING
## IN THE SOUTHERN HEMISPHERE

1. You need to be a good librarian. We catalogued every piece of information that came aboard with all the different systems. This saved us so many times. When something broke, we were able to grab the manual for the system and find the answer or, at least, the email address or phone number for technical support.

2. Any new noise is a bad noise. At sea, there is no such thing as a good new noise. It is always something grinding, rubbing, breaking, or otherwise coming apart. Something is always chafing somewhere. Find it, fix it, make it stop.

3. GPS and chart plotters can kill you. A good navigator should always be some-what paranoid. If your GPS is accurate to 30' and every chart in the world is up on your plotter, what could go wrong? Lots. Like new sand bars, inaccurate charts, uncharted meteorological buoys, mis-entered way points, making the center of a small island your way point and falling asleep with the autopilot on and hit the island exactly, within 30 feet.

4. It is OK to be a captain. I started off on the trip after twenty years of teaching Outward Bound. Many of the early group discussions were classic "What do you think?" group interaction efforts. Later I was much more ready to give orders. A boat works better with clear lines of command and responsibility.

5. Different countries work differently. Don't sit and fret that getting a load of diesel is not as easy as in the States. Relax and enjoy the cultural experience.

6. The two hardest things about cruising the globe are clearing in and out of Customs in different countries, and getting your propane tank filled up. Customs clearance is helped somewhat by fancy crew lists and Official Ship's Stamps, especially if you had a bright red stamp pad, or could seal your signature with engraved raised lettering like a notary. But propane is amazingly unstandardized. Metric, SAE, left handed, right handed, male, female, integral step down valves or external, rules against filling bottles not properly marked, etc., etc. We ended up with five different types of bottles on board and a huge mayonnaise jar full of different connectors.

7. Don't have anything onboard just because "that's how they did it in the old days," nor because "It's the latest and greatest!" Every piece of equipment has to "buy" its way on board and be the best thing for the job.

8. You want to choose what is going to break. Everything today is strong but some-thing is still going to break – you should choose where so that it will be a little deal, not a big deal. Say your boom can take 6000 pounds a third the way out from the mast, where you would put the preventer that helps keep the boom in place.

Sunk ship.

Make the attachment point to the preventer a line with a breaking strength of less than 5000 pounds. Better to break the line than the boom.

9. Meteorology is pretty good these days. You can get good advice anytime, anywhere. If you are paying attention, it is much, much harder to get into weather trouble than it used to be.

10. A schooner is a much safer boat offshore than a sloop, yawl or ketch, as discussed at length elsewhere.

11. A boat built by sailors will hold up much better in hard use than a boat built simply by good boat builders.

12. Simpler is better. There is lots of marvelous gear that looks great in a catalog or a store, but rope and knives and pulleys will win most days over some fancy specialized piece.

13. Modern materials are better and safer than what we had ten or twenty years ago. Carbon fiber, Spectra lines, Wooden masts and hemp sails are great for boat shows; just don't go offshore with them.

passage, though not a lot for spring in the North Atlantic! The first has just passed the island to the north and we knew we would catch a bit of it starting out. Then there would be a little gale and then there would be a big one, which we have to beat into Lunenburg.

We are close hauled, making for our Gulf Stream entry point at about 7.5 knots. We are headed north-northeast and the wind has backed a bit to the west-northwest, and diminished from 25 knots to 17–20. It is rather a rough ride. The waves aren't big—the biggest perhaps only 10 feet—but the period is short and we get occasional unpleasant vertical drops. We have come 172 NM from Bermuda and have 551 to go to Lunenburg. We anticipate arrival in Lunenburg at about noon on Saturday, May 10th.

We should enter the Gulf Stream about noon tomorrow. The wind should have backed to the west and the current flow is from the southwest, so hopefully there won't be too much excitement. It feels a bit as if the *Maggie B* is remembering the wave period of the North Atlantic and relearning how to best handle it. Like a skilled dancer going from Argentinean Tango to Brazilian Samba to Foxtrot. We hope that we won't be Charlestoning when we hit the Gulf Stream!

We are surprised that we haven't seen a single bird in the last day. This kind of weather usually brings out the stormy petrels, but none are about. Perhaps the Gulf Stream is just too interesting, or they haven't completed their pilgrimage back from the south yet. We did have a pod of about 15–20 striped dolphin (*Stenella coeruleo-alba*) playing around our bow yesterday. It was interesting that there was one spotted dolphin (*Stenella plagiodon*) with them. At first, we thought he was "Dad," with a bunch of teenagers. He didn't mix things up around the bow like the rest and stayed on the outskirts, like a distant cousin at a rowdy family swim party.


## 8 MAY 2008

We are in the Gulf Stream—water temperature 70 degrees, and making 10.2 knots for Lunenburg, which is 378 NM away. About 2 knots of our speed is the favorable Gulf Stream current. We are about half way. The wind is a nice 20-knot southwesterly, pushing us along at about 8 1/2 knots boat speed, with one reef in main and fore and the fixed prop tied off. We have the reefs in because the southwesterly is due to blow up to 30 knots tonight and we are getting plenty of boat speed. I'm hearing the characteristic "9-knot hum" from the centerboard.

The day is clear but with a high overcast coming in. The barometer is steady at

## WHAT MAKES THE BEST PORT?

I'm often asked which was my favorite port. There is no one answer, but my crew and I talked about what attributes make a port good or poor. Everyone values these factors differently. Here's a list of what we considered important.

1. Technically good anchorage or docking: good holding ground at anchor, no swells, shelter. It doesn't matter how pretty the beaches are if you are rolling out your masts in the anchorage, as we did in Fernando de Noronha.

2. Water quality and clarity. Lack of pollution.

3. Character of town: history, shops, artistic community, vibrant, culture. Not too big, not too small.

4. A welcoming attitude towards visitors.

5. Technical support and crew comforts: laundry, showers, Internet, phones, water, fuel.

6. Reasonable costs.

7. Distance from amateurs. Martinique is lovely, but 1,000 catamarans are rented each week and every nearby harbor is filled with charter boats, many manned by inexperienced sailors. Conversely, places that attract traveling boats and their seasoned crews are significantly more interesting. Puerto Williams, Chile, being a good example of the latter.

8. Food. Good restaurants and markets with all the staples as well as local specialties.

9. Yacht support. Can you get critical supplies and skilled help? Are there specialists who can make your life easier?

10. Security. Not just night watchmen at the marina; are the town and surrounding area safe?

Naiad.

1010 mb.

At this speed, the computer says that we will arrive in Lunenburg at about midnight on Friday the 9th. We expect the wind to slow down a bit tomorrow as this southwesterly blows out in anticipation of the next significant weather event, a very fast moving low. It is going to arrive in Nova Scotia as a proper spring northwesterly gale, sometime on Saturday, hopefully not cranking up until the evening. Needless to say, we are in scamper mode, and will not spare the Yanmar horses tomorrow as the wind eases. The center of the low, which should pass 150 NM south of Nova Scotia, is forecast to be 987 mb, a fairly severe storm. We will cross the track of the center of the low at about noon tomorrow, a day and a half ahead of its arrival. Timing is everything.

Right now we are still barefoot and in shirtsleeves. But we have spent the day reinforcing *Reep*'s lashings and doubling the anchor's tie down. I was shocked to find the anchor's shackle bolt was three turns unscrewed! We fitted vent covers and adjusted hatch clamps.

John Steele of Covey Island asked us to bring along some nice Bermuda weather with us, I'm afraid it will be more resembling Cape Horn for our Saturday night party!


**9 MAY 2008**

We are motorsailing at 7.1 knots directly for Lunenburg, which is just 176 NM away. We have come 556 NM from Bermuda.

We had the "little gale" last night. It didn't seem so little. Winds to 46 knots, with about eight hours of 35+ knots. We had the foresail down and the main with two reefs. *Maggie B* did fine and all were relatively comfortable. We were still in the Gulf Stream, so the facefuls of water were 71 degrees. This morning was quite different. The seawater is now 51 degrees, there was thick, dripping fog at dawn and the outside temperature is perhaps 45 degrees. T-shirts and bare feet are a distant memory. Tooks are on. And the wind has mostly died out, veering through the north to get set up for tomorrow's big easterly, heralding the "big gale." We hope to arrive in Lunenburg at about noon tomorrow, and beat the worst of the weather.

I know that things will become very busy tomorrow. Also that it will be some time before I can fully reflect on this trip. Today is very poignant for me, the last day when the circumnavigation is still alive. Tomorrow it will be a memory. We will have sailed the *Maggie B* about 38400 NM in 25 ½ months, leaving a temporary 5-meter-wide track behind us.

I am in full agreement with Tennyson's words for Ulysses: "I am a part of all that I have met."

At the start of each leg we do a little ceremony. We fill a glass with rum, pour the first over the side for a safe passage, and then each person makes a toast and takes a drink in turn. I always toast: "To the *Maggie B*, to those who built her and those who sail her." Right now, I also want to toast all those who supported us along the way: computer technicians in an office somewhere ashore; anonymous sailors who caught our dock lines just when we needed help; lighthouse keepers keeping their lights going; officials who made paperwork easy; and, especially, friends and family.

Psalms 107:23–24 says: "They that go down to the sea in ships, that do business in the great waters, these see the works of the Lord, and his wonders in the deep."

## 10 MAY 2008

The Schooner *Maggie B* docked in Lunenburg at 1100 on May 10th. We are back after 38400 NM.

# EPILOGUE

**13 JUNE 2008**

I have looked at our web statistics for the Schooner *Maggie B* web site. Successful requests between February and December 2007 are 1,939,211 including 35,017 in the last week.

The *Maggie B* was hauled out in Lunenburg and trucked over to Petite Rivere where she is sitting—standing—in the very spot where she was built. The plan is to make her ready for a few months' cruise, starting in August. We are doing all the steps to make her safe and whole, though not necessarily a full overhaul. There will be more time this winter to finish up.

Right now, her rig is out and being overhauled. There will be a lot of stainless steel welding to fix the mast top fittings. The Yanmar and the Onan are out and shipped for overhaul. The "sacrificial" part of the keel, the bottom ten inches behind the lead ballast, was mostly sacrificed when we ran aground in Brazil, and it will be replaced. New paint has been ordered and will be flown up to Nova Scotia next week. John has found the places where the rudder was loose and that should be fixed soon.

*Reepicheep* was trucked down to the ApprenticeShop in Rockland, where she was built, to be rebuilt. Close inspection showed that several ribs were cracked and will have to be replaced. Fixing *Reep* up will become a full training drill for the ApprenticeShop and it should be accomplished by fall, to have her ready for next year's adventures.

Hannah and Curtis have signed on to the *Elemiah*, a Covey Island boat that is headed to the Mediterranean soon. They may end up based

Damaged propeller opening being refit.

in Croatia! Rik and Danette are back at work in Lunenburg.

I hope to be up to see *Maggie* towards the end of June.


## 10 JULY 2008

The schooner *Maggie B* is in the Covey Island shed getting fixed up after her hard 38400 NM maiden voyage. It was quite a shock to see our home 'all tore up.' They aren't actually doing a lot, but it is hard to imagine that it will soon again be all back together and ready for the next adventure.

I often mentioned problems with the toilet. Curtis, Robert and I put in hundreds of hours to troubleshoot blockages in the black water tank and then to build a "work around." It turns out that a single tampon was the culprit—an all too familiar story to anyone who works with marine toilets.

Feathering props are an essential part of any traveling sailboat. For the *Maggie B* it made a 3/4 to one knot difference. At a very rough estimate, we probably saved 30 days of sailing with the extra speed—the difference between going 6 and 7 knots over 30,000 NM. Of the several alternatives out there, we selected the Italian J-Prop when the boat was new. We lost our first J-Prop when it simply came off somewhere between Barbados and Brazil on the way out. The distributor said that it had never happened before, which turned out to be a lie. But they did send us a

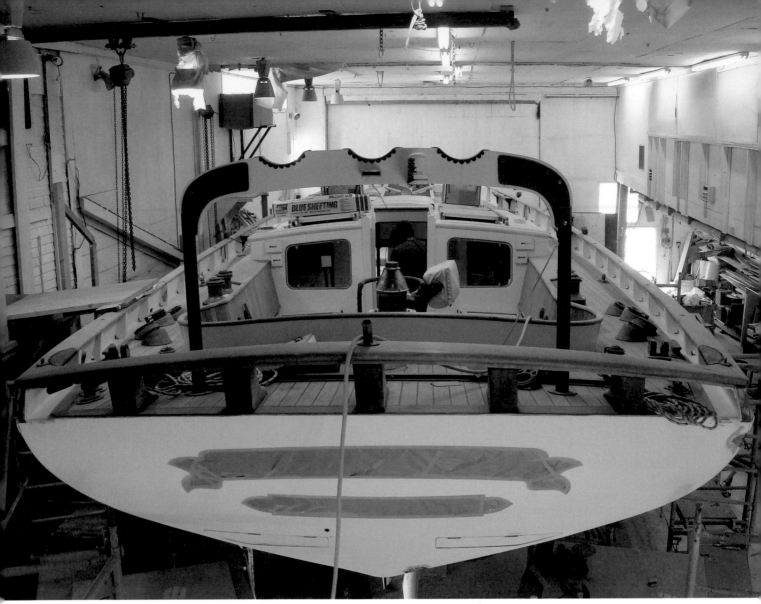

Repainting in the Covey Island shed.

free replacement. Free until Brazil customs demanded a 100% import tax due to mistakes J-Prop made in shipping. The replacement J-Prop failed in Martinique on our way back. When we took it apart, the gear teeth fell out as if it had been the loser in a bare-knuckle fight.

When we got back to Canada we were told 1) they had changed the warrantee period to one year from three, so it was out of warrantee, 2) that J-Props never fail unless they are abused. Ours failed, so therefore it must have been abused, so the warrantee is voided and 3) we could ship it to Italy to be rebuilt, but they had no idea how long it would take. Our next prop will be from someone else.

# CODA

### 15 AUGUST 2008

Today I received the shattering news that the Covey Island Boatyard in Petite Rivere burned to the ground last night. The Schooner *Maggie B* was completely destroyed. She was the only boat in the boatyard at the time. She was completely overhauled and was to be relaunched in three days.

I immediately flew from Maine to the Covey Island yard. It was still smoking. What is more than a total loss? Even the propeller melted.

### 4 SEPTEMBER 2008

The fire inspectors and the insurance specialists agree that the fire started in the area where the main electrical circuits come into the building. Most all of the boat gear was stored in the building and was also destroyed. The main, fore and jib sails were at North Sails for repair and will go to our friend Danette Eden to become high-end bags, but the storm sails and our beautiful "Bird" gennaker were burnt.

*Maggie B*'s prop and sternpost.

Ashes of the Covey Island boatyard.

### Losing the *Maggie B*

Even after four months, I can't speak articulately, politely or clearly about losing the *Maggie B*. I know that I'm expected to say, "She was just a boat," or "The insurance paid off" (which it did), or "I completed the voyage," or reply, "I'm glad to be back" when someone says, "Welcome Home." But I can't.

I used to say that I would give up my left arm to have her back. But then I met a charming single-armed young woman Paralympian cyclist back from Beijing, and I thought that my offer was insufficient to impress the gods.

I *am* glad that we made it all the way around together. I am glad that I have the insurance money so that I can build another great boat with Nigel and Covey Island, and set off with new and old shipmates to new horizons. And I am glad to be ashore for a spell.

I got so many lovely messages from all around the world after the fire. It was like being Tom Sawyer and present at your own funeral oration. While my great-grandchildren will never sail her, neither will she sit on the hard somewhere and rust and rot away unloved. We gathered up some of her ashes from the fire and will scatter bits all around the world.

## Nautical Lexicon—*Maggie B*

Sailing has a rich vocabulary assembled from many countries over many years. It may seem exclusionary to non-sailors, but on board a sailboat it can be critical. Most boats have their own terminology, depending on the captain and the ship's tradition.

In modern parlance, to "learn the ropes" means to come to understand the procedures of a business or situation. On a ship, it means, literally, to learn the ropes—which rope does what to the boat. Sometimes the cry "there's a hockle in the starboard foresheet—clear it or cut it!" must be instantly understood and obeyed for the safety of the ship.

The definitions used in this book may be unfamiliar to some readers. Other sailors may have different definitions. Great! But these are used on my boat.

\* \* \*

*Barrett's Privateers* – A modern drinking song written and performed by Stan Rogers, associated with Atlantic Canada. Sung often on *Maggie B*.

*Blue Water* – As a concept, this means far offshore where the water is blue rather than on-shore grey. Blue Water means no 911 emergency services, no cell coverage, no hardware store, no quick refuge.

*Bollard* – A short vertical post on a wharf, used to tie up the vessel. We came across some bollards made from old cannons set nose-first in the pier.

*Bunt* – The center, or the body of a sail. So "make fast the bunt of the fore" would mean to tie up the body of the foresail.

*Capstan Pawl* – The capstan is the (usually) vertical drum used to raise the anchor. In the old days the capstan was powered by sailors using long capstan bars; today, it is powered by an electric motor. The pawl is the pivoted catch mechanism that stops the ratchet from turning at the base of the capstan.

*Commanders' Weather* – Professional meteorologists located in Nashua, New Hampshire. They provide specialized weather reports: accurate and insightful forecasts and routing information for ships all around the world. www.commandersweather.com

*Courtesy Flag* – When in foreign waters, a ship should fly the flag of the country she is visiting from a hoist halfway up the forward mast.

*CQR Anchor* – An articulated plow-type of anchor developed in the 1930s. While much beloved by traditionalists, it has been outstripped by modern technology.

*Cringle* – A reinforced grommet at the corner of a sail.

*Cutlass Bearing* – Also called a stave bearing. It is the piece that carries a propeller shaft through the hull of a boat. It needs to be tight enough to minimize water egress into the boat, but free enough to not be damaged by the rotation of the shaft.

*Deadeye* – A component of traditional rigging used to tighten and adjust the standing rigging, often supplanted by the more modern turnbuckle. It is usually made from a hard piece of wood, with three holes in it.

*DIN* – *Deutsches Institut für Normung.* Basically, German and European standards and specfications. If you have a bolt that made to US standards, it will not fit a DIN nut.

*Directions, Current and wind* – If a wind is northerly, it is *coming from* the north. If a current is northerly, it is *going* north.

*EPIRB* – Emergency Position-Indicating Radio Beacon. These self-contained radios transmit emergency signals up to satellite repeaters. When activated, it transmits the unique number of its vessel together with geographic position. That signal is picked up by emergency services that can initiate immediate rescue efforts.

*Feathering prop* – Propellers for motorboats have fixed blades. The blades are always working to make the boat go. Modern sailboat propellers can feather or fold when the boat is under sail, and the propeller is not being used to propel the boat. They streamline with the flow of water. On a feathering prop the blades stay in place, but turn neutral to the water flow. On a folding prop, the blades close back and minimize their resistance. A folding or feathering propeller can make a big difference in boat speed when under sail.

*Fetch* – In ocean terms, it is the distance across the surface of the that waves have to build up height. If you are sheltered by a shoreline or island, waves are small; if you are a hundred miles out and a gale has been blowing for days, the waves build up over the distance and may be big. Fetch is also a term used when sailing close hauled, when you can make the mark you are trying to reach; "With this current, we can fetch the island on this tack."

*Fid* – A fid is an ancient and essential tool for a sailor. It is a conical tool, fine pointed at one end. A fid is also called a marlinspike, named after the bony nose on a marlin. It is used to open knots that are seized up tight, or to unlay ropes to splice them.

*Furuno* – Our navigational equipment was made by the Japanese company Furuno, known for their excellent radar systems.

*Gaff saddle* – Gaff-rigged boats have a large spar at the top edge of the sail. It holds the sail up from the mast to the upper, outer corner of the sail. That spar is called the gaff. It rests against the mast and slides along it. The gaff saddle fits between the gaff and the mast.

*Gennaker* – A sail that is a big, deep jib, useful for going downwind. It is shaped between a genoa jib and a spinnaker.

*Greenwich Mean Time (GMT)* – The day has come to be defined as relating to the time in Greenwich, England. Time of day varies around the world. It is called Zulu time in the US Navy, or UTC (Universal Time Clock) more modernly. A boat has to change her clocks ahead or back as she moves east and west.

*GRIB files* – GRIdded Binary data. This is the best meteorological forecast easily obtained around the world. GRIB files can be received by satellite radio or SSB (Single Side Band radio) or lower frequency radio, and converted by simple computer programs to offer excellent meteorological information and forecasts.

*Grommet* – An eyelet or reinforced ring in a sail. It has different names depending on different locations on the sail. See cringle.

*Grub screws* – The body of a bolt without a head, or a set screw.

*Hull speed* – Monohull boats, sail and power, can only go a maximum theoretical speed, unless pushed to surf or plane. It is a function of the length of the waterline; in general, it is 1.34 times the square root of the length of the waterline of the boat. For *Maggie B*, theoretical hull speed was about 10.2 knots.

*ITCZ* - Intertropic Convergence Zone – An area of the earth near the Equator, known to sailors as the Doldrums, where the northeasterly and southeasterly trade winds come together. It is an area of variable wind, significant rain and unsettled weather.

*Lanyard* – A short, light piece of line used to secure things on a boat.

*Lee-bow push* – If a current is from your leeward side and pushing your hull to windward, it can help you sail upwind.

*Magnetic and True* – The earth's magnetic north is close to the geographic North Pole, but not exactly. The difference in any one place between magnetic and true readings is called Variation. Some places on the globe, the difference is zero; at some places it is 20 degrees or more. It can make a big difference in course accuracy when steering by compass.

*Marae* – A religious and social meeting ground for Polynesians.

*MaxSEA software* – French marine navigation software that has excellent integration of weather and boat performance to allow sophisticated strategic and tactical planning.

*NM* – Nautical Miles are about 6076 feet. Statute miles are 5280 feet. From the Equator to the North Pole is 90 degrees. Each degree has 60 minutes. A minute of arc on the planet Earth is 1 nautical mile. For sailor and pilots, NM is the standard. Statute miles are related to the Roman one thousand paces, from the Legions.

*One o'clock* – Relative bearings are often related to a clock face with the boat positioned in the center, pointing to 12 o'clock. Six o'clock is right behind you. Nine o'clock is perpendicular to the left. On a ship, nine o'clock used to be called as "hard on the port beam." With modern crews, you get quicker understanding of direction by using the clock times.

*Parrel Beads* – Beads of a variety of sizes and materials tied together to roll against the mast, keeping a boom or gaff in place.

*Pink* – A type of sailing ship with a relatively narrow stern and a shallow draft.

*Pressure* – Pressure can refer to at least two things. A high Barometric pressure means calm weather and little wind. A low Barometric pressure means turbulent weather and high winds. Similarly, tactically on a sailboat, "pressure coming" means your tactician has seen a big puff of wind, increased air pressure, on the water. So, "expecting more pressure" is a way of saying "wind is coming." Conversely, saying "The pressure is up two millibars" means you are sailing out of a low-pressure system towards a high.

*Rude* – A quay where you dock in French Polynesia, generally stern-in and the bow held off by your anchor.

*Reef* – Make the sail smaller, but still useful. Reefing can be done in a number of ways, depending on what system is installed on the sails and the rig. Generally it can be done progressively, as in First Reef, Second Reef, etc. A reef can also refer to shallow depths, though still hidden under water, a real danger for sailors.

*Rhumb line versus Great Circle Navigation* – The earth is spherical and three-dimensional; maps are flat and two-dimensional. Rhumb line course means you keep a constant heading on the compass, Great Circle course means you adjust your compass heading to allow for the curvature of the earth. Great Circle is shorter, Rhumb line is easier. Over a short distance it doesn't matter, but over a long distance it can matter greatly. New York to Hong Kong by Rhumb Line is 9,400 NM, while a Great Circle course goes over the Pole, and is 7,000 NM.

*Right of Way Rules* – There are extensive and detailed rules, the Colregs, which every Watch Officer should know. Some parts are simple, such as between two similar ships converging, the one on the right has right of way. A motorboat must give way to a sailboat. A sailboat must give way to a fishing boat that has its gear out. It is generally simple during the day and with good visibility. At night and in poor visibility it can lead to confusion, "do they know we are a sailboat under sail" or "Oh, my god, we are crossing between a tug and its barge!"

*SAE* – Society of Automotive Engineers. It is the international standards setter. See DIN above. SAE bolts do not fit with DIN nuts, and so forth.

*SSB (Single Side Band* – lower frequency) radio propagation depends on many variables. Sometimes you can get a good signal 1000 miles away from a station, but not one 500 miles away, and it may change quickly. The basic marine radio is VHF radio, Very High Frequency radio.

*Solenoid* – A solenoid actuator can be used to turn something on and off remotely. An electric switch can provide power to an electromagnet, which will open a valve or door. Most are set to close when power is removed.

*Southern Ocean* – It is also called the Antarctic Ocean. For sailors, the Southern Ocean starts at 40 degrees South, but later proposed rules are 50 or 60 degrees south.

*Standing rigging* – The mast is supported by permanent, standing rigging made from rope, wire or rods. Running rigging are the lines that are routinely adjusted, such as halyards or sheets.

*Tack* – A sailboat is sailing on a tack defined by where the wind is coming from: when the wind is coming over the port side of the boat first, the boat is on the port tack. A sailboat under sail on the starboard tack has right of way over sailboats sailing on port tack.

*Steady Bearing Angle* – Collision course. If two boats are on a course to meet, and the bearing angle between them remains steady, ie., does not change, they are on a collision course. If a boat is on your right side and the angle to that boat moves more to the right, it will go behind you. If the vessel moves more toward the left, it will cross in front of you.

*Tiki* – Large wooden Polynesian carvings associated with religious sites.

Topsail breeze – Good sailing: enough wind to fill the topsails, which in older ships were sails that were higher and lighter, and would be furled in strong wind.

*VMG* – Velocity Made Good. How fast you are getting to your goal.

**Waka** – A Maori canoe. The biggest were the war canoes, *waka taua*, which were up to 120-feet lang. *Waka ama* had an outrigger or two. In the oral histories, there were *waka hourua* (catamarans) for long distance, interisland travel.

*Wind, backing and veering* – Wind backing means that the wind is changing direction in a counter clockwise direction in the Northern Hemisphere. Veering is a wind direction change in a clockwise direction. It is an important clue on how the weather is developing, differently interpreted in each hemisphere.

*Yard* – A horizontal spar on a sailing ship holding up a square sail.

*Yachtie* – In Australia and New Zealand, it is used to describe skilled boat professionals. (In US parlance, it is a pejorative, implying an excess of snobbism, empty pomp, and lack of sailing skill.) I use the former definition.

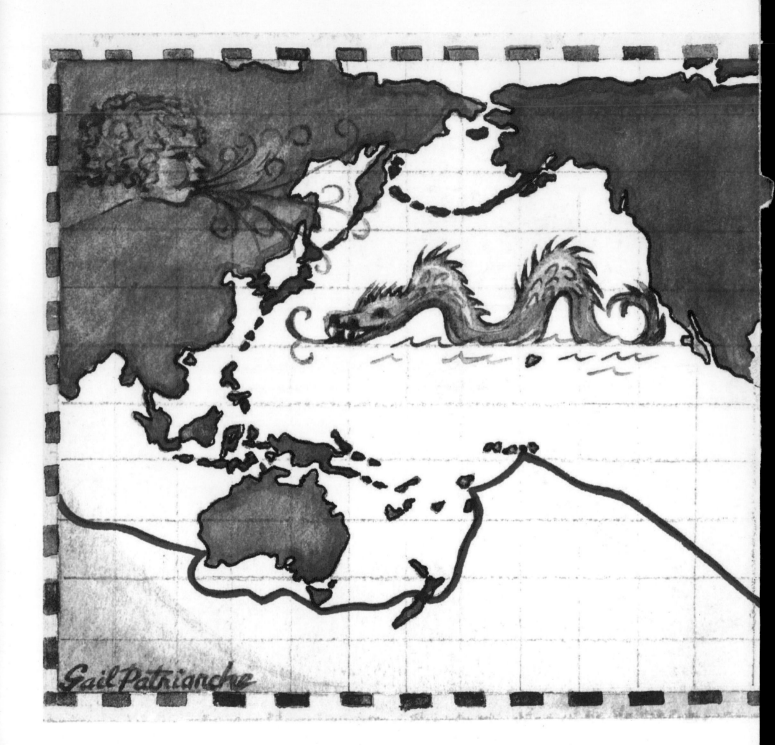

Gail Patriarche